World Book
Discovery Science Encyclopedia

Technology

WORLD BOOK

a Scott Fetzer company
Chicago
www.worldbook.com

For information about other World Book publications, please visit our website at www.worldbook.com or call **1-800-WORLDBK** (967-5325).

For information about sales to schools and libraries, please call **1-800-975-3250** (United States); **1-800-837-5365** (Canada).

World Book, Inc.
233 N. Michigan Ave.
Chicago, IL 60601
U.S.A.

The Library of Congress has cataloged an earlier edition of this title as follows:

Library of Congress Cataloging-in-Publication Data

Encyclopedia of technology.
pages cm. -- (World book discovery science encyclopedia)
Includes index.
Summary: "An exploration of technology, including discoveries, inventions and their inventors, the history of technology, and how technology is used in society. Features include drawings, diagrams, photographs, and activities"-- Provided by publisher.
ISBN 978-0-7166-7524-2
1. Technology--Encyclopedias, Juvenile. I. World Book, Inc.
T9.E463 2013
603--dc23

2013004570

This revised edition:
ISBN: 978-0-7166-7533-4

Printed in China by Shenzhen Donnelley Printing Co., Ltd., Guangdong Province
1st printing March 2015

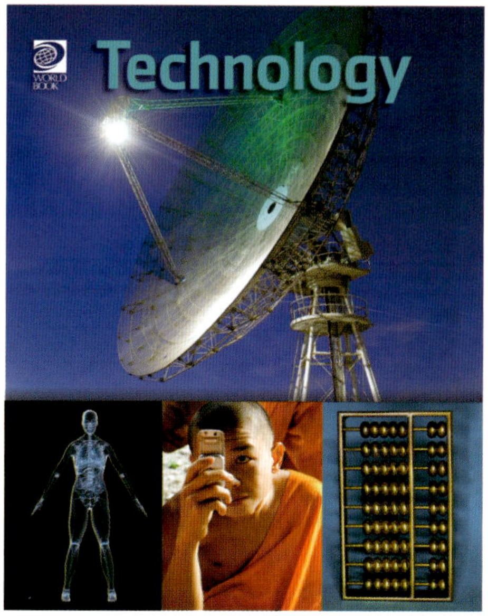

Front Cover:
© Everett Collection/SuperStock
© Shutterstock; © dbimages/Alamy Images;
Scott Camazine, Alamy Images

Back Cover:
© Ron Erwin, SuperStock; © Lloyd Sutton, Alamy Images; © John Miller, Alamy Images

Staff

Executive Committee

President
Jim O'Rourke

Vice President, Finance
Donald D. Keller

Vice President and Editor in Chief
Paul A. Kobasa

Vice President, School and Library Sales
Sean Lockwood

Director, Marketing
Nicholas A. Fryer

Director, International Sales
Kristin Norell

Director, Human Resources
Bev Ecker

Editorial

Associate Director, Annuals and Topical Reference
Scott Thomas

Managing Editor, Annuals and Topical Reference
Barbara A. Mayes

Manager, Sciences, World Book Encyclopedia
Jeff De La Rosa

Senior Editor, Annuals and Topical Reference
Christine Sullivan

Staff Editors
Michael DuRoss
Daniel Kenis
Nick Kilzer

Manager, Contracts & Compliance (Rights & Permissions)
Loranne K. Shields

Manager, Indexing Services
David Pofelski

Administrative Assistant
Ethel Matthews

Editorial Administration

Senior Manager, Publishing Operations
Timothy Falk

Graphics and Design

Art Director
Tom Evans

Coordinator, Design Development and Production
Brenda B. Tropinski

Senior Designers
Matt Carrington
Don Di Sante
Isaiah Sheppard

Contributing Designer
Lucy Lesiak

Media Researcher
Jeff Heimsath

Contributing Photographs Editor
Carol Parden

Manager, Cartography
Wayne K. Pichler

Senior Cartographer
John M. Rejba

Production

Director, Manufacturing and Pre-Press
Carma Fazio

Manufacturing Manager
Sandra Johnson

Production/Technology Manager
Anne Fritzinger

Senior Production Manager
Jan Rossing

Production Specialist
Curley Hunter

Proofreader
Nathalie Strassheim

How to use World Book Discovery Science Encyclopedia

- **Hundreds of illustrations**
- **Guide words**
- **Phonetic spellings**
- **Related article lists**
- **Experiments and activities**
- **QR codes**

World Book Discovery Science Encyclopedia is filled with information about basic science concepts, tools, and discoveries as well as the world around us. Entries on people who have made important contributions to science are included, too. All entries are written in a way that makes them easy to understand.

Finding entries is easy, too. They are arranged in alphabetical order. There is also an index in each volume. The index lists all the entries, as well as topics that are covered in the volume but that are not themselves entries.

Science experiments and activities are also included in this volume. These and the many other features of *World Book Discovery Science Encyclopedia* make it an encyclopedia that you can use for research as well as reading just for fun.

Easy alphabetical access
Each letter of the alphabet is highlighted to help you locate entries alphabetically.

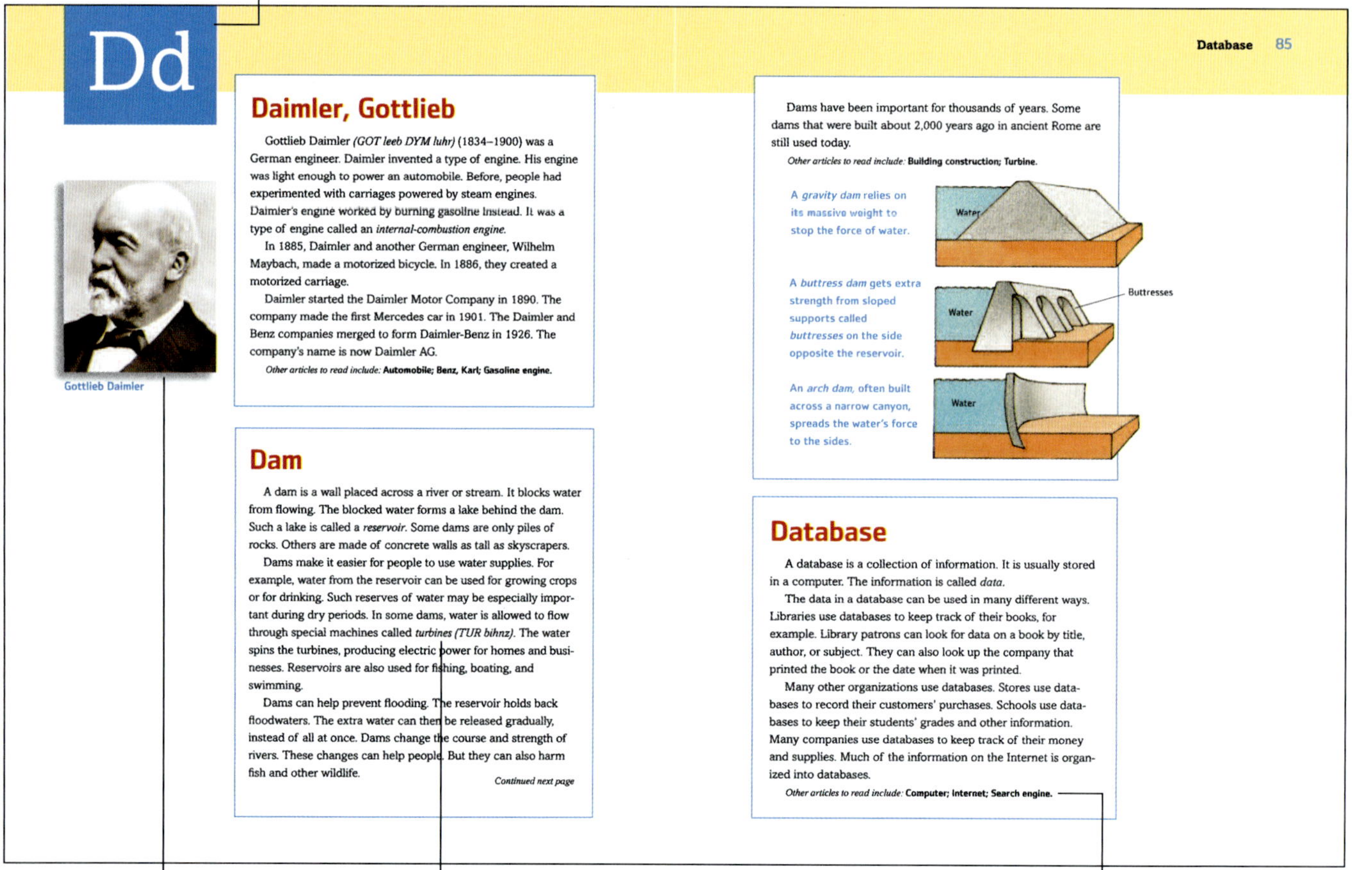
Dd

Database 85

Daimler, Gottlieb

Gottlieb Daimler *(GOT leeb DYM luhr)* (1834–1900) was a German engineer. Daimler invented a type of engine. His engine was light enough to power an automobile. Before, people had experimented with carriages powered by steam engines. Daimler's engine worked by burning gasoline instead. It was a type of engine called an *internal-combustion engine.*

In 1885, Daimler and another German engineer, Wilhelm Maybach, made a motorized bicycle. In 1886, they created a motorized carriage.

Daimler started the Daimler Motor Company in 1890. The company made the first Mercedes car in 1901. The Daimler and Benz companies merged to form Daimler-Benz in 1926. The company's name is now Daimler AG.

Other articles to read include: **Automobile; Benz, Karl; Gasoline engine.**

Gottlieb Daimler

Dam

A dam is a wall placed across a river or stream. It blocks water from flowing. The blocked water forms a lake behind the dam. Such a lake is called a *reservoir.* Some dams are only piles of rocks. Others are made of concrete walls as tall as skyscrapers.

Dams make it easier for people to use water supplies. For example, water from the reservoir can be used for growing crops or for drinking. Such reserves of water may be especially important during dry periods. In some dams, water is allowed to flow through special machines called *turbines (TUR bihnz).* The water spins the turbines, producing electric power for homes and businesses. Reservoirs are also used for fishing, boating, and swimming.

Dams can help prevent flooding. The reservoir holds back floodwaters. The extra water can then be released gradually, instead of all at once. Dams change the course and strength of rivers. These changes can help people. But they can also harm fish and other wildlife.

Continued next page

Dams have been important for thousands of years. Some dams that were built about 2,000 years ago in ancient Rome are still used today.

Other articles to read include: **Building construction; Turbine.**

A *gravity dam* relies on its massive weight to stop the force of water.

A *buttress dam* gets extra strength from sloped supports called *buttresses* on the side opposite the reservoir.

An *arch dam,* often built across a narrow canyon, spreads the water's force to the sides.

Database

A database is a collection of information. It is usually stored in a computer. The information is called *data.*

The data in a database can be used in many different ways. Libraries use databases to keep track of their books, for example. Library patrons can look for data on a book by title, author, or subject. They can also look up the company that printed the book or the date when it was printed.

Many other organizations use databases. Stores use databases to record their customers' purchases. Schools use databases to keep their students' grades and other information. Many companies use databases to keep track of their money and supplies. Much of the information on the Internet is organized into databases.

Other articles to read include: **Computer; Internet; Search engine.**

Illustrations
Each volume of *Discovery Science Encyclopedia* contains hundreds of photographs, drawings, maps, and other illustrations. Each illustration is labeled or explained in a caption.

Pronunciations
The phonetic spelling for unusual or unfamiliar words is given. A key to the pronunciation is in the front of each volume.

Related references
The references listed at the bottom of many articles tell you which other articles to read to find out more or related information.

Experiments
Many experiments are found in *Discovery Science Encyclopedia.* These experiments extend or enrich the subject of the article they accompany and are suitable for use at home or in the classroom.

Guide words
Guide words at the top of a page help you quickly find the entry you are seeking.

Activities
Many activities are found in *Discovery Science Encyclopedia.* These simple activities, which can be done at home or in the classroom, extend or enrich the subject of the article they accompany.

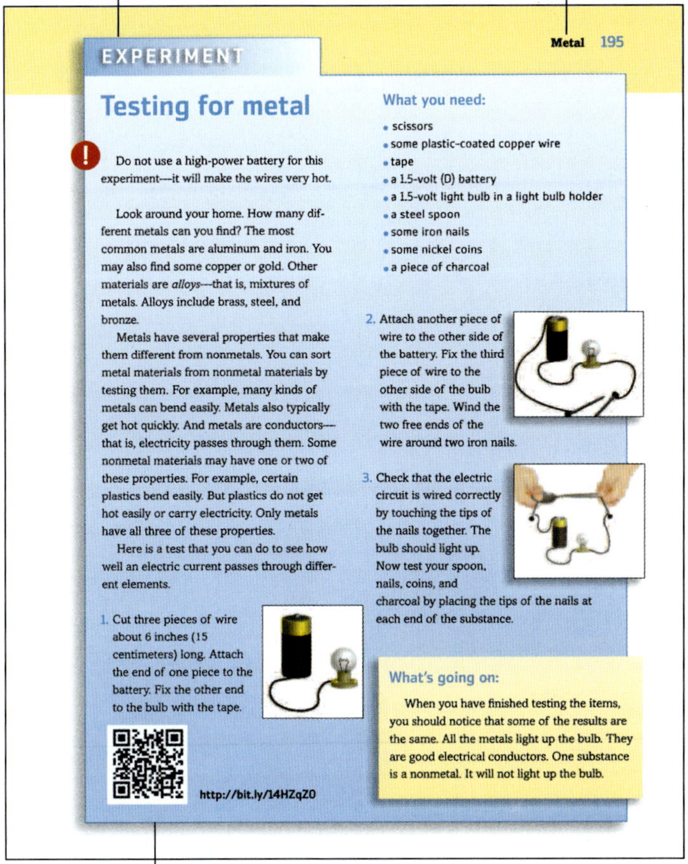
Metal 195

EXPERIMENT

Testing for metal

Do not use a high-power battery for this experiment—it will make the wires very hot.

Look around your home. How many different metals can you find? The most common metals are aluminum and iron. You may also find some copper or gold. Other materials are *alloys*—that is, mixtures of metals. Alloys include brass, steel, and bronze.

Metals have several properties that make them different from nonmetals. You can sort metal materials from nonmetal materials by testing them. For example, many kinds of metals can bend easily. Metals also typically get hot quickly. And metals are conductors—that is, electricity passes through them. Some nonmetal materials may have one or two of these properties. For example, certain plastics bend easily. But plastics do not get hot easily or carry electricity. Only metals have all three of these properties.

Here is a test that you can do to see how well an electric current passes through different elements.

1. Cut three pieces of wire about 6 inches (15 centimeters) long. Attach the end of one piece to the battery. Fix the other end to the bulb with the tape.

http://bit.ly/14HZqZ0

What you need:
- scissors
- some plastic-coated copper wire
- tape
- a 1.5-volt (D) battery
- a 1.5-volt light bulb in a light bulb holder
- a steel spoon
- some iron nails
- some nickel coins
- a piece of charcoal

2. Attach another piece of wire to the other side of the battery. Fix the third piece of wire to the other side of the bulb with the tape. Wind the two free ends of the wire around two iron nails.

3. Check that the electric circuit is wired correctly by touching the tips of the nails together. The bulb should light up. Now test your spoon, nails, coins, and charcoal by placing the tips of the nails at each end of the substance.

What's going on:

When you have finished testing the items, you should notice that some of the results are the same. All the metals light up the bulb. They are good electrical conductors. One substance is a nonmetal. It will not light up the bulb.

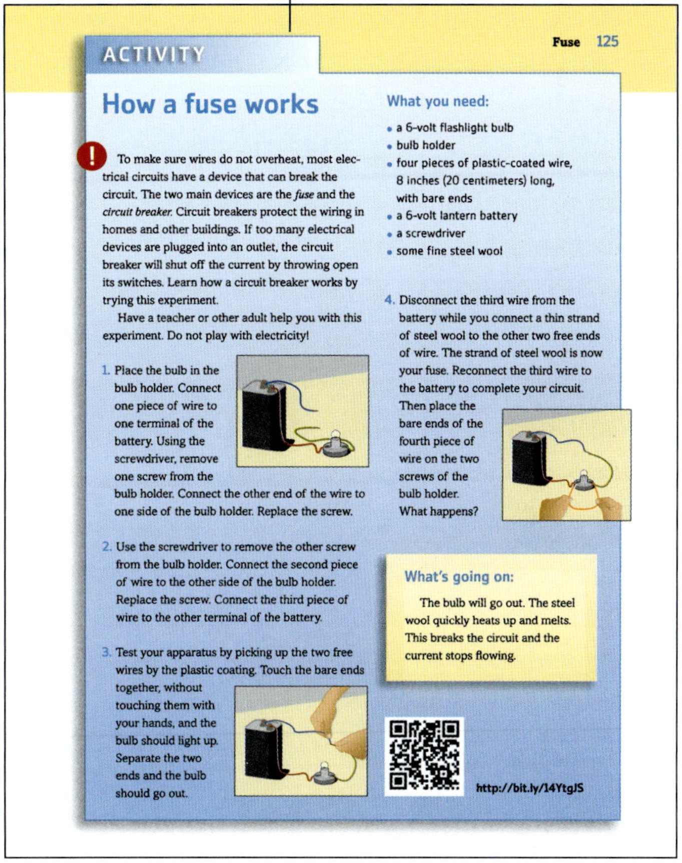
Fuse 125

ACTIVITY

How a fuse works

To make sure wires do not overheat, most electrical circuits have a device that can break the circuit. The two main devices are the *fuse* and the *circuit breaker.* Circuit breakers protect the wiring in homes and other buildings. If too many electrical devices are plugged into an outlet, the circuit breaker will shut off the current by throwing open its switches. Learn how a circuit breaker works by trying this experiment.

Have a teacher or other adult help you with this experiment. Do not play with electricity!

1. Place the bulb in the bulb holder. Connect one piece of wire to one terminal of the battery. Using the screwdriver, remove one screw from the bulb holder. Connect the other end of the wire to one side of the bulb holder. Replace the screw.

2. Use the screwdriver to remove the other screw from the bulb holder. Connect the second piece of wire to the other side of the bulb holder. Replace the screw. Connect the third piece of wire to the other terminal of the battery.

3. Test your apparatus by picking up the two free wires by the plastic coating. Touch the bare ends together, without touching them with your hands, and the bulb should light up. Separate the two ends and the bulb should go out.

What you need:
- a 6-volt flashlight bulb
- bulb holder
- four pieces of plastic-coated wire, 8 inches (20 centimeters) long, with bare ends
- a 6-volt lantern battery
- a screwdriver
- some fine steel wool

4. Disconnect the third wire from the battery while you connect a thin strand of steel wool to the other two free ends of wire. The strand of steel wool is now your fuse. Reconnect the third wire to the battery to complete your circuit. Then place the bare ends of the fourth piece of wire on the two screws of the bulb holder. What happens?

What's going on:

The bulb will go out. The steel wool quickly heats up and melts. This breaks the circuit and the current stops flowing.

http://bit.ly/14YtgJS

QR codes
This symbol is a QR code. You can find QR codes on all the pages with experiments and activities in the *World Book Discovery Science Encyclopedia.* Simply scan a code with your smartphone or tablet to see a video about the experiment or activity or related information about the subject of the project. (You will need to download a QR code reader to your device if you have not already done so.) If you do not have a mobile device, you can still access the videos linked to experiments and activities by keying in the URL beneath each QR code into a browser on your computer.

Key to pronunciation

World Book Discovery Science Encyclopedia provides the pronunciations for many unusual or unfamiliar words. In the pronunciation, the words are divided into syllables and respelled according to the way each syllable sounds. The syllables appear in *italic letters.* For example, here are an article title and the respelled pronunciation for it:

Absorption *(ab SAWRP shuhn)*

The syllable or syllables that get the greatest emphasis when the word is spoken are in capital letters *(SAWRP).*

Aa

Abacus

The abacus *(AB uh kuhs)* is a counting board used to solve arithmetic problems. It was used by the ancient Chinese, Greeks, and Romans.

An abacus has columns of beads. The first column on the right stands for ones. The second column stands for tens, the third for hundreds, and so on.

A crossbar divides the columns. The five beads below the crossbar each stand for one unit. The two beads above the crossbar each stand for five units. So in the first column, the lower beads stand for ones, and the upper beads stand for fives. In the second column, the lower beads stand for tens and the upper beads stand for fifties, or five tens. People moved the beads up or down to solve problems.

Other articles to read include: **Calculator.**

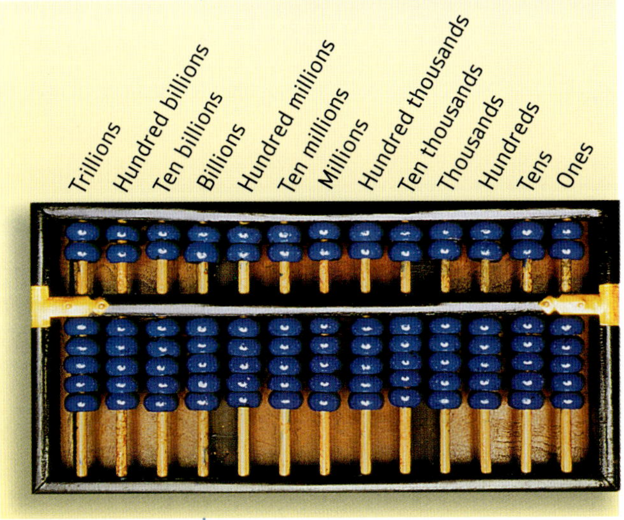

The beads on an abacus are used for counting. A column of beads stands for ones, the next for tens, and so on.

Adobe

Adobe *(uh DOH bee)* is the Spanish name for sun-dried bricks. People have used adobe to build houses and other buildings in desert regions for thousands of years. The ancient Egyptians and Babylonians used adobe.

To make adobe, workers mix sandy clay with water and a small amount of straw or grass. The straw holds the mixture together. Workers place the mixture into wooden forms. The forms shape it into bricks. Workers then remove the forms and bake the bricks in the sun.

Adobe houses are common in Mexico and in the southwestern United States. Traditional adobe houses are covered with mud. Modern adobe houses are covered with a plasterlike material called *stucco (STUHK oh).* Adobe houses are cooler than traditional homes made of wood or stone. But adobe is not suitable for cold or damp regions. The bricks will crumble if exposed to rain. Adobe is also damaged by freezing and thawing.

Other articles to read include: **Building construction.**

Adobe buildings are often covered with mud or stucco.

Air cleaner

An air cleaner is a device that removes *contaminants* (impurities) from the air or other gases. Solid contaminants include dust, lint, smoke, and pollens. Liquid contaminants include mist and fog. Other contaminants come in the form of vapors and gases.

Air cleaners serve many purposes. For example, makers of food processors and electronics use air cleaners to keep such items free of airborne dust. Air cleaners also help protect people from allergies caused by pollen and dust. Department stores may use air cleaners to keep merchandise clean. Air cleaners collect lint or other burnable material, reducing the risk of fire. Hospitals use air cleaners to prevent the spread of infection.

Other articles to read include: **Air conditioning.**

Air conditioning

Air conditioning keeps air inside a building or vehicle warm or cool enough for comfort. It also helps control the air's cleanliness and moisture. Air conditioning keeps people comfortable where they live, work, and play. It cools areas with many machines or computers, which give off much heat. Hospitals and certain

Continued on the next page

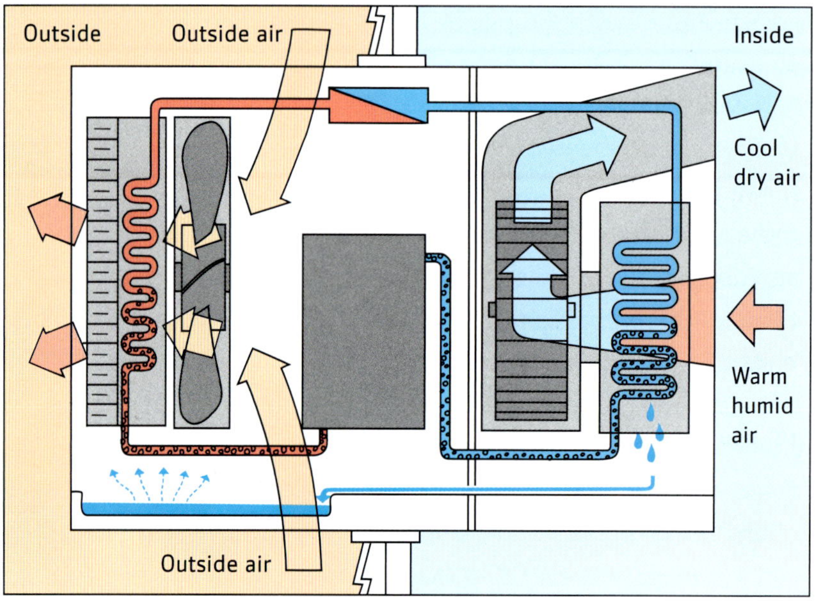

Inside a window air conditioner, refrigerated coils absorb heat from indoor air, cooling it. The heat absorbed by the coils is transferred to the air outdoors.

factories require clean and comfortable air provided by air conditioning.

Many air conditioners work by blowing air over coiled tubes. When filled with cool water or another liquid, the tubes draw heat from the air. Similarly, hot tubes or wire screens can add heat to air. Some air conditioners are small machines that fit in a window on warm days. *Central air conditioners* are larger. They can cool or warm entire houses or buildings.

Air conditioning was done even before modern machines were invented. The ancient Egyptians, Greeks, and Romans, for example, used wet mats to cool indoor air. They hung the mats over the doors to their tents and other dwellings. When wind blew through the mats, the water evaporated, cooling the air.

Other articles to read include: **Air cleaner; Refrigeration.**

Air cushion vehicle

An air cushion vehicle is a craft that floats just above the land or water on a layer of air. The air acts like an invisible cushion. It enables the craft to float. Air cushion vehicles can carry people, vehicles, and heavy cargo. They are mostly used for military missions.

An air cushion vehicle has one or more fans that suck air into the craft. The fans force the air underneath the vehicle. This action creates an air cushion between the craft and the land or water.

Propellers move the craft. Air cushion vehicles can travel backward, forward, or sideways. Some can travel very fast. Air cushion vehicles can also hover float in one place. For this reason, they are sometimes called *hovercraft.*

Other articles to read include: **Aircraft, Military.**

An air cushion vehicle floats on a layer of air just above the surface of a frozen lake.

Airbag

Airbag

An airbag is a cloth bag that fills with air during an automobile crash. It helps cushion the drivers and passengers. An airbag is most effective when used with lap and shoulder belts.

Airbags work with devices called *sensors.*The sensors measure the vehicle's speed. They can tell if a car crashes. Sensors on the car doors can detect crashes from the side.

If a car crashes, sensors send an electric signal to a computer. The computer can then send a signal to the car's airbags. The signal heats a wire. The heat sets off a tiny explosive capsule. The explosion burns pellets inside the airbag. When the pellets burn, they give off much nitrogen gas. This harmless gas blows up the airbag like a balloon.

The whole process takes a fraction of a second. Once puffed out, the airbag quickly starts to release the nitrogen gas.

Other articles to read include: **Automobile.**

Aircraft, Military

Military aircraft include airplanes, helicopters, and other flying machines. Armed forces use military aircraft for a wide variety of tasks in both combat and peacetime. During a war, these aircraft observe and attack enemy forces. They protect and transport troops and supplies. In peacetime, military aircraft can help rescue people. They can also help perform scientific experiments.

Fighters are fast-flying attack planes. They usually carry cannons, rockets, and missiles. Fighters shoot down other aircraft. They can also strike ground targets.

Bombers are another type of attack plane. Unlike fighters, they do not usually attack other aircraft. Instead, they attack targets on the ground. *Strategic* bombers fly over great distances. They

Continued on the next page

A *fighter* is a fast-flying plane that attacks other aircraft or ground targets.

can strike deep into enemy territory. *Fighter-bombers* have shorter ranges. *Stealth* bombers are designed to avoid detection by enemy radar.

Other aircraft are not used for direct attack. *Tankers* refuel other aircraft in flight. *Transport* aircraft carry people and equipment. Helicopters are widely used for both transport and for observing and attacking targets.

Unmanned aerial vehicles (UAV's) are remotely controlled and have no pilot onboard. They are also called *drones*. UAV's often have advanced camera equipment for observing targets. Some larger UAV's carry missiles.

Other articles to read include: **Airplane; Helicopter; Jet.**

Airplane

Commercial airliners are big planes used by airline companies. Most airliners carry passengers and some cargo.

An airplane is an engine-powered flying machine. Airplanes are much heavier than air. But the flow of air around an airplane's wing keeps the plane from falling. Airplanes quickly transport people around the world. They also carry mail and goods. In addition, airplanes are also major weapons of war.

There are many types of airplanes. They vary widely in size, speed, and use. Many modern airplanes use *jet engines*. Jets take in air and burn it with fuel. Some smaller planes, on the other hand, are powered by spinning blades called *propellers*.

Airliners are big planes used by airline companies. Most airliners carry passengers and some cargo. They usually fly 500 to 600 miles (800 to 970 kilometers) per hour.

The biggest airliners have four jet engines. Smaller three-engine and twin-engine airliners make shorter flights. The smallest airliners use propellers.

Continued on the next page

Airplane *Continued from the previous page*

Light planes are small planes with two to six seats. They can take off and land at small airports. Most light planes use propellers. Some people travel on light planes that they own. People also use light planes to take pictures, fight fires, and deliver cargo. Students often learn to fly on light planes.

Military planes are widely used by armed forces. *Bombers* attack targets on the ground. *Fighters* attack other planes in the air. *Tankers* can refuel other planes in flight. *Transport planes* carry troops and equipment.

Other kinds of planes have special designs. *Seaplanes* can take off and land in water. *Spray planes* are used to spray fertilizer or insect spray on crops.

Unmanned aerial vehicles (UAV's), also called *drones*, are remotely controlled planes. Military forces use UAV's to observe and attack distant targets without putting pilots at risk.

Continued on the next page

The main parts of an airplane are common to nearly all designs. They include a wing, a section called a *fuselage,* a tail, landing equipment, and engines. This light airplane is the Piper Cherokee.

The fastest planes, such as fighters, are *supersonic.* That means they can fly faster than the speed of sound.

Almost all planes have the same main parts. They have a wing, a main section called a *fuselage (FYOO zuh lahzh),* a tail, landing equipment, and an engine.

Most airplanes look like they have two wings. But it is actually a single structure. The wing sticks out from both sides of the fuselage.

The wing is nearly flat on the bottom and curved on top. This shape makes air flow around the wing in a special way. The airflow raises the plane off the ground and keeps it in the air.

Most airplane wings have moving parts that help balance the plane. The *ailerons* are hinged pieces on the back of the wing. They make the plane bank, tilt, and turn. Many planes also have *flaps* on the wing. The flaps help the plane lift up for takeoff and slow down for landing. The wing carries navigation lights. The left wing tip has a red light. The right has a green light. The two lights show which way the plane is traveling. The airplane's engines are usually on, or in, the wing.

The fuselage holds the controls, the crew, the passengers, and the cargo. In many small planes, the pilot and passengers sit in the same area. Large planes are divided into a *cockpit* and a *cabin.* The pilot and crew sit in the cockpit. Passengers and cargo are in the cabin. Most planes have a *yoke wheel* for steering. Some planes are steered with a stick.

The tail is the rear part of the airplane. It helps guide the plane and keep it balanced. Like the wing, it has moving parts. The *rudder* is a hinged plate on the back of the tail. It helps the plane turn left or right. A flap called the *elevator* helps raise or lower the plane's nose. It is connected to the *stabilizer,* which is the part of the tail that looks like a small wing.

All planes have landing gear for takeoff and landing. On high-speed planes, the landing gear is pulled up when the plane is flying.

Three main kinds of engines are used in airplanes. *Reciprocating engines,* also called *piston engines,* are much like automobile engines. The power from the engines turns propellers that move the plane through the air. Jet engines take in air and burn it with fuel. The burning pushes gases called *exhaust* out of

Continued on the next page

Airplane *Continued from the previous page*

the engine. As the exhaust shoots out, the plane is pushed in the opposite direction at high speed. The exhaust also spins a device called a *turbine,* which runs the other parts of the engine. A *turbo-prop* engine works somewhat like a jet engine. But a turboprop's exhaust spins a propeller. The propeller enables turboprop planes to fly slower than jet planes.

Gravity is a force that pulls planes toward Earth. For a plane to fly, its wing must create an upward force that is stronger than gravity. This upward force is called *lift.*

The special airflow around a plane's curved wing creates lift. For air to flow around a wing strongly enough, the plane needs to move fast. *Thrust* is the forward force produced by a plane's engine.

To *climb* (go higher), the pilot increases the engine power. To *descend* (go lower), the pilot decreases the engine power. To turn, the pilot *banks* (tilts) the plane.

During the 300's B.C., the Chinese discovered how to make kites. Later, large kites lifted people into the air. In the 200's B.C., the Greek mathematician and inventor Archimedes first described *buoyancy.* Buoyancy explains how objects float, even in air.

In 1783, two French brothers, the Montgolfiers, made a hot-air balloon. Two other Frenchmen floated over Paris in it. This was the first human flight. But balloons, unlike airplanes, float because they are lighter than air.

During the 1800's, many people experimented with *gliders* (planes without engines). They began to add engines and propellers. But these early machines could not be flown.

After experimenting with gliders, two brothers—Wilbur and Orville Wright—built a double-winged plane. On Dec. 17, 1903, Orville successfully flew it near Kitty Hawk, North Carolina. After that, many inventors built and flew planes.

Jet planes were developed during World War II (1939–1945). After the war, airliners began to use jet engines. The first *supersonic plane* flew in 1947. A supersonic plane is one that can fly faster than the speed of sound. A supersonic passenger plane called the Concorde flew from 1976 to 2003.

Other articles to read include: **Aircraft, Military; Engine; Glider; Jet.**

Airport

An airport is a place where airplanes and other aircraft take off and land. Planes also load and unload passengers and *cargo,* or goods, at airports.

Big city airports are exciting places. Overhead, planes come in for landing. On the ground, one plane after another takes off. Thousands of people crowd the *terminal* area—the place where planes and passengers arrive and leave. Cars, buses, and taxis pick up or drop off travelers at the terminal area.

The largest airports look like small cities. Many have hotels, restaurants, banks, post offices, and shops. Some may have their

Continued on the next page

Airplanes pick up and drop off passengers at an airport terminal.

The control tower houses workers that direct air traffic.

Airport *Continued from the previous page*

own police force, fire department, and medical office.

Passengers leave and *board* (get on) aircraft from areas in the terminal called *gates.* At most large airports, a covered walkway connects the gate with the aircraft. Passengers enter and leave an airplane by walking through the covered walkway. Terminals also have areas called *baggage claims* where arriving passengers collect their baggage.

Far away from the terminals are buildings called *hangars* where aircraft are stored and repaired. Some hangars are huge, big enough to hold several large jets at one time.

At the control tower, workers called *air traffic controllers* direct air traffic. They tell the pilots exactly where to fly. They decide when and where it is safe to land and take off.

Aircraft take off and land on *runways.* Runways must be long enough and wide enough to handle the largest planes that use the airport. Such runways are paved like roads. Small airports may use only strips of grass called *landing strips.*

Other articles to read include: **Airplane; Radar.**

Airline workers help travelers at an airport check-in counter.

Airship

Airships called *blimps* are often used for advertising.

An airship is a craft that floats in the air and can carry people and cargo. It is also called a *dirigible (DIHR uh juh buhl).* Unlike balloons, airships are powered and steered. An airship's engine turns propellers that push the ship through the air. Airships are shaped much like fat cylinders. Large passenger airships once had rigid solid support structures. *Blimps* are nonrigid airships.

An airship's *envelope* holds a gas that is lighter than air, usually helium *(HEE lee uhm).* The gas causes the ship to rise into the air. Early airships used hydrogen gas, which is lighter than helium. But hydrogen explodes easily.

Until the late 1930's, people often traveled in airships. In 1937, the hydrogen-filled *Hindenburg* airship exploded. The explosion killed 36 people. Later, most people traveled on airplanes.

Other articles to read include: **Balloon; Blimp.**

Buzz Aldrin

Aldrin, Buzz

Buzz Aldrin *(AWL drihn)* (1930–) is a United States astronaut. He was the second person to walk on the moon. On July 20, 1969, Aldrin and fellow astronaut Neil Armstrong landed their spacecraft on the moon. Armstrong then stepped onto the moon first and Aldrin followed him.

Buzz Aldrin was born in Montclair, New Jersey, on Jan. 20, 1930. He studied at the U.S. Military Academy at West Point, New York. The academy is a college for people who want to be military officers. In 1951, Aldrin joined the U.S. Air Force. He served as a fighter pilot in the Korean War (1950–1953) in 1952. In 1963, Aldrin became an astronaut. He then briefly returned to the Air Force before retiring from military service in 1972.

Buzz Aldrin's birth name was Edwin. He got the nickname "Buzz" when he was a toddler. His sisters called him their "baby buzzer" because they could not pronounce "brother." Aldrin legally changed his name to Buzz as an adult.

Other articles to read include: **Armstrong, Neil Alden; Astronaut; Space exploration.**

Alloy

Many pots and pans are made of an alloy called stainless steel.

An alloy *(AL oy* or *uh LOY)* is a mixture of a metal with one or more other materials. The main metal in an alloy is called the *base metal.* The materials added to an alloy may or may not be metals.

An alloy behaves differently than its base metal. A good alloy makes the base metal harder or stronger. For example, steel is an alloy of iron with a small amount of carbon mixed in. Steel is much stronger than iron. Stainless steel is an alloy of iron combined with a metal called *chromium (KROH mee uhm).* Things made of stainless steel do not rust.

People have made alloys for several thousands of years. The first alloy was *bronze,* a mixture of copper and tin. People first made bronze about 5,500 years ago.

Other articles to read include: **Bronze; Metal; Steel.**

Alternating current

Alternating current is easy to generate and to transport long distances by power lines.

Alternating *(AWL tuhr NAY tihng* or *AL tuhr NAY tihng)* current is a form of *electricity.* It is a kind of *electric current.* An electric current is a flow of extremely tiny particles called *electrons.* Electrons can move through metal wires somewhat like water flows through a pipe.

Alternating current is different from *direct current.* Direct current moves in only one direction through wires. It is abbreviated *DC.* Alternating current, on the other hand, keeps switching direction back and forth. Alternating current is abbreviated *AC.*

Many electronic devices use direct current. But alternating current is easier to generate. It is also easier to transport over long distances. In addition, alternating current can easily be changed into direct current. Large facilities called *power plants* generate alternating current. They send the current through power lines to homes, schools, and offices. Devices that plug into wall sockets use alternating current.

Other articles to read include: **Direct current; Electric power; Power plant.**

Anemometer

Anemometer

An anemometer *(AN uh MOM uh tuhr)* is an instrument used to measure wind speed. There are several types of anemometers.

The most common anemometer has three or four cone-shaped cups. The cups are at the end of short rods. The rods spin around a vertical shaft. When wind blows on the cups, it makes the rods spin. The wind pressure is greater on the inward curving side of the cups than on their outward curving side. For this reason, the cups will spin no matter the wind direction. The faster the wind blows, the faster the cups spin.

The wind speed is measured by the number of turns the cups make in a given time. This information is often shown on a dial on the anemometer. But it can also be sent to a computer.

Other articles to read include: **Weather forecasting.**

Apple Inc.

Apple Inc. is a leading computer and electronics company. Its products often have simple, attractive designs. Apple makes computers and the software programs that run on them. Apple's iPod is a popular portable media player. Its iPhone is a computerlike cell phone. In addition, the company also sells songs, videos, and software over the Internet. Apple's headquarters are in Cupertino, California.

Apple was started in 1976 by Steve Jobs and Steve Wozniak. Both men were computer hobbyists. In 1983, Apple introduced the first computer controlled using a *mouse*. The Macintosh computer was released in 1984. It was the first computer that could be controlled by clicking on images, rather than typing instructions.

In 2001, Apple started selling the iPod. In 2003, Apple started the iTunes Store. The store sells music and videos over the Internet. In 2007, Apple released the iPhone. The phone could also play music and videos like an iPod and access the Internet like a computer. People could control the iPhone simply by touching its screen. In 2010, Apple released a magazine-sized computer called the iPad. It also featured touchscreen-based controls. In 2014, Apple revealed the Apple Watch, a computerized wristwatch.

Other articles to read include: **Cellular telephone; Computer; Jobs, Steve; Wozniak, Steve.**

Aqueduct

Ancient Roman aqueduct

Aqueducts *(AK wuh duhkts)* are waterways that take water where it is needed. Aqueducts have been used since ancient times. The ancient Romans built many aqueducts. People today build aqueducts from brick, stone, concrete, cast iron, steel, and wood. People often tunnel through rock or dig canals to build them. Pipes have replaced many older aqueduct designs.

Sometimes aqueducts are built so that water flows downhill. Otherwise, the water can be pumped through the aqueducts.

As cities, farms, and industries grow, they need more water. Many American cities, such as New York City and San Francisco, rely on water brought by aqueducts. Winnipeg in Canada and Rio de Janeiro in Brazil also get water from aqueducts.

Other articles to read include: **Canal; Pump.**

Archimedes

Archimedes

Archimedes *(AHR kuh MEE deez)* (287?–212 B.C.) was an important ancient Greek scientist and inventor. He made many discoveries in mathematics and science. He also invented many machines. Archimedes lived on the island of Sicily in the Mediterranean Sea.

Archimedes explained how levers and pulleys work. Levers and pulleys are machines that can move heavy objects with little effort. Archimedes also explained why some things float in water.

Archimedes invented weapons to defend his city, Syracuse, against attacks by the Roman Empire. One weapon was a more effective *catapult.* The catapult is a machine that throws heavy rocks. Archimedes also invented a machine that could lift the Roman ships out of the water, shake them, and drop them. Eventually, the Romans captured Syracuse. According to one story, Archimedes was killed by a soldier while working on a geometry problem.

Other articles to read include: **Catapult; Lever; Machine; Pulley.**

Armor

Police wear bulletproof armor and hold shields for protection.

Armor is a covering used for protection in battle. In early times, people wore animal skins as armor. The Greeks and Romans wore metal armor over their chests and lower legs. They also carried metal shields and wore metal helmets.

During the Middle Ages, knights wore armor made of *mail.* Mail is made up of tiny rings of metal hooked together. However, by the 1300's, new weapons could pierce mail. So soldiers began to wear armor made of steel plates. Such armor was expensive. A full suit of armor cost as much as a small farm.

Guns changed the way people use armor. Metal armor that could stop bullets was too heavy to wear over the entire body. By the 1600's, only helmets and *breastplates* (chest armor) were widely used. Some officers and other soldiers wore additional armor, often for show. Today, thick metal armor is mainly used to cover ships, tanks, and other vehicles. Soldiers and police officers wear bulletproof armor made of artificial materials.

Other articles to read include: **Gun; Ship; Tank.**

Ancient Greek and Roman soldiers wore metal armor on their heads and torsos. During the Middle Ages, knights wore full suits of metal armor. Later soldiers wore chest armor or even just helmets.

Greek **Roman** **German** **European 1600's** **French 1800's**

Neil Alden Armstrong

Armstrong, Neil Alden

Neil Alden Armstrong (1930–2012) was a United States astronaut. He was the first person to set foot on the moon.

Armstrong was born on Aug. 5, 1930, on his grandparents' farm in Auglaize County, Ohio. He was a Navy pilot from 1949 to 1952. Later, he tested new aircraft. He became an astronaut in 1962.

After one space flight in 1966, Armstrong joined the Apollo 11 mission as mission commander. On July 20, 1969, Armstrong and Edwin E. Aldrin, Jr., landed the lunar module Eagle on the moon's surface. When Armstrong stepped onto the moon, he said, "That's one small step for a man, one giant leap for mankind."

Armstrong received the Presidential Medal of Freedom in 1969. From 1971 to 1979, Armstrong was a professor of engineering at the University of Cincinnati. In 1986, he was on the commission investigating the space shuttle Challenger disaster. Armstrong died on Aug. 25, 2012.

Other articles to read include: **Aldrin, Buzz; Astronaut; Space exploration.**

As commander of the Apollo 11 mission, Neil Armstrong became the first person to set foot on the moon.

Arrowhead

An arrowhead is the sharp tip at the end of an arrow. It is usually a separate piece fastened to the shaft or stem. Bows and arrows were invented in many different places in prehistoric times. The first arrowheads were made of stone. Later, arrowheads were made of iron.

American Indians made arrowheads of flint and other kinds of stone. First, the Indians split a stone to get a piece of the right size. Then they pressed the upper side with a tool. As a result, a small chip flaked off the underside. They repeated the process until the arrowhead was the right shape.

Indian arrowheads were made in many shapes, such as triangles and ovals. The largest were more than 2 inches (5 centimeters) long. Scientists can recognize where and when different types of arrowheads were made.

Other articles to read include: **Tool.**

Flint arrowhead

Artificial intelligence

Artificial intelligence is the ability of certain computers to "think" like a human. It is called *AI* for short. Research in AI helps computers solve problems and sort information. Many popular computer programs make use of AI. Such programs include Internet search engines and electronic games.

There are a number of approaches to AI. *Expert systems* work with strict, logical rules. However, humans often do not reason in this way. Other AI systems, called *neural networks,* are designed to work like the human brain. Certain AI systems can learn from their experiences.

Computers with advanced AI can defeat human experts in many games. AI also helps computers respond to human language. In addition, AI is important in robotics. Advanced robots use AI to "see" the world around them and control their motion.

Other articles to read include: **Computer; Robot.**

An artificial intelligence computer competes against a Russian chess champion.

Assembly line

An assembly line is a way of making things quickly and cheaply. Assembly lines are divided into stations. The item being made moves from station to station. At each station, workers perform one step in the manufacturing process. Each worker does one task over and over. Each item is made using the same parts.

Before assembly lines, skilled workers made items and parts by hand. No two finished products were exactly alike. Assembly lines, on the other hand, can employ unskilled workers. In addition, assembly lines produce products that are all the same.

The American automobile manufacturer Henry Ford famously used assembly lines in the early 1900's. Conveyor belts carried car parts between the workstations. A new car rolled out of Ford's factory every few minutes.

Other articles to read include: **Automobile; Ford, Henry; Robot.**

An assembly line is used to make many products quickly and cheaply. These illustrations show some key stages in an automobile assembly line.

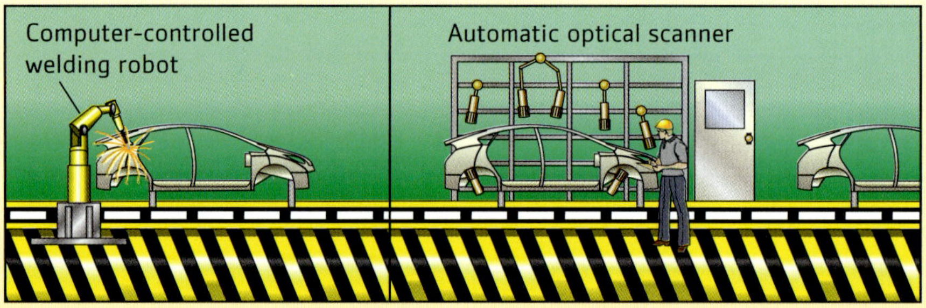

A robot welds the main parts of the automobile body together. Then, a device called an *automatic optical scanner* examines the body. It uses lasers and cameras to make sure the parts are assembled properly.

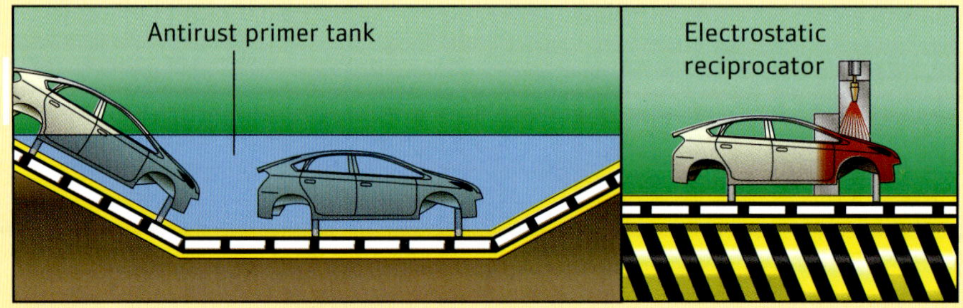

The body is then dipped in a tank of *primer.* Primer is a paint that helps protect the body from rust. Devices called *electrostatic reciprocators* spray on the final coats of paint.

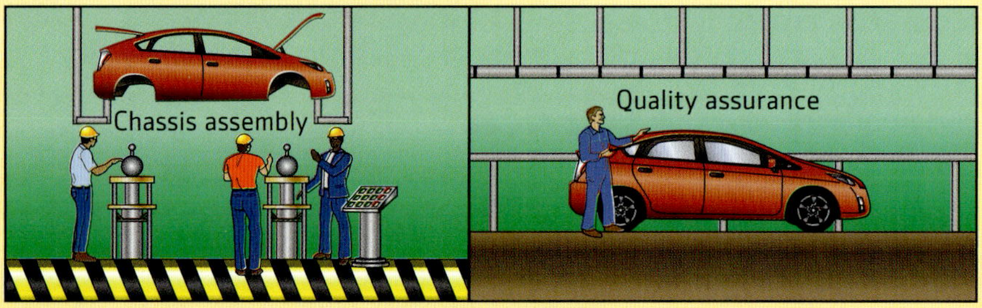

The painted body is attached to the *chassis.* The chassis includes the car's base and wheels. The windows, seats, and trim are also added. At a *quality assurance* station, workers make a final check of the automobile inside and out.

Astronaut

An astronaut works outside a spacecraft using a jet-powered backpack.

An astronaut is a person who pilots a spacecraft or works aboard one. *Astronaut* is the name used in the United States. *Cosmonaut* is the name used in Russia. Chinese astronauts are often called *taikonauts (TY kuh nawtz).*

Most U.S. astronauts work for the National Aeronautics and Space Administration (NASA). NASA chooses two basic kinds of astronauts: pilots and mission specialists.

Pilots must have more than 1,000 hours of jet-flying experience before they begin training. They command and pilot the spacecraft.

Mission specialists must have at least three years of experience in the work they will do in space. They take care of the spacecraft, do experiments, launch satellites, and walk in space.

NASA sometimes also chooses astronauts called *payload specialists.* They are scientists who do experiments in space. Payload specialists do not go through full NASA astronaut training.

The astronauts train at the Lyndon B. Johnson Space Center in Houston, Texas. They study science, spacecraft tracking, and other subjects. They also have flight training. Mission specialists are not normally pilots, but they learn how airplanes work and get some flying practice.

All astronauts learn survival skills. They need to know what to do if the spacecraft lands in the sea or in a hard-to-reach area on land. Astronauts also have mission training. They study the spacecraft and its equipment.

Astronauts are not always sent on space flights right away. While they are waiting, they work on engineering and other jobs. But once they are chosen for a crew, they begin training in machines called *simulators.* These machines are as much like a spacecraft as possible. The astronauts learn to solve problems that might come up in space. They also train in models of the spacecraft.

Sometimes astronauts get special training for a space flight. For example, they may practice working with jet-powered backpacks. During a mission, the packs are used to fly outside the

Continued on the next page

An astronaut works inside a spacecraft.

Astronaut *Continued from the previous page*

spacecraft without a safety line.

Astronauts may also work on the ground. They give information and instructions to crews in space. They work with engineers and scientists. They also suggest changes to improve the spacecraft and equipment.

On April 12, 1961, cosmonaut Yuri Gagarin of the Soviet Union became the first person to travel in space. The Soviet Union was a nation that included what is now Russia. Gagarin made one *orbit,* or trip, around Earth. Twenty-three days later, on May 5, Alan B. Shepard, Jr., became the first U.S. space traveler, but he did not go into orbit. John H. Glenn, Jr., was the first American to go into orbit. He circled Earth three times on Feb. 20, 1962. The first woman in space was the Soviet cosmonaut Valentina Tereshkova. She was in space for three days in 1963. Astronauts from many countries have flown on missions with the Russians and the Americans. On Oct. 15, 2003, Yang Liwei became the first astronaut sent into space by China. Only a few hundred people have ever gone into space.

Other articles to read include: **Aldrin, Buzz; Armstrong, Neil Alden; Gagarin, Yuri Alekseyevich; Glenn, John Herschel, Jr.; International Space Station; Lucid, Shannon Wells; McAuliffe, Christa; National Aeronautics and Space Administration; Ride, Sally Kristen; Shepard, Alan Bartlett; Tereshkova, Valentina Vladimirovna; Space exploration; Yang Liwei.**

Highly trained astronauts go outside their spacecraft on "spacewalks" to repair equipment.

Automated teller machine (ATM)

An automated teller machine (ATM) is a computer terminal used for banking. ATM's enable people to access their bank accounts at any time. Customers can use an ATM to make a bank deposit. They can withdraw cash and transfer money. ATM's also display account information.

To use an ATM, a customer must have a special plastic card. The card has a magnetic strip across the back or a computer chip inside it. The customer inserts the card into the ATM or swipes it through a special slot. The machine reads the customer's account number from the magnetic strip or computer chip. Then the customer enters a *personal identification number* (PIN). Having to know the PIN prevents other people from using a person's card.

ATM's are located at banks, airports, stores, and many other public places. Most ATM's are connected to a computer network. This enables the customer to receive the same service at any ATM.

Machines that dispense cash came into use in the late 1960's. ATM's were first introduced in the early 1970's. They became popular in the 1980's. By the early 2000's, many people did most of their banking at ATM's.

Other articles to read include: **Computer.**

Automobile

The automobile is the most important way to travel for millions of people around the world. People drive about 600 million passenger cars along the world's roads and highways. That is nearly 1 car for every 10 people. Few inventions have changed the world as much as cars have.

Automobiles are wheeled machines. When a driver steps on the gas pedal, the car moves forward. This action and reaction seems simple. But a number of complex systems must work together to make it happen. Each system has many moving and computerized parts.

The *power system* includes the car's engine. Engines have hollow parts called *cylinders.* Other parts called *pistons* move up and down inside the cylinders. Most engines run on

Continued on the next page

Automobile *Continued from the previous page*

gasoline. Burning gasoline inside the cylinders pushes the pistons up and down. Some cars have electric motors. These motors are powered by large batteries. *Hybrid cars* have both an electric motor and an engine that burns gasoline.

The *power train* is another automobile system. It is also called the *drive train*. It connects the car's power system to the wheels. The car's engine or motor creates spinning motion. This same motion eventually spins the wheels. But first, it is channeled into the car's *transmission*. The transmission makes sure the motion has the right speed and force before it reaches the wheels.

Control systems are used to drive the automobile. The *steering system* controls the front wheels. The driver uses the steering wheel to turn the front wheels and steer the car. The *brake system* slows or stops the car. All four wheels have brakes.

The *support system* supports the weight of the car. It includes wheels and axles, tires, and springs. Most cars have shock absorbers to keep the car riding smoothly.

The *electrical system* ties many of the other systems together. It helps start the car. It also powers the car's lights, radio, and other special equipment. All cars have batteries for their electrical systems. Hybrid and electric cars also have more powerful batteries for their motors.

Many people work at making cars. It takes several years to design and build a new car. Engineers design new cars on computers. Then they build model cars called *prototypes*. The prototypes must go through many safety tests. Some leading carmaking countries include Japan, the United States, Germany, France, Spain, and South Korea.

A car is a complex machine, with many different systems that work closely together. This diagram shows some of the important parts of a car.

Continued on the next page

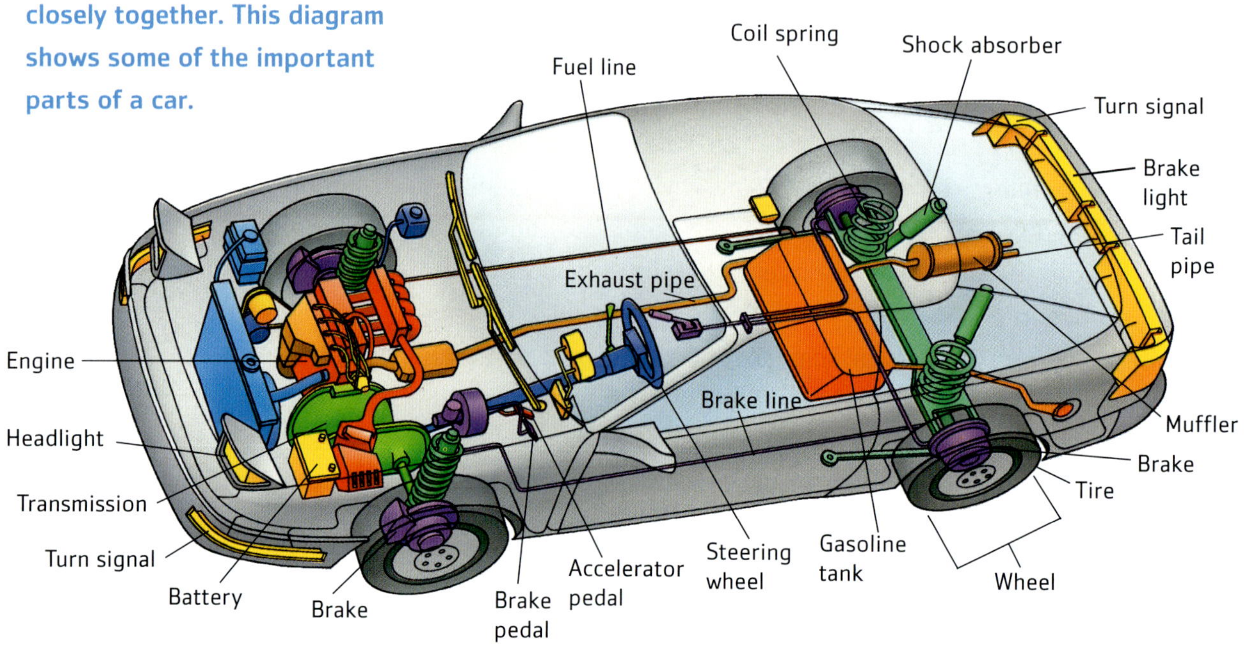

Ford's Model T was one of the first inexpensive cars. It was made on moving assembly lines starting in 1913.

Automobiles provide jobs for more than just automakers. Gas stations, fast-food restaurants, and motels are all businesses that depend on automobiles.

But cars cause problems, too. Millions of people have died in car accidents. Many more are injured. Today, cars have seat belts, airbags, and other equipment that makes them safer.

Automobiles also pollute the air we breathe. Many cars are now designed to give off less pollution. But cities still have air pollution problems caused by automobiles.

Nicolas-Joseph Cugnot, a French engineer, built the first car in the late 1700's. This car ran on steam instead of gasoline. By the late 1800's, several American companies were making steam-powered cars. But these cars were expensive to make and to run.

In the 1890's, electric cars became popular. They used batteries. They were quiet, clean, and easy to run. But they could not travel very fast or very far. In 1885, two German inventors built a gasoline-powered engine for cars. Soon other inventors were using gasoline engines in cars.

Early cars were luxury items. By 1910, the United States was making more cars than were being made in Europe. American carmakers figured out how to quickly produce large numbers of cars and keep the cost down. Cars soon became cheap enough for ordinary people to own.

By the 1930's, three big U.S. companies had most of the automobile business. They were Ford Motor Company, Chrysler Group LLC, and General Motors. People still buy cars from these companies.

The use of cars grew after World War II (1939-1945). More roads and highways were built. Many people moved to the suburbs around big cities. These people needed cars to get from place to place. U.S. cars of the 1950's and 1960's were often big and powerful.

There was a worldwide petroleum shortage during the 1970's. It caused gasoline shortages and high gasoline prices. Many families switched to smaller, lightweight cars. Such cars are more fuel efficient. This shift led more cars to be imported into the United States from other countries.

Light trucks and sturdy sport utility vehicles (SUV's) became popular in the late 1990's and early 2000's. But as the 2000's continued, gas prices soared. More consumers purchased fuel-efficient vehicles, including hybrid cars and electric cars.

Other articles to read include: **Benz, Karl; Brake; Daimler, Gottlieb; Ford, Henry; Gasoline engine; Tire; Truck.**

Bb

Babbage, Charles

Charles Babbage *(BAB ihj)* (1791–1871) was an English mathematician. He created two early computer designs. His designs were geared machines. Modern computers are made using circuits, not gears. But they make use of many of Babbage's ideas.

Babbage's first design was called the *difference engine*. It was supposed to work out and print simple math tables. He never completed the machine. Instead, he worked on another machine. It was called the *analytical engine*. He designed it to do more difficult math problems. It followed a series of directions. Babbage never finished this machine, either. But his designs helped lead to the invention of modern computers.

Other articles to read include: **Computer.**

The *difference engine* was an early computing machine invented by Charles Babbage. Babbage never finished building it. The device in this photograph is a model based on his design.

Balance

A balance is a device used to weigh things. One of the simplest balances is a horizontal bar. A pan is suspended from each end. The bar is held up at its center. To weigh an object, a person can place it in one of the pans. The person then puts objects of known weight in the other pan. The beam tilts toward the heavier pan. When the two pans are in balance, the weights are equal.

Today, many balances use only one pan. An object is placed in the pan. Built-in weights measure the heaviness of the object. Such balances often show the object's weight on a small electronic screen.

Other articles to read include: **Scale.**

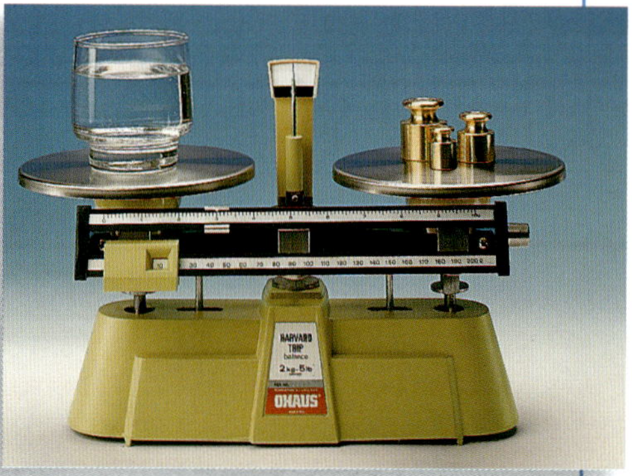

Many balances have two *pans* or trays. One pan holds the objects to be weighed (above left). The other holds units of standard weight.

Balloon

A balloon is a floating bag. It is filled with heated air or with a light gas. Hot air is lighter than normal air. Certain gases, such as hydrogen and helium, are also lighter than air. A balloon filled with any of these is lighter than the air around it, so it floats.

Balloons come in many sizes, shapes, and colors. They have many uses. Children play with toy balloons. People pilot *sport balloons* for fun. Large balloons have attached baskets to carry people. Scientists use balloons to gather information about the weather. These balloons carry instruments high up into the sky. They measure such things as the temperature of the air.

There are two main kinds of large balloons: *hot-air balloons* and *gas balloons*. Hot-air balloons are used mainly for sport ballooning. Hot-air balloons use a gas called *propane* to make a flame. The flame heats the air inside the balloon, causing the balloon to rise.

Gas balloons often carry scientific equipment. They are also used by the military. They may be filled with hydrogen, helium, or natural gas. Hydrogen is the lightest gas. But it explodes easily. Most gas balloons use helium because it is much safer.

Continued on the next page

Hot-air balloons float because the warm air inside the balloon is less dense, or lighter, than the surrounding, cooler air.

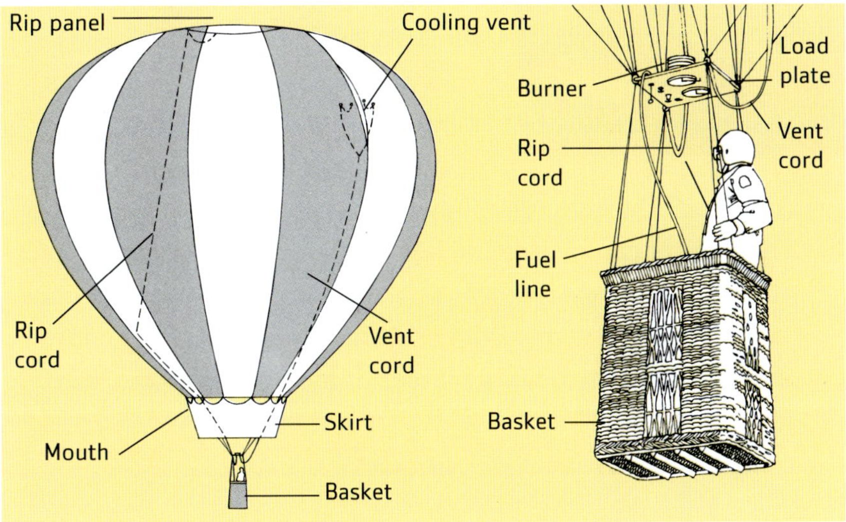

In a hot-air balloon, fuel is burned to heat air, making the balloon rise. To lower the balloon, the pilot turns down the burner or opens the *cooling vent.* Upon landing, the pilot pulls open the *rip panel* to quickly let the hot air out of the bag.

Balloon *Continued from the previous page*

The first human flights were on balloons. The hot-air balloon was invented by two French brothers, Jacques Étienne Montgolfier and Joseph Michel Montgolfier. The first balloon passengers were a duck, a rooster, and a sheep. They were launched on a balloon by the Montgolfier brothers. In 1783, Jean-François Pilâtre de Rozier, a French scientist, became the first human to fly in a hot-air balloon. Hot-air balloons are still used for flying today.

Other articles to read include: **Airship; Montgolfier brothers; Pilâtre de Rozier, Jean-François; Radiosonde; Weather balloon.**

Scientists launch gas balloons that carry instruments high into the sky.

A scanner reads a bar code by shining light on the pattern of bars. It sends the pattern to a computer.

Bar coding

Bar coding is a way of labeling items. Stores often use bar codes on products for sale. A bar code is made up of a pattern of lines and bars. The pattern stands for information about the item, such as its price.

A *scanner* is a device that shines light on the bar code's pattern. The scanner sends the pattern to a computer. The computer may be part of a store's cash register. The register can display the item's price, brand, and other information. Warehouses, hospitals, and factories also use bar codes to keep track of items. Driver's licenses often have bar codes with information about the driver. Some mobile phones can scan bar codes.

Other articles to read include: **Computer.**

Barometer

The barometer *(buh ROM uh tuhr)* is an instrument that measures *air pressure.* Air is very light, but it does have weight. Air pressure results from the weight of air pressing down. Weather forecasters use barometers to measure changes in air pressure. A change in air pressure usually means that the weather will change.

The barometer was invented in 1644 by Evangelista Torricelli, an Italian scientist. He filled a long glass tube with mercury, a liquid metal. He stood the tube on end in a cup of mercury. When air pressure above the mercury in the cup got higher, it pushed the mercury higher up in the tube. When air pressure went down, the mercury in the tube went down.

There are two kinds of barometers used today. One is a *mercury barometer.* It makes use of the same basic principle as Torricelli's device. The other kind of barometer is called an *aneroid (AN uh royd) barometer.* An aneroid barometer measures air pressure with a metal chamber. Some of the air has been taken out of the chamber. The sides of the chamber get pushed in when air pressure rises. They get pushed out when the air pressure falls. The changes move a needle around a dial. The number on the dial that the needle points to is the air pressure.

Pilots in airplanes use a kind of barometer called an *altimeter (al TIHM uh tuhr* or *AL tuh MEE tuhr).* It uses air pressure to measure *altitude* (height above Earth). The higher a plane flies, the lower the air pressure. The altimeter measures the air pressure but shows the measurement as height.

Other articles to read include: **Weather forecasting.**

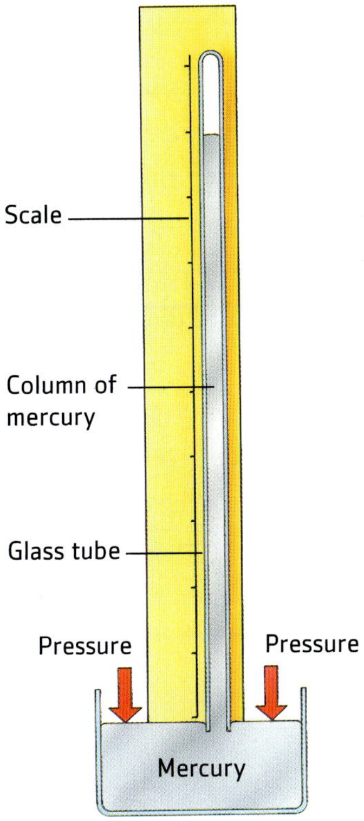

A mercury barometer is a glass tube filled with a liquid metal called *mercury.* The tube is closed at one end. Changes in air pressure cause mercury in the tube to rise or fall. The scale measures the pressure.

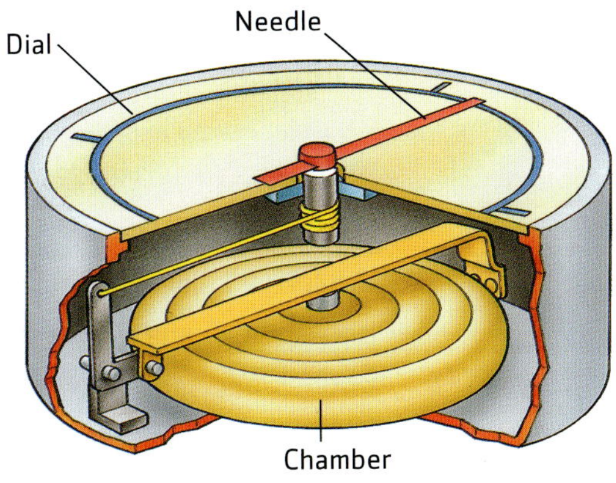

An *aneroid barometer* measures air pressure using a metal chamber. Air pressure pushes against the chamber, moving a needle around a dial.

Battery

A battery is a device that stores energy. The energy is stored in chemicals inside the battery. Batteries can release this energy as electric energy. Batteries power many devices, from small toys to large automobiles.

There are two main types of batteries: *primary* and *secondary* batteries. Primary batteries must be replaced when they wear out. Secondary batteries can be recharged. They can thus be used over and over again. Many computers, cell phones, and other electronic devices have built-in secondary batteries. Automobiles also use secondary batteries.

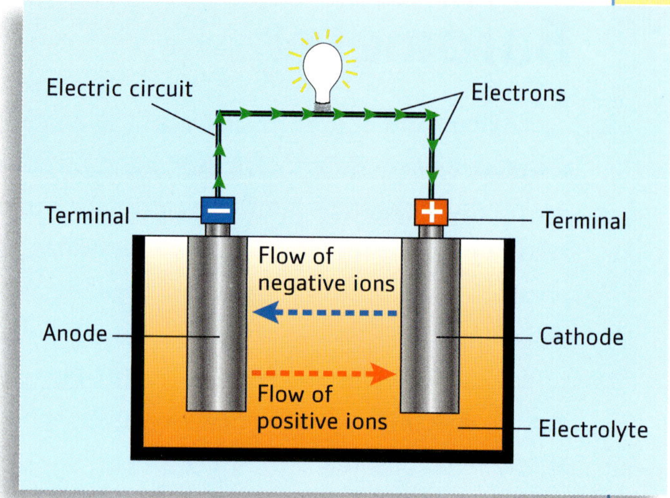

Chemical reactions inside a battery "push" charged particles called *electrons* around a circuit. The moving electrons form an electric current.

All batteries are filled with a substance called *electrolyte*. Electrolytes contain acids, bases, or salts. The electrolyte lies between two other main battery parts. They are the *anode* and the *cathode*. The anode is usually marked with a minus (–) sign. The cathode usually has a plus (+) sign. Batteries are often named for the kinds of materials in their anodes, cathodes, and electrolytes. For example, a *lithium-ion battery* uses the element lithium in its electrolyte.

Chemical reactions take place among the battery's anode, cathode, and electrolyte. The reactions "push" electric charges out through the anode. These charges have energy. They travel into an *electric circuit* connected to the anode. An electric circuit is looping path. The charges power devices connected to the circuit. Then the charges come back inside the battery through its cathode.

In a secondary battery, the charges can be "pushed" the opposite way by an electric current. This process restores the battery's chemicals so they can react again.

Other articles to read include: **Electric circuit; Electric current; Electrode.**

Batteries come in many shapes and sizes. Some devices, such as phones and laptop computers, have built-in batteries.

ACTIVITY

Energy from a lemon

Caution: This experiment requires adult assistance and supervision!

Did you know you can make a battery from a lemon? It's true! This experiment will show you how to make a simple battery from two pieces of metal and a lemon. The two metals react with the citric acid in the lemon to produce an electric current. You'll see how you can even use this battery to power an electrical device.

1. Use the scissors to cut the cardboard into three strips about ½ inch (12 millimeters) wide and about 2 inches (5 centimeters) long. Wrap aluminum foil around the cardboard strips.

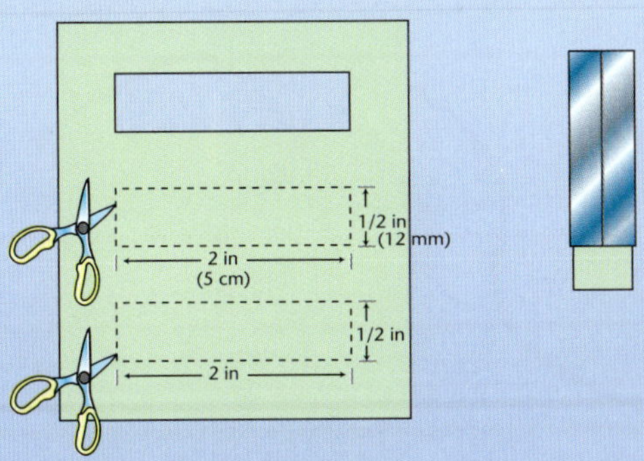

2. If you are using a copper sheet, have an adult use tin snips to cut three strips about ½ inch wide and about 2 inches long. If you are using copper tubing, have an adult use a hacksaw to cut three 2-inch long pieces of tubing. Have the adult use pliers to squeeze one end of each section of tubing flat.

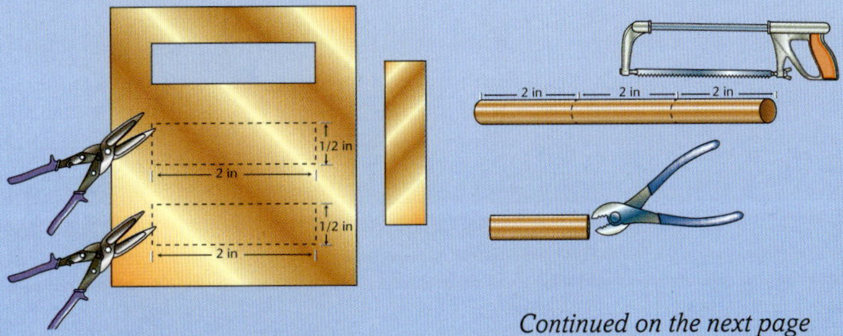

What you need:

- scissors
- a piece of thin cardboard
- aluminum foil
- a sheet of copper or some ½-inch (12-millimeter) copper tubing
- tin snips, a hacksaw, or pliers
- some thin, insulated copper wire
- three lemons
- a table knife
- metal paper clips
- a button-battery powered LCD (liquid crystal display) clock
- electrical tape or adhesive tape

Caution: These tools should be handled only by an adult. Copper can be sharp or jagged after being cut and must be handled carefully.

3. Have an adult cut two pieces of copper wire about 6 inches (15 centimeters) long and two pieces about 12 inches (30 centimeters) long. Have the adult strip about ½ inch of insulation from each end of each wire.

Continued on the next page

ACTIVITY

4. Squeeze the lemons gently without breaking the skin. You may do this by rolling them on the table with the palm of your hand. Squeezing breaks some of the tiny sacs inside a lemon that hold the juice. Have an adult cut two parallel slits about 1 inch (2.5 centimeters) apart in each lemon with the table knife.

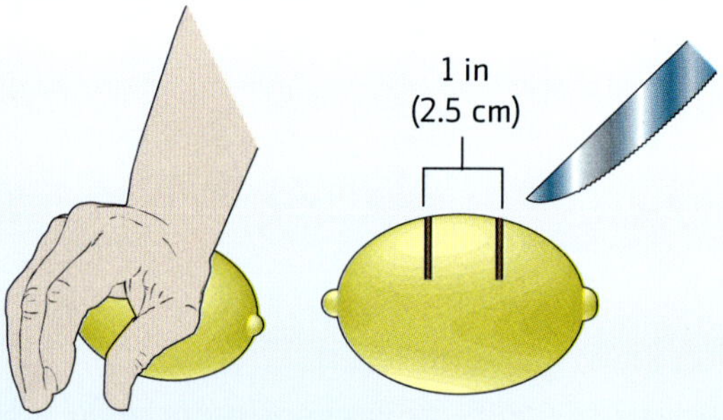

5. Insert an aluminum-covered strip into one of the slits in each of the lemons. Insert a copper strip, or the flattened end of a piece of copper tubing, into the other slit in each lemon. The pieces of metal will be the terminals of your lemon batteries. Be sure that the two metals do not touch inside the lemons.

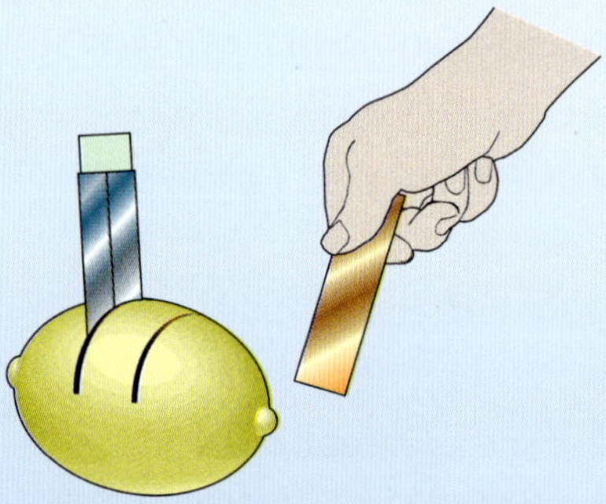

6. Use paper clips to attach a stripped end of each of the two short wires and one of the long ones to the aluminum-covered strips. Be sure that the metal of the wire is touching the metal of the strip.

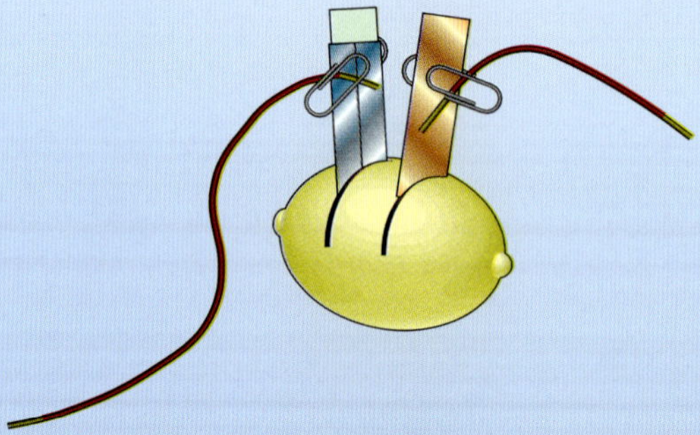

7. Line the lemons up and use paper clips to connect the free ends of the short wires and one end of the unused long wire to the copper pieces as shown in the illustration.

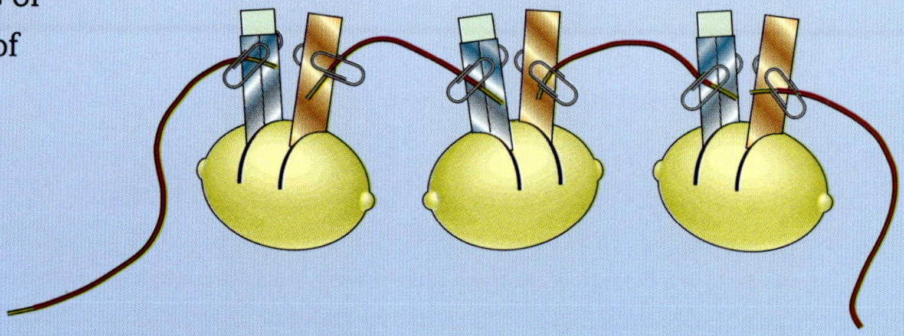

Continued on the next page

ACTIVITY

8. Open the battery compartment of the clock and observe the position of the battery before you remove it. Make a note of which side of the battery is marked with a plus sign (+). Use tape to connect the long wire attached to the piece of copper to the clock's positive terminal, the metal part that had been touching the side of the battery with the plus sign.

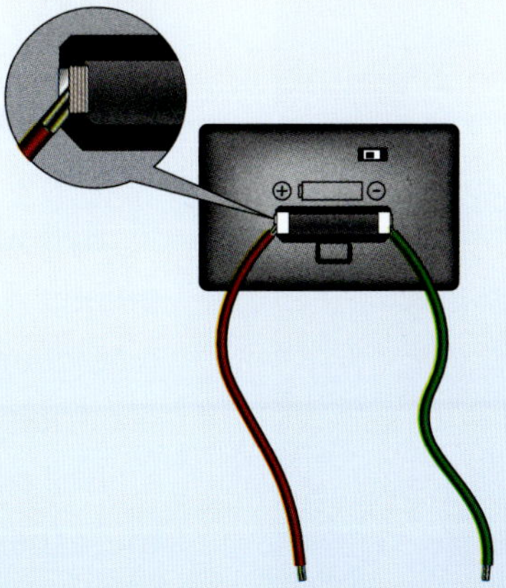

9. Use tape to connect the long wire attached to the aluminum-covered strip to the clock's negative terminal, the metal part that had been in contact with the other side of the button battery.

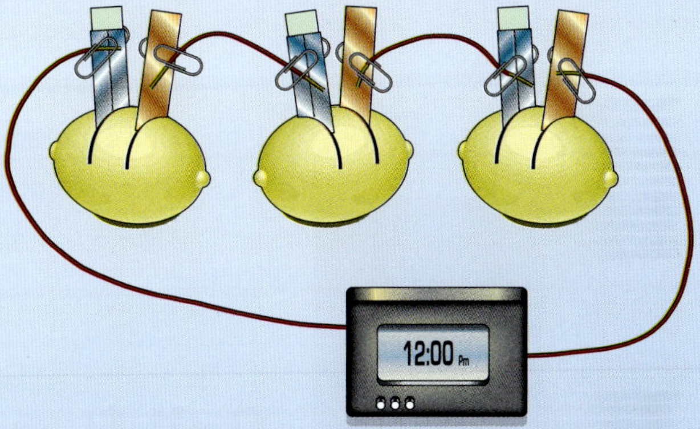

It will take a while for the reaction to produce a high enough voltage to run the clock. If the clock does not begin running within a minute, check to make sure that the bare copper wire is in contact with the metal of each of the terminals on the lemons and on the clock.

Additional activities:

A single lemon battery produces about 0.5 volt. Most small flashlight bulbs require about 2.4 volts to light brightly. You can light a flashlight bulb by connecting additional lemon batteries to the series. By using a total of four or five lemon batteries, you should be able to light the bulb when you touch one of the two free wire ends to its base and the other to its side.

You can perform the original activity using other kinds of citrus fruits, such as grapefruit, limes, or oranges. How many of each of these fruits do you need to use to power the clock? The weaker the acid is in the fruit, the more fruit batteries will be needed to make the clock work.

http://bit.ly/WWORxy

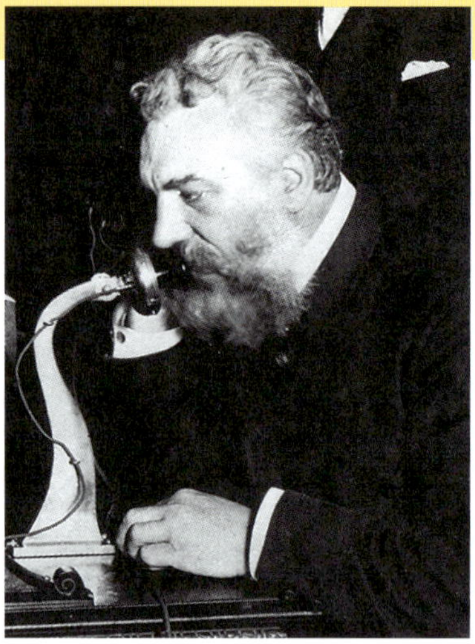

Alexander Graham Bell

Bell, Alexander Graham

Alexander Graham Bell (1847–1922) was a Scottish-born inventor. He is most famous for inventing the telephone.

Bell was born in Edinburgh, Scotland. His mother was a painter. His father taught deaf people to speak. Bell also became a teacher and taught deaf students. He also experimented with electricity.

Bell tried to invent a better *telegraph.* A telegraph sends messages over a wire as a series of clicks. Bell wanted to send a human voice over a telegraph wire. An assistant, Thomas A. Watson, helped Bell make a machine that could send certain sounds. In March 1876, Bell spilled acid on his clothes. He called, "Mr. Watson, come here. I want you!" Watson was in another room. But he heard Bell's voice coming from the machine.

Bell's invention helped start the telephone industry. But Bell spent much of the rest of his life working to help the deaf.

Other articles to read include: **Telegraph; Telephone.**

Jocelyn Bell Burnell

Bell Burnell, Jocelyn

Jocelyn Bell Burnell (1943–) is a British astronomer. She was the first person to detect a *pulsar.* A pulsar is a relatively tiny star. Pulsars do not shine like other stars. Instead, they send out two narrow beams of radio waves. As the star spins, the beams sweep over Earth like the light from a lighthouse. Pulsars get their name from these passing "pulses" of energy.

Pulsars are a type of star called a *neutron star.* Since the 1930's, astronomers had thought that neutron stars existed. But they had never found one. Bell first found a pulsar in 1967. She was using a type of telescope that detects radio waves from space. Her discovery helped prove that neutron stars exist. This proof led to many new ideas about how stars form and change.

Susan Jocelyn Bell was born on July 15, 1943, in Belfast, Northern Ireland. She received a Ph.D. degree from the University of Cambridge in 1968. In 1982, she joined the Royal Observatory in Edinburgh, Scotland. During her long career, she worked as a professor at several universities in the United Kingdom and the United States. She also served as the vice president of the Royal Astronomical Society in England.

Benz, Karl

Karl Benz and his daughter Clara take a drive in the Benz Victoria, the first four-wheeled Benz automobile, built in 1893.

Karl Benz *(behnts)* (1844–1929) was a German engineer and inventor. Benz was a pioneer in building motor-driven vehicles. He founded Benz & Company in Mannheim, Germany, to manufacture gasoline engines.

Benz started to build his first gasoline engine in 1878. He made his first motor vehicle in 1885. The car did not look much like modern automobiles. It had a small front wheel and two big back wheels. But it used many devices that are still in cars today. For example, its engine started with an electric spark. Water also cooled its engine, as in modern engines. And like modern cars, Benz's car used special gears that let its wheels turn at different speeds. He also designed a type of carburetor and a transmission system.

Benz was born on Nov. 25, 1844, in Karlsruhe. He died on April 4, 1929.

Other articles to read include: **Automobile; Daimler, Gottlieb; Gasoline engine.**

Berners-Lee, Tim

Tim Berners-Lee

Tim Berners-Lee (1955–), a British computer scientist, developed the World Wide Web. The World Wide Web, or Web for short, is part of the Internet. The Internet is the worldwide network of computers. The Web allows computer users to make and view "pages." Web pages may contain pictures, sounds, and videos, in addition to words. The Web made the Internet much easier for ordinary people to use.

Berners-Lee developed the Web while working at the European Organization for Nuclear Research (CERN) near Geneva, Switzerland. In 1980, he created a system called *hypertext.* Hypertext links words in one computer file to other files. About 1989, he developed the World Wide Web. It was used at first by scientists. In 1991, the Web became part of the Internet. Berners-Lee created a coding system for building web pages. He also developed a system for organizing web pages on the Internet.

Other articles to read include: **Computer; Internet; Website.**

People ride bicycles to travel, to exercise, and just to have fun.

Bicycle

The bicycle is a vehicle powered by the pedaling of a rider. A bicycle has two wheels and a frame. One wheel is set behind the other. The rider pushes two pedals around in a circle to make the bike move. People ride bicycles to travel, to exercise, and just to have fun.

Bicycles are popular around the world. Most countries have more bicycles than cars. Brazil, China, Italy, Japan, South Korea, Taiwan, and the United States make the most bicycles.

Bicycles come in many sizes. Children's bicycles are measured by the wheel size. Adult bicycles are measured by the length of the tube that holds the seat. There are also many styles of bicycles.

Mountain bikes have strong frames and flat handlebars. They have wide, rough tires. They are good for riding on dirt tracks and forest paths. *Road bikes* are made to ride on smooth roads. They have curved handlebars. *Hybrids* are a bit like mountain bikes and a bit like road bikes. Many people ride hybrid bikes to work. A hybrid's tires are wider than those of a road bike but thinner than mountain bike tires. Hybrid bikes have flat handlebars.

BMX bikes are made for a sport called *bicycle motocross,* in which riders race on dirt tracks. *Freestyle bikes* are used for trick riding. *Specialty bicycles* have unusual designs. *Tandem bikes,* for example, carry two riders, one in front of the other. Each rider has a set of pedals. To ride a *recumbent bike,* a person lies back in a special seat and pedals with the legs in front.

To ride a bike, the rider pushes the pedals in a circle. The pedals are attached to a *sprocket* (toothed wheel) called the *chainring.* A chain wraps around the chainring and around a smaller sprocket on the rear wheel. When the rider pedals, the chainring turns. The turning of the chainring pulls on the chain. The chain in turn turns the small sprocket and the rear wheel.

Continued on the next page

A bicycle's gear system often has sprockets of different sizes. This allows the rider to switch between low and high gears. Low gear makes it easier to pedal. But in low gear, each turn of the pedals moves the wheel just a little. So low gear is slower. The rider has to pedal faster to make the same speed. Low gear may be used to pedal uphill.

High gears are used for fast speeds on level roads. They are also used in bicycling downhill. In high gear, each turn of the pedal makes the rear wheel turn many times around a smaller sprocket.

The rider uses the handlebars to steer the bicycle and keep it steady. The brakes are used to stop. Most bicycles have brakes that are connected to levers on the handlebars. To use the brakes, the rider squeezes these levers. Brake pads then press against the rims of the wheels and slow their spinning motion. If the bicycle has *coaster brakes,* the rider stops by pushing backward on the pedals.

In the United States, all bicycles must have certain safety features. These features include front and rear reflectors. Reflectors bounce back light. They make the bicycle easier to see at night. The wheels must also have reflectors that can be seen from the side. The tires should always be properly inflated. The brakes and gears should work easily. Bells or horns are not required. But they can warn people that a bicycle is coming and help prevent accidents.

Continued on the next page

Parts of a bicycle

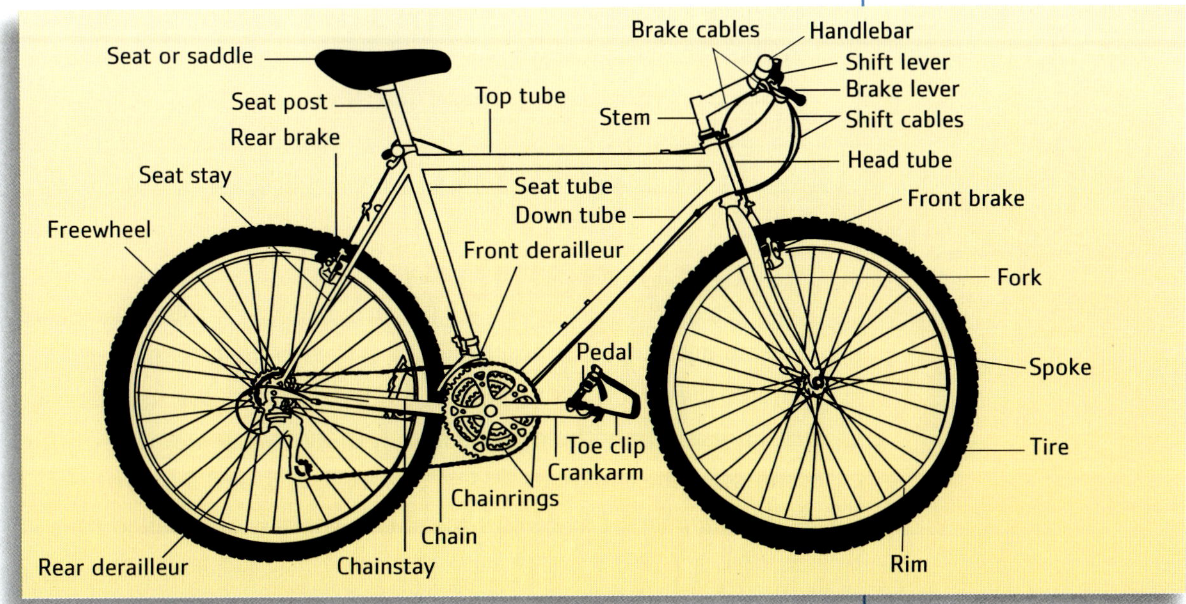

Development of the bicycle

The draisienne, about 1817

Pierre Lallement's pedal-powered bicycle, 1866

High-wheeler, 1870's

Safety bicycle, 1880's

Bicycle *Continued from the previous page*

Bicyclelike vehicles first appeared in Europe during the 1800's. In 1817, Baron Karl von Drais of Germany invented the *draisienne*. It had two wheels and a seat, but no pedals. The rider pushed on the ground with his or her feet to make it move. A Scottish blacksmith named Kirkpatrick Macmillan added pedals in 1839.

High-wheeler bikes appeared about 1870. They had a huge front wheel and a tiny rear wheel. The big wheel turned once for each turn of the pedals. So the bicycle went a long way with a single turn of the pedals.

About 1885, an English bicycle maker made the first successful *safety bike*. Its wheels were the same size, so it was easier and safer to ride than a high-wheeler. It also had a chain and sprockets, like modern bicycles.

By 1890, bicycles had air-filled rubber tires. Before that, tires were solid and usually made of metal or rubber. The hard, solid tires made the ride bumpy and rough. Air-filled rubber tires made the ride less bumpy.

Some bicycles by that time also had coaster brakes and adjustable handlebars. About 4 million Americans were riding bicycles by then. But as cars became popular, many people stopped using bikes.

Bicycles became popular again in the 1970's. At that time, people began riding bikes for exercise and for fun. Many cities now have special lanes for bicycles in parks and along many city streets.

Other articles to read include: **Brake; Gear; Motorcycle; Tire.**

Binary number

A binary number is written with only two *digits*. Digits are symbols used to write numbers. Binary numbers are usually written using only the digits *0* and *1*. In everyday life, we commonly use the digits *0, 1, 2, 3, 4, 5, 6, 7, 8,* and *9* to write *decimal numbers*. The binary number system is also called *base 2*.

Continued on the next page

The decimal system, on the other hand, is called *base 10.*

Any decimal number can also be written as a binary number. For example, the decimal number 5 is written *101* in binary. The first *1* is in the "fours" place. The zero is in the "twos" place. And the second *1* is in the "ones" place (4 + 0 + 1 = 5).

Computers use binary numbers to store data and perform calculations. A computer's circuits can be switched either "on" or "off." The switch lets an electric current pass through or not. These two positions work like the two digits in binary numbers. A binary number in a computer can stand for letters and words. It can even represent pictures, sounds, and videos. Modern computers can perform huge numbers of binary calculations at extremely fast speeds.

Gottfried Wilhelm Leibniz, a German philosopher and mathematician, developed the binary number system in the late 1600's. But binary numbers were not widely used until the 1940's, when people developed the first electronic computers.

Other articles to read include: **Byte; Computer.**

Binoculars

Binoculars make faraway objects look larger and closer. Binoculars are made up of two tubes, joined side by side. Each tube is a small telescope. Each telescope has a large lens at one end. The large lens gathers light from an object and *magnifies* the image—that is, it makes the object look bigger. The magnified image is upside down and reversed. In some binoculars, a prism flips the image back over and right side up. In others, another lens does this. The image's light then travels to lenses at the eyepiece. These lenses magnify the image even more.

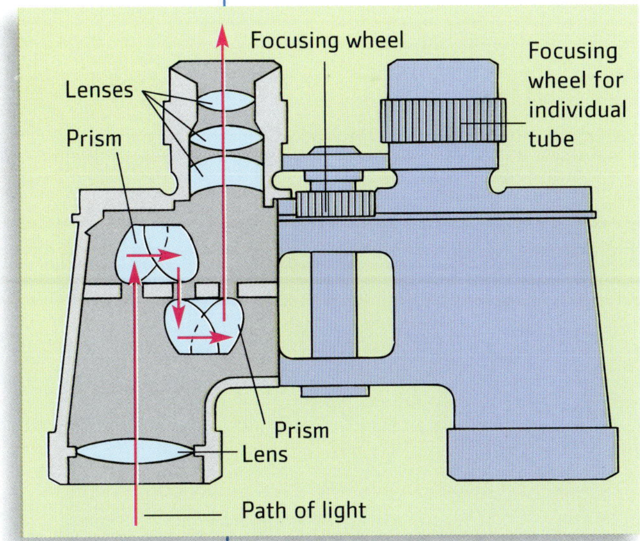

The parts of binoculars

On most binoculars, two small wheels can be turned to let the person see objects at different distances. One wheel between the tubes adjusts the lenses in both tubes. The other wheel, placed on an eyepiece, adjusts the lenses in only one tube.

Other articles to read include: **Lens; Prism; Telescope.**

Biodegradable material

Biodegradable *(BY oh dih GRAY duh buhl)* materials can be broken down by *microbes.* A microbe, or *microorganism,* is a tiny living thing. Materials made from living things are often biodegradable. Metals and most plastics are not.

Biodegradable products may help reduce waste. Such products break down when properly thrown away. This reduces the waste in *landfills* (garbage dumps).

Biodegradable materials need certain conditions to break down. These conditions are often available in a *compost* pile. Compost *(KOM pohst)* is a mixture of dead plant parts and other material. Biodegradable materials can be composted.

Other articles to read include: **Landfill; Plastics.**

Day 0

Day 12

Day 33

Day 45

This biodegradable fork, made out of a corn-based plastic, breaks down in about 45 days.

Blimp

Blimps are huge, tube-shaped airships. They are similar to large balloons. But they have engines that move them through the air. They are usually filled with helium gas. Blimps are used mainly for advertising. Military forces also use blimps.

The name *blimp* comes from the United States Navy's B-class *nonrigid* airships, built in 1917. These airships—unlike *rigid* airships—had no solid support structure. They became limp when their gas was let out. People called them *B-limps,* or *blimps* for short.

Other articles to read include: **Aircraft, Military; Airship.**

A blimp is an airship without a rigid support structure.

Bluford, Guion Stewart, Jr.

Guion Stewart Bluford *(GY uhn STOO urt BLOO furd),* Jr. (1942–), was the first African American to travel in space. On Aug. 30, 1983, Bluford and four other astronauts began a six-day flight aboard the space shuttle Challenger. During the flight, Bluford launched a satellite for India. He also helped test the shuttle's robotic arm. The astronauts used the arm to move a heavy weight from the cargo area into space and back again.

Bluford was born on Nov. 22, 1942, in Philadelphia. He entered the Air Force in 1964. He began training to become an astronaut in 1978. Bluford continued to serve on space shuttle flights until 1993. In that year, he resigned as an astronaut and retired from the Air Force.

Other articles to read include: **Astronaut; Space exploration.**

Guion Stewart Bluford, Jr.

Bolden, Charles Frank, Jr.

Charles Frank Bolden, Jr. (1946–), became administrator of NASA in 2009. *NASA* stands for *N*ational *A*eronautics and *S*pace *A*dministration. Bolden, a pilot and astronaut, was appointed by President Barack Obama. He became the first African American to head the agency.

Bolden was born in Columbia, South Carolina, on Aug. 19, 1946. He studied at the U.S. Naval Academy. Bolden, a Marine Corps fighter pilot, served in the Vietnam War (1957–1975) from 1972 to 1973. He also served as a commander in the Persian Gulf War of 1991.

Bolden joined the NASA astronaut corps in 1980. He flew on four space shuttle flights and served as mission commander on two of the flights. After his final space shuttle flight in 1994, he left NASA to return to active duty in the Marine Corps as the Deputy Commandant of Midshipmen at the Naval Academy. He retired from the Marines in 2003.

Other articles to read include: **National Aeronautics and Space Administration.**

Charles Frank Bolden, Jr.

Bomb

Bombs are weapons that explode. Most bombs are used in war. People called *terrorists* also use deadly bombs to spread fear and alarm.

Most bombs are made up of a metal container filled with a material that explodes. The explosion creates a burst of pressure called a *blast wave*. The blast wave destroys buildings, vehicles, and living things. The explosion also shatters the bomb's container. Pieces of the container fly out at high speeds, also causing damage.

Many bombs are dropped from airplanes. Some bombs are small enough to carry in the hand. Other bombs may be thrown or fired from special guns. Unlike a missile, a bomb does not fly through the air under its own power. But some bombs have fins or wings that can guide them as they fall.

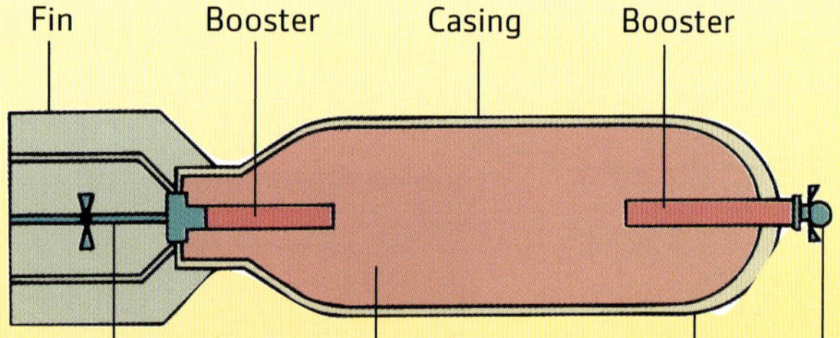

This diagram shows the parts of a type of bomb usually dropped from high in the air. A fuse in the nose or tail can trigger the explosion. Fins help steady the bomb in flight.

Bombs may have special designs. Bombs with heavy steel noses can pierce thick armor on battleships. *Incendiary bombs* are designed to start fires. *Nuclear bombs* are the most powerful kind by far.

The first bombs to be dropped from the sky were used in 1849 by Austria. Italy was probably the first country to drop bombs from an airplane. It did so in a war against Turkey in 1911.

During World War I (1914–1918), Germany, France, the United States, and Britain dropped bombs from airplanes. During World War II (1939–1945), bombs destroyed much of Europe and Japan. Incendiary bombs set fire to entire neighborhoods and cities. In 1945, the United States dropped two atomic bombs on Japan. These were the two most powerful and deadly bombs ever used in war.

During the Vietnam War (1957–1975), the United States used huge bombs nicknamed "daisy cutters" to clear thick jungle. Modern bombs are often guided by electronics and satellite signals. They are called *smart bombs*. Such bombs were widely used in the Persian Gulf War of 1991, the Iraq War (2003–2011), and the Afghanistan War, which began in 2001.

Other articles to read include: **Explosive; Guided missile; Nuclear weapon.**

Bondar, Roberta

Roberta Bondar

Roberta Bondar *(BAHN dahr)* (1945–) was the first Canadian woman to travel into space. She is a doctor of medicine. In January 1992, she and six other astronauts took an eight-day flight aboard the space shuttle Discovery. During the mission, Bondar studied how space flight affects human beings. She also examined how gravity affects and helps shape materials and living things. Bondar worked on tools and methods for doing research in the weightless state of space flight.

Roberta Lynn Bondar was born on Dec. 4, 1945, in Sault Sainte Marie, Ontario. She earned a medical degree from McMaster University in Hamilton in 1977. Her medical specialty is *neurology (nu ROL uh jee)*, the study of the nervous system and its diseases. Bondar served as an astronaut from 1983 to 1992. After leaving the astronaut program, Bondar educated people about science. From 2003 to 2009, she served as the chancellor of Trent University in Peterborough, Ontario.

Other articles to read include: **Astronaut; Space exploration.**

Boomerang

Boomerang

A boomerang is a flat, curved object thrown for sport or as a weapon. People often think of boomerangs as weapons of the Aborigines *(ab uh RIHJ uh neez)*. The Aborigines were the first people to live in Australia. They used boomerangs for hunting. They also used them as weapons, tools, and trading pieces. However, many groups of people throughout history have used boomerangs.

Most boomerangs are made of plastic or wood. They measure from 12 to 36 inches (30 to 90 centimeters) long. There are two types of boomerangs: returning and nonreturning. A returning boomerang may come back to a person after it is thrown. This type of boomerang is used mostly for sport. A nonreturning boomerang does not come back. But it can travel for about 650 feet (200 meters). People use nonreturning boomerangs for hunting. The spinning boomerang hits with more force than a thrown rock or stick.

Other articles to read include: **Tool.**

Brake

A brake is a device that slows or stops a moving object. Vehicles use a variety of brakes. A pedal or other control makes the brake work.

Brakes have a part called a *brake pad* or *brake shoe.* This part presses against a wheel or other moving part. Movement is slowed or even stopped by *friction* (rubbing) between the brake pad and the moving part.

There are several different kinds of brakes. For example, a bicycle has *mechanical brakes.* Most bicycle brakes are controlled with levers on the handlebars. The rider squeezes a lever. A cable transmits this squeezing force to the brake. There, it pushes the brake pad against the wheel rim. Cars have hydraulic *(hy DRAW lihk) brakes.* In these brakes, a liquid called *brake fluid* pushes the brake pads against the wheels. Buses and large trucks have *air brakes.* These brakes use the force of air to push the brake pads against the wheels.

Other articles to read include: **Automobile; Bicycle; Motorcycle.**

Most bicycles have *mechanical brakes.* Squeezing a lever on the handlebar causes two brake levers to press rubber pads against the wheel rim, slowing the wheel.

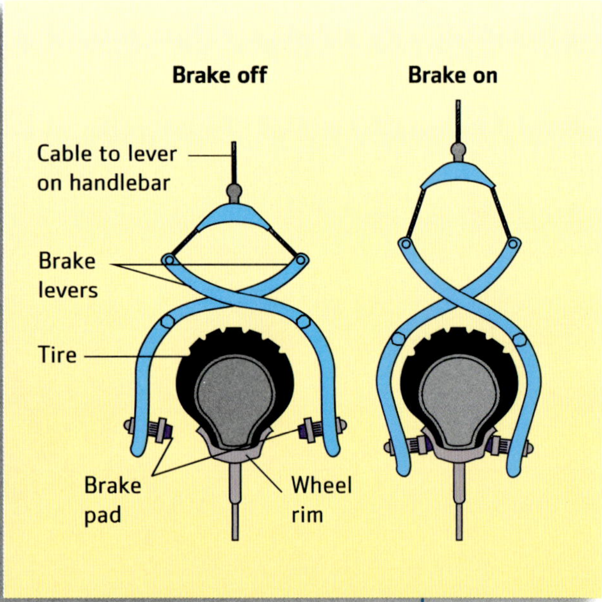

Cars use *hydraulic brakes.* A liquid called *brake fluid* pushes against brake pads or shoes. In *disc brakes,* the brake pads squeeze the sides of a wheel's disc, slowing the wheel. In *drum brakes,* curved brake shoes press against the inside of a wheel's drum.

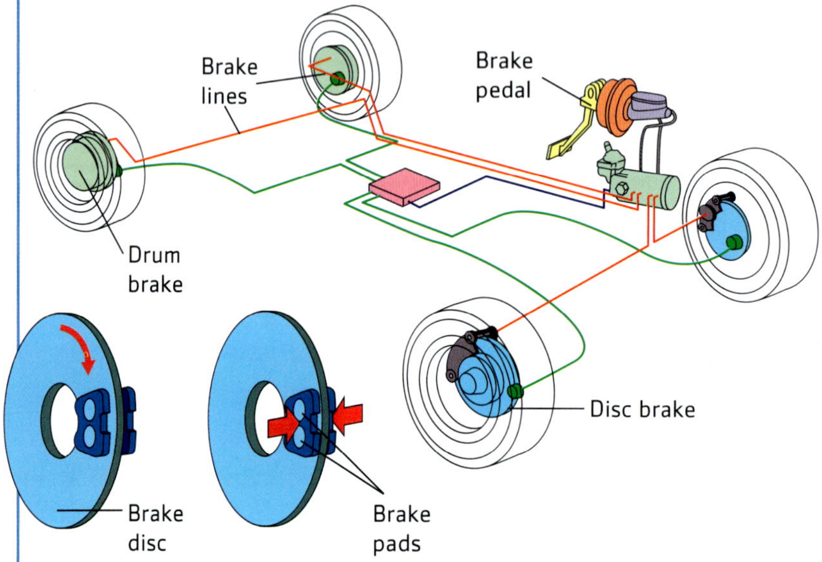

Brass

Brass is a metal *alloy* (mixture) of copper and zinc. It is often used in hardware, jewelry, and musical instruments.

Brass is yellow to coppery-red. By itself, copper is a soft metal. But copper becomes stronger when mixed with zinc. Other metals may be added to brass for various reasons. For example, adding lead makes brass easier to cut.

Brass was probably first made by accident when people heated rock that contained copper and zinc. Brass was used in ancient Rome about 2,000 years ago. The Romans made brass coins, pots, and ornaments.

Other articles to read include: **Alloy; Metal.**

Brass has been used since ancient times. This brass shield is decorated with figures of humans and animals.

Breakwater

A breakwater is a wall that protects beaches and harbors from strong waves. A wave loses much of its energy in hitting a breakwater. Breakwaters thus create an area of calm water near the shore. Ships can safely anchor behind a breakwater. People can also safely work in the calm water.

Some breakwaters are made of piled-up soil or rocks. Others are made from long pieces of wood, concrete, or steel. These pieces are driven into the sea bottom like fence posts. Breakwaters must be able to withstand waves from the strongest local storms.

Other articles to read include: **Building construction.**

A breakwater protects beaches and harbors from strong waves.

Bridge

Bridges enable people to cross rivers, canyons, railroads, or highways. Without bridges, people would often have to travel many miles or kilometers out of their way.

A bridge must be strong. It must hold up its own weight and that of the people and vehicles that cross it. Bridges must stand up to fierce winds, rough seas, and even earthquakes. In ancient times, people made bridges of stone and brick. Today, bridge builders use steel and concrete.

Most bridges are held up by supports at each end called *abutments.* Some bridges also have one or more supports between the abutments. These extra supports are called *piers.* The length of bridge between any two supports is called a *span.* The longer the bridge, the more supports it needs. A bridge's *roadway* is the part on which people and vehicles travel.

Bridges are built in a variety of ways. One of the oldest types of bridges is the *arch bridge.* The arch bears the weight of the bridge. The roadway can be either on top of the arch or underneath it.

A *cantilever (KAN tuh LEEV uhr) bridge* has two sections called *cantilevers.* The cantilevers stretch out from opposite sides of a river. They rest on piers. The cantilevers are joined in the middle by a connecting section.

Suspension (suh SPEHN shuhn) bridges are used to cross long distances. They may be built across deep canyons, ocean bays, and wide rivers. In this kind of bridge, the roadway is hung, or suspended, from thick steel cables. These *main cables* stretch from one end of the bridge to the other. They are held high in the air by two tall towers. The towers stand on piers. The roadway hangs from vertical cables attached to the main cables. The Golden Gate Bridge in California is a famous suspension bridge.

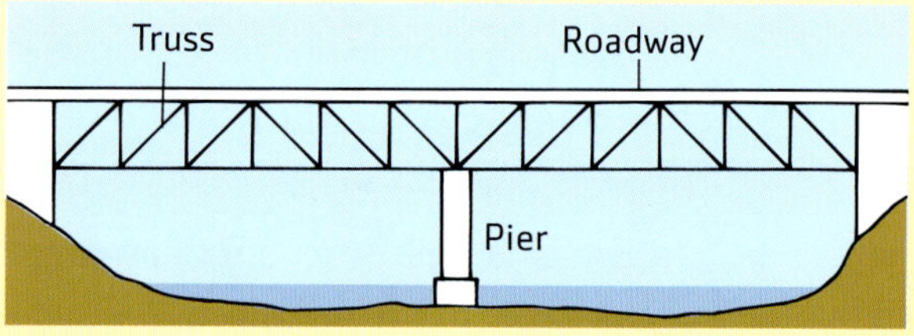

A *truss bridge* is supported by a frame called a *truss.* The parts that make up the trusses are set up in the shape of triangles.

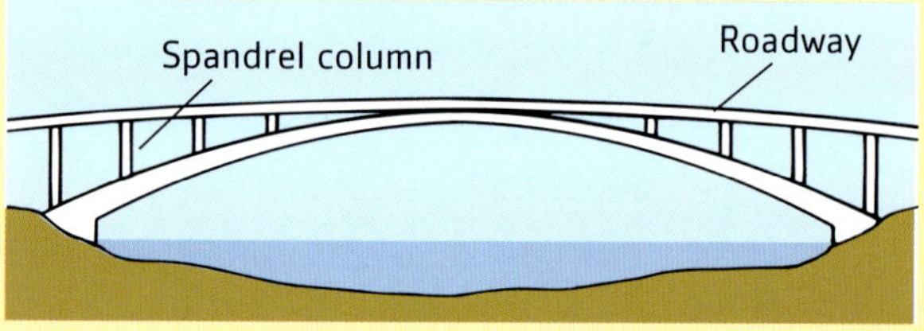

Some *arch bridges* have a roadway on top of supports called *spandrel columns.*

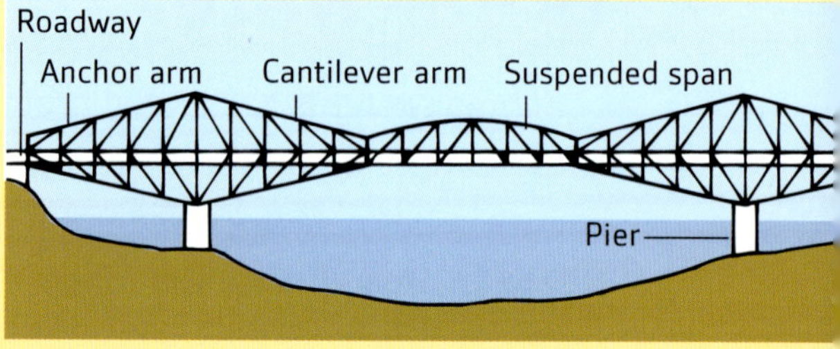

A *cantilever bridge* uses sections of beams called *cantilevers.* Each has two parts—an *anchor arm* and a *cantilever arm.*

A *cable-stayed bridge* is like a suspension bridge. But the cables holding the roadway are connected directly to the towers.

Other kinds of bridges can move. Part of the bridge swings open or lifts up to let large ships pass through.

Other articles to read include: **Building construction; Transportation.**

Continued on the next page

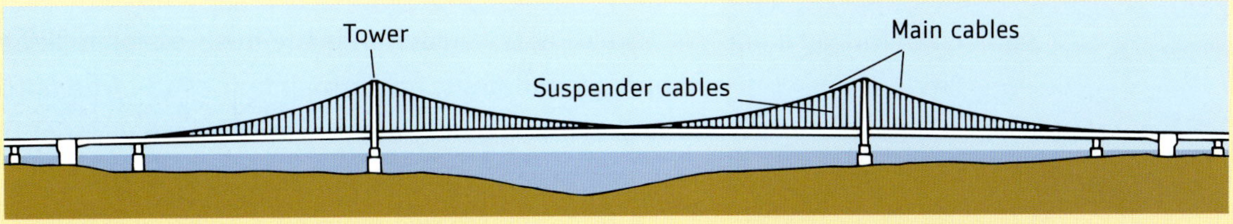

A *suspension bridge* has a roadway that hangs from *suspender cables.* The suspender cables hang from *main cables.* The main cables are held up by towers. The towers are on piers. Suspension bridges can span great distances.

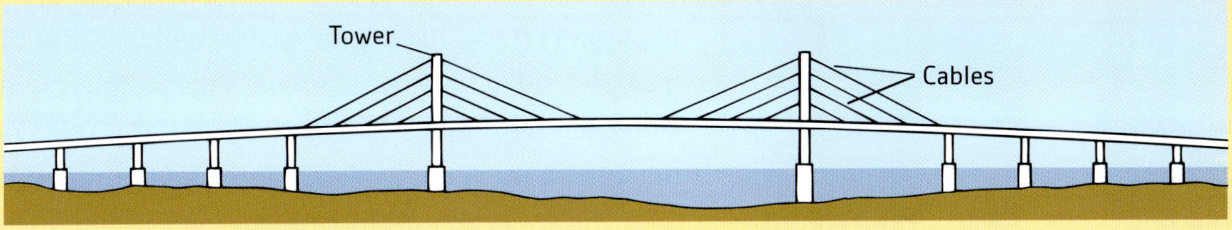

In a *cable-stayed bridge,* the cables that hold up the roadway are attached directly to the bridge's towers.

Bronze

Bronze is an *alloy*—a mixture of metals. It is mostly copper and tin. Sometimes other metals are added.

Bronze is easy to cast into large shapes, such as statues and bells. Such objects are made by melting the metal and pouring it into a mold. Bronze bells have a rich sound.

Bronze objects may last hundreds of years. In time, the surface of bronze turns brown or green.

People learned to make bronze about 3500 B.C. Ancient people crafted bronze cups and vases. They battled with bronze shields, helmets, axes, and swords. The time when bronze was commonly used is called the Bronze Age.

Other articles to read include: **Alloy; Metal.**

People have made objects from bronze since about 3500 B.C. This bronze statue is from Algeria in Africa. The statue was made before 100 A.D.

The frame of a skyscraper is built up one floor at a time. Building materials are lifted into place by cranes.

Building construction

Building construction is the business of making all kinds of buildings, from small homes to large office towers. It has been an important industry since ancient times.

A building has two main parts. The part below ground is the *foundation*. It supports the building. The foundation includes the basement walls, even if they are partly aboveground. The part of the building aboveground is called the *superstructure*.

Both the foundation and the superstructure help to support the *load* (weight) of the building. Buildings may also have to withstand wind, the weight of snow, and earthquakes. In some buildings, walls help to support the load. In skyscrapers and other buildings, the walls do not hold up anything. Such buildings use a *skeleton construction*. A sturdy framework holds up the walls, floors, and roof.

Architects and engineers design a building before construction begins. Large buildings, such as skyscrapers, require a great deal of planning. Computers help building designers figure out how to make a building safely.

Continued on the next page

Workers build up a framework of concrete reinforced with steel. The framework will support the building's walls, floors, and roof.

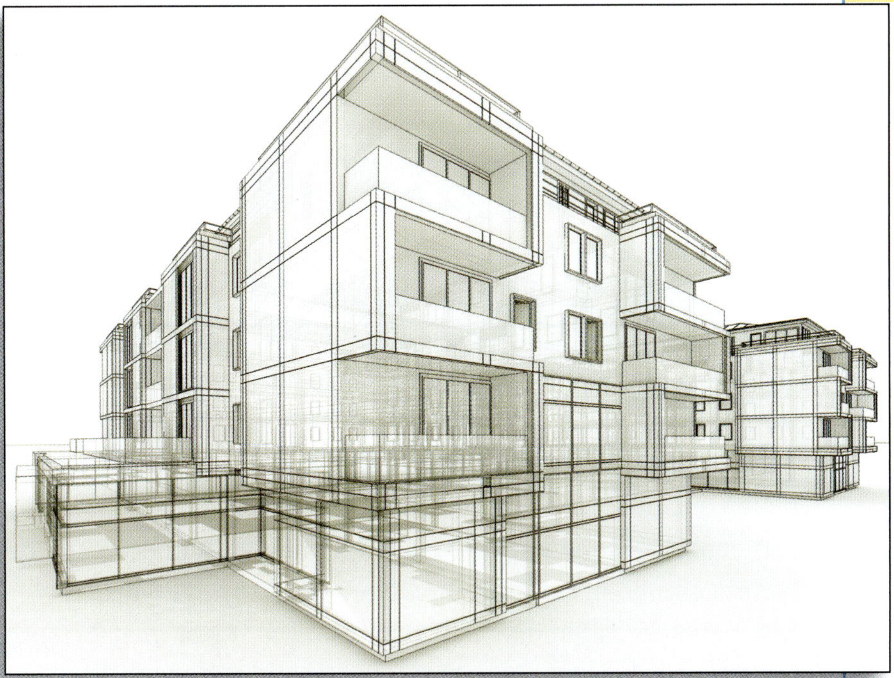

Architects and engineers design buildings before construction begins. This design for a new building was created using a computer.

Some buildings are *prefabricated (pree FAB ruh kay tuhd)*. That means all the parts are made to exact measurements in a factory. They are delivered to the building's location. There, workers put the parts together. Prefabricated buildings usually take less time and cost less to build.

Other articles to read include: **Cement and concrete; Engineering; Materials; Plumbing; Skyscraper; Steel; Welding.**

Some buildings are made with *prefabricated* parts. Workers put the parts together as they construct the building.

Byte

The byte is a unit of computer memory. A byte is made up of eight *binary digits,* or *bits.* A bit is one digit (either *0* or *1)* in the *binary system.* The binary system is the counting system used by computers.

A byte is any binary number between 00000000 and 11111111. There are 256 different combinations. A byte can stand for a numeral, a letter of the alphabet, a punctuation mark, or some other symbol. Computers string together bytes to form words and sentences. But bytes can stand for any kind of information, including sounds, pictures, and videos.

A computer's memory is measured in bytes. A photograph or the text of a book both take up about 1 *megabyte* (1,048,576 bytes). A short video may take up 1 *gigabyte* (1,024 megabytes). Computers often store hundreds of gigabytes of information.

Internet connection speeds are also measured using bytes. For example, a connection speed of 10 Mbps enables a user to download 10 megabytes of information per second.

Other articles to read include: **Binary number; Computer; Internet.**

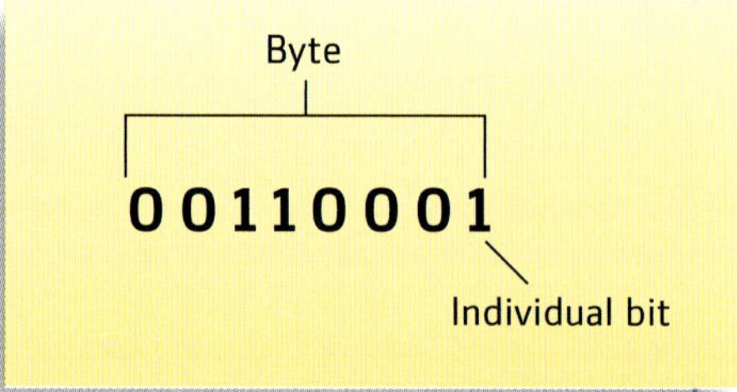

A *byte* is a group of eight *bits.* Each byte can represent a number, a letter, or another symbol. Computer memory is measured in bytes.

Cable

A cable is a wire or bundle of wires. Cables are widely used in electronics and communication. For example, they carry Internet and television signals around the world.

Most cables are made of metal wires. The wires *conduct* (carry) a flow of electricity called *electric current.* Rubber or plastic surrounds the cables, helping to keep the electric current from skipping the cable. A kind of cable called *coaxial cable* has two conductors separated by an insulator.

Another kind of cable is called a *fiber-optic* cable. It contains a bundle of glass fibers. The fibers carry pulses of light.

Billions of miles or kilometers of cable carry communications signals and electric power throughout the world. Specialized cables are used with computers and other devices.

Some cables have been replaced by *wireless communication*. Wireless communication is the sending of signals via radio or other invisible waves. However, cables are often the fastest way to send communications signals.

Other articles to read include: **Electric current; Fiber optics; Wire.**

Electric power cables

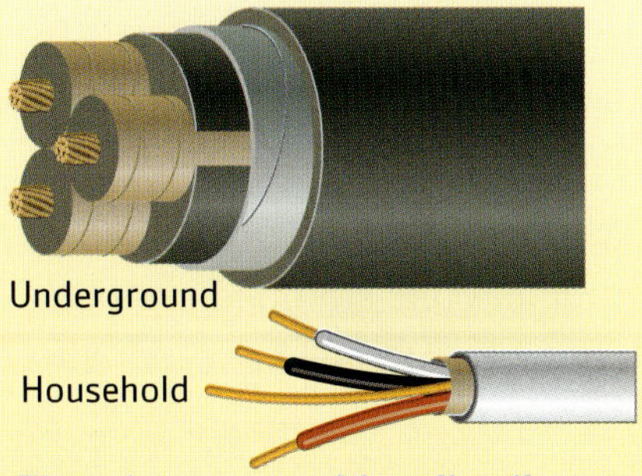

Electric power cables distribute electric power from utility companies to customers.

Communication cables

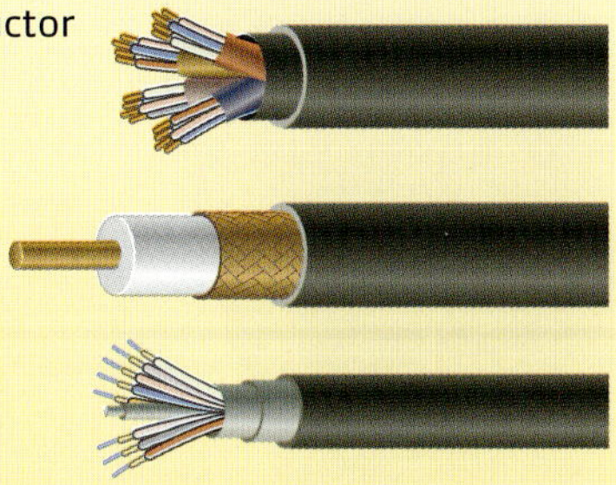

Communications cables carry telephone and television signals.

Computer cable

Special-purpose cables are used in computers and other electronic devices.

Cable car

Cable car

A cable car is a vehicle pulled along by a moving cable. A cable is a strong, thick rope made of wires twisted together. Cable cars can carry passengers from place to place.

Most cable cars move on the ground on rails, as do trains. The cable runs in a groove beneath the street. An engine in a central station moves the cable at a steady speed of about 9 miles (14 kilometers) per hour. An operator clamps a car onto the cable to move it. The clamp is opened to stop the car's movement.

Other cable cars move through the air. This type of cable car runs on cables that hang between tall towers. Many ski lifts are this kind of cable car.

Other articles to read include: **Cable; Train; Transportation.**

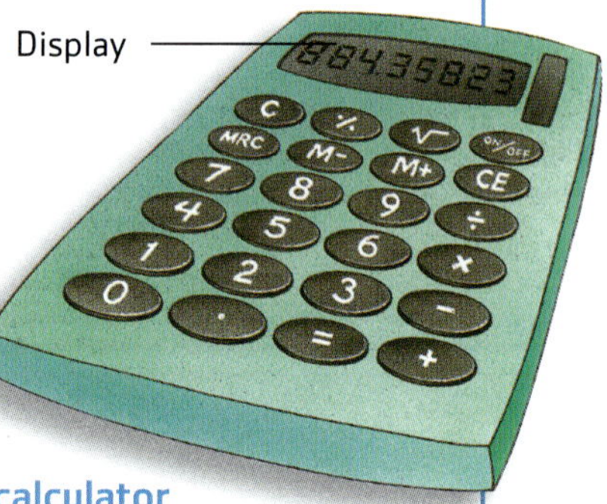

Pocket calculator

Calculator

A calculator is a machine that quickly performs mathematical operations. Modern calculators are small devices that contain computer chips. The computer chips have tiny electronic circuits stamped on them. The circuits can be switched on or off, like light switches. Certain patterns of "on" and "off" circuits represent certain numbers.

Simple calculators show numbers on a small window called a *display*. These calculators can add, subtract, multiply, and divide numbers. More complex calculators can run computer programs to solve math problems. They can also display images, such as graphs. Computers and many cell phones have built-in calculators.

Other articles to read include: **Abacus: Cellular telephone; Computer.**

Calendar

Calendars are used to measure and record the passing of time. Early people noticed that the seasons of the year came in a regular pattern. This discovery changed their lives greatly. People soon planned their lives around the seasons. They knew what they needed for each season and when they could get food from plants. People needed a way to keep track of time. Such a tool would help them prepare for long, cold winters and other harsh seasons. People developed calendars to serve this purpose.

Before clocks were invented, people told time by watching the sun, the moon, and the stars. The daily rising of the sun gave them a short unit of time. It was called the *day*. The cycle of seasons gave them a longer unit of time. It was called the *solar year* or simply *year*. People also watched how the moon moved and changed shape. The time between full moons gave them the *month*.

Today, most people in North and South America use a calendar called the Gregorian *(grih GOHR ee uhn)* calendar. It was worked out in the 1580's under the direction of Pope Gregory XIII. It has 12 months. Eleven of the months have 30 or 31 days. The other month, February, normally has 28 days. In nearly every fourth year, called *leap years*, February has 29 days.

The Gregorian calendar is based on the year that Jesus Christ was born. Many people refer to dates before that year as B.C., or *before Christ*. They use A.D., *anno Domini,* for dates after that year. *Anno Domini* means *in the year of our Lord* in the Latin language.

Other calendars include the Hebrew calendar, the Islamic calendar, the Chinese calendar, and the Maya calendar. The Hebrew calendar begins at what was thought to be the moment the world began. Scholars had placed this moment at 3,760 years and 3 months before the birth of Jesus Christ. So, to find a year in the Hebrew calendar, we add 3,760 to the date in the Gregorian calendar. The Islamic calendar begins with A.D. 622, by the Gregorian calendar. The Islamic year is based on the moon. It has 12 months. Six of these months have 29 days and 6

Continued on the next page

Days of the week	Months of the year
Sunday	January
Monday	February
Tuesday	March
Wednesday	April
Thursday	May
Friday	June
Saturday	July
	August
	September
	October
	November
	December

The days and months of the Gregorian calendar

The Egyptians were probably the first people to make a calendar based mainly on the sun.

Calendar *Continued from the previous page*

months have 30 days. The Chinese calendar begins at 2637 B.C. That was the year that calendar was invented. The Maya used a combination of calendars. One was a 260-day record of sacred events. The Maya also had a 365-day calendar based on the solar year. Combining the two gave a 52-year cycle called the Calendar Round. The longest Maya calendar, called the Long Count, was based on a 5,128-year cycle.

Other articles to read include: **Clock.**

The Maya of Central America had several calendars. Their calendars were used for special purposes, such as marking religious festivals.

Camera

A camera is a device for taking photographs and videos. Older cameras were dark boxes that held film. Newer cameras are *digital.* They use sensors rather than film to record images. Such images can be viewed using a computer.

In both types of cameras, light from a scene enters through a glass lens. In film cameras, the light reacts with chemicals on film. The reaction makes an image. In digital cameras, the light strikes

Continued on the next page

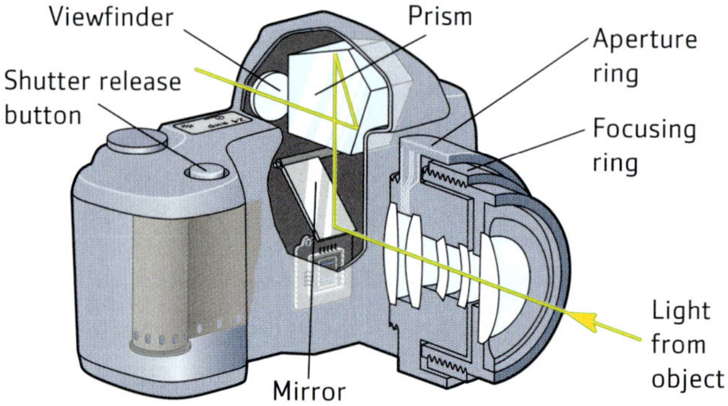

Light enters a camera through the lens. A mirror lets the photographer see the scene by looking through the viewfinder. Taking a picture lifts the mirror, letting the light shine on the film.

tiny electronic sensors. The sensors record the image as a computer file.

Photography is the art of using a camera. Photographers must position the camera to capture a scene. They must use the right amount of light. They also must make sure the camera is focused. Otherwise, the picture will be blurry. Many digital cameras automatically focus and make other adjustments.

Other articles to read include: **Lens; Photography.**

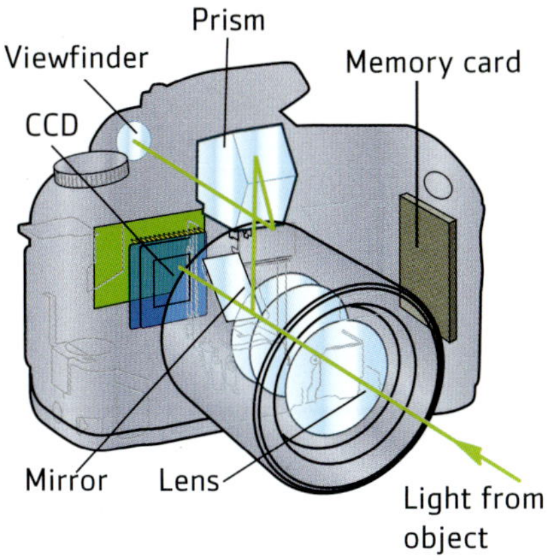

A digital camera focuses light on a light-sensitive part called a charge-coupled device (CCD) instead of film. The CCD converts captured light patterns into a computer file.

Canal

A canal is a waterway dug across land. Canals enable boats or ships to travel between large bodies of water. They also carry water to farms and cities.

Canals may connect bodies of water, such as lakes and oceans. Such canals work as "shortcuts" for ships and boats. Canals may also help control the course of a river, making it easier for vessels to travel on the river.

The ancient Babylonians and Egyptians made canals more than 4,000 years ago. The Panama and Suez canals are the most important canals in the world today. Both provide important shortcuts.

The Panama Canal is in Central America. It links the Atlantic and Pacific oceans through the nation of Panama. It is the busiest canal in the world. About 12,000 ships pass through it each year.

The Panama Canal is about 51 miles (82 kilometers) long. It shortens the sea route between New York City and San Francisco by more than 7,800 miles (12,600 kilometers).

The Suez Canal lies between Port Said, Egypt, and the Gulf of Suez, an arm of the Red Sea. It is about 118 miles (190 kilometers) long. The Suez Canal allows ships to move between the Mediterranean and Red seas. It shortens the sea route between Europe and Asia.

Other articles to read include: **Aqueduct: Panama Canal.**

Canal locks make it possible for vessels to move between bodies of water that have different water levels. While the boat is between two locked gates, the water level is raised or lowered.

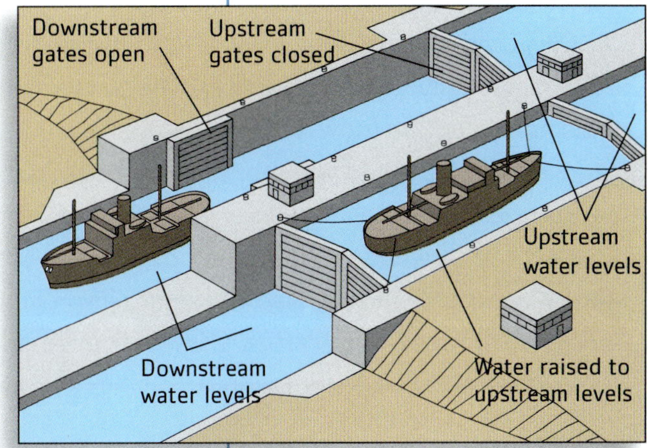

Cannon

Cannon

A cannon is a powerful, tube-shaped gun too large to be carried by hand. *Cannon* comes from the Latin word *canna*, meaning *tube* or *reed*. Large bronze and iron cannons were first used in warfare about 1350. Cannons firing heavy balls were widely used in the American Civil War (1861–1865).

Other articles to read include: **Firearm; Fuse; Gun.**

Carver, George Washington

George Washington Carver (1864?–1943) was a pioneering African American scientist. He became famous the world over for his research on soil and crops.

Carver was best known for his work with peanuts. He made more than 300 products from peanuts. These products include face powder, printer's ink, and soap.

Carver was born a slave on a farm in Missouri. When he was a baby, his father was killed in an accident. His mother was kidnapped. George was raised by Moses and Susan Carver. The Carvers had been his owners until 1865, when slavery became illegal in the United States. The Carvers taught young George to read and write. When he was 11, he went to a school for African American children in Missouri.

George Washington Carver, (right), won worldwide fame for agricultural research. He taught at Tuskegee Institute in Alabama.

Carver went to college at Iowa State Agricultural College (now Iowa State University). He then moved to Alabama to teach at the Tuskegee Institute (now Tuskegee University). At Tuskegee, he studied soil. He found ways for farmers to get more from their crops. He also taught Southern farmers, especially black farmers, how to use modern farming methods.

In 1910, Carver began his study of peanuts. He traveled around the United States to talk about the value of peanuts. He also worked to improve relations between black people and white people. Throughout his career, Carver received many awards for his work.

Other articles to read include: **Invention.**

Cassini

Cassini is a spacecraft sent to Saturn. It was launched by the United States in 1997. It arrived at Saturn in 2004. Cassini has helped scientists learn about Saturn, its rings, and its moons.

Cassini carried a probe named *Huygens (HOY gehns)*. It dropped Huygens onto Saturn's moon Titan. Huygens studied Titan's atmosphere and surface. It landed on the surface.

Cassini has taken thousands of photos of Saturn and its moons. Cassini has made many discoveries. For example, it found jets of water on the moon Enceladus. It also discovered *moonlets* (tiny moons) hidden inside the rings.

Other articles to read include: **Space exploration.**

This illustration shows the Cassini spacecraft orbiting the planet Saturn.

Catapult

The catapult *(KAT uh puhlt)* is a war machine that flings heavy stones and other objects. Ancient armies often used catapults to attack walled cities.

Catapults work somewhat like giant slingshots. People loaded stones, spears, or other deadly objects on one end of a long beam. The beam was attached to a twisted rope or stretched-out fibers. When the beam was released, the rope or fibers acted like a spring. They caused the beam to snap forward, hurling the objects through the air. Some catupults were made from young trees. Soldiers bent the trees back and released them to fling deadly objects. Burning materials were sometimes shot from catapults. So were cans filled with explosives or poison gas.

The first effective catapults were built in the 300's B.C. Catapults were used to attack castles during the Middle Ages (A.D. 400's through 1400's). Today, specialized catapults are used to launch airplanes from the decks of large ships called *aircraft carriers*.

Other articles to read include: **Archimedes; Machine.**

Catapults were used in ancient times and during the Middle Ages to fling heavy stones at cities and castles. The weapons worked like a giant slingshots.

ACTIVITY

Make a catapult

! Have a teacher or other adult help you with this experiment.

1. Ask an adult to hammer four nails into the block of wood. The two large nails should be placed about 1 inch (2.5 centimeters) behind the small nails. .

2. Place a rubber band around the two large nails. Make sure it is stretched tight. Twist another rubber band so it is tightly coiled and place it around the small nails.

3. Put the spoon's handle through the twisted-up rubber band. Let the spoon rest against the higher rubber band.

What you need:

- a hammer
- two small nails
- two large nails
- a block of wood about 4 in (10 cm) across and 9 in (22.5 cm) long
- two wide rubber bands
- a plastic spoon
- paper

4. Place a small piece of crumpled paper in the bowl of the spoon. Pull the spoon down, stretching against the rubber band. Then, release! The paper should go flying.

1.
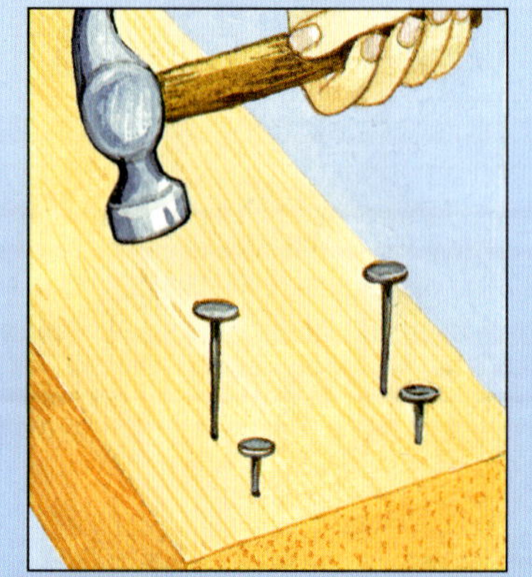

2.
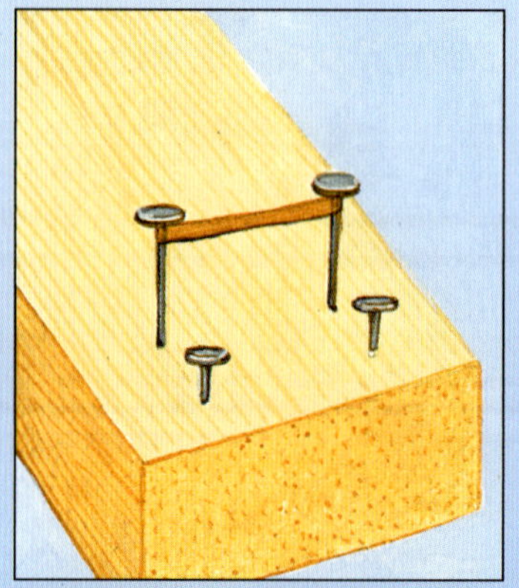

3.

4.

http://bit.ly/YfNQz9

Cayley, Sir George

Sir George Cayley's "aerial carriage," with its circular wings, was never built. This model is based on his 1843 original design.

Sir George Cayley *(KAY lee)* (1773–1857) was a British engineer. He is often called the father of modern *aeronautics (AIR uh NAW tihks).* Aeronautics is the study of designing, making, and flying aircraft.

Cayley came up with many early ideas about aviation flight . He wrote about helicopters, parachutes, and making aircraft streamlined. He also came up with the idea for the *biplane.* A biplane is an airplane with double wings. He built a glider that flew 900 feet (270 meters) through the air.

Cayley believed that only craft that were lighter than air could make long flights under engine power. He suggested using a tube-shaped balloon, much like a modern blimp.

Cayley was born on Dec. 27, 1773, near Scarborough, England. He died on Dec. 15, 1857.

Other articles to read include: **Airplane; Airship; Balloon; Glider.**

Cellular telephone

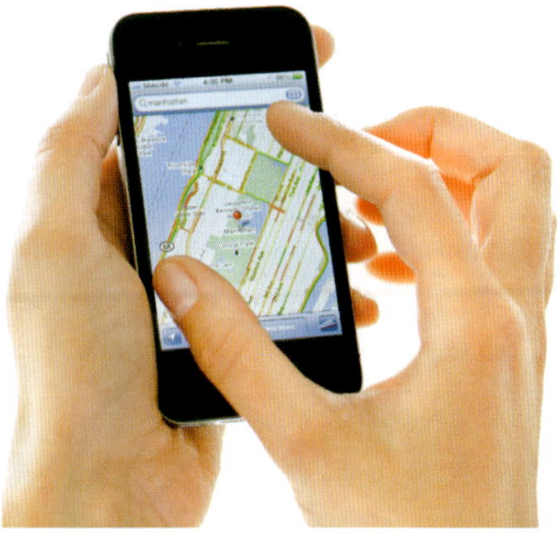

Some cell phones, called smartphones, also work as tiny computers. People use such phones by touching their screens.

Cellular telephones, or *cell phones,* are phones that work through radio signals. The signals travel between the phone and special towers called *base stations.* People use cell phones to make voice calls, send text messages, and connect to the Internet.

The area around a base station is called a *cell.* A cell can range from less than a kilometer to several dozen kilometers wide. When a person moves from one cell to another, the phone's connection switches to a new base station.

Cellular phones are powered by rechargeable batteries. Some phones can receive signals from the Global Positioning System (GPS) satellites. Such a phone can pinpoint the user's location. *Smartphones* are cell phones that work much like small computers. Such phones often have built-in cameras. They can play music, videos, and games.

Continued on the next page

Cellular telephone *Continued from the previous page*

The first cellular phones were used in the United States in 1983. During the 2000's, cell phones became more popular than phones that use telephone wires.

Other articles to read include: **Apple Inc.; Communication; Radio; Telephone.**

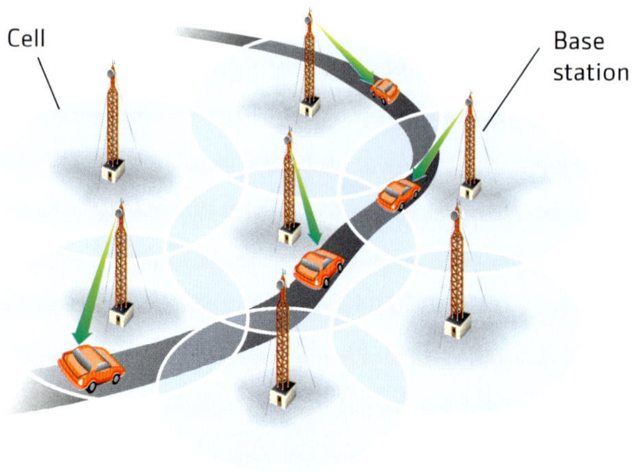

Radio waves travel between cell phones and special towers called base stations. The area around each base station is called a cell. If a person on a cell phone moves from one cell to another, the phone switches to the new tower.

A cement truck pours wet concrete into special forms. The forms hold the concrete in place until it hardens.

Cement and concrete

Cement and concrete are among the most important building materials. Cement is a fine, gray powder. The powder is mixed with water to form a paste. This paste is used to bind sand, crushed stone, or other materials together. The resulting mixture is called *concrete*. Wet concrete is soft like mud. But it hardens into a rocklike mass.

A tall skyscraper is held firmly in the ground by tons of concrete. The walls, floors, and roofs of many buildings are made of concrete. Many sidewalks, highways, tunnels, and bridges are also made of concrete. Steel rods or cables can be put into the mixture while it is still wet. This process is used to make extra-strong concrete for tall buildings, bridges, and other large structures.

Continued on the next page

Two thousand years ago, the ancient Romans made cement and concrete. They mixed lime and water with ash from a volcano to make cement. Some of their concrete buildings, roads, and bridges still stand. The Roman Empire fell in the 400's. Knowledge of cement was lost for hundreds of years. In 1756, John Smeaton, a British engineer, again found how to make cement. Modern cement is called *portland cement.* It is the same color as a kind of stone found in Portland, in southern England. Portland cement was invented in 1824 by a British bricklayer named Joseph Aspdin.

Other articles to read include: **Bridge; Building construction; Skyscraper.**

Challenger disaster

This photograph shows the crew of the Challenger shuttle. All seven died in the accident.

The Challenger disaster was a deadly space shuttle accident. It was one of the worst accidents in the history of space flight.

On Jan. 28, 1986, the space shuttle Challenger launched from the Kennedy Space Center in Florida. The trouble began about four minutes into the flight. A problem in one of the rocket engines led the shuttle to break apart in midair. The pieces landed in the Atlantic Ocean.

None of the seven crew members survived the accident. The crew included the first schoolteacher to fly on a shuttle, Christa McAuliffe. It also included the first Asian-American astronaut, Ellison Onizuka. The other crew members were Francis R. (Dick) Scobee, Michael J. Smith, Judith A. Resnik, Ronald E. McNair, and Gregory B. Jarvis.

The accident prompted a long investigation into possible flaws in the shuttle. Space shuttles did not start flying again until Sept. 29, 1988.

Other articles to read include: **Columbia disater; McAuliffe, Christa; Space exploration.**

Chandra X-ray Observatory

The Chandra *(SHAHN druh)* X-ray Observatory is an artificial *satellite*. A satellite is an object that *orbits* (circles) another body, in this case, Earth. Chandra carries an X-ray telescope and two cameras. Chandra was built to look at very hot objects in the universe. These objects give off X rays. The National Aeronautics and Space Administration (NASA) launched Chandra from the space shuttle Columbia on July 23, 1999. Chandra has helped us learn more about how stars and galaxies form.

Gas gives off X rays when heated to millions of degrees. Such X rays can come from *supernovae* (exploding stars), colliding galaxies, and matter swirling around *black holes*. A black hole is an object whose gravitational pull is so strong nothing can escape it. In December 1999, Chandra produced evidence that tens of millions of galaxies have huge black holes at their centers.

The Chandra X-ray Observatory was launched by space shuttle Columbia in 1999. Chandra was designed to detect X rays from high-energy areas of the universe.

The Chandra X-ray Observatory was named for the Indian-born American *astrophysicist (AS troh FIHZ uh sihst)* Subrahmanyan Chandrasekhar *(SU brah MAN yuhn SHAHN druh SAY kahr)*. An astrophysicist studies stars and other objects in space.

Other articles to read include: **Satellite, Artificial; Space exploration; Telescope.**

This image of the Milky Way galaxy's core combines data from Chandra and other observatories. X-ray sources detected by Chandra are shown in blue.

Chang-Díaz, Franklin

Franklin Chang-Díaz (1950-) was a United States astronaut. He flew on seven NASA space shuttle missions between 1986 and 2002.

Chang-Díaz was born in San José, Costa Rica. He moved to the United States during high school. He remained in the United States for college. Chang-Díaz studied engineering and physics in college. He later worked to develop rocket engines. Chang-Díaz left the space shuttle program in 2005. He continued his rocket research. He also began teaching physics to college students.

Other articles to read include: **Astronaut; Space exploration.**

Franklin Chang-Díaz

Chanute, Octave

Octave Chanute *(ok TAYV shuh NOOT)* (1832–1910) was a French-born American engineer. He developed a double-winged glider.

Chanute began studying *aerodynamics (AIR oh dy NAM ihks)* in his late 30's. Aerodynamics is the study of designing and flying aircraft. Chanute did not build and fly a glider until after age 60. He built gliders with more than one wing. He then built a *biplane* (double-winged) glider. This glider could be controlled by shifting the wings. Chanute built the lightest, strongest glider frameworks of his day.

The first airplane used a biplane wing design. It was built by the Wright brothers in 1903. Chanute was born in Paris.

Other articles to read include: **Airplane; Glider; Wright brothers.**

Octave Chanute developed a double-winged glider.

Claude Chappe's telegraph used wooden beams mounted on high towers. People arranged the beams to send coded messages.

Chappe, Claude

Claude Chappe *(shap)* (1763–1805) was a French engineer. He invented a signaling system called the *semaphore (SEHM uh fawr) optical telegraph* during the 1790's. Chappe coined the word *telegraph*. It means *distant writer*.

The semaphore telegraph used wooden beams. The beams were mounted on high towers. The beams had wings on the ends. The beams and wings could be arranged at different angles. Each position stood for a letter, number, or coded word. People could spot the signals many miles or kilometers away using telescopes.

By 1794, Chappe built 15 tower stations. Messages could be sent from station to station over 130 miles (210 kilometers). But people could not see the messages in bad weather. The electric telegraph was invented in 1840. It replaced Chappe's invention.

Other articles to read include: **Communication; Semaphor; Telegraph.**

Sundials are the oldest known objects used for telling time. They measure the lengths of shadows cast by the sun.

Clock

A clock is an instrument that shows the time. Clocks also decorate homes and other buildings.

There are many kinds of clocks. Some clocks have hands that show the time. The hands point to numbers on a dial. Other clocks, called *digital clocks,* show the time in numbers on the clock face. Many clocks have chimes or sound an alarm. Others have mechanical birds or dancing figures that mark the hours.

Every clock has two main parts—the *works* and the *case*. The works are the functional parts of the clock, and they do three jobs. They show the time. They supply power to run the clock. And they keep time. The case covers and protects the works.

Timekeeping in most clocks is done by counting some regularly repeated action. One example is the swing of a pendulum. *Quartz* clocks count certain vibrations of a quartz crystal. Clocks with a very steady repeated action keep time better than other clocks. The most accurate clocks are atomic clocks. They measure vibrations of certain atoms and molecules.

Continued on the next page

Mechanical clocks are run by various mechanical parts that must be wound up. Some have to be wound every day, but others run for seven or eight days without rewinding. Electric clocks run on batteries or on electricity from an outlet.

Sundials are the oldest known objects used for telling time. They were first made more than 4,000 years ago. As the sun crosses the sky, it casts a shadow on the dial. A sundial tells time by measuring the length or the angle of the shadow. Other early clocks measured the steady flow of sand or water out of a container.

The first mechanical clocks in Europe were probably developed during the late 1200's. They had no hands and no dial. Instead, they told the hour by ringing a bell. By the mid-1700's, inventors had developed most of the mechanisms used in today's mechanical clocks. Digital clocks first became popular in the 1970's.

Other articles to read include: **Pendulum; Sundial.**

A steadily swinging weight called a pendulum keeps time in some clocks.

Columbia disaster

The Columbia disaster was a major space shuttle accident in 2003. It was the second shuttle accident to end in death. The first was the Challenger accident in 1986.

On Feb. 1, 2003, the space shuttle Columbia was returning to Earth from space. The shuttle broke apart while still 40 miles (65 kilometers) above the ground.

This photo shows the crew of the Columbia shuttle. All died in the accident.

The accident was caused by a damaged wing. The wing had been hit by a chunk of foam during take-off. The foam fell off the shuttle's *external* (outside) fuel tank. The foam made a small hole in the wing. As the shuttle returned to Earth, the hole got worse. The wing failed, leading the shuttle to tumble out of control and break apart.

All seven crew members died. The crew included Ilan Ramone, the first Israeli astronaut. The other crew members were Rick D. Husband, William C. McCool, Michael P. Anderson, Kalpana Chawla, David M. Brown, and Laurel Blair Salton Clark.

The accident led to a long investigation. A space shuttle did not fly again until July 26, 2005.

Other articles to read include: **Challenger disaster; Space exploration.**

Smoke signals were one of the earliest forms of long-distance communication.

Communication

Communication is the sharing of information. People communicate mainly by speaking and writing. They also communicate without words. They use their faces, for example, to smile or frown. They use their hands to wave.

Most of our everyday communication is *personal communication.* In this kind of communication, one person talks to or writes to another person or a small group of people. *Mass communication* is when information is shared with many people. Books are a form of mass communication. So are newspapers, magazines, television, and radio. Mass communication does not always require words. Artists communicate through paintings, music, and dance. Both personal and mass communication take place on the Internet.

Communication systems are called *media.* Millions of people work in media companies. They make news, entertainment, and advertisements. Governments also rely on media. In some cases, governments and other organizations use media to spread *propaganda.* Propaganda is communication meant to control people's thoughts and actions.

Communication has its roots in language. Human babies can quickly learn language. Experts think that people started using language around 150,000 years ago. Language helped early

Continued on the next page

Communication throughout history

Cuneiform writing consists of wedge-shaped characters stamped into clay. This clay cylinder was made during the 500's B.C. in Babylon.

Printing from movable type was invented in Asia during the 1000's and in Europe during the 1400's. A printing shop of the 1600's is shown here.

Samuel F. B. Morse developed one of the first successful electric telegraphs in 1840. He also developed Morse code, a system for sending messages.

Alexander Graham Bell designed one of the first successful telephones. He patented it in 1876.

people work together. It helped them make tools and shelters.

Early people communicated mostly by speaking to one another. Runners carried messages from village to village. Early people also beat drums and made smoke signals to communicate. Later, people marked things on clay tokens, probably as a way of keeping records. People also communicated by drawing pictures. Over time, some pictures were used as symbols for other objects or ideas.

The Sumerians developed the first writing system around 3300 B.C. The Sumerians lived in what is now Iraq. Their writing system was called *cuneiform*. It made use of wedge-shaped markings. Some of the markings were based on pictures.

Other cultures also developed their own writing systems. Over time, some markings became more like modern alphabet letters. They stood for sounds, not objects or ideas. They could be combined to form words and ideas.

Ancient cultures used writing to record laws. They sent letters from town to town. But for thousands of years, few people knew how to read or write. Writing materials were expensive.

During the Middle Ages (A.D. 400–1500), artists called *scribes* copied books by hand. A single book could take months to copy.

Printing was invented in Asia during the 1000's. Europeans learned to print books during the 1400's. Printing was much faster and easier than writing by hand. Printed Bibles spread far and wide throughout Europe. More people learned to read.

Continued on the next page

Thomas A. Edison developed the first practical *phonograph* in 1877. It recorded sound on a cylinder covered with foil.

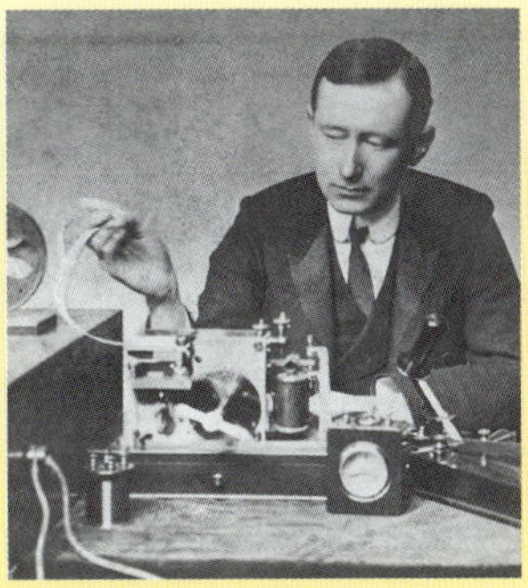

Guglielmo Marconi invented the wireless telegraph in 1895. The invention led to modern radio.

Motion-picture cameras were developed by several inventors in the late 1800's and early 1900's.

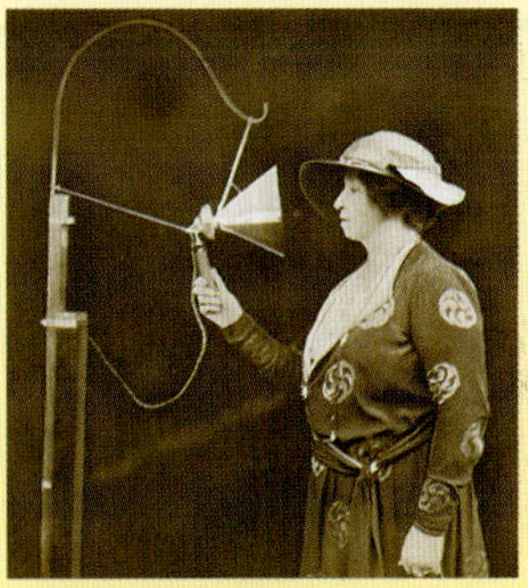

Radio became a major source of information and family entertainment during the 1920's.

Communication *Continued from the previous page*

In the 1600's, businesspeople throughout Europe used newssheets called *corantos.* Corantos were almost like today's newspapers. They told which ships had landed and what the ships carried.

In the early 1800's, new inventions made communications faster and easier. Using steam power, printing presses could print books faster and cheaper. Steamships and trains carried news long distances.

During the 1830's, an American painter and inventor named Samuel F. B. Morse made the first telegraph. It used electric signals. The telegraph sent messages over wires in a code of dots and dashes. This code became known as Morse code. In 1866, the first underwater telegraph cable was laid across the Atlantic Ocean.

In the late 1800's, new inventions led to new forms of communication. Some inventions could display sounds and images. They included the photograph, the phonograph, and the motion-picture projector. Telephones enabled distant people to talk to one another. Typewriters made it even easier to write.

In 1895, Guglielmo Marconi, an Italian inventor, invented the first radio. Like the telegraph, it made use of Morse code.

Continued on the next page

An experimental television broadcast of the late 1920's showed a statue of the comic strip character Felix the Cat.

Telstar I, a satellite launched in 1962, relayed telephone calls, TV shows, and other communications.

Computers sped communication in the 1960's and 1970's. They gave workers such as airline ticket agents access to large amounts of constantly changing data.

E-mail (electronic mail) enables users to send and receive messages on their computers. Individuals, businesses, and schools use e-mail widely.

But it did not rely on wires. It could send messages over the air. In 1906, Reginald A. Fessenden, a Canadian scientist, attached a telephone mouthpiece to Marconi's instrument. He was able to send spoken words over the radio for the first time.

In 1925, John Logie Baird, a Scottish engineer, showed television to the public for the first time. In 1936, the British Broadcasting Corporation (BBC) made the world's first TV broadcast. By the early 1950's, there were TV stations all over the United States. Major industries formed around TV and radio.

In 1979, the first cellular telephone system was built in Japan. Cell phones quickly became an important way to communicate.

People began using computers to communicate in the second half of the 1900's. During the 1960's, the United States government linked many computers together. This system eventually became the Internet. In 1991, a British computer scientist named Tim Berners-Lee developed the World Wide Web. The Web made it much easier for regular people to use the Internet. During the 2000's, the Internet became much faster. Music and videos spread through the Internet. Many cell phones could connect to the Internet by the 2010's.

Other articles to read include: **Cellular telephone; Computer; E-mail; Internet; Printing; Radio; Telegraph; Telephone; Television.**

Short written messages, such as ***text messages*** sent and received by cell phone, are widespread in modern communication.

Compact disc

A compact disc, or *CD* for short, stores *digital* (computerized) information. A CD is a flat, thin platter of hard plastic and metal, usually aluminum. The platter holds a spiral of extremely tiny pits. The pattern of pits works as a code. On many CD's, the code represents music. On other CD's, the code can stand for words, pictures, videos, an electronic game, or any other kind of information.

Compact disc

A CD player reads the information on the disc. It shines a laser on the disc as the disc spins around. The metal coating reflects the laser. As the laser passes over pits, the reflec-

Continued on the next page

Compact disc *Continued from the previous page*

tion becomes weaker. The changing laser reflection forms a pattern, which stands for information.

A full CD might contain two billion pits. It can store a relatively short video. A *DVD* can store much more information than can a CD. DVD's are used mainly for movies.

Other articles to read include: **Computer storage disk; DVD; Laser.**

Compass

A compass is a tool for finding directions. It can help you find your way when there are no signs to guide you. Hikers use compasses. Ships use compasses to guide them across the ocean. Airplanes use compasses to guide them through the air.

A simple pocket compass looks a little like a clock. It has a needle that swings around. The face of the compass has letters that stand for direction. *N* stands for north, *S* stands for south, *E* stands for east, and *W* stands for west. These are called the *cardinal points* of a compass.

A pocket compass has a magnetic needle that points north.

A *compass rose* is the circle on the face of a compass. It is usually marked with degrees. On a compass, degrees are used to divide north, south, east, and west into smaller sections. Compass roses are also printed on some maps and city streets.

The needle in the compass is a magnet. It always points to Earth's *north magnetic pole*. The north magnetic pole is a point at the top of Earth, near the North Pole. So the compass needle always points north.

A *gyrocompass* does not use Earth's magnetism to tell direction. This device always points north. It uses spinning mechanisms, weights, and balances. Ships and aircraft use gyrocompasses, because they are more accurate than magnetic compasses.

Other articles to read include: **Gyrocompass; Magnet; Navigation.**

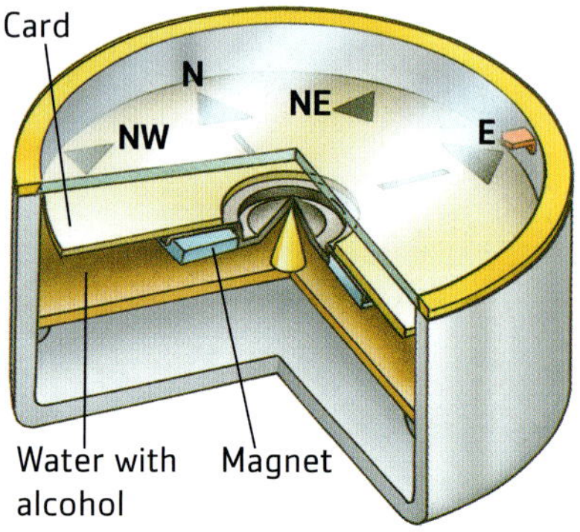

In some compasses, a magnet and a card float in a bowl of water mixed with alcohol. The magnet can spin freely. The card shows direction.

Computer

Laptop computers are powered by rechargeable batteries. They often connect to the Internet wirelessly.

A computer is a machine that handles information. Such information may include numbers and words. It may also include pictures, sounds, videos, and games. People around the world use computers every day. Many devices—such as clocks, cameras, and cars—have small computers inside them. Computers around the world are linked together to form the Internet.

Computers are made of *hardware.* Hardware includes all the physical parts of a computer. Hardware also includes other machines that are attached to computers. Computers work using *programs.* A program is a set of instructions that tells the computer what to do. Programs are also called *software* or *applications.*

There are many kinds of computer programs. People write text using *word processors.* They organize business information on *spreadsheets.* Electronic games are an important kind of software. *Web browsers* are programs that people use to explore Internet websites. The most important programs of all are *operating systems.* These programs control the computer's basic functions and all the other programs. Popular operating systems include Windows, Mac OS, and Linux.

Almost all computers today are electronic. They store information *digitally*—that is, in the form of numerical code. Computers calculate with billions of extremely small electronic switches called *transistors.* Like a light switch, a transistor can be switched "on" or "off." These two states stand for the numbers 1 and 0. The numbers form a code. The code can stand for words, pictures, videos, games, or other information.

There are a number of different types of computers. *Personal computers* are probably the most familiar. They have screens and—usually—keyboards. *Desktop computers* are larger machines that must stay plugged in. *Laptop computers* are smaller and use rechargeable batteries. They open on a hinge, with a screen on top and a keyboard on bottom. *Tablet computers* have only a screen. People touch letters and images on the

Continued on the next page

Computer *Continued from the previous page*

screen instead of using a keyboard. *Smartphones* are cell phones that also work as personal computers.

Mainframes are the largest and most powerful computers. They can hold more information and do more difficult tasks than can personal computers. Large numbers of people can use a mainframe at the same time. The most powerful mainframes are called *supercomputers.* Scientists use supercomputers to solve very complex problems, such as modeling Earth's climate.

A *dedicated* computer can do just a few different tasks. A *video game console* is an example of a dedicated computer. It is designed mainly for playing games. *Server computers* are common on the Internet and smaller computer networks. They store information, such as the code for websites. They are designed to quickly send this information to other computers on the network.

Embedded computers are small computers built into other machines. They help the machine do its job. Embedded computers in cars, for example, help the car brake and switch gears. Embedded computers in airplanes help the pilot fly the plane. Embedded computers also help control robots, spacecraft, and missiles.

The "brain" of the computer is called the *microprocessor* or *central processing unit.* The microprocessor controls the other parts of the computer. It switches transistors on and off. In this way, the computer processes works with information. Microprocessors are often about the size of a fingernail. They are made from plates of silicon. Billions of transistors are carved into the silicon plate. The transistors are so small that you can only see them with powerful microscopes. Microprocessors work closely with memory chips. The memory chip holds information and programs used by the microprocessor.

Computers are vital to all modern industries, including building construction.

Continued on the next page

A hurricane specialist studies weather models on computers.

Other devices store computer information, too. Most computers have built-in *hard drives*. Hard drives can store huge amounts of information. They use spinning magnetic platters to encode information. *Flash drives,* also called *solid-state drives,* have no moving parts. DVD's are used to store such information as movies and games.

The earliest computers were calculating machines. In 1642, the French scientist Blaise Pascal made a geared machine that could do simple math. During the 1670's, the German philosopher Gottfried Wilhelm Leibniz improved Pascal's calculator. He also developed the binary number system. This system could represent any number with just two symbols—*1* and *0*. Modern computers use this same system.

The first electric computers were built in the 1930's and 1940's. They were huge, expensive machines. They took up whole rooms. During World War II (1939–1945), the British used electronic computers to break the Nazis' secret codes.

Transistors were developed in 1947. Computer chips were developed in 1959. Soon after, engineers learned to fit all of a computer's workings on a handful of chips. They also learned to fit more and more transistors on a single chip. Computers quickly became smaller, cheaper, and more powerful. The first microprocessor, developed by Intel in 1971, held around 2,500 transistors. Modern microprocessors have billions of transistors.

The first personal computers were invented in the 1970's. Personal computers became extremely popular in the 1980's and 1990's.

In the 1990's, household computers began connecting through the Internet using the World Wide Web. In the early 2000's, portable computing with smartphones and tablets became increasingly popular.

Other articles to read include: **Apple Inc.; Artificial intelligence; Babbage, Charles; Berners-Lee, Tim; Computer chip; Computer graphics; Computer simulation; Computer storage disk; Computer virus; Database; Electronic game; Gates, Bill; Internet; Jobs, Steve; Microsoft Corporation; Modem; Shannon, Claude Elwood; Turing, Alan Mathison; Virtual reality; Wozniak, Steve.**

Computer chip

A computer chip is a tiny piece of material that holds a complex electronic *circuit.* A circuit is a pathway for electrical signals. Parts of the circuit called *transistors* can be switched "on" and "off," like light switches. Computer chips are usually made of a material called *silicon (SIHL uh kuhn).* Most chips are only the size of a fingernail.

There are two main kinds of computer chips: (1) *microprocessors (MY kroh PROS uhs uhrz),* and (2) *memory chips.* Microprocessors serve as the computer's "brain." They carry out the instructions in computer programs. Memory chips store computer programs and other data. Most computers use both kinds of chips.

The first computer chips were made in 1959 by two Americans—Jack Kilby, an engineer, and Robert Noyce, a scientist. They figured out how to fit all the parts of a computer circuit onto a single piece of silicon. During the 1960's, scientists developed chips for guided missiles and satellites. The first microprocessors were made in 1971 for use in desktop calculators. By the 2010's, computer chips often contained billions of transistors.

Other articles to read include: **Computer; Electronics; Transistor.**

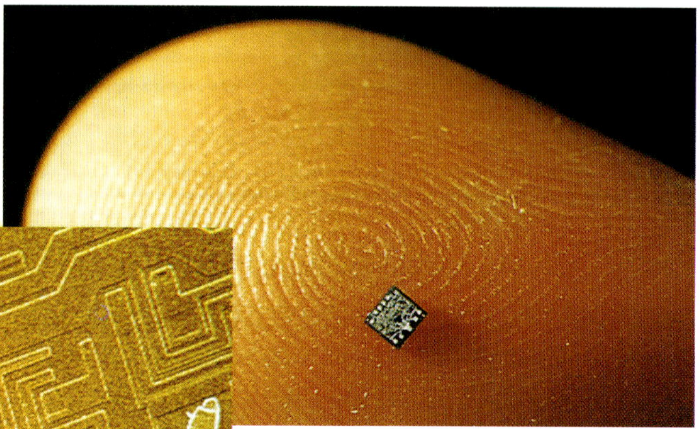

A tiny silicon chip (above) holds a complex electronic circuit (left). Parts of the circuit called *transistors* can be switched on or off, like light switches.

Computer graphics

Computer graphics are images made with computer programs. *Computer graphics* also means the art of making such images. Computer graphics are widely used in television, movies, and electronic games. Scientists also use computer graphics.

Images on a computer screen are made up of many tiny dots called *pixels*. Pixel is short for *picture element*. If you look closely at a computer screen, you can often see the individual pixels.

Computer graphics are flat images. But they often give the illusion of depth. Computer graphics are usually designed in three dimensions. Artists create backgrounds that work like virtual dollhouses. Artists also create three-dimensional models of characters. They can then pose the characters at any angle. Artists create lights that shine on the characters and background. Computer graphics images are somewhat like photographs of such scenes. The process of taking such a "photograph" is called *rendering*.

Filmmakers string rendered images together to create animations that seem to move. In electronic games, a virtual "camera" often follows the player's movements through a three-dimensional environment. The game must render the scene's graphics many times per second.

Scientists use similar techniques. Computer graphics can show the structures of molecules inside cells. People use computer graphics to make and work with three-dimensional models of cars, buildings, and many other objects.

Other articles to read include: **Computer; Electronic game; Virtual reality.**

Engineers use computer graphics to make three-dimensional models of devices.

Scientists use computer models to simulate things in the real world, such as weather.

Computer simulation

Computer simulation involves making models of real-world objects or ideas. For example, people create weather simulations on computers. The simulation helps people predict how weather will change. Engineers simulate new automobile designs on computers. They can thus test a design without building it. Scientists use simulations to model the behavior of distant stars. Pilots train on computer simulations called *flight simulators*. These simulations re-create different kinds of aircraft. They challenge pilots to respond to bad weather or combat conditions. Extremely powerful computers, called *supercomputers*, can make the most lifelike simulations.

Other articles to read include: **Computer; Electronic game; Virtual reality.**

An optical disk, such as a DVD, stores data as a series of tiny pits on its surface.

Computer storage disk

A computer storage disk is a device for storing *data* (information). The disk itself looks like a round, flat platter. There are two main kinds of storage disks: (1) *magnetic disks* and (2) *optical disks*. A magnetic disk is made of magnetic material. Data can be stored by changing magnetic patterns on the disk's surface. On an optical disk, data is stored in a pattern of tiny pits.

A device called a *disk drive* reads the data on a disk. Many disk drives can also write data on a disk. The drive spins the disk. A magnetic disk is spun near a magnetic *head*. The head writes magnetic patterns on the disk. The patterns represent the 0's and 1's of computer language. This is how information is stored on a computer. The

Continued on the next page

head can also read the patterns, turning them back into computer language. This is how data is retrieved.

One common kind of magnetic disk is called a *hard disk*. It is built into a drive called a *hard drive*. Many computers have hard drives built into them. An *external hard drive* is a separate device. It can be plugged into various computers.

One type of optical disk is the *CD-ROM* (Compact Disc-Read Only Memory). To store data on a CD-ROM, a laser beam cuts patterns of tiny pits into the disk. The patterns represent 0's and 1's. To read the data, a laser beam shines on the pits and flat spaces. The reflected pattern is read in computer language. DVD's are another kind of optical disk. A DVD can store much more information than a CD can.

Other articles to read include: **Compact disc; Computer; DVD; Laser.**

Computer virus

A computer virus is a harmful computer program. It spreads among computers somewhat like a disease. A computer virus can attach itself to other computer programs and files. These programs and files may be passed from computer to computer. The virus spreads with them.

A computer virus can delete, change, or store information on a computer. It can get into a computer through data storage devices, such as disks. It can also spread through the Internet. Some computer viruses can even take control of a computer's e-mail software. They can use it to e-mail copies of themselves to other computers. People can use special *antivirus* programs to protect their computers from viruses.

Viruses are not the only kind of harmful computer program. *Trojan horses* are like viruses, but they do not copy themselves. *Worms* spread without attaching themselves to other programs. Viruses and other harmful programs are sometimes referred to as *malware*, short for *malicious software*.

Other articles to read include: **Computer; Internet.**

Contact lens

A contact lens is a small plastic disk worn in the eye. Contact lenses are most often worn to correct vision problems such as nearsightedness or farsightedness. Contact lenses are made of hard or soft plastic. They float on a thin layer of tears on the surface of the *cornea (KAWR nee uh)*. The cornea is the clear front surface of the eyeball.

Contact lenses are curved to focus light rays on the *retina (REHT uh nuh)*. The retina is the part of the eyeball that is sensitive to light. It receives light from the things we look at. When the light rays are properly focused, a person sees clear images.

Many people wear contact lenses because they do not like wearing glasses. Some may feel they look better without glasses. Many athletes and other active people also prefer contact lenses. Contact lenses cannot fall off, get in the way, or break as easily as can glasses. Unlike glasses, contact lenses also provide normal side vision.

Contact lenses are placed on the eye. The lenses float on the eye's natural layer of tears.

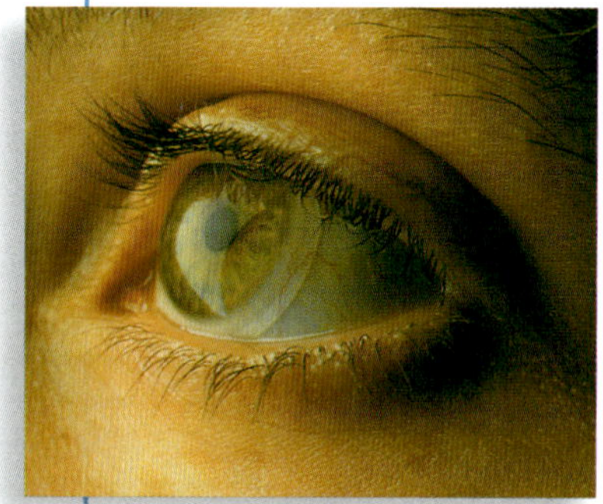

Most types of contact lenses must be taken out after a day's wear. Some types can be thrown out after a day. One type of contact lenses can be worn for a week or more without removing them.

Other articles to read include: **Lens; Plastics.**

Copying machine

Copying machines make copies of writings, drawings, and photographs, and other printed material. Office workers use copying machines to copy business documents. Teachers may use copying machines to make lessons and tests for students.

Most copiers use a process called *xerography*. The name *xerography* comes from two Greek words meaning *dry* and *writing*. The machine passes light over the original document.

Continued on the next page

The document's white paper reflects light. But dark areas—such as letters or pencil marks—absorb light. The machine's surface is charged with static electricity. The dark areas form a pattern of electric charges.

The machine can then print this same pattern on other sheets of paper. Copiers usually print copies with powdered ink called *toner*. The toner sticks to parts of the paper with static charge. Heat melts the toner to the paper, forming a permanent copy.

Other articles to read include: **Fax machine; Laser printer.**

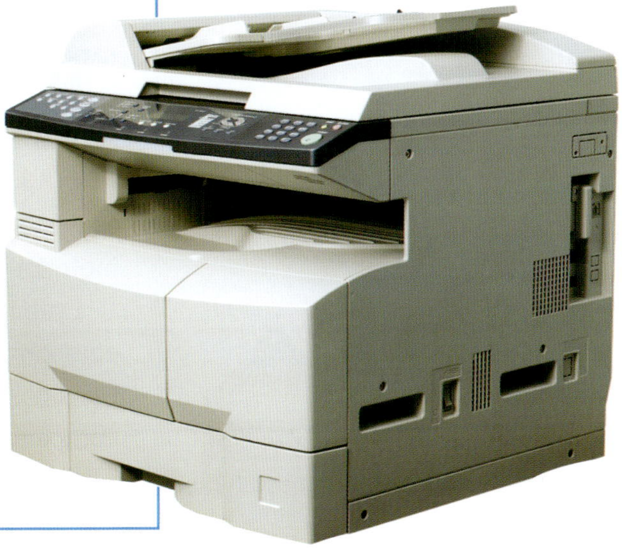

Copying machine

Cotton gin

The cotton gin is a machine that removes seeds from cotton fibers. The American inventor Eli Whitney is famous for his cotton gin. However, simple cotton gins had existed for centuries. In 1793, Whitney invented a faster, cheaper way of separating cotton seeds from fibers. His cotton gin helped make the United States the world's leading grower of cotton.

Earlier cotton gins could remove the seeds from a variety of cotton called *long-staple*. But they did not work as well with the *short-staple* cotton commonly grown in the American South. Whitney's cotton gin worked with short-staple cotton. It could process as much cotton in a day as could 50 people working by hand. After Whitney's invention, Southern farmers quickly grew much short-staple cotton for sale.

Other articles to read include: **Whitney, Eli.**

Eli Whitney's *cotton gin* quickly and cheaply separated cotton seeds from the fibers.

Gottlieb Daimler

Daimler, Gottlieb

Gottlieb Daimler *(GOT leeb DYM luhr)* (1834–1900) was a German engineer. Daimler invented a type of engine. His engine was light enough to power an automobile. Before, people had experimented with carriages powered by steam engines. Daimler's engine worked by burning gasoline instead. It was a type of engine called an *internal-combustion engine.*

In 1885, Daimler and another German engineer, Wilhelm Maybach, made a motorized bicycle. In 1886, they created a motorized carriage.

Daimler started the Daimler Motor Company in 1890. The company made the first Mercedes car in 1901. The Daimler and Benz companies merged to form Daimler-Benz in 1926. The company's name is now Daimler AG.

Other articles to read include: **Automobile; Benz, Karl; Gasoline engine.**

Dam

A dam is a wall placed across a river or stream. It blocks water from flowing. The blocked water forms a lake behind the dam. Such a lake is called a *reservoir*. Some dams are only piles of rocks. Others are made of concrete walls as tall as skyscrapers.

Dams make it easier for people to use water supplies. For example, water from the reservoir can be used for growing crops or for drinking. Such reserves of water may be especially important during dry periods. In some dams, water is allowed to flow through special machines called *turbines (TUR bihnz)*. The water spins the turbines, producing electric power for homes and businesses. Reservoirs are also used for fishing, boating, and swimming.

Dams can help prevent flooding. The reservoir holds back floodwaters. The extra water can then be released gradually, instead of all at once. Dams change the course and strength of rivers. These changes can help people. But they can also harm fish and other wildlife.

Continued on the next page

Dams have been important for thousands of years. Some dams that were built about 2,000 years ago in ancient Rome are still used today.

Other articles to read include: **Building construction; Turbine.**

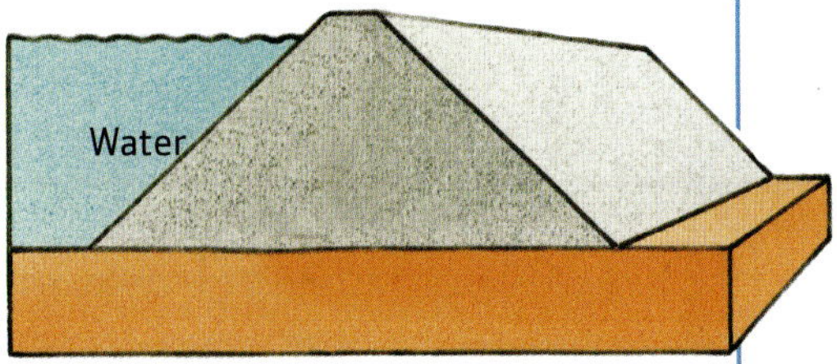

A *gravity dam* relies on its massive weight to stop the force of water.

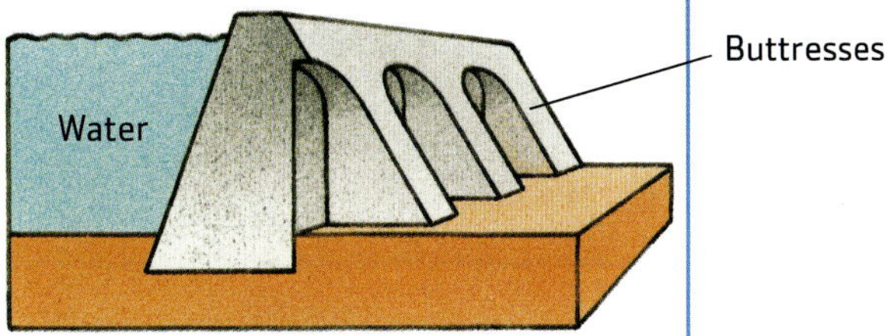

A *buttress dam* gets extra strength from sloped supports called *buttresses* on the side opposite the reservoir.

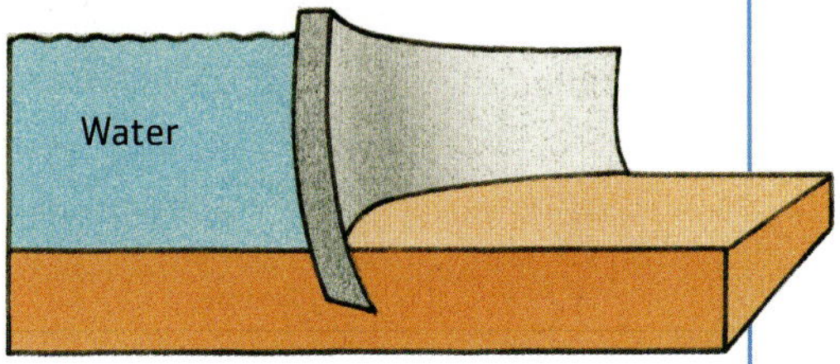

An *arch dam,* often built across a narrow canyon, spreads the water's force to the sides.

Database

A database is a collection of information. It is usually stored in a computer. The information is called *data*.

The data in a database can be used in many different ways. Libraries use databases to keep track of their books, for example. Library patrons can look for data on a book by title, author, or subject. They can also look up the company that printed the book or the date when it was printed.

Many other organizations use databases. Stores use databases to record their customers' purchases. Schools use databases to keep their students' grades and other information. Many companies use databases to keep track of their money and supplies. Much of the information on the Internet is organized into databases.

Other articles to read include: **Computer; Internet; Search engine.**

Dehumidifier

A dehumidifier *(DEE hyoo MIHD uh FY uhr)* is a machine that removes *moisture* (wetness) from the air. Warm air holds more moisture than does cool air. Excess moisture can make people feel uncomfortable. A dehumidifier makes air in a room feel cooler by making it drier. A dehumidifier can also help stop mold and mildew from growing indoors.

A dehumidifier uses two sets of *coils* (twisted parts). A fan draws air in across a set of cold coils called the *evaporator*. The coldness makes the air lose its moisture. Another set of coils, called the *condenser*, reheats the air to room temperature. Then the air blows back into the room. Moisture taken from the air may drain out through a hose or collect in a special container.

Other articles to read include: **Air conditioner.**

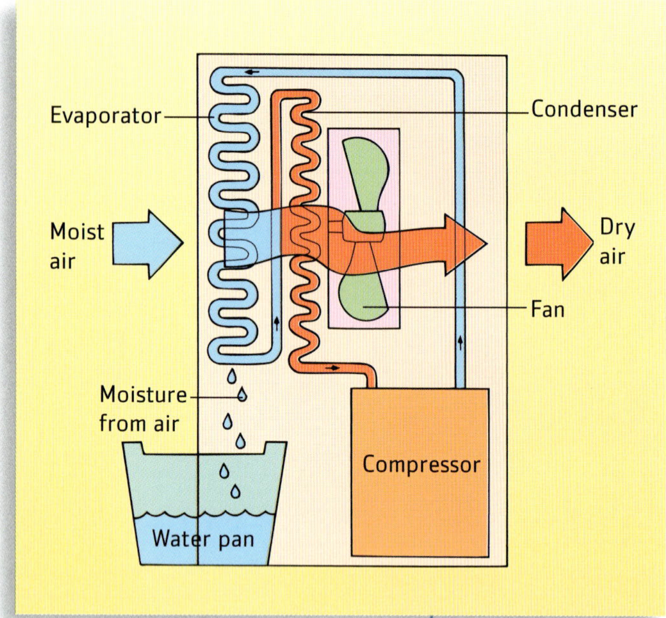

A dehumidifier removes moisture from the air. The fan draws in moist air. The air loses its moisture as it passes over the *evaporator.* Then the air is reheated by the *condenser* and released.

Dehydrated food

Dehydrated food is food preserved by drying. Some dehydrated foods can be used dry. Others must have water added before eating or cooking. Dehydrated food products include dried milk and milk products, soups, coffee, tea, spices, gelatin and dessert mixes, and pasta. Other common dehydrated foods are yeast, potatoes, and snack products.

Dehydrated foods are lightweight and compact. Over 90 percent of their water is removed during drying. Correctly packaged dehydrated foods can be kept for several months if stored below 75 °F (24 °C).

Other articles to read include: **Food preservation.**

Dried pasta is a common dehydrated food.

Desalination

Desalination *(dee SAL uh NAY shuhn)* is the process of removing salt, usually from seawater. Water in the ocean is salty. But people and many animals can drink only fresh water. Most plants also need fresh water. People use desalination to prepare seawater for drinking or for watering crops.

There are several methods of desalination. Seawater is boiled in a method called *distillation*. The water turns to steam. As it does, it leaves the salt behind. When the steam cools, it becomes liquid water again. This fresh water can be collected and used. This process has been used for thousands of years.

Another method of desalination is called *reverse osmosis*. In this method, salt water is forced under pressure to flow through a special barrier. The barrier does not let salt through. Fresh water collects on the other side of the barrier.

Electrodialysis is a third method of desalination. It makes use of electric currents. The currents can separate salt from water.

Other articles to read include: **Electrolysis.**

A *desalination* facility removes salt from seawater. The water can then be used for drinking, watering crops, and other uses. Desalination is used in areas with little fresh water.

Detergent and soap

Detergent and soap are substances used to clean dirty items. Soap is a type of detergent. Detergents and soaps come in many shapes. They include bars, flakes, grains, and liquids.

People use detergents and soaps to wash their skin and shampoo their hair. Doctors clean sores and wounds using detergents that kill germs.

People use detergents and soaps around the house, too. They use them to wash dishes and to do laundry. People also use detergents to scrub floors and clean windows.

Detergents and soaps are important in industry. For example, soap helps new tires slip out of their molds. Some motor oils contain detergents. The detergents break down dirt and other small materials that can harm engines. Soap is also used to polish jewelry and soften leather.

Continued on the next page

Detergent and soap

Continued from the previous page

All detergents and soaps need water to work. They contain molecules called *surfactants,* or *surface active agents.* One side of the molecule is attracted to bits of dirt. The other side is attracted to water. The surfactants form a thin layer around bits of dirt. The outside of this layer is attracted to water. When wetted, they pull dirt out of the material and into water. Dirt can then be easily rinsed away.

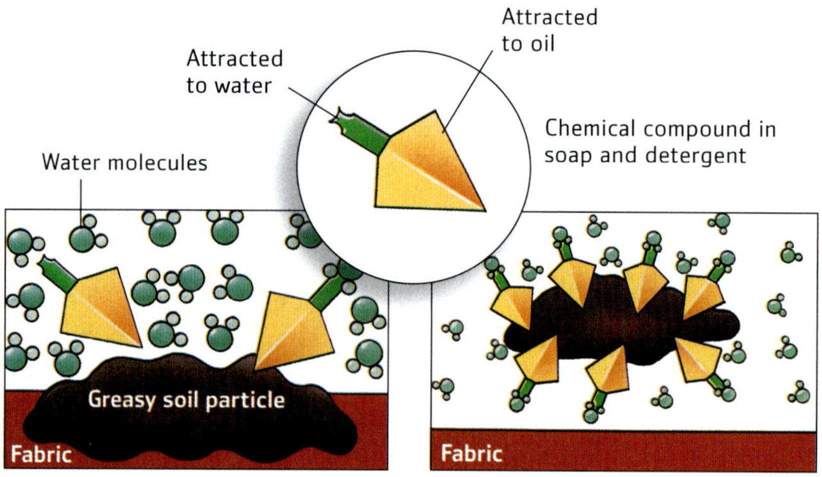

Special chemical compounds give soap and detergent their cleaning power. The molecules of these compounds have two ends. One end can attach to water, and the other end can attach to oil, grease, and other kinds of dirt. The end attracted to oil attaches to dirt. The other end then pulls the dirt out into the water.

Diesel engine

The diesel *(DEE zuhl* or *DEE suhl)* engine is a kind of engine often used for heavy-duty work. Like a gasoline engine, a diesel engine burns fuel. The burning heats gases in the engine. The heated gases *expand* (spread out). They push against parts of the engine, causing the parts to move. These parts, in turn, move parts outside the engine. Such parts may be the wheels of a motor vehicle or the propeller of a boat.

Gasoline engines use a spark to *ignite* (start the burning of) fuel. Diesel engines ignite their fuel using pressure.

Diesel engines are heavy and *efficient.* Efficient engines make much energy for the amount of fuel they use. Diesel engines are used in buses, freight trucks, heavy construction equipment, locomotives, ships, and tractors. They can also be used to make electricity or pump water. Some automobiles have diesel engines.

Other articles to read include: **Automobile: Gasoline engine; Truck.**

Digital video recorder

A digital video recorder (DVR) stores television shows. People can watch the shows later. A DVR records shows as *digital files.* Digital files are the types of data used by computers.

A common type of DVR connects to a cable television system for recording. A DVR can often store 100 or more hours of programs.

A user can replay any part of a stored program on a DVR right away. Users can also watch programs as the DVR records them. The first DVR's for home use became available in 1999. In the late 2000's and 2010's, some DVR's could also download shows from the Internet.

Other articles to read include: **Compact disc; Television; Videotape recorder.**

Direct current

Direct current is a form of *electric current.* An electric current is the movement of electric charges. It comes from the movement of tiny, fast-moving *particles* (small bits of matter) called *electrons.* Electrons move through wires somewhat like water flows through a pipe. This flow is an electric current.

Direct current flows in only one direction. It is different from another kind of electric current, *alternating current.* Alternating current moves back and forth through a wire.

Batteries produce direct current. Power stations, on the other hand, provide alternating current to homes. Alternating current is easier to transmit over long distances.

Many devices use direct current. Electric parts in cars and motors on trains run on direct current. Radios and televisions use both direct current and alternating current.

Other articles to read include: **Alternating current; Electric current; Short circuit.**

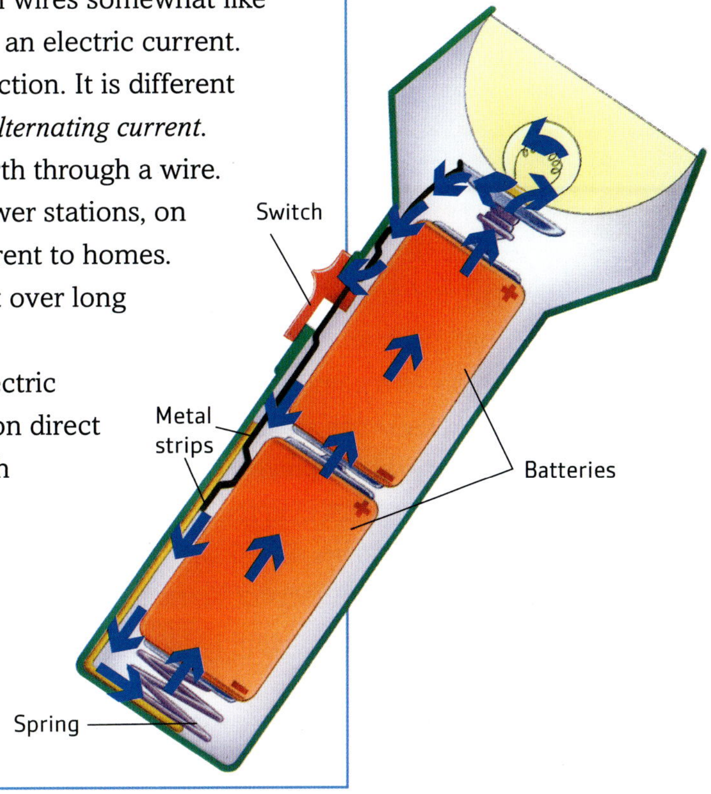

A flashlight uses *direct current,* a flow of electricity in only one direction. Current flows from the batteries to the light bulb and back.

The dome of the Cathedral of Florence, Italy, was built in 1436.

Dome

A dome *(dohm)* is a part of some buildings. It looks like a big, upside-down cup on top of a building. The earliest domes covered huts. They were made of brick or stone. The ancient Romans used domes to cover some of their temples. The most famous Roman dome covers a temple called the Pantheon.

In the early 500's, people learned how to make domes over square buildings. Earlier domes had to cover circle-shaped buildings. The Hagia Sophia is a famous square-shaped building with a dome. It was built in Constantinople (now Istanbul) in 537.

During the Renaissance, people in Europe built taller domes. The Renaissance was a cultural movement that began in the 1300's. St. Peter's Basilica, in Rome, has a famous Renaissance-style dome. The United States Capitol has a dome based on the Basilica's.

The Muslims built many domes. Most *mosques* (Muslim places of worship) have domes. So do many Islamic tombs. The Taj Mahal is a beautiful example of a domed tomb. It was built in Agra, India, between 1630 and 1650.

Some of the largest domes cover huge sports stadiums. They include the Astrodome in Houston and the Louisiana Superdome in New Orleans.

Other articles to read include: **Building construction; Geodesic dome.**

DVD

A DVD is a round, flat disk that stores information. DVD's are mainly used to hold movies. But computer programs and other information may also be stored on a DVD. A DVD is the same size as a compact disc (CD). Both are about 4 ¾ inches (12 centimeters) across. But a DVD can store much more information than can a CD. A DVD is read by a special disk drive or player.

Information is stored on a DVD in the form of a *digital* (numeric) code. A single DVD can store up to 17 *gigabytes (GIHG uh byts)* (billion bytes) of information.

DVD is often said to stand for *Digital Versatile Disc* or *Digital VideoDisc*. But there is no evidence that the letters were meant to stand for anything. DVD's first became available in 1996.

Other articles to read include: **Compact disc; Computer storage device; Digital video recorder.**

Dye

Dyes are chemicals used to color things. People use dyes to color cloth. They also dye ink, leather, paper, and plastic. People also use dyes to color hair. Many dyes are toxic.

There are two kinds of dyes. *Synthetic (sihn THEHT ihk)* dyes are made from artificial chemicals. Most synthetic dyes work best on certain kinds of fibers, such as cotton or nylon. Some dyes fade little. They are used for clothes that must be washed often.

Natural dyes come from plants. A bright yellow dye comes from the crocus plant. Other natural dyes come from animals. A bright red dye comes from insects found in Mexico and Central America.

To color cloth, the dye must first be *dissolved,* or mixed into a liquid. Then the cloth is placed in the liquid. The cloth may be treated with chemicals to keep the colors from running or fading.

Dyes are used at different stages in the making of cloth. Sometimes the fibers are dyed before being spun into yarn. Sometimes the yarn is dyed before being made into cloth. Often, the cloth is dyed after weaving. Sometimes a machine prints different colors of dye in different areas to make a design.

Yarn takes on a bright red color by being pulled through large vats of dye.

Dynamite

Dynamite is an *explosive*. It can blast away rock in building dams and roads. Miners use dynamite to help dig for gold, silver, coal, and other materials. Dynamite has been used in war. But it is not much used today.

The main part of dynamite is a chemical called *nitroglycerin (ny truh GLIHS uhr ihn)*. Nitroglycerin is a heavy, oily liquid. It explodes easily. Other chemicals are added to nitroglycerin. They make the explosive safer to handle and use.

Dynamite was invented in 1867 by the Swedish chemist Alfred Nobel. Nobel mixed nitroglycerin with a type of chalky soil. He found this mixture safer to handle. It was also more powerful than gunpowder explosives used at the time. Nobel started the Nobel Prizes, awards given every year to scientists and others.

Other articles to read include: **Explosive; Nitroglycerin.**

Dynamite is packaged into cylinders made of waxed paper or plastics (inset). Dynamite may be used to tear down buildings. The explosion triggers the building to collapse in on itself (above).

Ee

E-mail

E-mail is a kind of message sent over a computer network. *E-mail* is short for *electronic mail*. To use e-mail, a person must have an *e-mail address*. An e-mail address works somewhat like a street address for package delivery or paper mail. But unlike these kinds of mail, e-mail travels almost instantly. People can send e-mails to many people at once over the Internet. They can also e-mail digital photos and other files.

An e-mail address may include the name of its user and of an organization. It often takes the form *name@organization.com*. Many organizations and websites offer e-mail addresses. They also offer virtual "mailboxes" to store a person's e-mails.

Other articles to read include: **Computer; Internet.**

Earth observing satellite (EOS)

An Earth observing satellite (EOS) is a spacecraft that studies Earth's surface and atmosphere. *Satellites* are objects that *orbit* (travel around) Earth or other planets. Scientists and researchers use EOS's to study changes in the environment over time. The satellites can also help forecast the weather. They may also provide information on the effects of natural disasters.

Other articles to read include: **Satellite, Artificial; Weather forecasting.**

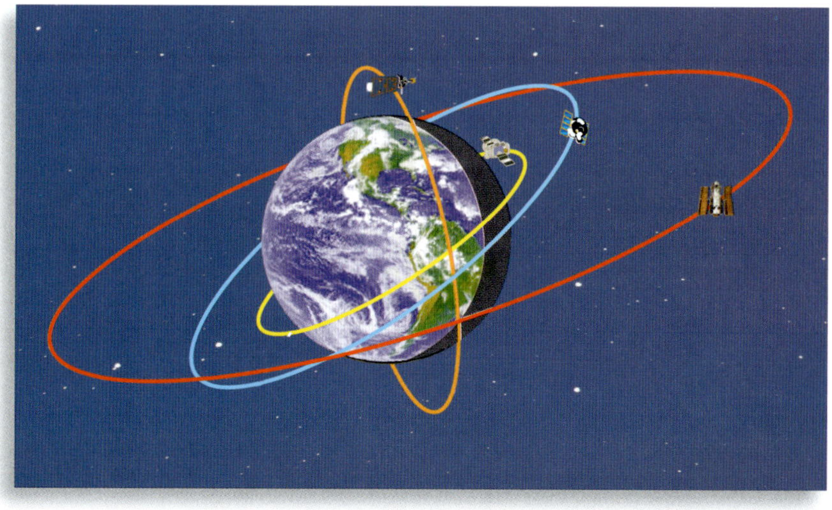

Earth observing satellites can travel around the planet in several different kinds of *orbit* (path).

Eastman Kodak Company

George Eastman

The Eastman Kodak Company became famous as one of the world's largest manufacturers of photographic equipment. It makes cameras, film, photographic chemicals, and other equipment. It also makes *digital cameras.* Digital cameras take photographs that can be viewed on a computer. The company also produces computer scanners and X-ray equipment and film.

The American businessman George Eastman founded the company in 1880. At the time, photography was difficult and expensive. Eastman developed new kinds of film. His company introduced a simple camera in 1888. These products made it easier and cheaper for ordinary people to take photographs. The company was successful for many years. But digital photography became more popular than film in the early 2000's. The company struggled to adapt. It filed for bankruptcy in 2012. The company's headquarters are in Rochester, New York.

Other articles to read include: **Camera; Photography.**

Edison, Thomas Alva

Thomas Edison with the phonograph he invented

Thomas Alva Edison (1847–1931) was one of the greatest American inventors of all time. He invented the first practical electric light bulb. He invented the *phonograph,* a machine to play and record music. He made important improvements to the telegraph and the telephone. Edison also helped found the motion picture industry. In all, Edison was awarded 1,093 United States *patents.* A patent is a legal document that helps prevent others from copying an invention.

Edison was a successful businessman. He created new companies to make and sell his products. His work helped the United States become a world industrial power in the late 1800's.

Edison also developed the modern research laboratory. Some people think this was his greatest achieve-

Continued on the next page

Edison's first incandescent electric light (above) was an important invention.

Edison, Thomas Alva *Continued from the previous page*

ment. At his laboratories, Edison and his assistants performed many experiments. They worked on many problems in physics and chemistry. They also built on the work of others.

Edison was born on Feb. 11, 1847, in Milan, Ohio. His family later moved to Port Huron, Michigan. Edison did not receive much formal schooling. His mother, who had been a teacher, guided his education. He liked reading science books. He performed his own experiments and built models.

In 1863, Edison began to work as a telegraph operator. Over the next few years, he learned all he could about telegraphy. He worked to improve telegraph equipment and made several other inventions. He also met with business leaders. In 1870, he started a company that made *stock tickers.* Stock tickers are machines that track the price of stocks on a stock market.

In 1876, Edison built a laboratory in Menlo Park, New Jersey. There, he and his assistants developed inventions that made him famous. They included an improved telephone system, the phonograph, and the electric light. Edison created electric power companies, too. They supplied power for his lights. In 1886, he built a larger laboratory in West Orange, New Jersey.

Edison continued to work and experiment until his death on Oct. 18, 1931. Edison received honors from around the world.

Other articles to read include: **Electric light; Invention; Light bulb; Phonograph; Telegraph; Telephone.**

Electric car

An electric car is an automobile that runs on electric power. Most automobiles have an engine that burns gasoline or another fuel. An electric car has an electric motor. The motor usually gets its power from rechargeable batteries. It may also use batterylike *fuel cells.*

Electric cars are quieter than cars with gasoline engines. When an electric car brakes, the battery recharges a little bit. Electric cars also do not give off harmful *exhaust* (waste gases).

Continued on the next page

However, electric cars also have disadvantages. They can take hours to fully recharge. Often they cannot travel very far on a single charge.

A *hybrid car* is a mix between a gasoline car and an electric car. It has both a gas engine and a battery-powered motor. It can run on either one.

Many early automobiles were electric. But by the early 1900's, gasoline-powered cars were much more popular. Few electric cars were made again until the 1970's. In 2010, General Motors released an electric car called the Chevy Volt. It included a small gasoline engine. But unlike hybrid cars, the Volt only used the engine to recharge the battery.

Other articles to read include: **Automobile; Electric motor; Hybrid car.**

The Tesla Model S, an electric car, is powered by rechargeable batteries.

Electric circuit

An electric circuit is a path followed by an *electric current*. An electric current is a flow of electricity. The current has energy. Many modern devices, such as lights and computers, make use of this energy.

One part of a circuit is called the *source*. The source produces the electric current. The source can be a battery or a machine called a *generator*. Another part is called the *output device*. The output device uses the current's energy. For example, lights glow with the energy. Toasters get hot. The source and the output device are connected, usually by wires.

A circuit makes a full loop. Electricity flows from the source to the output device and back again. Many circuits have a *switch*. The switch is a part that can break the loop. This stops the flow of current.

Other articles to read include: **Battery; Electric current; Electric generator; Electric power; Short circuit.**

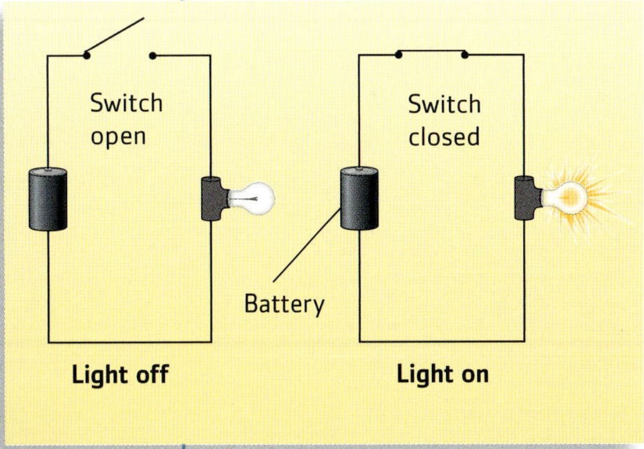

Electric current flows around a path called a *circuit*. The circuit must be closed for the current to flow and power devices, such as light bulbs.

Electric current

An electric current is a flow of electric charges. Currents power many modern devices, such as lights, televisions, and computers.

Currents are typically made of tiny bits of matter called *electrons.* Electrons are parts of atoms. They have a negative charge.

Electric current flows easily through some kinds of material. Such materials are called *conductors.* Metal wires are good conductors. In a metal wire, electrons move easily from atom to atom. This flow of electrons carries energy. An *electric circuit* is a path on which current travels. The current can power devices on the circuit, such as light bulbs and computers.

Other materials do not conduct current well or at all. Such a material is called an *insulator.* Wires are often covered in insulators such as rubber or plastic. The insulator helps keep the current from leaving the wire.

An electric current is either direct or alternating. *Direct current* always flows in the same direction. Direct current is abbreviated DC. Batteries produce direct current. *Alternating current* changes its direction of flow back and forth. Alternating current is abbreviated AC. It is produced by power plants. It travels over power lines to homes and other buildings.

Other articles to read include: **Alternating current; Direct current; Electric circuit; Insulator, Electric.**

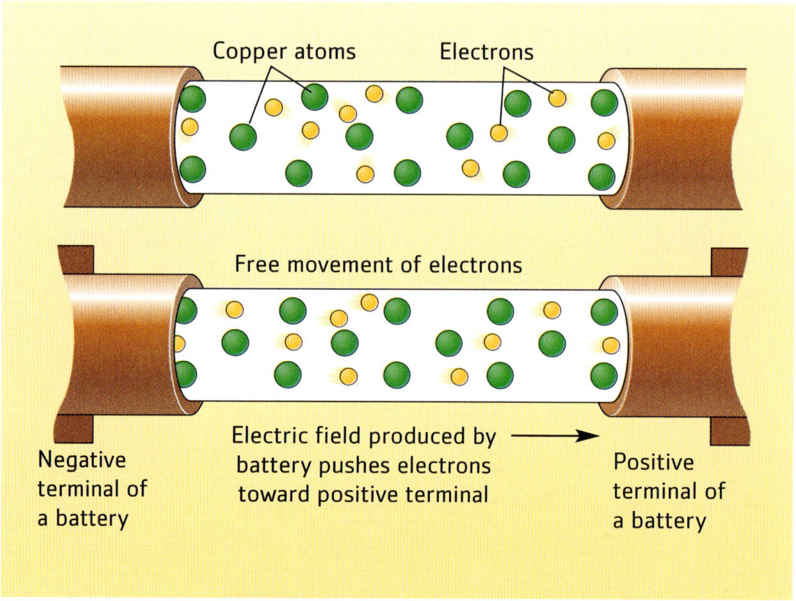

Electrons flow through a copper wire, forming an *electric current.* The wire is connected to a battery. The battery's energy "pushes" free electrons through the wire.

Electric generator

An electric generator is a machine that makes electric power. Generators make much of the electric power people use each day. Electric power runs machines in factories. It powers lights in home and offices. Refrigerators, televisions, and computers work with electric power from generators.

Some generators are small enough to hold in one hand. A bicycle may use such a generator. It may be used to power the bike's headlight. Other generators are bigger than houses. They are used in power plants. These generators can supply power for as many as 1 million homes.

A generator does not create energy. Rather, it changes the energy of motion into electric energy. It does this using magnets. Some generators spin a magnet near a loop of wire. Others spin the wire loop near a magnet. Electricity and magnetism are closely related. Either of these movements causes an electric current to be "pushed" through the wire. The current is a flow of tiny particles called *electrons*. This flow carries energy through the wire to distant homes and other buildings.

The energy to spin the generator's magnet or wire must come from some other source. Burning fuel, for example, can create steam. The steam spins a device called a *turbine* that connects to the magnet or wire.

There are two main kinds of generators. *Alternating-current* (AC) *generators,* or *alternators,* make an electric current that changes direction many times every second. Nearly all power plants use AC generators. *Direct-current* (DC) *generators* make an electric current that always flows in the same direction. Some kinds of factories, trains, and ships use DC generators.

Other articles to read include: **Electric power; Electromagnet; Power plant.**

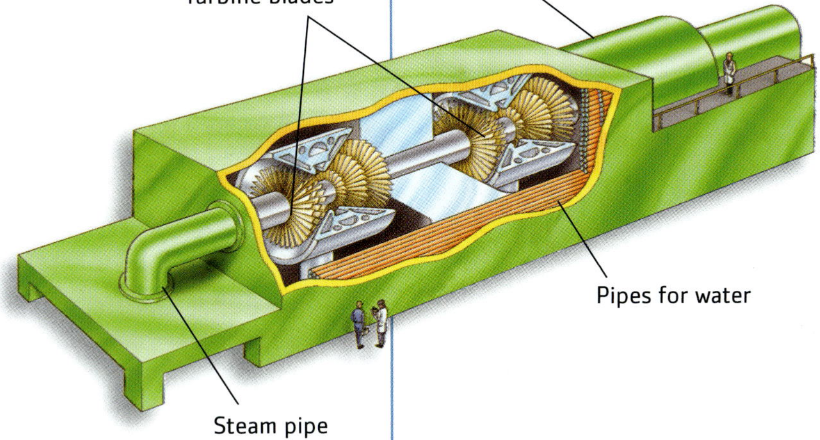

Hot steam spins the blades of *turbines* at a power plant. The spinning motion works with magnets in a *generator* to produce electric power.

Electric guitar

Electric guitar

The electric guitar is a musical instrument with metal strings. It changes the motion of the strings into electrical signals. Electric guitars are popular in rock, country, jazz, and other forms of music. They are almost always used with a device called an *amplifier.* The amplifier can change the guitar's sound and make it much louder.

Plucking the string of an electric guitar creates an electrical signal. The amplifier strengthens this signal. It can also distort the signal to make it sound "heavier." Many rock songs use such distortion. Amplifiers can also make echoing sounds and other effects. A speaker turns the amplified signal into sound that people can hear.

Compact fluorescent light

Electric light

An electric light changes electric energy into light. Electric lights connect to *electric circuits.* An electric circuit carries a flow of electric energy called a *current.* There are two main kinds of electric lighting: (1) *incandescent lighting* and (2) *gaseous-discharge lighting.*

The light of an incandescent lamp comes from the glow of a hot metal wire. The wire is called a *filament.* When the lamp is switched on, electric current flows through the filament. The current's energy heats the filament. The heat causes the filament to glow, much like a red-hot poker. A bulb surrounds the filament. The bulb keeps air away from the filament. Air would cause the filament to burn up. The bulb is filled with a special mixture of gases instead of air.

Gaseous-discharge lamps pass electric current through a gas instead of a filament. They are also called *electric-discharge* lamps. In most such lamps, the gas is held in a tube or a bulb. There are several different kinds of gaseous-discharge lights. *Fluorescent*

Continued on the next page

lamps are widely used in homes and offices. *Compact fluorescent lights* (CFL's) are the same size as common incandescent light bulbs. Sodium and mercury *vapor lights* are often used in streetlights. *Neon lights* glow red-orange or other colors, depending on their mixture of gases. Gaseous-discharge lights are often more expensive than incandescent lights. But they last longer and use less energy.

Before electric lights, people could see at night only with candles, fires, gaslights, or oil lamps. During the mid-1800's, a number of inventors tried to create light from electric energy. Several lighting pioneers developed incandescent lamps. These lamps operated with batteries and burned out quickly.

The American inventor Thomas A. Edison invented an improved electric light in 1879. He also developed electric power stations. The stations made electric current and could channel it to many buildings. With this cheap source of electric power, electric lights became popular.

In the early 1890's, Nikola Tesla, an American inventor from Austria-Hungary, demonstrated the earliest versions of fluorescent and neon lighting. During the early 1900's, engineers began to experiment with gaseous-discharge lamps containing mercury. In the 1970's, researchers developed energy-saving light sources, such as metal halide lamps and high-pressure sodium lamps.

In the early 2000's, *light-emitting diodes* (LED's) began to replace other kinds of electric lights. These lights have no bulbs. They make use of the same materials found in computer chips.

Other articles to read include: **Edison, Thomas Alva; Electric power; Fluorescent lamp; Lamp; Light bulb.**

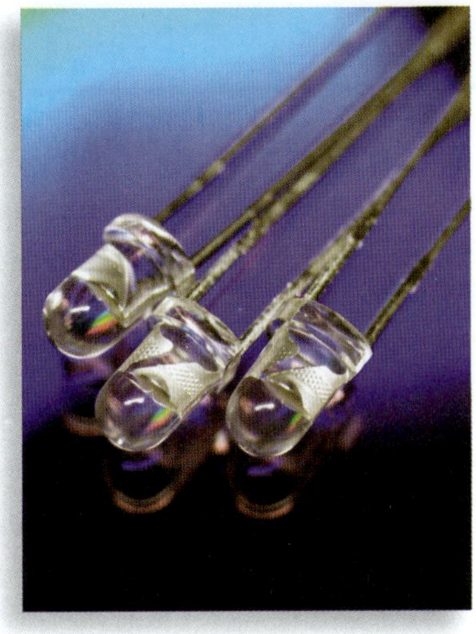

Neon lights (top) make use of gases to give off light. *Light-emitting diodes* or LED's (above left) make use of materials found in computer chips. *Incandescent bulbs* (above right) contain a glowing wire called a *filament.*

Electric motor

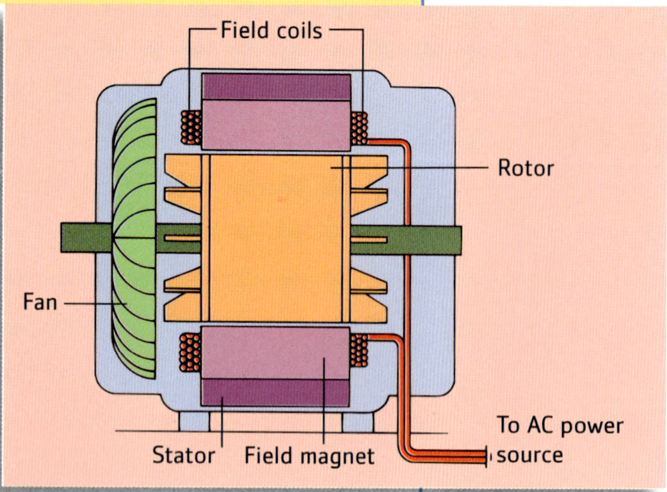

The interaction between electricity and magnetism makes electric motors move. This electric motor uses alternating electric current (AC). The current interacts with the field magnet to spin a rotor, which in turn spins a fan.

An electric motor is a device that changes electric energy into motion. Many home appliances use electric motors. These devices include hair dryers, electric razors, and food processors. Some kinds of trains and automobiles use electric motors.

A simple electric motor makes use of a loop of wire. The loop is held between the two ends of a horseshoe magnet. Electricity flows through the wire. It turns the wire into a kind of magnet called an *electromagnet.*

The ends of a magnet are called *poles.* The poles of magnets push or pull on each other. In the simple electric motor, the poles of the wire loop push and pull against the poles of the horseshoe magnet. This pushing and pulling makes the loop of wire spin. The spinning motion can do useful work. It can spin the blades of a food processor or the wheels of a car or train, for example.

Other articles to read include: **Alternating current; Electric current; Electromagnet; Engine; Magnet; Wire.**

Electric power

Electric power is the use of electric energy to do work. Electric power runs much of our technology. It lights, heats, and cools our homes. Machines called *generators* make electric power. They produce a flow of energy called an *electric current.* The current moves through wires and into buildings. Huge generators in power plants produce enough electric current for millions of homes.

Power plants do not create energy out of nothing. Instead, they change another kind of energy into electric energy. Many power plants use the energy of *fossil fuels.* Fossil fuels include coal, oil, and natural gas. These materials release heat when burned. Power plants use the heat to boil water, creating steam. The hot steam, in turn, spins wheellike machines called *turbines.* The spinning motion of the turbines is a form of energy. Generators change this spinning energy into electric energy.

Continued on the next page

Nuclear power plants also use steam to spin turbines. But they make steam from the heat of nuclear fuels. *Hydroelectric plants* use the energy of falling water to spin turbines. *Wind turbines* spin from the energy of blowing wind. Solar panels do not use turbines. They change the energy of sunlight directly into electric energy.

Electric power is measured in units called *watts.* For example, it takes 100 watts of electric power to operate a 100-watt light bulb. The world's power plants produce billions of watts at any given time.

Other articles to read include: **Electric generator; Nuclear reactor; Power plant; Solar energy; Turbine; Wind power.**

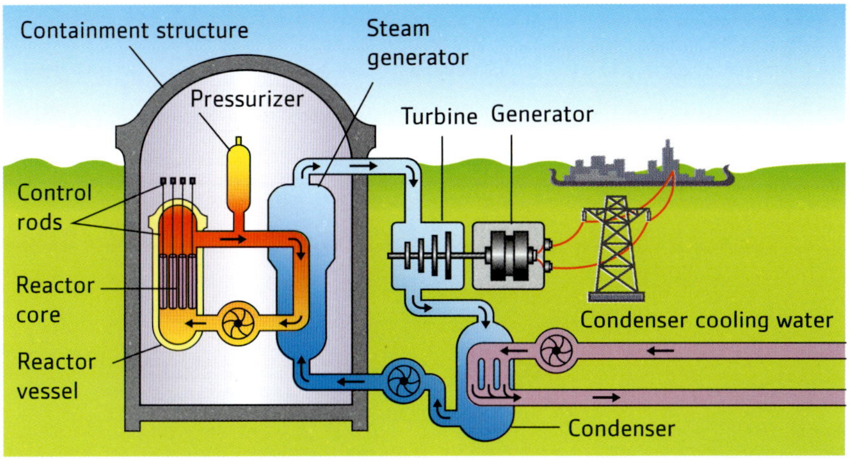

A *nuclear power plant* makes steam using the great heat from nuclear reactions. The steam moves a *turbine,* powering an electric *generator.* The nuclear reactions take place in a reactor core sealed inside a containment structure.

Electrode

An electrode carries electric current into or out of a device. Electric current is a flow of electricity. Electrodes are made of *conductors.* A conductor is a material that carries electricity well. Most electrodes are pieces of metal. They may be shaped into plates, rods, wires, or wire mesh.

A battery has two electrodes. One is positively charged. The other is negatively charged. The electrodes can be connected to a circuit. The battery makes current that powers devices on the circuit. Other electronic devices also have two or more electrodes.

Other articles to read include: **Battery; Electric circuit; Electric current.**

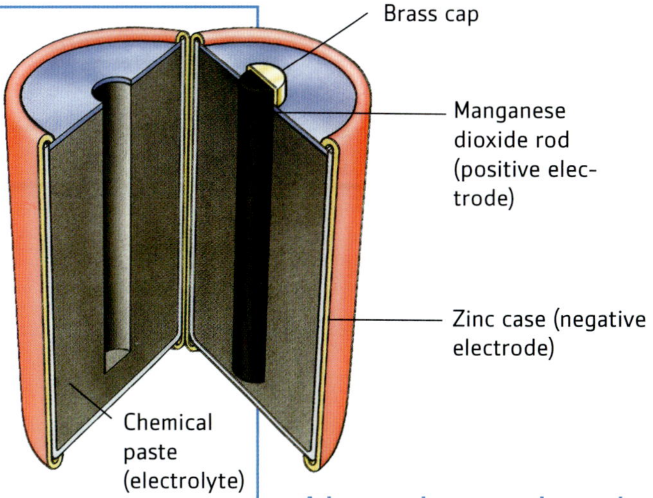

A battery has two *electrodes.* Electric current is "pushed" out of the battery from the negative electrode. It re-enters the battery at the positive electrode.

ACTIVITY

How to make copper move through vinegar

! Ask a teacher or other adult to help you with this experiment.

What you need:

- two plastic-coated, copper wires, each about 12 inches (30 centimeters) long
- electrical tape
- lead from a mechanical pencil, about 2 inches (5 centimeters) long
- a 1.5-volt battery
- a small glass jar, filled with vinegar

1. Take the two coated wires and carefully cut ½ inch (1.25 centimeters) of the plastic coating from three ends.

2. Cut 4 inches (10 centimeters) of the coating from the fourth end, and bend the bare copper wire into a U shape. Connect the other piece of wire to the pencil lead.

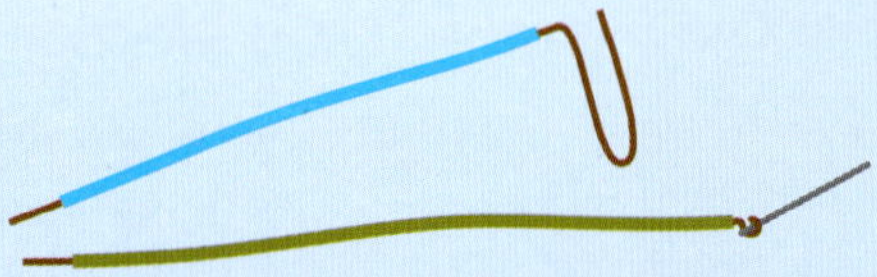

3. Now join the two free ends to the battery. Tape the other end of the wire with the pencil lead to the negative (–) terminal of the battery. Connect the other end of the piece of wire with the U-shape to the positive (+) terminal.

4. Put the pencil lead and the U-shaped wire into the vinegar. Move these two electrodes closer together until you notice bubbles in the vinegar. Move them apart again until the bubbles stop. .

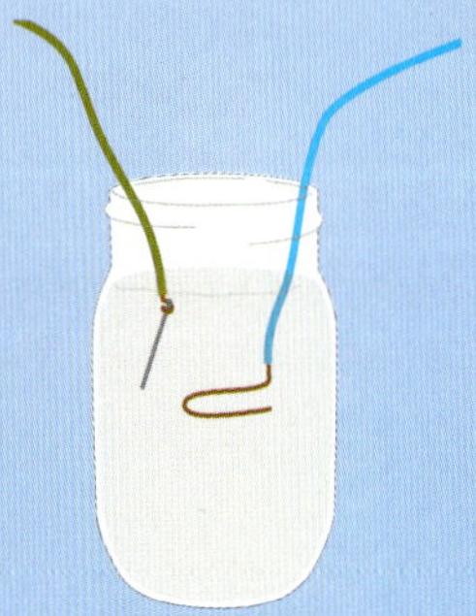

5. Move the two electrodes close together again until you notice the bubbles. After about 10 minutes, disconnect the battery and take the electrodes out of the vinegar. What changes do you notice?

6. Now you can make the coating disappear again. Put your electrodes back into the vinegar. This time connect the pencil lead to the positive connection and the U-shaped wire to the negative connection.

What's going on:

The copper wire is cleaner and brighter than before, and the pencil lead has a grayish or pinkish-brown coat. The electric current has taken copper from the U-shaped wire through the solution, and coated it onto the pencil lead.

http://bit.ly/TUZgvi

Electrolysis

Electrolysis *(ih lehk TROL uh sihs)* is a process in which an *electric current* passes through a liquid. An electric current is a flow of electric charges. In electrolysis, the passing of current causes certain *chemical reactions* to occur. A chemical reaction is the change of a substance into one or more different substances. Electrolysis can break particles of a substance into two or more pieces. The word *electrolysis* means *splitting with electricity.* Electrolysis has many uses, especially in industry.

A simple example of electrolysis involves passing electric current through water. Electrolysis breaks the water molecules into hydrogen gas and oxygen gas. Some uses of electrolysis do not involve a chemical reaction. For example, electrolysis can remove metals from some liquids.

Other articles to read include: **Electric current; Electrode.**

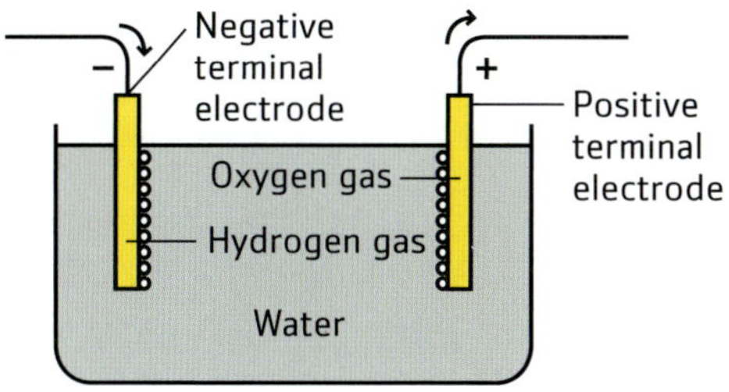

***Electrolysis* can be used to break water molecules into hydrogen and oxygen. An electric current passes through the water. Hydrogen gas collects at the negative electrode. Oxygen gas collects at the positive electrode.**

Electromagnet

An electromagnet is a kind of temporary magnet. It forms when *electric current* flows through an object. Electric current is the movement of electric charges.

A common kind of electromagnet is made from an iron bar. The bar is wrapped in a *coil* (twist) of wire. Electric current is passed through the wire. It turns the bar into a temporary magnet. When the current is removed, the bar stops being a magnet.

Electromagnets are used in many household appliances, such as refrigerators, vacuum cleaners, and doorbells. They are used in electric motors and generators. Powerful industrial electromagnets lift heavy pieces of scrap iron. Electromagnets are also used in scientific equipment, including huge machines called *particle accelerators.*

In 1820, the Danish physicist Hans Oersted discovered that electric current produces a magnetic field. The American physicist Joseph Henry built the first practical electromagnet in the late 1820's.

Other articles to read include: **Electric current; Electric generator; Electric motor; Magnetic levitation train.**

Powerful industrial electromagnets lift heavy pieces of iron.

ACTIVITY

Make an electromagnet

An ordinary bar magnet has a magnetic field around it all the time. We call this kind of magnet a *permanent magnet.* You can also make a magnet by wrapping wire around an iron rod or bolt. When an electric current passes through the wire, the rod works like a magnet. We call this kind of magnet an *electromagnet.* We use electromagnets in many household appliances, such as refrigerators and vacuum cleaners.

What you need:

- a small compass
- a plastic or wooden ruler
- two large iron bolts
- 2 pieces of thin, plastic-coated wire, 20 inches (50 centimeters) and 40 inches (1 meter), with bare ends
- a 1.5-volt ("D") battery
- a felt-tip pen
- a 6-volt battery
- adhesive tape

1.

1. Line up the compass needle so that it points to the north. Place it near one end of the ruler, with the ruler facing east-west.

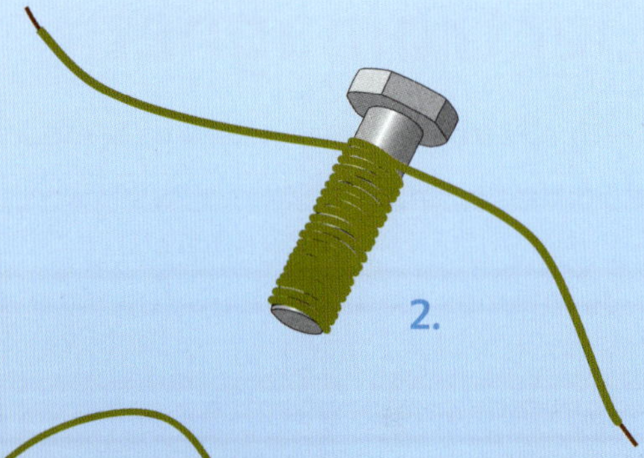
2.

2. Wind the 20-inch (50-centimeter) wire many times around one of the bolts. Always wind the wire in the same direction. Leave about 4 inches (10 centimeters) of wire free at each end. Place the bolt facing east-west on the ruler near the compass.

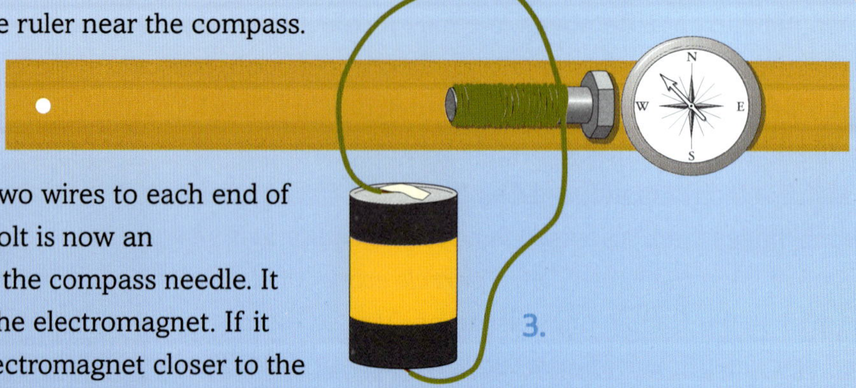

3.

3. Tape the ends of the two wires to each end of the "D" battery. The bolt is now an electromagnet. Watch the compass needle. It should swing toward the electromagnet. If it does not, move the electromagnet closer to the compass. Where does the electromagnet have to be on the ruler to make the compass needle point halfway between the *N* and the *W?* Mark this point on the ruler.

4. Now make a second electromagnet with the longer wire, leaving about 6 inches (20 centimeters) of wire free at each end. Disconnect the first electromagnet. Place the second one on the ruler at the mark you made earlier, and connect it to the "D" battery.

   What happens to the compass needle? Does it swing around farther than before? Twice as much wire means twice as much resistance. This makes the current half as strong.

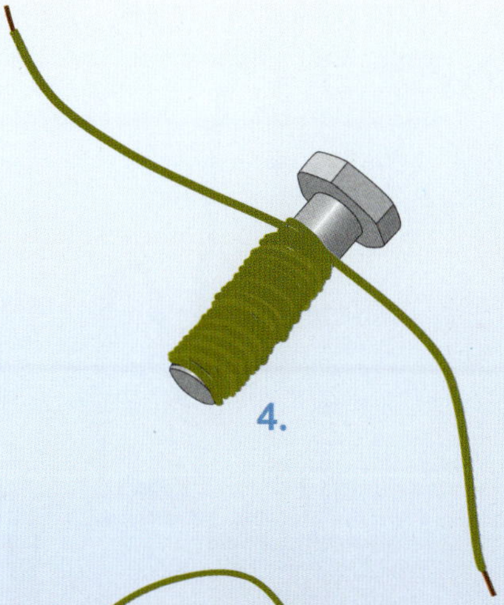

4.

5. Now disconnect the wires from either end of the "D" battery and connect one wire to the positive (+) terminal of the 6-volt battery and one wire to the negative (–) terminal. Place the electromagnet at the mark on the ruler. What happens?

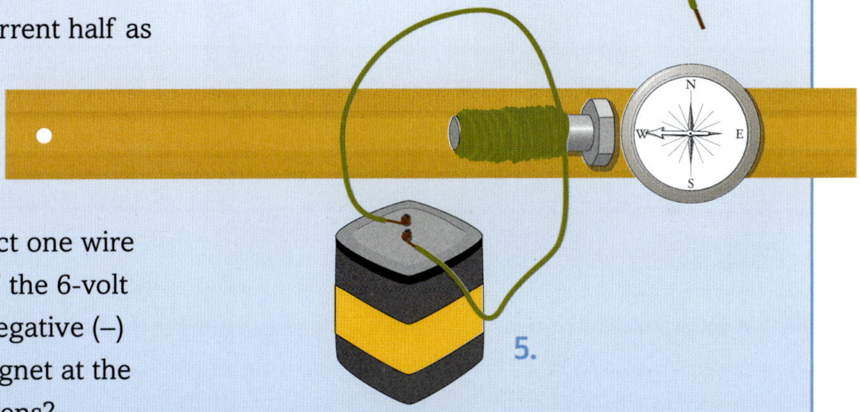

5.

Making an electromagnet stronger:

What can you learn from this experiment? The strength of an ordinary bar magnet is permanent and fixed. But we can make the magnetism around an electromagnet weaker or stronger, and we can even turn it off completely. How can you make an electromagnet stronger? How did you increase the magnetism in the electromagnet?

What's going on?

The electromagnet has become stronger because the 6-volt battery is sending more electric current through it. More electric current makes an electromagnet stronger. The needle moves farther than before.

http://bit.ly/XeJ8EG

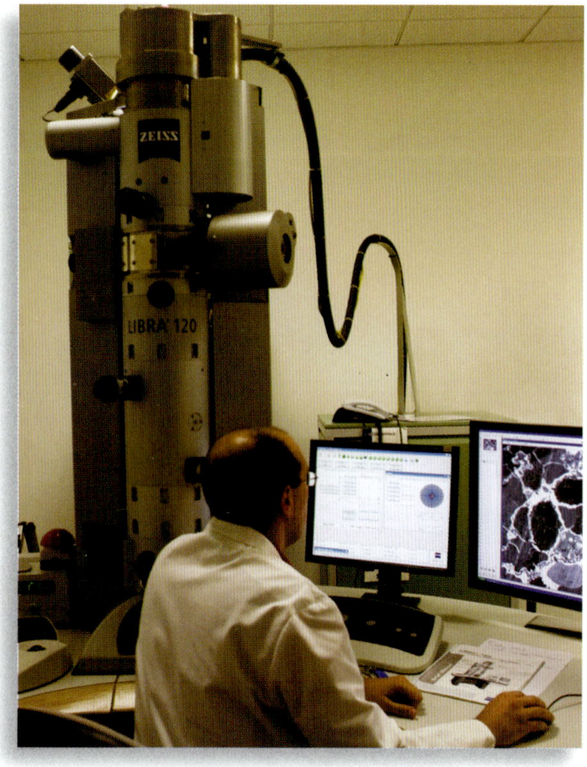

Electron microscope

An electron microscope is a device used to see very tiny things. It works by shooting the object with a beam of *electrons.* Electrons are tiny particles smaller than atoms. Electron microscopes can make objects look millions of times bigger than they really are. Scientists use them to see things too small to be seen with *optical microscopes.* Optical microscopes use light instead of electrons. Electrons are smaller than waves of light.

One kind of electron microscope is the *scanning electron microscope.* It shoots the object with a beam of electrons. As the electrons hit the object's surface, they knock other electrons off it. A device called a *collector* gathers these electrons. It uses them to make an image of the object. The image can be shown on a computer screen.

An electron microscope produces an image of extremely tiny objects using a beam of electrons. The image may be displayed on a computer.

Another kind of electron microscope is the *transmission electron microscope.* In this kind of microscope, the electron beam passes through the object. But the object scatters or absorbs some of the electrons. A collector gathers the electrons that pass through. It uses them to make an image of the object.

Other articles to read include: **Microscope.**

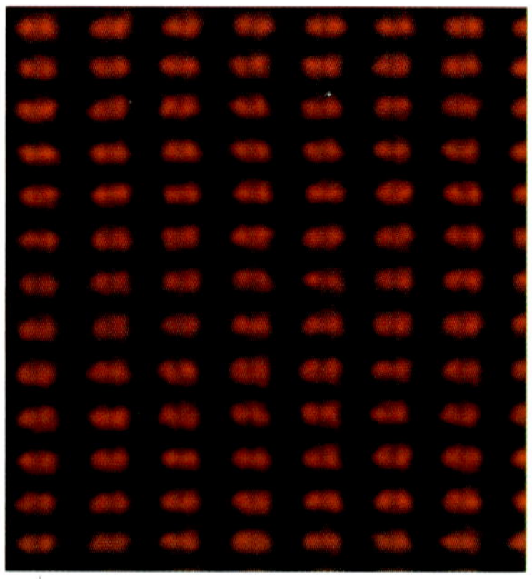

This electron microscope image shows pairs of atoms in a silicon crystal.

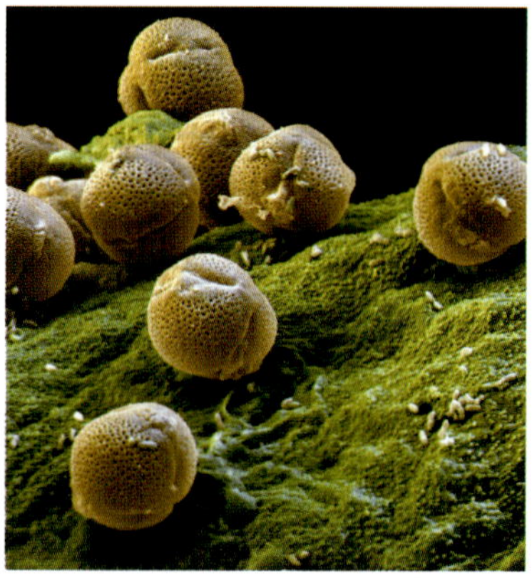

Pollen grains from a rowan tree have a hard outer coating that can be seen with an electron microscope.

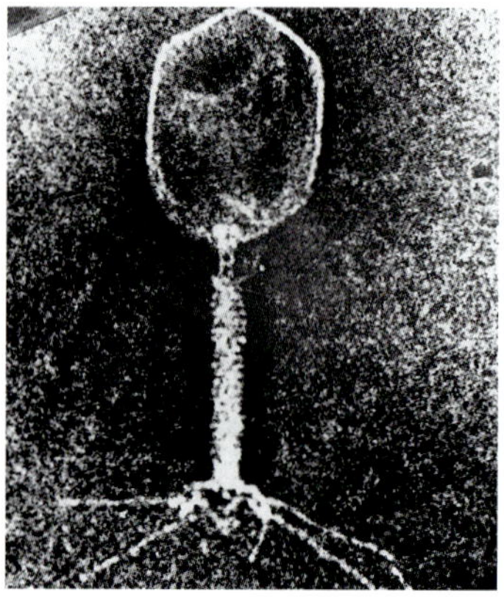

An electron microscope magnified this virus specimen to 190,000 times its actual size.

Electronic game

Nintendo's Wii video game console enables people to control video games by moving a wandlike controller.

An electronic game is a game played with a computer and video screen. Such games are also called *video games* or *computer games.* They are a popular form of entertainment. Unlike many other forms of entertainment, they are *interactive.* This means that the player helps guide the action. Electronic games let players battle monsters or fly spaceships. Some games let players explore huge, complex worlds.

Each game is designed to work on a certain type of computer. Many games are played on *video game consoles.* These machines generally hook up to a television. Other games are played on *handheld game systems.* These systems are miniature consoles with built-in screens. Many games are played on personal computers or cell phones. Some electronic games are stored on cartridges or special discs. People can also download games from the Internet.

A player uses a device called a *controller* to play an electronic game. Many controllers have buttons and leverlike joysticks. Some controllers track the player's movements and gestures. Computer games are usually controlled with a computer keyboard and mouse. Handheld game systems have built-in controllers.

Many people work together to create electronic games. *Game designers* create the rules and goals of the game. They also determine how the player controls the game. Artists, musicians, and sound engineers create the look and sound of a game. *Programmers* combine all the parts of the game into the game's *code* (computer instructions). *Playtesters* test the game to make sure it works properly.

Many games involve moving from one end of an obstacle course to another. In many games, the player takes on the role of a character in a story. The player may be in charge of building cities or commanding armies. Other games focus on exploration or solving puzzles.

Continued on the next page

Electronic game *Continued from the previous page*

Graphics are how the game looks. The graphics in some games are almost lifelike. Other games look like cartoons. Some games have *two-dimensional* graphics. The parts of the game are represented by flat images. Many modern games have *three-dimensional* graphics. In these games, the characters and objects are more like dolls in a dollhouse.

One of the first electronic games was *Tennis for Two* (1958). Players could bounce an electronic "ball" back and forth over a "net." In the early 1970's, engineers began to develop simple *arcade games.* These games were built into special cabinets. People often had to pay with coins to play them. One of the most popular was *Pong* (1972), a game based on table tennis. It was released by a company called Atari. In 1977, Atari made the first video game console for the home.

Electronic games got a major boost in popularity in 1985. In that year, the Japanese company Nintendo released the game *Super Mario Bros.* on its new console, the Nintendo Entertainment System. The game featured colorful graphics, catchy music, and fun gameplay. In 1986, Nintendo released *The Legend of Zelda.* It was the first game to let players save their progress so they could continue the adventure later. In the late 1980's, Nintendo released the first handheld system, called the Game Boy.

Many important games appeared on personal computers. They included strategy games like *Sid Meier's Pirates!* (1987) and *Sid Meier's Civilization* (1991). Games such as *Wolfenstein 3D* (1992) and *Doom* (1993) featured intense shooting gameplay. In *The Sims* (2000), players controlled neighborhoods full of imaginary characters.

By the 2000's, many computer games worked over the Internet. Among the most popular was the 2004 game *World of Warcraft.* It features a vast fantasy world that players explore together online. In 2006, Nintendo released the Wii console. By the early 2010's, simple games played on the Internet or cell phones had also become popular.

Other articles to read include: **Computer; Computer graphics; Internet; Virtual reality; Wright, Will.**

Many cell phones can play games downloaded over the Internet.

Electronics

Electronic readers can hold the text of thousands of books.

Electronics is working with electric signals to do useful things. Phones, radios, televisions, and video games are all electronic products. Computer chips are made of electronic circuits.

Electronics uses electricity to carry signals. The signals often work as a code. They may stand for numbers, words, sounds, images, or other kinds of information. A website, for example, consists of electric signals. These signals travel over the Internet. A computer screen displays the signals as the website's words and pictures.

Electricity involves tiny particles called *electrons.* Electrons have a negative electric charge. Other particles have positive electric charges. The two kinds of charge attract each other. An *electric current* is a flow of charges. Currents can flow through metal wires and other materials. A *circuit* forms a path for electric current.

A change in electric current can act as a signal. For example, an electric circuit can be switched on or off. This change is a signal. A change in *voltage* can also be a signal. A voltage is a force that "pushes" an electric current.

Electronic devices can change currents and voltages at amazing speeds. Some electronics parts are so small that you need a microscope to see them. A fingernail-sized computer chip may contain billions of circuit switches.

Other articles to read include: **Computer; Computer chip; Electric circuit; Electric current; Invention**

Elevator

Elevators

An elevator is a machine that carries people or freight up and down inside a building. The *car* is the part in which people or freight travel. It moves up or down the elevator's *shaft.*

Most elevators use long, heavy steel cables to raise and lower the car. One end of each cable is attached to the top of the car. The other end is attached to a heavy weight. The weight balances the weight of the car. An electric motor pulls the cables. A safety device prevents the car from falling if a cable breaks.

Elevators became common in the 1800's in the United States and England. But they were slow and dangerous. An inventor named Elisha G. Otis built the first elevator with a safety device in 1854. Elevators led to the development of skyscrapers.

Other articles to read include: **Electric motor; Escalator; Otis, Elisha Graves.**

Engine

An engine is a machine that uses energy to do useful work. Many engines use energy produced by the *combustion* (burning) of fuels, such as gasoline. Other engines get energy from steam or from high-pressure air or water.

Engines are used in many ways. They power airplanes, cars, trains, and ships. They are also used in factories.

One of the first engines was the *steam engine.* It was developed in the 1700's. A steam engine burns fuel to heat water. The water boils, creating steam. The hot steam, in turn, pushes or spins other devices. This pushing or spinning motion can do work.

Another kind of engine is the *internal-combustion engine.* This type of engine burns fuel inside a hollow chamber called a *cylinder.* The cylinder also contains a rod called a *piston.* When the fuel burns, hot gases push the piston in the cylinder. The piston's up-and-down motion can spin the wheels of a car. Most cars use *gasoline engines.* These engines use a spark to burn gasoline inside the cylinder. Other vehicles use *diesel engines.* In a diesel engine, the fuel in the cylinder explodes because it is put under high pressure.

Other articles to read include:
Automobile; Diesel engine; Gasoline engine; Piston; Steam engine.

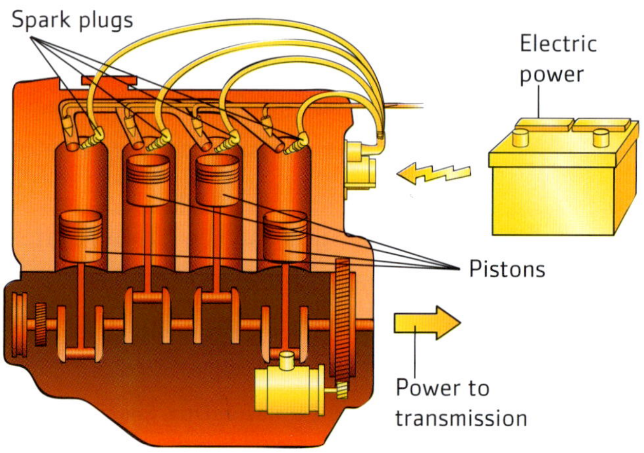

A gasoline engine uses an electric spark to ignite a mixture of gasoline and air in a *cylinder.* The exploding fuel mixture pushes a *piston.* The motion of the pistons can spin a car's wheels.

Engineering

Civil engineers inspect a building site.

Engineering involves using science to make useful things. Engineers design airplanes, bridges, and computers. They design huge dams and tiny electric circuits. They also help make useful chemicals, medicines, and artificial limbs and organs.

There are many different kinds of engineers. For example, an *aerospace engineer* might plan, test, and fix rockets, missiles, spacecraft, or aircraft. *Civil engineers* plan and help build dams, highways, railroads, buildings, and many other projects. *Computer engineers* build computers and create the software programs that run on them. But areas of engineering knowledge often overlap. Also, different kinds of engineers may work closely together on certain projects.

Early engineers made use of *simple machines,* such as pulleys, wedges, and wheels-and-axles. Ancient Egyptians used these simple tools to build the great pyramids of Giza around 2500 B.C. During the 1700's and 1800's, engineers created machines powered by steam engines. This period was known as the Industrial Revolution. Since that time, scientific knowledge has hugely increased. By the 2000's, engineers had to study constantly to keep up with new knowledge.

Other articles to read include: **Building construction; Computer; Machine.**

Escalator

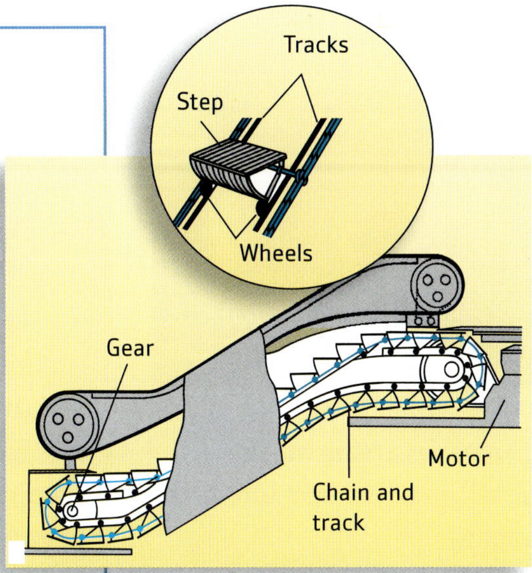

An escalator is a set of steps that are pulled along tracks.

An escalator is a moving stairway. It takes people from one floor or level in a building to another. Escalators are found in airports, subway stations, stores, and other buildings.

The steps of an escalator have wheels under them. The wheels run on tracks. The tracks flatten the steps at the top and bottom of the escalator. The flattening helps people get on and off easily. The flattened steps slide under the floor and loop back to the other end.

George H. Wheeler and Jesse W. Reno created designs that led to the first escalators. One was first used in 1900, in a New York City elevated train station.

Other articles to read include: **Elevator.**

The Ariane 5 rocket was developed by the European Space Agency and a group of European companies known as Arianespace. The rocket is used mainly to launch satellites.

European Space Agency (ESA)

The European Space Agency (ESA) is a space program run by the nations of Western Europe. It was created in 1975. Members of the ESA are Austria, Belgium, the Czech Republic, Denmark, Finland, France, Germany, Greece, Ireland, Italy, Luxembourg, the Netherlands, Norway, Portugal, Romania, Spain, Sweden, Switzerland, and the United Kingdom.

The ESA combines parts of the space programs of its member countries. It directed the building of Spacelab, an orbiting laboratory. Spacelab was carried aboard the U.S. space shuttle on various missions between 1983 and 1998. The ESA also built Columbus, a laboratory module for the International Space Station. The ESA has launched many objects into space, including probes to other planets.

The ESA and NASA, the United States space agency, have partnered on many space missions. For example, they are partners in the Hubble Space Telescope.

Other articles to read include: **International Space Station; Space exploration.**

Explosives create hot, high-pressure gases that spread rapidly.

Explosive

An explosive is a substance that is designed to explode. It may be a solid, a liquid, or a gas. When a powerful explosive is heated or hit hard, it quickly changes into a hot gas that spreads out in a big, loud blast.

Explosives are dangerous, but some are useful. They can blast tunnels through mountains or clear away rocks and tree stumps so that people can build roads.

Fireworks are one use of explosives. The gunpowder in fireworks sends them into the air and makes them explode. On exploding, fireworks make bright, beautiful colors in the sky. But all explosives can hurt people. Explosives are also used to make gunpowder, bombs, and land mines. These explosives are made to destroy buildings and kill people.

Other articles to read include: **Bomb; Dynamite; Fireworks; Gunpowder.**

Facebook

Facebook is a *social networking website.* People on Facebook can connect with other Facebook users. They can also share photos and information about themselves. Millions of people around the world use Facebook. Businesses, charities, and politicians also use the website.

Users create *profile pages.* They can post pictures, their interests, and other information on their profiles. Users connect with each other on Facebook by becoming *friends.* Friends can see each other's profiles and easily keep track of each other.

Facebook has changed the way many people communicate. Users can spread messages and ideas instantly through "word of mouth." Facebook is also important in modern politics.

Mark Zuckerberg, a student at Harvard University, founded Facebook in his dorm room in 2004. At first, the website was available only to college students. In September 2006, Facebook opened to anyone over 13 with an e-mail address. Its headquarters are in Palo Alto, California. It also operates out of Dublin, Ireland, and Seoul, South Korea.

Other articles to read include: **Internet; Website.**

Factory

A factory is a place where products are made. Some factories are the size of garages. Others are groups of buildings covering whole city blocks. Inside a factory, workers and machines put parts together to make finished product. This process is called *manufacturing.* Most of the products we use are made in factories.

About one-fourth of the world's people work in manufacturing. Factories make use of the idea of *division of labor.* Work in a factory is divided into several parts or tasks. A worker might work on one part or task over and over. The next worker does the next part or task, and so on. Factories also use computers and robots to manufacture products.

Before factories, people made products by hand in homes or workshops. Each product was different from the next. In the late 1700's and 1800's, people invented power-driven machines. These machines made factories possible. Modern factories turn out products that are more or less identical.

Other articles to read include: **Assembly line; Machine; Materials.**

A fax machine sends a copy of a document over telephone lines.

Fax machine

Fax machines send and receive written words and pictures over telephone lines. The word *fax* comes from the word *facsimile (fak SIHM uh lee),* which means an exact copy. A fax machine sends a copy of any *document (DAHK yoo muhnt),* such as a letter, picture, map, or report.

Both the sender and the receiver must have a fax machine. The sender puts the document to be sent into the machine. Then the sender dials the telephone number of the receiver's fax machine. The sender's machine scans the document. Scanning converts the document's contents into an electric signal. Telephone lines carry this signal to the receiving fax machine. The receiving machine uses the signal to print an exact copy of the document.

The first fax machine was built in 1842 by Alexander Bain, a Scottish scientist. In the 1930's, news companies began using fax machines to send photographs. Many businesses started using fax machines in the 1980's. At that time, fax machines could only print on special paper. Today, most machines use regular paper. Today's fax machines can send a page in 10 to 30 seconds. But for many purposes, fax machines have been replaced by e-mail and other Internet communication.

Other articles to read include: **Copying machine; Telephone.**

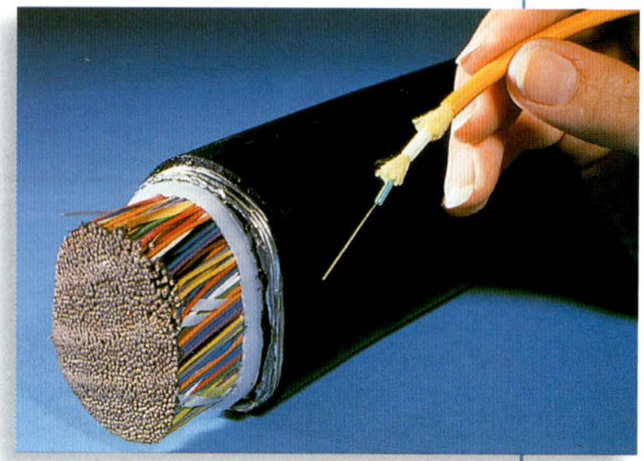

An optical fiber thin enough to hold between two fingers can carry several times as much data as a large cable of wires.

Fiber optics

Fiber optics is the sending of signals using light and thin glass or plastic threads. The threads, called *optical fibers,* may be thinner than a human hair. Pulses of light carry the signals. The light pulses travel through the fibers at extremely high speeds. Fiber-optic cables form a major part of the Internet. They carry the Internet's information around the world. Optical fibers are also used in medicine and in many other industries.

Optical fibers can bend without breaking. To send a signal, a pulse of laser light is sent into the fiber. The inside wall of the

Continued on the next page

fiber reflects light. The light bounces around inside the fiber and quickly comes out the other end. The signal comes through even if the fiber is many miles or kilometers long.

In communications, the patterns of light pulses form a *digital* (numeric) code. The code may stand for words, pictures, sounds, or videos. Doctors also use fiber optics to gather information about human bodies. The fibers are thin enough to fit into blood vessels and other hollow parts of the body.

Other articles to read include: **Cable; Internet; Wire**

Fiberglass

Fiberglass is glass in the form of fine *fibers* (threads). A glass fiber may be much thinner than a human hair. Fiberglass can look and feel like silk. But the fibers are flexible and stronger than steel. They will not burn, stretch, rot, or fade.

Fiberglass makes good insulation. It traps air and prevents the movement of heat. Fiberglass insulation is used to keep heat in buildings. Fiberglass can also work as insulation against sound and electricity. Firefighters wear clothes made with fiberglass to keep away the heat of fire.

Fiberglass is combined with plastic to make a strong, lightweight material. This material is used in automobile bodies, boat hulls, building panels, fishing rods, and aircraft parts.

Other articles to read include: **Glass; Insulator, Electric; Plastics.**

This worker is making fiberglass parts for mobile homes. Fiberglass can be combined with plastic to make a strong, lightweight building material.

Some security systems require fingerprint identification to unlock certain doors.

Fingerprinting

Fingerprinting is a method of identification based on marks left by the fingers and thumbs. The skin on the ends of the fingers and thumbs forms a distinctive pattern of ridges. These ridges can leave impressions on things that a person touches. Fingerprints are used for identification because each person's fingerprints are unique. Fingerprints remain the same throughout a person's life, except for rare cases involving disease or injury.

Fingerprints are used in the investigation of crimes. They are often presented as evidence in criminal trials. They also may help identify victims of wars and violent disasters. Some governments and companies use fingerprinting in efforts to prevent crime. For example, many airports, banks, military bases, and government buildings have systems for checking fingerprints before allowing people to enter certain areas.

In the 1860's, Sir William J. Herschel, a British colonial administrator, began using fingerprint identification to prevent fraud in India. In 1880, Henry Faulds, a Scottish doctor, proposed the use of fingerprint identification to help solve crimes. During the 1880's and 1890's, Francis Galton, a British scientist, worked to develop the scientific foundations for fingerprint identification.

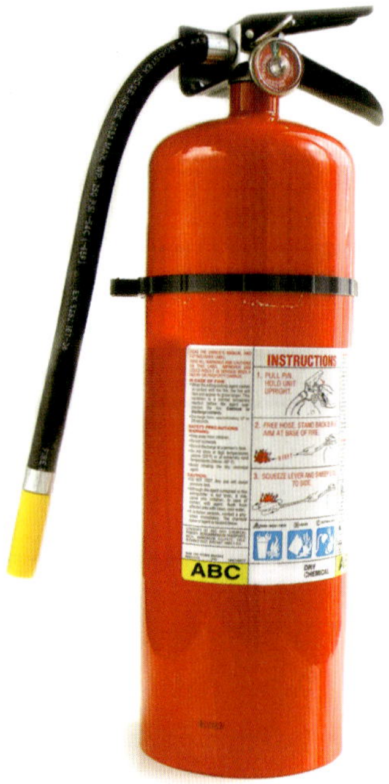

Fire extinguishers are useful for putting out small fires, such as those that can start in home kitchens.

Fire extinguisher

A fire extinguisher is a special container filled with water or chemicals. It is used to put out fires. Fire extinguishers are easy to carry and use. They can put out small fires before the flames spread. Fire extinguishers contain one of four substances: water, foam, liquefied gas, or dry chemicals.

In the United States, state and local fire laws require all public buildings to have fire extinguishers. They must be kept in easily seen places. School buses, boats, and most public vehicles also must carry extinguishers.

There are several kinds of fire extinguishers. The kind used depends on the type of fire. Fire prevention experts divide fires

Continued on the next page

into four classes. These are *A, B, C,* and *D.* The class depends on what material is burning. *Class A* fires involve such materials as cloth, paper, rubber, or wood. *Class B* fires involve flammable gases or liquids. Flammable liquids include cooking grease, gasoline, and oil. *Class C* fires involve motors, switches, or other electrical equipment. *Class D* fires involve metals that can catch fire, such as magnesium chips or shavings. Most extinguishers are labeled with the class, or classes, of fire that they can safely put out.

Firearm

A firearm is a device that uses gunpowder to fire a bullet or shell. When people say *firearms,* they often mean *light firearms.* Light firearms include rifles, machine guns, shotguns, and pistols. Light firearms are often called *small arms.* Heavier firearms such as cannons are generally referred to as *artillery.*

A modern firearm has four essential parts. These are (1) the barrel, (2) the chamber, (3) the breech mechanism, and (4) the firing mechanism. The *barrel* is a long tube. The bullet or shell is fired through this tube. The *chamber* is a widened hole at the rear end of the barrel. It holds the *cartridge* (explosive charge). The *breech mechanism* closes the rear end of the barrel. This holds the cartridge in the chamber. The *firing mechanism* sets fire to the charge.

The Chinese invented gunpowder before A.D. 900. By 1100, the Chinese may have used firearms that looked like small, handheld cannons. Travelers brought gunpowder from Asia to Europe in the 1200's. Beginning in the 1300's, Europeans developed cannons. Then they created handheld firearms. Firearms led to great changes in warfare. Armored knights and castle walls could not withstand firearms. The rifle was invented about 1500. It could shoot bullets more accurately than other firearms. Many improvements since then have resulted in high-powered firearms.

Other articles to read include: **Cannon; Gun; Gunpowder; Rifle.**

Types of firearms

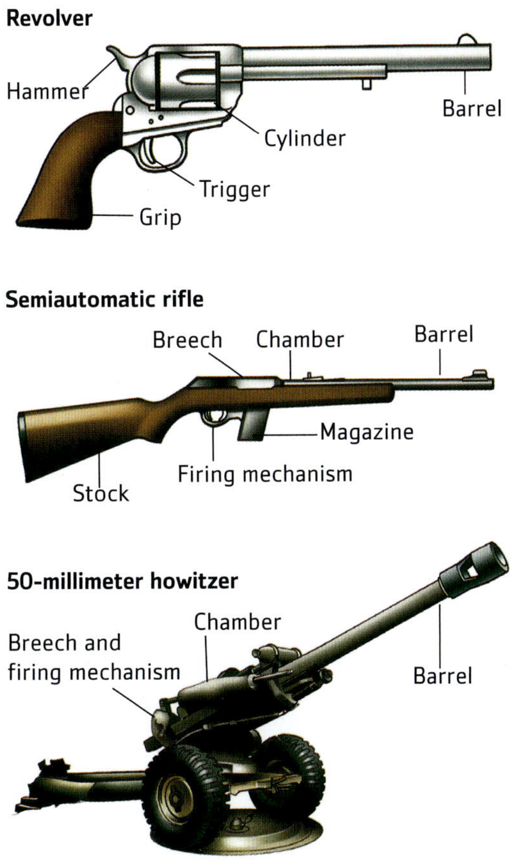

Fireworks are often used in celebrations.

Fireworks

Fireworks are explosives chiefly used for entertainment. They contain a mixture of gunpowder and other ingredients. Fireworks explode with loud noises and often colorful sparks and flames. Some fireworks, called *firecrackers,* only make loud noise. Fireworks can be dangerous. They should be used only by people who are trained to handle them safely.

People use some small fireworks at home. Large fireworks displays are part of many holiday celebrations.

Most fireworks are made by packing gunpowder into hollow paper tubes. Some of the gunpowder shoots the fireworks into the air. Then the rest of the gunpowder explodes. Special chemicals mixed with the gunpowder make colors and designs.

Fireworks have other uses, too. One kind is used as a danger signal on highways and railroads.

Other articles to read include: **Explosive; Gunpowder.**

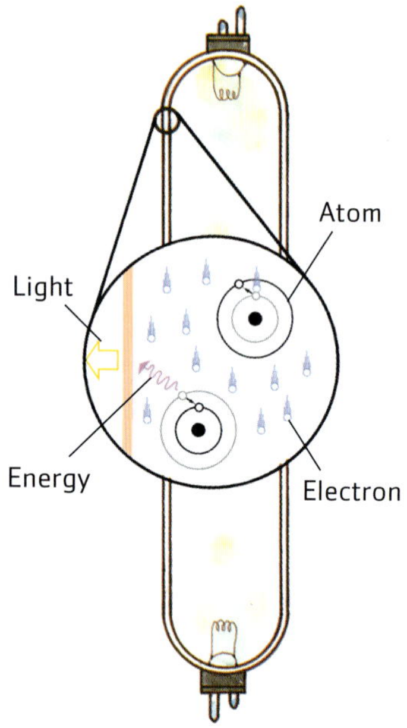

In a fluorescent lamp, electric current passes through a gas-filled tube. It makes atoms in the gas give off energy. This energy, in turn, makes the glass tube's coating glow.

Fluorescent lamp

A fluorescent *(FLOO uh REHS uhnt)* lamp is a kind of electric light. In a fluorescent lamp, electricity passes through a gas-filled glass tube. Such lamps differ from *incandescent lights.* In an incandescent light, electricity passes through a wire. A fluorescent lamp uses less electricity than does a similar incandescent light bulb. The fluorescent lamp also produces less heat.

A fluorescent lamp's tube is filled with a mixture of gases. One kind of gas, usually argon, *conducts* (carries) electricity. When the lamp is turned on, electricity flows through the tube.

The tube also contains mercury vapor. Mercury vapor is the gas form of the element mercury. The electricity causes the mercury vapor to give off *ultraviolet* (UV) *light.* UV light is

Continued on the next page

invisible to human eyes. But it reacts with chemicals called *phosphors* that coat the inside of the lamp's glass tube. It causes these chemicals to glow with visible light.

Long, tube-shaped fluorescent lamps are often used in schools, offices, and factories. Fluorescent lamp tubes can also be twisted into a shape like a traditional light bulb for home use. Such bulbs are called *compact fluorescent lamps* (CFL's).

Other articles to read include: **Electric light; Light bulb.**

Food preservation

Food preservation means keeping food from spoiling. Spoilage can change a food's odor and flavor. Spoiled food can also cause illness. Many methods are used to prevent spoilage. They include canning, drying, freezing, and using chemicals called *additives*. *Curing* is the use of salt and other chemicals to preserve foods.

All foods will eventually spoil. Food is spoiled by pests or by *microorganisms* (*MY kroh AWR guh nihz uhmz*). Microorganisms are tiny living things such as bacteria, molds, and yeasts. Pests include insects and rodents.

Some methods of food preservation kill microorganisms with heat or radiation. *Fermentation,* on the other hand, is a method that makes use of microorganisms. The microorganisms chemically change food so that it lasts longer. Fermented foods include wine, cheese, and pickles.

The modern food industry relies on food preservation. Many kinds of food are transported over long distances. Without preservation, much of this food would spoil before it could be eaten.

Other articles to read include: **Dehydrated food.**

Canned foods resist spoilage, enabling them to kept on the shelf longer than fresh foods.

Henry Ford developed assembly lines to manufacture affordable cars.

Ford, Henry

Henry Ford (1863–1947) was the leading automobile maker in the United States in the early 1900's. He started the Ford Motor Company. From 1908 to 1927, more than half the cars sold in the United States were Fords.

Henry Ford was born on a farm in what is now Dearborn, Michigan. He became an engineer at an electric company. He built his first gasoline engine in 1893. In 1896, he built a car.

In 1903, Ford started the Ford Motor Company. At first, the company made only expensive cars. But Ford wanted cars to cost less. He hoped that more people could afford to buy one. In 1908, he began selling the Model T.

The first Model T's cost only $850. This price was less than that of European cars of the time. But many people could not afford a Model T even at this price. So Ford and his workers found ways to make them cost even less. The company used a new method called an *assembly (uh SEHM blee) line.* The parts were carried to workers on a moving belt. Each worker did only one job. This method shortened the time it took to make a car. By 1924, a Model T cost only $290.

Ford paid his workers more than did many other companies. He also let them work fewer hours and shared the company's profits with them. Skilled workers flocked to Ford's factories, and he could choose the best ones.

Ford's company kept making Model T's. But other companies were making many kinds of cars. Finally, Ford introduced the Model A in 1927. In 1932, Ford introduced a low-priced car with a powerful engine. But by that time, General Motors was selling more cars than Ford. One of Ford's grandsons took over Ford's company in 1945.

Henry Ford was also interested in politics. He ran for Congress but was not elected. He gave time and money to many projects and charities. He and his son Edsel started the Ford Foundation. It gives money for education and research.

Other articles to read include: **Assemby line; Automobile.**

Fort

A fort is a building or a place that is strong and well protected. In the past, people built forts for safety and to defend themselves.

In the United States and Canada, European settlers built small, square forts called *blockhouses.* They used the forts to defend against Indian attacks. These forts were usually two-story buildings. People fired at enemies through small openings in the walls.

The ancient Romans made many forts. In Europe, early castles were earthen forts built on hills. Later castles had thick stone walls, iron gates, and towers. Strong castles were very hard to capture.

Today, the name *fort* is used for U.S. Army bases. Some cities have *fort* in their names because the cities were built around forts.

A castle in Wales (left) features thick walls and towers for archers. During the Revolutionary War in America, colonists attacked a fort in Indiana held by British troops (bottom).

Benjamin Franklin

Franklin, Benjamin

Benjamin Franklin (1706–1790) was an American *statesman* (leader). He helped write the Declaration of Independence. He was also a printer, a scientist, and an inventor.

Scientist and inventor

Franklin was always interested in science. He was one of the first people in the world to experiment with electricity. He conducted his most famous electrical experiment at Philadelphia in 1752. The experiment proved that lightning was a huge electric spark. It was a very dangerous experiment. Franklin said he flew a homemade kite during a thunderstorm. A bolt of lightning struck a pointed wire fastened to the kite. Franklin said the lightning traveled down the kite string to a key fastened at the end. There, it caused a spark. Franklin invented the lightning rod to protect buildings from lightning.

Franklin also invented *bifocal eyeglasses.* Bifocal eyeglasses combine regular glasses and reading glasses in a single frame. Franklin invented a new kind of heating stove that wasted little fuel. He was also the first scientist to study the movement of the Gulf Stream, a major current in the Atlantic Ocean.

Other articles to read include: **Electric current; Invention; Lightning rod.**

Franklin and his kite showed the world that lightning is actually an enormous electric spark.

The Franklin stove gave more heat than the other stoves, and used much less fuel.

Franklin's lightning rod saved many buildings from fires caused by lightning.

Bifocal eyeglasses feature two-part lenses for both reading and distance vision.

Fuel cell

A fuel cell is a device that produces electric energy from chemical reactions. It is similar to a battery. A fuel cell works without *combustion* (the burning of fuel). Instead, the electric energy comes from different chemical reactions.

Unlike batteries, fuel cells cannot produce energy on their own. They need two additional substances to work. One substance is called the *fuel.* The other is called the *oxidizer.* Each substance causes chemical reactions at one end of the fuel cell. The fuel reaction pushes charged particles called *electrons* out of the cell. The electrons flow around a circuit and then back into the cell. The oxidizer reacts with electrons as they come back. The loop of flowing electrons is called an *electric current.* It can power devices connected to the circuit, such as motors or lights.

One type of fuel cell uses only two gases. Hydrogen is the fuel, and oxygen is the oxidizer. Unlike a combustion engine, it produces no air pollution. It only makes water and a small amount of heat.

Fuel cells have been used to power spacecraft. Cheaper fuel cells could replace gas-burning engines in cars, reducing pollution.

Other articles to read include: **Battery; Electric current; Electric power.**

This power plant uses devices called *fuel cells* to produce electric power for homes.

Fuller, Buckminster

Buckminster Fuller (1895–1983) was an American engineer, architect, and inventor. He designed buildings to work with technology and the needs of modern life.

In 1940, Fuller came up with a new idea for a domed structure. This structure is called a *geodesic (JEE uh DEHS ihk) dome.* A geodesic dome is large and lightweight. It covers a vast open space with no inside supports.

Richard Buckminster Fuller was born in Milton, Massachusetts. He made many designs for automobiles, buildings, and cities.

Other articles to read include: **Geodesic dome.**

Buckminster Fuller with a structure he designed called the *geodesic dome*

Robert Fulton

Fulton, Robert

Robert Fulton (1765–1815) was an American inventor and artist. He built a famous *steamboat.* A steamboat is a boat powered by a steam engine.

Fulton was born in Lancaster County, Pennsylvania. He began inventing things at an early age. He later studied art. But he found that he was more interested in science and engineering.

Fulton's first important inventions were new kinds of boats that could travel in canals. He also invented machines for making ropes and cutting rock.

In the early 1800's, Fulton decided to build a steamboat. He built a working steamboat called the *Clermont.* It began carrying passengers on the Hudson River in New York state in 1807. The *Clermont* was not the first steamboat. However, it was the first one that worked well and made good money.

Other articles to read include: **Ship; Steam engine.**

Fuse

A fuse is a small device that protects an *electric circuit.* An electric circuit is a path followed by electricity. The fuse protects the circuit from too much *current* (flow of electricity).

A fuse contains a wire. The wire is made of a metal that melts easily. When too much current flows in the circuit, the wire gets hot and melts. That makes a gap in the circuit. The gap stops the current from flowing through the circuit. To restore the circuit, the fuse must be replaced.

Two types of fuse that protect electric circuits are the *plug fuse* (below left) and the *cartridge fuse* (below right).

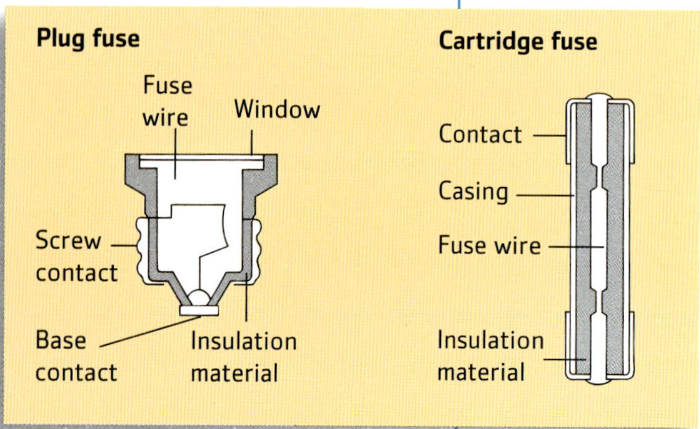

Older homes used fuses to prevent overloading their electric systems. Most newer homes use *circuit breakers* rather than fuses. Like a fuse, a circuit breaker stops a current that is too strong. But a circuit breaker does not melt. Instead, it switches the circuit off. A circuit breaker can be reset any number of times.

Other articles to read include: **Electric circuit; Electric current; Wire.**

ACTIVITY

How a fuse works

To make sure wires do not overheat, most electrical circuits have a device that can break the circuit. The two main devices are the *fuse* and the *circuit breaker.* Circuit breakers protect the wiring in homes and other buildings. If too many electrical devices are plugged into an outlet, the circuit breaker will shut off the current by throwing open its switches. Learn how a circuit breaker works by trying this experiment.

Have a teacher or other adult help you with this experiment. Do not play with electricity!

What you need:

- a 6-volt flashlight bulb
- bulb holder
- four pieces of plastic-coated wire, 8 inches (20 centimeters) long, with bare ends
- a 6-volt lantern battery
- a screwdriver
- some fine steel wool

1. Place the bulb in the bulb holder. Connect one piece of wire to one terminal of the battery. Using the screwdriver, remove one screw from the bulb holder. Connect the other end of the wire to one side of the bulb holder. Replace the screw.

2. Use the screwdriver to remove the other screw from the bulb holder. Connect the second piece of wire to the other side of the bulb holder. Replace the screw. Connect the third piece of wire to the other terminal of the battery.

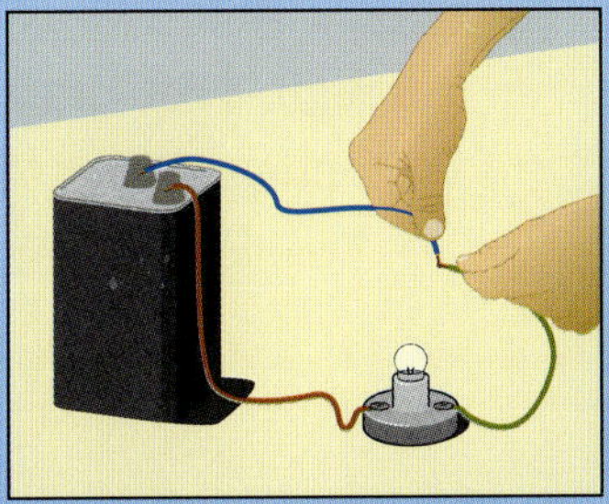

3. Test your apparatus by picking up the two free wires by the plastic coating. Touch the bare ends together, without touching them with your hands, and the bulb should light up. Separate the two ends and the bulb should go out.

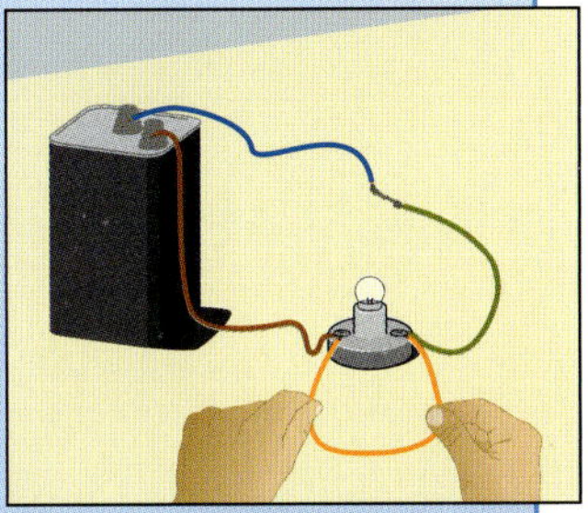

4. Disconnect the third wire from the battery while you connect a thin strand of steel wool to the other two free ends of wire. The strand of steel wool is now your fuse. Reconnect the third wire to the battery to complete your circuit. Then place the bare ends of the fourth piece of wire on the two screws of the bulb holder. What happens?

What's going on:

The bulb will go out. The steel wool quickly heats up and melts. This breaks the circuit and the current stops flowing.

http://bit.ly/14YtgJS

Gg

Gagarin, Yuri Alekseyevich

Yuri Alekseyevich Gagarin *(YOOR ee ah leh KSEH yuh vihch gah GAHR ihn)* (1934–1968) was the first human being to reach space. He was a pilot in the Soviet Union's air force. Gagarin circled Earth once on April 12, 1961. His trip was short. Gagarin was in orbit for 89 minutes. The entire trip lasted 1 hour and 48 minutes. During his trip, Gagarin traveled at a speed of more than 17,000 miles (27,000 kilometers) per hour. At one point, he was about 203 miles (327 kilometers) above the ground. Gagarin's spacecraft was named Vostok 1.

Gagarin was born on March 9, 1934, in Gzhatsk, near Moscow. He entered the Soviet air force in 1955. In 1959, he began training to become an astronaut. He was killed in a plane crash on March 27, 1968.

Other articles to read include: **Astronaut; Space exploration.**

Yuri Alekseyevich Gagarin

Galleon

A galleon *(GAL ee uhn)* is a big, fast sailing ship armed with large guns. Galleons sailed the seas beginning in the mid-1500's.

The first galleons were used by Italian traders. They carried goods across the sea. In 1570, an English sea captain named John Hawkins turned the galleon into a warship. Twelve large guns stuck out of the sides of the English galleons. Smaller guns were attached to the top deck.

Spanish galleons were used to bring back gold and silver from colonies in North and South America. They were difficult to sail, though. They often fell victim to pirates in the Caribbean Sea.

Other articles to read include: **Gun; Ship.**

The galleon was a big, fast, armed ship of the 1500's.

Garneau, Marc

Marc Garneau

Marc Garneau *(gahr NOH)* (1949–) was the first Canadian to travel in space. He is a captain in the Royal Canadian Navy. Garneau flew with six American astronauts aboard the United States space shuttle Challenger from Oct. 5 to 13, 1984. Garneau also made shuttle flights in 1996 and 2000.

Garneau was born on Feb. 23, 1949, in the city of Quebec. He earned a doctor's degree in electrical engineering from the Imperial College of Science and Technology in London. Garneau joined the Royal Canadian Navy in 1965. He became an expert on communications and weapon systems. In 1983, Garneau was chosen to be one of Canada's first six astronauts. He served as president of the Canadian Space Agency (CSA) from November 2001 to November 2005. Garneau became the *chancellor* (head) of Carleton University in Ottawa in 2003. Garneau was elected to the Canadian Parliament in 2008.

Other articles to read include: **Astronaut; Space exploration.**

Gas mask

Gas masks are often worn by workers in mines and in the chemical industry.

A gas mask protects people from breathing harmful substances. The mask fits tightly over the face. Air can enter only through special filter pads. The filters clean the air.

In World War I (1914–1918), troops shot poison gas at one another. Soldiers wore masks to protect themselves. Gas was not used in World War II (1939–1945). However, armies had masks in case gas warfare began. During the Persian Gulf War of 1991 and the Iraq War (2003–2011), troops and civilians had gas masks. The Iraqi army had used poison gas in earlier conflicts. But during these two wars, Iraqis did not actually use such weapons. Gas masks are also often worn by miners, workers in chemical industries, and firefighters.

Other articles to read include: **Mining.**

A woman fills the tank of her car with gasoline. Almost all automobiles have gasoline engines.

Gasoline engine

A gasoline engine burns gasoline to produce motion. Gasoline engines are lighter and more powerful than other kinds of engines. They are found in nearly all automobiles. Gasoline engines are also used in lawn mowers, motorcycles, motor scooters, snowmobiles, and small tractors. They power many trucks, buses, airplanes, and small boats. Gasoline engines can also be used to make electric power or to pump water.

Inside the engine, burning gasoline makes hot gases. The gases *expand* (spread out). They push against parts of the engine, causing them to move. The moving parts connect to other devices. Their movement might spin the wheels of a car. Or it might spin the propeller of a plane.

Burning gasoline gives off certain harmful gases. These substances contribute to pollution. Many cars filter out some of these substances. Some vehicles use battery-powered motors instead of gasoline engines.

Other articles to read include: **Automobile; Electric power; Engine; Truck.**

Gates, Bill

Bill Gates (1955–) is a cofounder of Microsoft Corporation. The company became the world's largest publisher of *software* (computer programs). Its success made Gates one of the richest people in the world.

William Henry Gates was born in Seattle on Oct. 28, 1955. He started his first computer software company when he was 15. He worked with a schoolmate, Paul Allen. In 1975, Gates began making programs for personal computers, which were new at the time. That year, he also started a company called Microsoft.

Microsoft developed *operating systems*—master control programs—for personal computers. In 1980, Gates made the

Continued on the next page

MicroSoft Disk Operating System (MS-DOS). It ran on popular computers made by International Business Machines Corporation (IBM). In 1985, Microsoft introduced the Windows operating system. It let people control other programs using boxes or windows on the computer screen.

In 2000, Gates and his wife established the Bill & Melinda Gates Foundation. It became the world's largest charity foundation.

Other articles to read include: **Computer; International Business Machines Corporation; Microsoft Corporation.**

Bill Gates

Gear

A gear is a wheel or disk slotted with "teeth" around the edge. Gears work in pairs. One gear's teeth *mesh* (fit together) with the teeth of the other gear. When one gear turns, so does the other.

Gears have many shapes and sizes. Tiny gears move the hands of wristwatches. Huge gears drive the propellers of oil tankers. Most gears are made of steel. Some are made of other metals or plastic.

Each gear has a metal bar called an *axle* in its center. The axle of one gear is connected to a power source, such as an electric motor. When this axle turns, its gear turns. This turning causes the second gear to turn. As the second gear turns, its own axle drives the machinery or does some other useful work.

Gears can change a machine's speed and spinning force. For example, consider a small gear turning a larger gear. The large gear turns more slowly. But it also turns with more force.

Other articles to read include: **Machine; Wheel and axle.**

A gear consists of an *axle* and a wheel or disk with slots called *teeth.* Turning one gear causes another to turn.

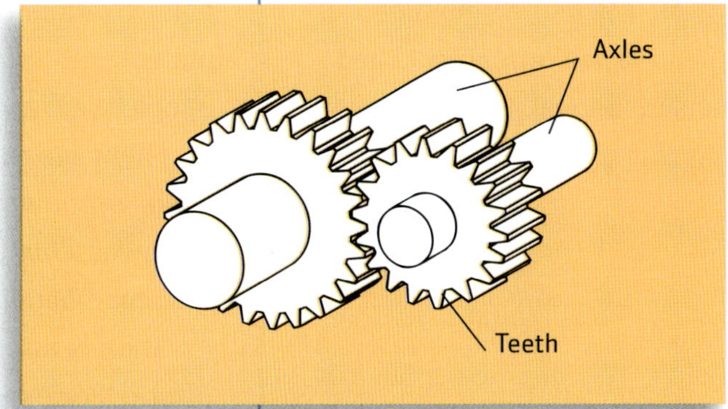

This geodesic dome houses a science museum in Vancouver, Canada.

Geodesic dome

A geodesic *(JEE uh DEHS ihk)* dome is a many-sided structure. It looks like a ball or part of a ball. The frame of a geodesic dome is made up of many triangles. The dome has no supports on the inside. The arrangement of triangles holds the dome up. The triangles can be arranged in more than one way.

Geodesic domes are strong. They lose little heat to the wind. They can be used to enclose vast open spaces.

Geodesic domes were made popular in the 1940's by an inventor named Buckminster Fuller. He thought the domes could solve housing shortages. Companies have used the domes for stadiums and other buildings.

Other articles to read include: **Dome; Fuller, Buckminster.**

Glass is made by mixing sand, limestone, and soda ash and heating the mixture until it melts. The molten mixture is then shaped into objects and cooled (above).

Glass

Glass is one of the most useful materials in the world. It is made by melting sand and other materials together. Glass takes on many forms. It can be finer than a spider web or stronger than steel. Most glass is clear. But it can be made any shade of any color.

Glass is also one of the most beautiful materials in the world. People have admired the stunning colors in church windows for hundreds of years. Some people collect delicate animals and other objects shaped from glass. Glass is used every day, too. We drink from glass containers. Windows in homes, offices, and schools are made of glass. Cars and other vehicles have glass windows. Some people wear eyeglasses to help them see better.

There are many different kinds of glass. *Flat glass* is used to make windows. *Heat-resistant glass* is used in cookware and industrial gear. *Optical glass* is used in eyeglasses, cameras, and telescopes. *Fiberglass* consists of tiny glass threads.

Glass is also combined with other kinds of materials, such as plastic. For example, *safety glass* is made with layers of plastic and

Continued on the next page

Glass forms an important part of many modern buildings.

flat glass. The outside layer of glass may shatter, but the inside layer of plastic does not break. The plastic holds the broken glass together and keeps it from flying around. Safety glass is used in windshields.

At a glass factory, huge bins hold the sand and powders for making the glass. Furnaces melt the materials to a white-hot liquid. Glass melts at 2600 to 2900 °F (1427 to 1593 °C).

The melted mixture is then shaped. It may be blown into a bulb shape, squeezed, and stretched. It may be drawn into thin rods or fibers. Or it may be pressed or cast into a desired shape. Most glass made today is what is called *float glass.* It is made by drawing a wide sheet of molten glass onto a bath of molten tin. The melted glass "floats" above the tin. It forms a perfectly even layer. Hot glass must be evenly cooled into a solid, or the solid glass will easily shatter.

Glass occurs in nature. Slender glass tubes called *fulgurites* can form where a lightning strike melts sand. Volcanic eruptions sometimes melt rocks and sand into a glass called *obsidian.*

People probably first used glass around 3000 B.C. as a glaze on pots. The first glass vessels were made in 1500 B.C. in Egypt and Mesopotamia. Early glassmaking was slow, hard, and expensive. The ancient Romans improved glassmaking. By the 1200's, the city of Venice in what is now Italy had become the center of glassmaking. In the late 1600's, the English made glass with lead. It was useful for such instruments as telescopes. After 1880, glassmakers began widely using natural gas as a fuel for furnaces. It worked much better than coal and wood. They built huge factories and learned to make stronger and better glass. Scientists continue to study and develop glassmaking.

Other articles to read include: **Lens; Fiberglass; Materials; Skyscraper.**

Glass can be formed into many different shapes and colors.

Astronaut John H. Glenn, Jr., became the first American to orbit Earth. He made his historic flight in a spacecraft named Friendship 7.

Glenn, John Herschel, Jr.

John Herschel Glenn, Jr. (1921–), was the first American to orbit Earth. On Feb. 20, 1962, he circled Earth three times. The trip lasted less than five hours. Glenn's spacecraft was named Friendship 7.

Glenn was born on July 18, 1921, in Cambridge, Ohio. He entered the U.S. Marine Corps in 1942. He served as a pilot in World War II (1939–1945) and the Korean War (1950–1953). He later became a *test pilot.* A test pilot is someone who flies new aircraft to aid in their development. In 1959, Glenn was selected to become an astronaut. He resigned as an astronaut in 1964. From 1974 to 1999, Glenn served as a U.S. senator from Ohio. In 1984, Glenn ran for U.S. president. He left the race after failing to win any first-round elections.

Glenn returned to space in 1998. In that year, he traveled aboard the space shuttle Discovery. He became the oldest person to travel in space.

Other articles to read include: **Astronaut; Space exploration.**

Glider

A glider resembles a small airplane without an engine.

A glider resembles a small airplane, but it has no engine. People mainly use gliders for fun and sport. They are sometimes called *sailplanes.* The Wright brothers experimented with gliders. Their experiments helped them invent the first airplane.

Both airplanes and gliders must fly fast to stay in the air. The speed keeps enough air moving around their wings. The movement of air around the wings creates a lifting force. An airplane's engine pushes it fast enough to take off and fly. A glider must use other methods to take off and stay in the air. But gliders are much lighter than airplanes. It thus takes less lift to keep them in the air.

In the United States, gliders are usually towed into the air by an airplane. Then they are released. In Europe, gliders are usually pulled into the air like kites by a vehicle on the ground. Glider pilots use rising flows of air to stay in the air for long periods. Most glider flights last one to five hours.

Other articles to read include: **Airplane; Lilienthal, Otto; Wright brothers.**

Global Positioning System

The Global Positioning System (GPS) is a group of satellites that circle Earth. The satellites send radio signals to Earth's surface. Many electronic devices can pick up these signals. Such a device can use the signals to calculate its location on Earth. Many automobiles, ships, airplanes, and cell phones use GPS.

The GPS has 24 satellites, called Navstars. They follow six *orbits* (paths) around Earth. They orbit at a height of about 12,500 miles (20,200 kilometers). The United States Air Force operates the satellites. But the signals are used both inside and outside the military. A GPS device can usually find its location to within 33 feet (10 meters). The U.S. military began developing the GPS in the early 1970's. People were able to fully use the system in 1995.

Other articles to read include: **Navigation; Radio; Satellite, Artificial.**

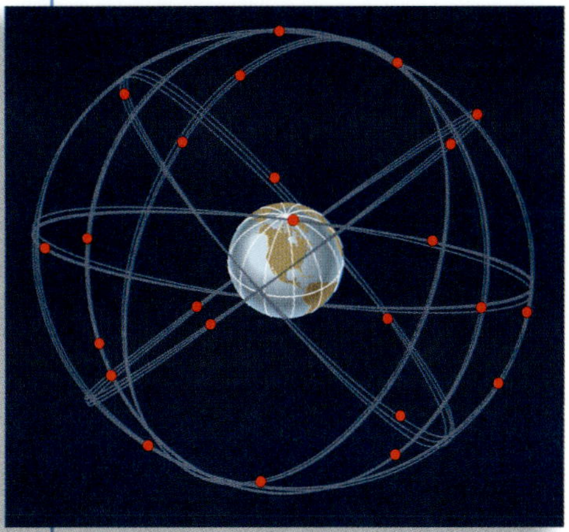

Global Positioning System (GPS) satellites broadcast radio signals down to Earth. Many vehicles and devices can use these signals to determine their own locations.

Globe

A globe from the early 1600's, (above left) shows sea routes for ship navigation. A modern globe (above) is mounted on a center axis to show how Earth rotates.

A globe is a map shaped like a *sphere* (ball). The map is usually printed on strips of paper. The strips are pasted onto a hollow cardboard sphere. Sometimes the map is printed on pieces of plastic that are shaped into a sphere.

There are different kinds of globes. A *terrestrial (tuh RES tree uhl) globe* shows the surface of Earth. A *celestial (suh LES chul) globe* is a map of the sky. There are also globes of the moon and some of the planets.

A globe can show a truer picture of a planet than can a flat map. When features from a round planet are put onto a flat map, some features must be *distorted* (taken out of shape).

Other articles to read include: **Map.**

Glue

Glue is a sticky substance made from animal parts.

Glue is a sticky substance made from animal parts. It is a kind of *adhesive.* Adhesives are used to stick things together. Many people use the word *glue* for any adhesive. This article talks about only the glue made from animals.

Glue is made by boiling animal skin, bones, and other parts. It is placed on two surfaces to be joined. The objects are then pressed together. The glue fills tiny holes in the surfaces. When glue dries, it makes a hard bond.

People have made glue for centuries. It is still one of the most popular adhesives. Many wooden items, such as furniture, toys, and musical instruments, are held together with glue.

Goddard, Robert Hutchings

Robert Hutchings Goddard launched the first successful liquid-fueled rocket.

Robert Hutchings Goddard (1882–1945) was an American rocket scientist. His experiments led to the development of rocket engines for spacecraft and missiles.

Goddard wrote a report about flying to the moon in 1919. It was called "A Method of Reaching Extreme Altitudes." He described the kind of rocket flight needed. At the time, many people thought it would be impossible to fly to the moon.

In 1926, Goddard launched the world's first liquid-fueled rocket. The rocket climbed 41 feet (12.5 meters) in the air. It flew at a speed of about 60 miles (100 kilometers) per hour. It landed 184 feet (56 meters) away. During World War II (1939–1945), Goddard helped the United States Navy develop rocket engines for airplanes.

Goddard was born in Massachusetts on Oct. 5, 1882. He died on Aug. 10, 1945.

Other articles to read include: **Rocket; Space exploration.**

Goodyear, Charles

Charles Goodyear (1800–1860) was an American scientist. He invented a treatment for rubber. This treatment is called *vulcanization.* Vulcanization makes rubber stronger. Vulcanized rubber is also resistant to heat and cold.

In 1832, Goodyear began experimenting with a type of rubber called *India rubber.* India rubber breaks easily when cold. It becomes sticky when hot. Goodyear found that sulfur makes India rubber less sticky.

In 1839, Goodyear accidentally spilled the rubber-sulfur mix on a stove. It did not melt. Goodyear realized that heat helped make the rubber-sulfur mix stronger. This vulcanized rubber could be used to make many useful things.

Charles Goodyear developed a way to make rubber stronger.

Google, Inc.

Google Inc. is a major Internet and technology company. Its main feature is an Internet search engine. It helps people find websites and other useful information. Google sells advertisements that run alongside its search engine. It runs the popular video-sharing website YouTube. Google also makes special *software* (computer programs) for cell phones and other devices.

Google officially launched in 1998. It was started by two computer science students at Stanford University, Larry Page and Sergey Brin. The name *Google* comes from the very large number, *googol.* Googol is written as a 1 followed by a hundred 0's. The name Google refers to the huge amount of information on the Internet.

Other articles to read include: **Internet; Search engine; Website.**

Guided missile

Guided missiles are powered by jet or rocket engines. They can strike distant targets.

A guided missile *(MISS uhl)* is a flying weapon that is steered to its target. Most fly with a jet or rocket engine. Guided missiles are launched from the ground, from ships, and from airplanes and helicopters. Some guided missiles steer themselves. They contain a computer that guides them. Some of these missiles can even chase and destroy a moving target, such as an airplane or another missile. Others fly under human control, though they carry no pilot. They follow directions from radio controllers on the ground.

Most guided missiles look like rockets. Some have stubby wings. Most have one or more exploding parts called *warheads.* Guided missiles range in size from 4 feet (1.2 meters) to 60 feet (18 meters). The largest ones can travel up to 9,200 miles (15,000 kilometers). Germany developed the first guided missiles during World War II (1939–1945). After World War II, the United States and the Soviet Union made thousands of nuclear-armed guided missiles. In the 2000's and 2010's, the United States attacked many suspected terrorists with guided missiles. Many of the missiles were launched from unmanned aircraft called *drones.*

Other articles to read include: **Aircraft, Military; Jet; Rocket.**

Gun

Guns carried by hand, such as this rifle, are called *small arms.*

Guns are weapons that fire solid objects at deadly speeds. Small guns include pistols, rifles, and shotguns. They shoot bullets. Large guns fire shells that explode when they hit the target. *Gunpowder* provides the force that shoots bullets or shells. When the gunpowder burns, it creates an expanding gas. The gas pushes the bullet or shell out of the gun at high speed. Some guns, called *machine guns,* can fire up to a thousand bullets every minute and more. Large guns are used on warships, tanks, and aircraft.

No one knows who invented the gun. By the 1100's, China had cannonlike weapons. During the 1300's, Arabs of North Africa used early guns.

Other articles to read include: **Aircraft, Military; Cannon; Gunpowder; Handgun; Rifle; Tank.**

Gunpowder

Gunpowder is an explosive material. It burns rapidly to form high-pressure gas. This gas expands inside the barrel of a gun. It can propel a bullet at great speed. Gunpowder is used in all sorts of ammunition and explosives.

The first kind of gunpowder, called *black powder,* was first developed in Asia. Black powder is a mixture of *saltpeter* (potassium nitrate), charcoal, and sulfur. It created much smoke and damaged gun barrels. *Guncotton,* an early kind of smokeless gunpowder, was invented in the 1840's. It exploded powerfully but was dangerous to make. A more useful smokeless powder was invented in 1864. About 1887, the Swedish chemist Alfred Nobel created another kind of smokeless powder.

Other articles to read include: **Explosive; Fireworks; Gun.**

Gun cartridges use burning gunpowder to fire a bullet.

Gutenberg, Johannes

Johannes Gutenberg *(yoh HAHN uhs GOOT uhn BURG)* (1395?–1468?) was a German inventor and printer. He invented a printing press.

Gutenberg's press used letters stamped on metal pieces. The letters could be reused and rearranged to create new pages. Other presses had used letters carved into plates. The plates were hard to make. They could not be reused.

Gutenberg's invention changed the way that books were printed. Using his press was much faster than copying books by hand.

Gutenberg was born in Mainz, Germany. He learned how to work with metal as a young man.

Other articles to read include: **Invention; Printing.**

Johannes Gutenberg (above right) invented a printing press with movable type.

A gyrocompass points to true north. It is more reliable than a traditional magnetic compass.

Gyrocompass

A gyrocompass *(JY roh KUHM puhs)* is a device that tells direction. It is used to *navigate* (direct) many kinds of ships. Some aircraft and land vehicles also use gyrocompasses. The German engineer Hermann Anschutz-Kampfe invented the gyrocompass in 1908.

A gyrocompass is more accurate than a *magnetic compass.* A magnetic compass makes use of Earth's *magnetic field,* the region of magnetic influence surrounding the planet. A magnetic compass points to *magnetic north.* Magnetic north is nearly—but not quite—true north. A gyrocompass points to true north. A gyrocompass is not affected by magnetic fields or by the movement of a vehicle.

A gyrocompass makes use of a *gyroscope.* A gyroscope is a spinning device like a wheel. It is powered by an electric motor. A gyroscope resists changes to the direction of its spinning. This helps a gyrocompass always point in the same direction.

Other articles to read include: **Compass; Gyroscope; Magnet; Navigation.**

Gyroscope

A gyroscope's rotor tends to keep spinning in the same direction, even if the rest of the device moves.

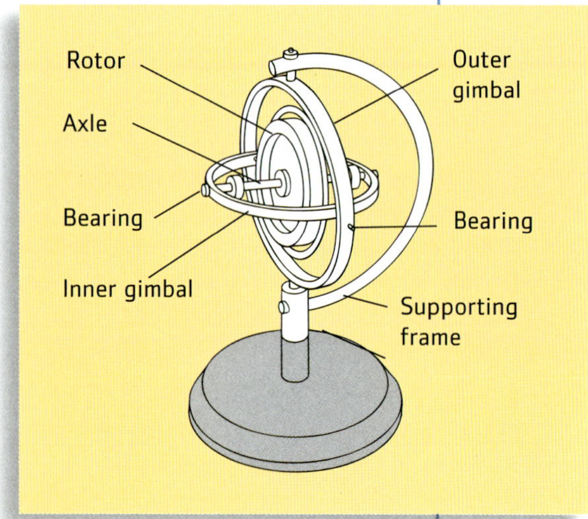

Gyroscope *(JY ruh skohp)* is a device that spins in a steady direction. It is sometimes called a *gyro.* Gyroscopes help keep ships and airplanes moving straight. Gyroscopes are also used on rockets and other spacecraft.

Most gyroscopes have a spinning wheel, called a *rotor.* The rotor is attached to pivoting rings called *gimbals.* When the rotor starts to spin, it tends to keep spinning in the same direction. It resists changes in its spin, even if the base becomes pointed in another direction. For this reason, a gyroscope can be used to steer an airplane or other craft.

Other articles to read include: **Airplane; Gyrocompass; Ship.**

Hh

Hammer

A hammer is a tool used to pound nails and other objects. Hammers are also used to bend and shape metals and other materials. Hammers are made in different shapes and sizes for different tasks.

Carpenters often use a *claw hammer.* One side of the claw hammer's head is blunt. It is used to pound nails into wood or some other material. The other side is curved and split down the middle. That end is used to pull nails out of a material. It is called the *claw.*

A *sledgehammer* has a long handle and a heavy, stubby head. It is used to smash things. A *ball peen hammer* has a rounded head for working with metal.

Other articles to read include: **Tool.**

A carpenter pounds in a nail with a claw hammer.

Handgun

A handgun is a firearm that can be used with one hand. Other types of guns, such as rifles and machine guns, require both hands or a support.

The police and the armed forces carry handguns. Some citizens use handguns for target shooting, hunting, or protection. Others collect antique or classic handguns. Thousands of handgun-related deaths occur in the United States, Canada, and many other countries each year. These deaths include suicides, murders, self-defense killings, and accidents.

Handguns come in many shapes and sizes. Different handguns use different *ammunition* (bullets). However, they all include the same basic parts. These parts are the *frame,* the *grip,* the *barrel,* the *sights,* and the *action.* The frame is the main body of the gun. It connects the other parts. The grip is the handle of the gun. The barrel is the metal tube through which the bullet is fired. The shooter uses the sights to line up the handgun with the target.

Continued on the next page

The Colt .45 is an automatic handgun.

Handgun *Continued from the previous page*

The action consists of the main working parts of the handgun. It includes the trigger and other parts that fire the bullet. The action of a handgun has a *safety.* The safety is a switch that prevents the gun from going off accidentally.

Probably as early as the 1100's, the Chinese used a handheld gun that resembled a cannon. The first gun operated with one hand was the *matchlock,* which appeared in the 1400's. The gunpowder was touched off using a slow-burning wick called *match*. In the early 1500's, the *wheel-lock gun* was invented. Its revolving metal wheel set off sparks. With the wheel lock, soldiers no longer had to carry flames to ignite the gunpowder.

One of the first practical *revolvers* was the Colt Paterson. A revolver can quickly shoot several bullets. The Paterson was patented in England in 1835 by Samuel Colt, an American inventor. In 1897, the American inventor John M. Browning patented an automatic pistol. It could be fired even faster. The gun became the basis for later automatics, including the Colt .45.

Other articles to read include: **Firearm; Gun; Gunpowder.**

John Harrison developed an extremely accurate clock.

Harrison, John

John Harrison (1693–1776) was an English clockmaker. In 1735, he built an extremely accurate clock called a *chronometer (kruh NOM uh tuhr).* Sailors could use the chronometer to help figure out their location. The invention helped them to sail farther than before without getting lost.

Many clocks at the time used a *pendulum (PEHN juh luhm* or *PEHN dyuh luhm).* A pendulum is a weight that swings back and forth. But heat or cold can make a pendulum longer or shorter. This can cause a clock to keep poor time.

Harrison invented the *gridiron compensating pendulum.* This pendulum could adjust to heat and cold without changing in overall length. It remained accurate even in cold temperatures. Harrison used it in the chronometer.

Harrison was born on March 24, 1693, in West Yorkshire, England. He died on March 24, 1776.

Other articles to read include: **Clock; Navigation; Pendulum.**

Hazardous wastes

Hazardous wastes are unwanted chemicals that can harm people or the environment. They can be solids, liquids, or gases. Hazardous wastes can come from places such as power plants, factories, mines, and hospitals.

Hazardous wastes can get into the air, water, and ground. They can also get into food and poison people or animals.

Laws limit the amount of hazardous wastes that people can make. These laws also limit how people can *dispose* (get rid of) hazardous wastes. People may dispose hazardous wastes by burying, burning, or recycling.

Other articles to read include: **Nuclear waste; Power plant; Recycling.**

People must wear protective clothing when handling hazardous wastes.

Helicopter

A helicopter is a flying machine. It is lifted into the air by spinning wings called *rotors.* The name *helicopter* comes from Greek words meaning *spiral* and *wing.*

Helicopters can fly straight up or down. They can fly forward, backward, or sideways. They can even *hover,* or stay in one spot in the air.

Helicopters are different from airplanes in many ways. Most airplanes need a long runway to take off. But helicopters can take off and land in small spaces. Helicopters can safely fly slower and lower than airplanes. However, they cannot fly as fast as most planes.

Continued on the next page

Helicopter *Continued from the previous page*

Helicopters are used for many purposes. They are often used to rescue people. Helicopters can hover above a burning skyscraper or a sinking ship. They can lower a rope to people below and lift them to safety. Helicopters are also used as flying ambulances. They can rush people to a hospital much faster than can an ambulance on the ground.

Police officers use helicopters to chase criminals and look for lost people. Radio and TV stations use helicopters to look for traffic jams and report them on the air. Scientists use helicopters to study large areas of wilderness. Helicopters carry people back and forth to regions that may be hard to get to with a car, train, or airplane.

Farmers sometimes use helicopters to spread seed on their farmland and fertilizers on their crops. Companies that make forest products use helicopters to carry logs out of the forest.

The armed forces also use helicopters in many ways. Helicopters serve as flying ambulances, especially for soldiers injured in battle. They also carry soldiers and battle equipment to places where they are needed. Army attack helicopters are armed with missiles, cannons, and machine guns.

Most flying machines have wings. Wings produce a force called *lift*. Lift carries airplanes, helicopters, and other aircraft into the air and keeps them there.

Continued on the next page

A helicopter has wings that spin rapidly. The special motion of air around the wings lifts the helicopter.

Helicopters have rotary wings. These are blades that spin very fast. As the wings spin around, air flows over them and under them. The special airflow gives the helicopter lift.

The single-rotor helicopter is the most common type of helicopter. It has one main rotor mounted above its body. It also has a second, smaller rotor on its tail. Twin-rotor helicopters have two main rotors.

Pilots make the helicopter go up or down by adjusting the amount of lift. They do so with instruments in the *cockpit*. The cockpit is the place in the helicopter where pilots sit. The control instruments change the way the wing pushes against the flow of air.

Other articles to read include: **Aircraft, Military.**

A helicopter pilot sits in the cockpit.

Holland, John Philip

John Philip Holland developed the submarine. He is shown in one of his early subs.

John Philip Holland (1841–1914) was the main inventor of the submarine. He built a submarine called the *Holland* in 1898. It became a model for later submarines.

Holland was born in Ireland. He began work on the idea of a submarine as a schoolteacher there. He later moved to the United States. He sent his submarine plans to the U.S. Navy in 1875. But the plans were rejected. A group of Irish patriots supported Holland's experiments. They hoped to oppose England's sea power. They gave him money to build two submarines.

The inventor built the *Holland* privately. He launched it in 1898. In 1900, the Navy bought the *Holland*. Holland's company has continued to build submarines for the U.S. Navy and for other countries.

Other articles to read include: **Submarine.**

Holography

Holography *(huh LAWG ruh fee)* is a way of making a flat image that seems to have depth. The image is called a *hologram*. It seems to hover in space. Some credit cards have holograms printed on them. The holograms make it hard for people to make fake credit cards. Holography has other important uses too. For example, it is used to detect flaws in tires, lenses, airplane wings, and other products.

To make a hologram, a beam of laser light is bounced off an object. The light that bounces off makes a picture on a special material, called a *plate*. At the same time, another laser beam is directed onto the plate. The two laser beams make a pattern where they cross. The pattern helps show the depth of the object.

A hologram works by changing the direction of the light that shines on it. It makes it look like light is coming from the original object. In certain kinds of light, the hologram shows rainbowlike bands of color.

Dennis Gabor, a Hungarian-born scientist, invented holography in 1947. For this work, he won the 1971 Nobel Prize in physics, an important award.

Other articles to read include: **Laser.**

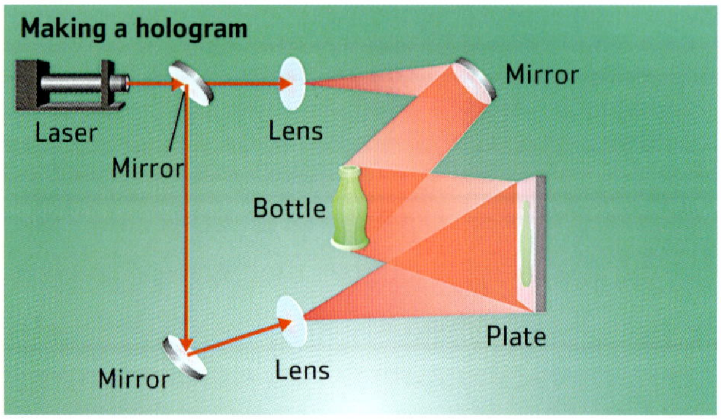

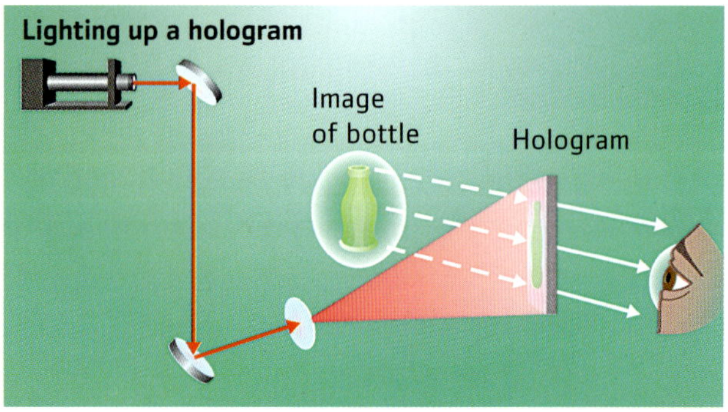

To make a hologram of a bottle, laser beams strike both the bottle and a special material called a *plate.* The beams make a pattern where they cross. The pattern shows the depth of the object. A person looking at the hologram sees the bottle appear to float in space.

Hooke, Robert

Robert Hooke (1635–1703) was an English scientist. He did a variety of experiments. He studied how some objects return to their original shape after being stretched or bent. This ability is called *elasticity.* Hooke came up with a rule of elasticity called Hooke's law. This rule is still accepted by scientists today.

Hooke also built the first *Gregorian telescope,* an early reflecting telescope. In addition, he used an early microscope to look at a piece of cork. In doing so, he discovered plant cells.

In another experiment, Hooke watched the motion of a vibrating spring. He saw that this motion was similar to the motion of a swinging pendulum. This observation led him to develop a balance spring for use in watches. Hooke also stated the *law of inverse squares,* a rule that governs the brightness of light.

Other articles to read include: **Microscope; Telescope.**

Robert Hooke

The Hoover Dam (below) is one of the highest concrete dams in the world. ▼

Hoover Dam

Hoover Dam is one of the highest concrete dams in the world. It helps prevent floods and *erosion* (the wearing away of soil). It also supplies water and electric power. The dam stands in the Black Canyon of the Colorado River on the Arizona-Nevada border. It is about 25 miles (40 kilometers) southeast of Las Vegas. Water falling through the dam generates much of the electric power used in Arizona, Nevada, and southern California.

Hoover Dam is 726 feet (221 meters) high and 1,244 feet (379 meters) long. The concrete base is 660 feet (200 meters) thick. The dam contains about 4 ½ million cubic yards (3.4 million cubic meters) of concrete. That amount is enough to pave a two-lane highway from New York City to San Francisco.

The dam holds back a *reservoir* (body of water) called Lake Mead. It is one of the world's largest artificially created bodies of water. It is about 115 miles (185 kilometers) long and 589 feet (180 meters) deep. The reservoir supplies water for cities in southern California through an aqueduct that is 240 miles (390 kilometers) long.

Hoover Dam was completed in 1935. It was named to honor President Herbert Hoover.

Other articles to read include: **Dam; Electric power.**

Grace Murray Hopper

Hopper, Grace Murray

Grace Murray Hopper (1906–1992) was an American computer scientist. She worked in the field of *programming languages.* A programming language is a set of symbols, letters, words, and numbers. It gives instructions to a computer.

Hopper was born on Dec. 9, 1906, in New York City. She graduated from Vassar College in 1928. She received a Ph.D. degree in mathematics from Yale University in 1934. Hopper joined the United States Navy in 1943, during World War II. Her work on computers began in the Navy. Later, she continued her work in private industry.

Early programming languages were often hard to understand and use. Hopper thought that these languages should be more like everyday languages. In 1952, she developed a translating system. It changed everyday language into instructions that a computer could process. Later, she directed the work that led to COBOL, one of the most widely used early computer programming languages. COBOL stands for *C*ommon *B*usiness *O*riented *L*anguage.

Hopper retired from the Navy in 1986. She died on Jan. 1, 1992.

Other articles to read include: **Computer.**

The Hubble Space Telescope orbits about 380 miles (610 kilometers) above Earth.

Hubble Space Telescope

The Hubble Space Telescope is a powerful instrument that orbits about 380 miles (610 kilometers) above Earth. It takes sharp pictures of objects in outer space such as stars, comets, and the sun. The telescope is named after the American astronomer Edwin P. Hubble.

Continued on the next page

This picture, taken by the Hubble Space Telescope, shows many stars at different stages in their life cycles.

The Hubble Space Telescope is a *reflecting telescope*. The telescope has a large mirror that collects light. The mirror is 94 inches (240 centimeters) wide. The light is reflected to a small lens that focuses it for a camera. The telescope enables scientists to see some of the farthest objects in the universe.

The Hubble Space Telescope views the sky without having to look through Earth's atmosphere. The planet's atmosphere distorts and dims light. Hubble is much smaller than the biggest telescopes on Earth. But because it does not look through the atmosphere, Hubble can see about as far as any telescope on Earth.

The space shuttle Discovery launched the telescope into orbit in 1990. Over several missions, astronauts have put new parts on the telescope, such as special devices to make its images clearer. The last mission to Hubble was in 2009.

Other articles to read include: **Space exploration; Telescope.**

The Cat's Eye Nebula, captured by the Hubble Space Telescope

Hybrid car

A hybrid car is an automobile that uses more than one source of energy to move. A common type has a gasoline-powered engine and a battery-powered electric motor.

A hybrid car's wheels may use power from the gasoline engine, the electric motor, or both. When the car speeds up, both systems may supply power. When the car cruises, the electric motor may supply all the power. If the gasoline engine is not needed, it may charge the battery. During braking, the motor uses the energy from the car's motion to charge the battery. This process is called *regenerative braking.*

A common type of hybrid car uses both a gasoline-powered engine and a battery-powered electric motor.

Hybrid cars use less fuel than do similar-sized cars with only gasoline engines. However, hybrids are more complex and expensive. Toyota Motor Corporation sold the first mass-produced hybrid car, the Prius, starting in Japan in 1997. During the 2000's and 2010's, hybrid cars became popular with consumers.

Other articles to read include: **Automobile; Battery; Brake; Electric car; Gasoline engine.**

Hydrofoil

A *hydrofoil (HY droh foyl)* is a boat that can travel above the surface of the water. Hydrofoils have wings called *foils.* The foils move under the water. The foils work like airplane wings. They help create a lifting force.

The foils are attached to the *hull,* or body, of the boat by long thin supports. At low speeds, the hydrofoil moves through the water on its hull, like a regular boat. When the hydrofoil reaches higher speeds, water rushes over the foils at a faster rate. The shape of the foils causes the water to flow in a special way. This special flow creates a lifting force. The hull of the hydrofoil then "flies" above the water on its foils. Hydrofoils can move smoothly over rough water at high speeds.

Continued on the next page

Hydrofoils can travel fast while using less power than other kinds of boats. They can do this because their hulls do not have to be pushed through the water. Hydrofoils usually travel at about 35 to 65 miles (56 to 96 kilometers) per hour—about as fast as a car.

Hydrofoils range in length from about 15 to 200 feet (4.5 to 60 meters). Large commercial hydrofoils carry people and goods. Commercial hydrofoils travel between the islands of Greece, across the English Channel, and in many other parts of the world. High-speed military hydrofoils patrol, track enemies, and fire missiles. Russia has the world's largest fleets of military and commercial hydrofoils.

Other articles to read include: **Ship.**

A hydrofoil has wings, called *foils,* that move under the water. At high speeds, they lift the boat's *hull* (body) out of the water.

Hygrometer

A hygrometer *(hy GROM uh tuhr)* is used to measure moisture in the air. The moisture is water vapor. Scientists use hygrometers to determine *relative humidity.* Relative humidity is the amount of water vapor in the air, compared with the amount the air can hold.

One of the most common types of hygrometer is the *psychrometer (sy KROM uh tuhr).* It has two thermometers mounted on the same frame. One of the thermometers has its tip kept wet. The other thermometer's tip is kept dry. The psychrometer is spun around in the air for a few minutes. The dry tip measures the air temperature. The wet tip gets cooler as the water *evaporates* (turns to vapor). How much water evaporates depends on how much vapor is already in the air. Scientists can compare the two temperatures to determine the humidity.

Other articles to read include: **Weather forecasting.**

A forest service worker uses a kind of hygrometer called a *psychrometer* to test humidity in the Big Cypress Swamp in the Florida Everglades.

Ii

Imhotep

Imhotep *(ihm HOH tehp)* was an ancient Egyptian architect. He was also a doctor and a high-ranking government worker.

Imhotep designed and built the Step Pyramid, the earliest known Egyptian pyramid. It was built around 2650 B.C. for King Zoser. It consists of a series of giant *terraces* (steps). The Step Pyramid still stands near Cairo. It is considered one of the most important buildings of the ancient world.

There are no records of Imhotep's medical work. But scholars know of his fame as a physician from the ancient Greeks. The Greeks identified Imhotep with their god of healing, Asclepius. They made shrines and statues in Imhotep's honor. Today, he is honored in medicine as the first physician known by name.

Other articles to read include: **Pyramid.**

A statuette shows Imhotep, the earliest known architect and physician.

Inclined plane

An inclined plane is a slanted surface, such as a ramp. It is one of the six simple machines.

An inclined plane can be used to raise heavy loads. Pushing a load up an inclined plane takes less force or *effort* than lifting the load straight up. For example, imagine a box weighing 200 pounds (90 kilograms). An average person could not lift the box 3 feet (90 centimeters) into the back of a truck. But an average person could push the box up a ramp 10 feet (3 meters) long and into the truck. The box travels a longer distance with the ramp. But it takes less force to move. As an inclined plane gets longer, the force needed to move a load grows less.

Other articles to read include: **Machine.**

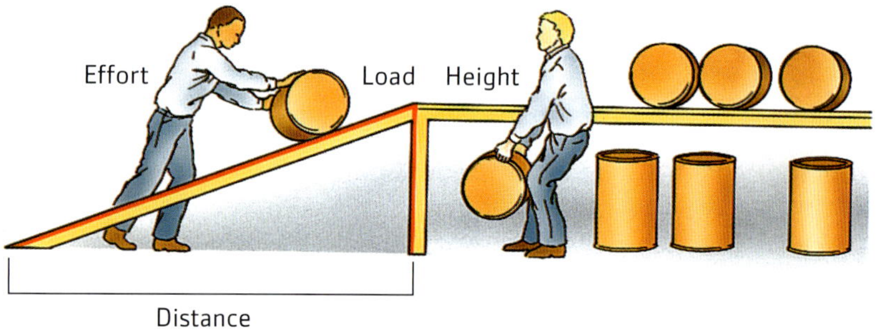

Pushing a barrel up an inclined plane takes less force than does lifting it straight up.

Insulation

Insulation is the control of the flow of heat or sound. Insulation can keep buildings cool in the summer and warm in the winter. People also use insulation to reduce noise in buildings.

Special materials, such as fiberglass or plastic, can be used in a house as insulation against the cold. Heat cannot travel well through these materials. They can thus help stop heat flowing into or out of a room.

People also use materials as insulation against noise. Some insulation blocks sound from spreading to another room. Other types absorb sound, reducing the level of noise in a room. Carpeting, drapery, and furniture can act like insulation by absorbing sound.

Other articles to read include: **Building construction; Fiberglass; Noise pollution; Plastics.**

Insulation prevents heat or sound from moving through a building's walls.

Insulator, Electric

An electric insulator is a type of material. Electric insulators carry almost no *electric current* (flow of electricity). Other insulators block the flow of heat.

Electric insulators prevent the unwanted or dangerous flow of current. They include dry wood, glass, the mineral mica, plastics, and rubber. Electric conductors, on the other hand, easily carry electric current. Metals, for example, are good conductors.

Conductors are often covered with insulators to prevent the leaking of electric current. For example, metal wires are often covered with rubber or plastic. Electricians and construction workers use tools with plastic or rubber handles. This helps them avoid injury from electric shock. Insulators are also used in many kinds of electrical and electronic equipment.

Other articles to read include: **Cable; Electric current; Wire.**

Wires are often covered by insulators, such as rubber or plastic tubes.

International Business Machines Corporation (IBM)

The International Business Machines Corporation (IBM) is a major computer technology company. IBM makes a number of important computer parts. They include *microprocessor* chips that form the "brains" of computers. The company also makes advanced computers and software programs for large businesses and other organizations.

International Business Machines Corporation grew out of an earlier firm, the Computing-Tabulating-Recording Company. It adopted its present name in 1924. The company made such devices as tabulating machines, time clocks, and electric typewriters.

In the 1950's, the company began making computer technology. In the 1960's, IBM's main business was making *mainframes* (large, powerful computers). In 1981, IBM began marketing a *personal computer* (PC). It was smaller and cheaper than a mainframe. People bought PC's for both homes and businesses. But other companies soon made similar computers. IBM faced intense competition. In 2005, IBM sold its PC division to Lenovo Group Limited.

Other articles to read include: **Calculator; Computer; Computer chip.**

International Space Station

The International Space Station is about 250 miles (400 kilometers) above Earth.

The International Space Station is a large *artificial satellite* in space. An artificial satellite is an object made by people that orbits a body, in this case Earth. More than 15 countries worked together to build the International Space Station. The first part of the station was launched in 1998. The space station was completed in 2011. Astronauts continue to add improvements to the station.

Continued on the next page

An astronaut floats as he works on a service module on the space station.

Three astronauts live in the International Space Station at one time. For a short period in 2009, 13 people were aboard the station at the same time. People first lived on the station in 2000. The International Space Station is about 250 miles (400 kilometers) above Earth.

The International Space Station is used to conduct scientific experiments. Some of these experiments measure how conditions in space can affect living things, including the astronauts.

A major advantage of a space station is that much of the equipment needs to be carried into space only one time. Spacecraft from several countries regularly visit the station. They bring new supplies and astronauts. In 2012, SpaceX became the first private company to send a spacecraft to the station.

Other articles to read include: **Astronaut; European Space Agency; National Aeronautics and Space Administration; Satellite, Artificial; Space exploration.**

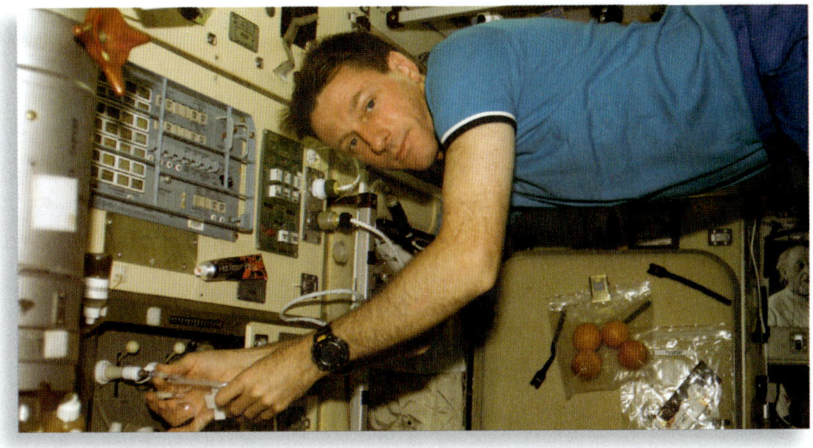

Astronauts aboard the space station live and work in weightless conditions.

The Internet has changed how people work, shop, and communicate.

Internet

The Internet is a system of computer networks. It links together billions of computers, mobile phones, and other devices. Almost a third of the world's people have Internet access.

The Internet is like a vast library. It stores a huge amount of information. This information includes text, such as books and news articles. It includes music, images, and videos. Computer programs are also available on the Internet. Such programs include electronic games.

Much information on the Internet is organized on *websites.* All the Internet's websites, linked together, form the World Wide Web. Unlike some parts of the Internet, the web is easy for nonexperts to use and explore.

The Internet does not just store information. People work, shop, and play on the Internet. They share artwork and ideas. People use the Internet to communicate in many ways. They can e-mail one another. They can also have face-to-face conversations using special cameras. *Social networking* websites help people stay in touch with their friends and families.

The Internet includes computers, mobile phones, and other devices and the wires that connect all these things together. These objects are called *hardware.* They link together, forming a "net." Electronic signals move quickly over the Internet's hardware. The signals carry information, such as text, photos, and videos.

The Internet's hardware would be useless without *software protocols.* Software protocols are special sets of rules. They control how signals move over the Internet. They work much like traffic laws guiding traffic on the streets.

However, information does not move on the Internet in the same way that a car moves on roads. For example, you might send a photo from your phone to a friend's computer over the Internet. But this photo does not stay in one piece. Instead, the photo is cut up into chunks. The chunks are called *packets.* Each packet can take a different path over the Internet. If a path is slow or broken, the packet switches to a new path. This concept

Continued on the next page

is called *packet switching.* Eventually, all the packets arrive at your friend's computer. They are put back together. The computer then displays the photo.

Development of the Internet began during the 1960's. At that time, the United States government worried about nuclear attacks from the Soviet Union. Such attacks could have crippled the U.S. communication system. The U.S. military worked with computer scientists. They developed the early Internet. With packet switching, communications could still work in case of an attack.

In the 1990's, a computer scientist named Tim Berners-Lee developed the World Wide Web. The Web made the Internet much easier to use.

During the 2000's, the Internet connections became much faster. New websites encouraged ordinary people to publish their own writing, photos, and videos. By the 2010's, many mobile phones and other wireless devices could connect to the Internet.

Other articles to read include: **Berners-Lee, Tim; Cellular telephone; Computer; Computer virus; Google Inc.; Website.**

Information, such as this photo of a cat, travels over the Internet in chunks in a process called *packet switching.*

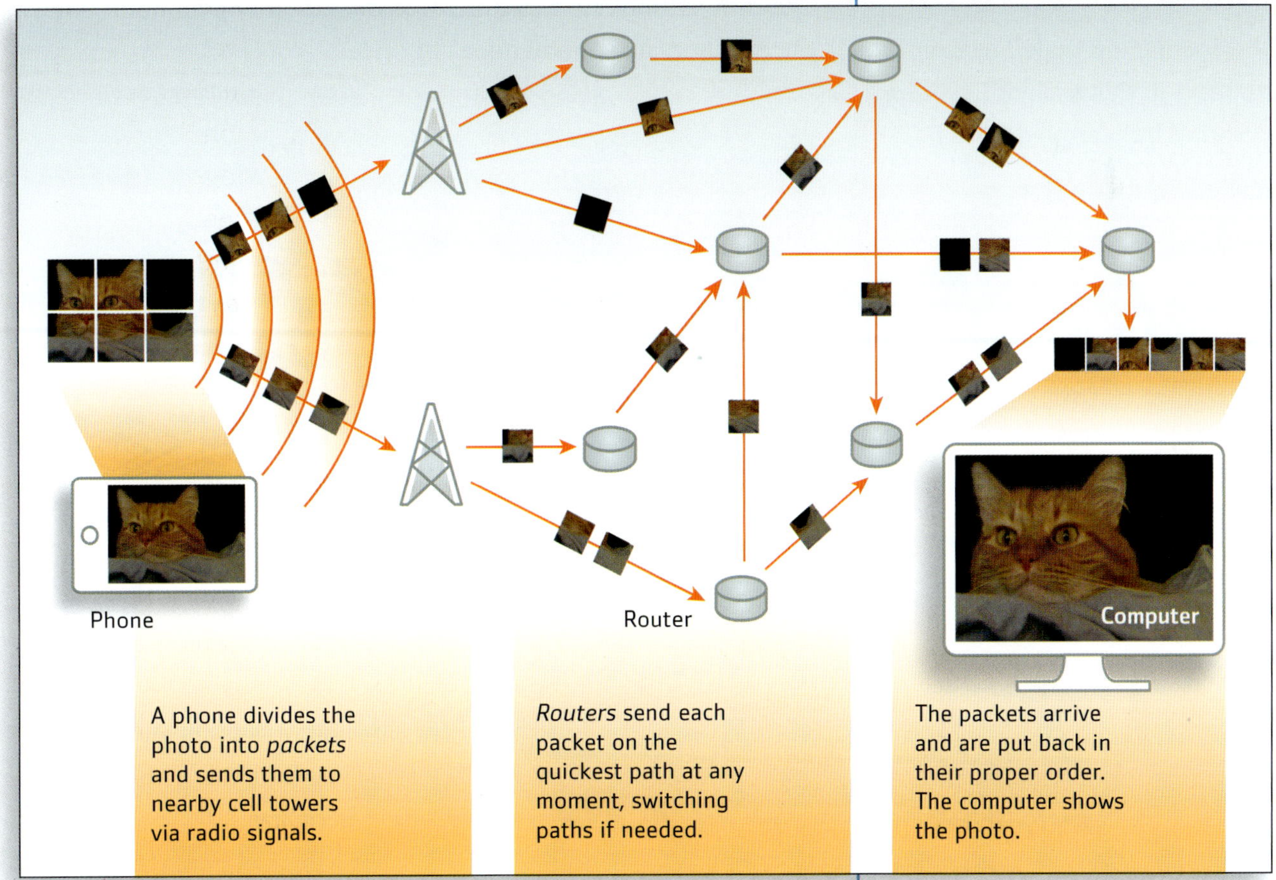

Invention

An invention is something new that has been created. An invention can be a tool, a machine, or a new way of getting work done. Inventions change the way that people live. The first inventions were simple weapons and tools. They made it easier to hunt, travel, or farm. Later inventions, such as writing and the printing press, helped people spread ideas far and wide. During the late 1700's and early 1800's, people invented many steam-powered machines and industrial processes. Modern society depends on such inventions as the automobile, the electric light, and the computer.

An invention is different from a *discovery.* Discovery is seeing something that already exists for the first time. An invention is the making of something that never before existed. For example, people discovered fire. But they invented the match to start fires.

Inventions succeed when they fill a need. For example, some inventions make it easier to farm crops or make products. Inventions may help people to communicate or to treat disease. Other inventions help nations win wars. Some inventions, such as the airplane, fill several needs at once.

Continued on the next page

The wheel is one of the most important inventions. It first appeared about 3500 B.C.

A wooden plow pulled by oxen appears in this ancient Egyptian painting from around 1300 B.C.

The printing press was invented by Johannes Gutenberg about 1440 in Germany.

People do not invent things out of thin air. Inventors must have some practical understanding of how their inventions will work. They also must have the right tools. Many modern inventions, such as televisions and computers, depend on earlier inventions involving electric power and circuits. Inventors must also be creative and willing to experiment.

Other articles to read include: **Machine; Tool;** *and those on individual inventions and inventors.*

The first successful airplane was invented and built in 1903 by the American brothers Wilbur and Orville Wright.

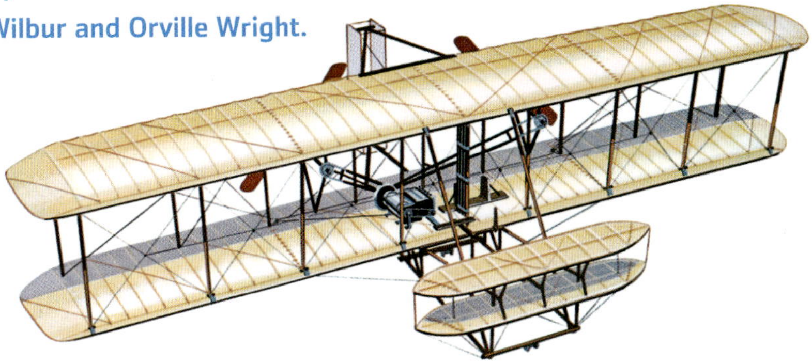

The gasoline-powered automobile was invented in 1885 by Karl Benz and Gottlieb Daimler, two German inventors working independently.

Iron Age

The Iron Age is a time in history. It began when people started widely using tools and weapons made of iron. In most regions, the Iron Age followed the Bronze Age.

Some people in the Middle East began to use iron tools as early as 3500 B.C. But true ironworking began in Asia Minor (now part of Turkey) between 1500 and 1000 B.C. It spread through Europe, Asia, and Africa.

Iron became popular because *iron ore* (rock that contains iron) is abundant. People learned how to remove the metal from the rocky ore. They also learned how to make iron into tools. They made knives, plows, hammers, saws, weapons, and other tools from iron. People soon replaced their stone or bronze tools with stronger, longer-lasting iron tools.

There is no clear end to the Iron Age. Iron continues to be useful to the present day.

Other articles to read include: **Bronze; Tool.**

These iron spearheads were made during the prehistoric Iron Age.

Mae Carol Jemison

Jemison, Mae Carol

Mae Carol Jemison (1956–) is an American doctor who became an astronaut. She was the first African American woman to travel in space.

Jemison was born in Decatur, Alabama. She grew up in Chicago and studied medicine at Cornell University in Ithaca, New York. For two years, she worked for the Peace Corps in Africa.

In September 1992, Jemison flew on the space shuttle Endeavour. She spent eight days in space. While on the Endeavour, she performed many scientific experiments.

Jemison left the space program in March 1993. She went to work on other projects, including the improvement of health care in western Africa.

Other articles to read include: **Astronaut; Space exploration.**

William Le Baron Jenney designed the first skyscraper with a metal frame, the 10-story Home Insurance Building, in Chicago. It was built in 1884 and 1885.

Jenney, William Le Baron

William Le Baron Jenney (1832–1907) was an American architect and engineer. He is best known as the designer of the Home Insurance Building in Chicago. It was the first skyscraper with a metal frame.

Before Jenney's work, tall buildings were supported by thick walls of stone and brick. Metal columns and beams helped to create much taller buildings. The Home Insurance Building had 10 stories. It was built in 1884 and 1885. It was torn down in 1931.

Jenney was born in Fairhaven, Massachusetts. He opened an office in Chicago in 1868. There, he trained other famous architects, including Daniel Burnham and Louis Sullivan. These architects developed a style of architecture known as the Chicago School.

Other articles to read include: **Engineering; Skyscraper.**

Jet

A jet is a kind of airplane. The word *jet* describes the plane's engines. A plane with jet engines can fly at high speeds for long distances.

There are two main kinds of jet engines: *turbojets* and *turbofans.* Turbojets are the oldest kind. They mix air with burning fuel to make exhaust. The exhaust moves backward through the engine. This pushes the plane forward. Some military planes use turbojet engines.

Turbofans are like turbojets. But, they have a fan at the front. The fan pulls in extra air. This air is then mixed with the exhaust. Turbofans are quieter and more powerful than turbojets. They also use less fuel. Most modern commercial airliners and military planes have turbofan engines.

Some airplanes use *turboprop* engines. A turboprop engine uses turbojet exhaust to turn a propeller. Turboprop planes can fly at low speed with great power. Some small business planes are turboprops.

Many military jets are *supersonic.* They can fly faster than the speed of sound. Some military jets can fly two and even three times the speed of sound. No commercial jet airliner is supersonic. There have been only two supersonic commercial airliners, the British-French Concorde and the Soviet TU-144. Both used turbojets. Both are retired.

Other articles to read include: **Aircraft, Military; Airplane; Engine; Jet propulsion.**

Military jet airplanes (top) can fly at high speeds for long distances. Most commercial airliners use *turbofan* engines (above).

Jet propulsion

Jet propulsion is movement by releasing a stream of gas at high pressure. The gas shoots out one end of a jet engine. It causes the engine to move in the opposite direction. Rockets, guided missiles, and many airplanes use jet propulsion. Jet-propelled airplanes can fly much faster than airplanes that use propellers. Some jet aircraft fly through the air faster than sound. Rockets use jet propulsion to fly through outer space.

Jet engines burn fuel in a *combustion chamber.* The burning fuel creates hot gases. These gases then rush out through a *nozzle.* Jet engines burn fuel with oxygen from the

Continued on the next page

Jet propulsion *Continued from the previous page*

air. Rocket engines, on the other hand, carry a supply of oxygen with them. Thus, rocket engines can work in outer space.

The English scientist Sir Isaac Newton described the basic idea behind jet propulsion in 1687. It is his third law of motion. It states that for every action, there is an equal and opposite reaction. Thus, forcing out gas pushes a jet in the opposite direction. The first jet-propelled airplane was flown in Germany in 1939. Since then, people have built many types of jet-propelled aircraft.

Other articles to read include: **Airplane; Engine; Jet; Rocket.**

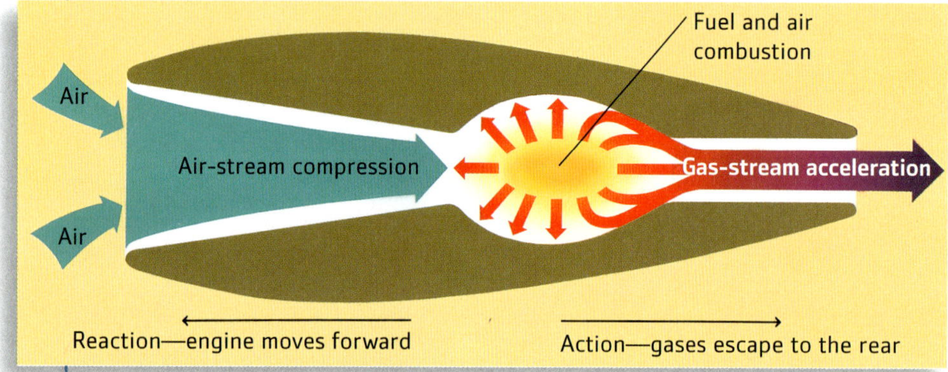

A jet engine draws in air, mixes it with fuel, and burns it. Hot gases are pushed out the other end. The force of the gases exiting pushes the engine in the opposite direction.

Steve Jobs

Jobs, Steve

Steve Jobs (1955–2011) was the cofounder of Apple Inc. (originally Apple Computer, Inc.). He was one of two men who started the company. Apple makes personal computers and also develops and publishes computer software. Under his leadership, Apple introduced the iMac computer and iPod music player.

Steven Paul Jobs was born in Los Altos, California, on Feb. 24, 1955. Paul and Clara Jobs of Mountain View, California, adopted Steve that same year. While in high school, Jobs took a summer job at a company where he met Stephen Wozniak, an engineer. In 1975, Jobs and Wozniak started Apple Computer. In 1984, Apple introduced the popular Macintosh personal computer. In the late 1990's and early 2000's, Jobs oversaw the development of many popular Apple devices. These included the iMac, the iPod, and the iPad tablet computer. Jobs died on Oct. 5, 2011.

Other articles to read include: **Apple Inc.; Cellular telephone; Computer; Wozniak, Steve.**

Keck Observatory

The Keck Observatory includes two giant telescopes. It is on Mauna Kea *(MOW nuh KAY uh)*, a mountain on the island of Hawaii. At the observatory, scientists called *astronomers* study planets, stars, and other objects in the sky. The Keck telescopes are among the largest *optical telescopes* in the world. An optical telescope collects visible light.

The telescopes at the observatory are called Keck I and Keck II. Along with visible light, the Keck telescopes also see *infrared* (heat) waves from space. Keck I and II are *reflecting telescopes*. Each uses a large mirror to collect and focus light.

Each of the two mirrors actually consists of 36 smaller mirrors mounted together. Together, the 36 mirrors form a reflecting surface 33 feet (10 meters) in diameter. The two telescopes are sometimes used together. Used this way, they act like a single larger telescope.

Keck I was completed in 1992. Keck II was built in 1996. The full name of the station is the W. M. Keck Observatory. It is named for a charitable foundation established by the American businessman William Myron Keck. The W. M. Keck Foundation funded the observatory's construction.

Other articles to read include: **Observatory; Telescope.**

The Keck Observatory is on Mauna Kea, a mountain in Hawaii.

The Keck Observatory includes two giant telescopes, called Keck I and Keck II.

The Kennedy Space Center, on the east coast of Florida, is a launch facility of the National Aeronautics and Space Administration (NASA).

Kennedy Space Center

The Kennedy Space Center is a launching place for spacecraft. It is on the east coast of Florida.

The full name of the center is the John F. Kennedy Space Center of the National Aeronautics and Space Administration (NASA). It is on Merritt Island, across from a point of land called Cape Canaveral. The center used to be at Cape Canaveral. For this reason, people sometimes refer to the center as Cape Canaveral.

NASA tests, fixes, and launches spacecraft at the Kennedy Space Center. Parts of the center are available for tour by the public.

Other articles to read include: **National Aeronautics and Space Administration; Space exploration.**

Kerosene

Kerosene is a liquid fuel that burns easily. It is clear and colorless and has a strong odor. Kerosene comes from petroleum.

Today, kerosene is used as airplane fuel. Farmers mix kerosene with other chemicals to kill weeds and insects. Before electric lights, many houses used kerosene lamps for light.

Kerosene is obtained from crude oil through *distillation*—that is, it is separated from the oil by heating or boiling.

Other articles to read include: **Lamp.**

Kerosene lamps were common in houses before electric lights.

Lamp

Lamps are devices that give off light. People have used lamps for thousands of years. With lamps, people can work, read, or do other activities after the sun goes down.

Long ago, lamps burned oil or fat. They used a wick, or cord, made of fibers. The wick soaked up the oil or fat. When the wick was lit, the oil or fat burned and gave off light.

Gas lamps were used in the 1800's. The gas was piped into the lamp. It burned as it rushed out of a small opening and mixed with the air. Today, gas lanterns are sometimes used by campers. Such lamps provide light in places with no electric power.

Thomas Alva Edison, an American inventor, made the first workable electric lamp in the late 1800's. Electric lamps give more light than earlier lamps. They also cost less and are easier to use.

Other articles to read include: **Electric light; Fluorescent lamp; Light bulb.**

Electric lamps provide bright light and are cheap and easy to use.

Oil lamp

Gas lamp

Oil lamps (left) were the earliest kind of lamp. Gas lamps (below left) were widely used during the 1800's.

Landfill

A landfill is a place for disposing trash and other wastes. There are two main types of landfills. *Sanitary landfills* are sealed off to prevent leaking. *Unsanitary landfills* are open dumps.

Open dumps are considered *unsanitary* (unclean). Wastes leaked from them can cause health problems. Such wastes can also harm the environment. Chemicals from open dumps can *contaminate* (pollute) soil, water, and air.

Sanitary landfills are designed to be safer for the environment than are open dumps. Sanitary landfills seal off waste material from the outside environment with layers of clay or plastic. The seals prevent leaks. A drainage system collects rain water from the landfill. The water can be pumped out and cleaned.

Other articles to read include: **Hazardous wastes; Recycling; Water pollution.**

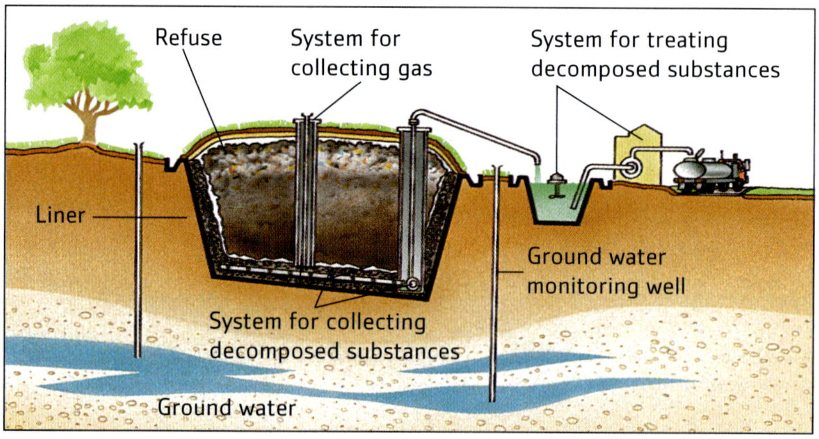

A *sanitary landfill* is tightly sealed to protect the environment. A liner prevents leaks from entering the surrounding soil or water supply. As trash breaks down, it gives off gases. These gases are collected to keep them from dirtying the air.

Laser

A laser is a device that makes a strong, narrow beam of light. Some laser beams are powerful enough to burn holes in diamonds. Other laser beams are so narrow that they can drill 200 holes on a pinhead. Lasers have many uses in modern technology.

Normal light travels in many directions. For example, light from a light bulb shines on all parts of a room. Light from the sun also travels in all directions. When the sun shines, its light covers

Continued on the next page

one-half of Earth's surface. Light from a laser is a different kind of light. Laser light travels in only one direction. It travels in a narrow beam, like an arrow.

Light is made of *electromagnetic waves.* Like ocean waves, electromagnetic waves can have different lengths—called *wavelengths.* The sun and light bulbs produce light with many different wavelengths. We see different wavelengths as different colors of light. When different colors combine, we see white light.

Lasers, on the other hand, produce light waves with almost the exact same wavelength. Thus, lasers make light of one color. Laser light is called *coherent light* because the waves move in a highly organized way. Laser light waves are like marchers in a parade, moving with the same stride in the same direction.

Laser light is made by giving energy to a special arrangement of *atoms.* Atoms are the building blocks of matter. They are far too small to be seen even with most microscopes. When given energy, atoms release light. When you heat up a metal poker, for example, it glows. The heat's energy causes the poker's atoms to release light.

The atoms in a laser take in energy—and release light—in a special way. They are arranged in a particular pattern, such as a crystal. When one atom takes in energy, it releases light. The light, in turn, gives energy to another atom. Then that atom releases light, and so on. Each time light is released, it has the same energy and wavelength. The light is caught between two mirrors. It is reflected back and forth. The waves of light "line up." Then they are released as a laser beam.

Continued on the next page

Laser light waves "line up" with one another, forming a strong, narrow beam. A laser relies on a special arrangement of atoms, such as a ruby crystal.

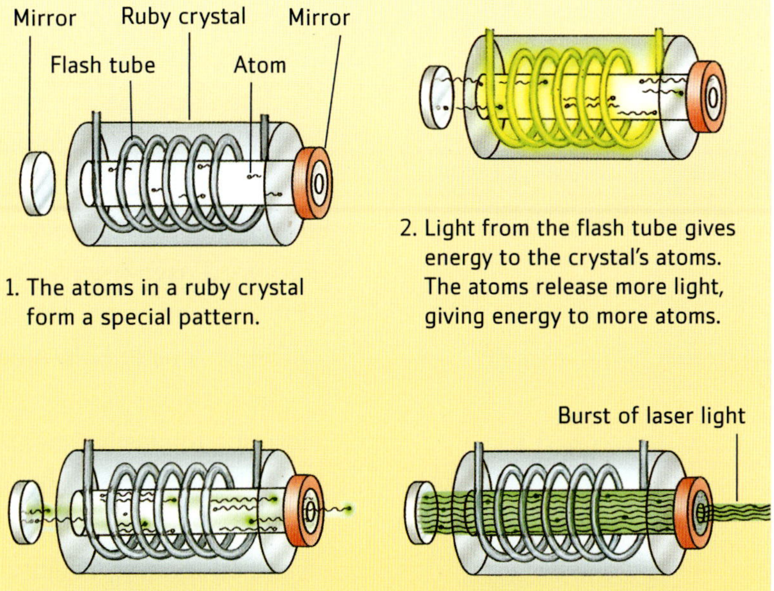

1. The atoms in a ruby crystal form a special pattern.

2. Light from the flash tube gives energy to the crystal's atoms. The atoms release more light, giving energy to more atoms.

3. Each time the ruby crystal atoms release light, the light has the same energy and wavelength.

4. The light is caught between two mirrors. It "lines up." It is released as a laser beam.

Colorful laser beams can shoot out into the sky or trace spectacular patterns of light on buildings or other surfaces.

Laser *Continued from the previous page*

Lasers are used for many purposes. Laser light can carry television and Internet signals. Laser signals may travel through *fiber-optic cables.* Such cables are made of tiny glass or plastic tubes that carry the light. Lasers also read and write patterns of pits on CD's and DVD's. The patterns stand for sounds, videos, or other information. In addition, lasers scan *bar codes* on products sold at stores. The bar code contains information about a product, such as its price.

Lasers are also used for measuring distance. The speed of light—including laser light—is known exactly. This knowledge helps people measure distances exactly. People can measure how long a laser beam takes to reflect from a distant object. The time it takes—usually a small fraction of a second—can be used to figure out the distance. Scientists measured the exact distance to the moon in this way. They bounced a laser beam off mirrors that astronauts left on the moon's surface.

Lasers help guide ships and airplanes. Because they are straight, laser beams can help detect changes in direction. Lasers are also used to guide bombs and missiles to targets.

Some laser beams create great heat. These beams can be used as precision cutting tools. Doctors sometimes use lasers in place of knives in surgery. Lasers are more precise than knives, and they cause less bleeding. Lasers are especially useful in eye surgery. Laser beams can pass through the clear front of the eye. But they can burn away tissues beneath it. They can also reshape the eye's lens to help a person see better.

The famous scientist Albert Einstein was the first person to describe the laser. Scientists began to use the idea in the 1950's. The first working laser used a ruby rod to create laser light. It was built in 1960. Since then, lasers have become widespread. The National Ignition Facility (NIF) operates the world's largest and most powerful laser system. It was completed in 2009. Its lasers are used for nuclear energy research.

Other articles to read include: **Compact disc; DVD; Holography.**

Laser printer

A laser printer uses powdered ink called *toner.* The toner sticks to electrically charged patterns made by a laser.

A laser printer uses lasers to create words and pictures on paper. Laser printers use a dry powdered ink called *toner.* The toner is electrically charged. It sticks to a barrel-shaped device called a *drum*. But it only sticks to certain areas of the drum. It sticks to areas where the charge has been altered by a laser.

The laser creates a pattern on the drum that looks like words or pictures. The toner sticks to this pattern. Then, the toner is pressed onto a sheet of blank paper. It sticks to the paper. Now the paper has the pattern of words or pictures.

In the last step, the paper passes through rollers. The rollers heat the paper and melt the toner powder. The melted toner sticks to the paper permanently.

Laser printers can print several pages of text per minute. They print complex images and photographs at a slower rate. Many laser printers print in color.

Other articles to read include: **Computer; Laser; Paper.**

Lawrence, Robert Henry, Jr.

Robert Henry Lawrence, Jr.

Robert Henry Lawrence, Jr. (1935–1967), was an American test pilot and scientist. Lawrence was the first African American selected as an astronaut. However, he died before making a space flight.

Lawrence was born on Oct. 2, 1935, in Chicago. In 1956, he graduated from college and entered the United States Air Force. After completing pilot training, Lawrence served as a fighter pilot and flight instructor. In 1965, he earned a Ph.D. degree in chemistry. He worked for a short time as a research scientist.

In 1967, Lawrence graduated from the Air Force Flight Test Pilot Training School. He was chosen as an astronaut for a project to build a small space station. On Dec. 8, 1967, Lawrence was killed in a plane crash.

Other articles to read include: **Astronaut; Space exploration.**

Lens

A lens is a clear object that bends light in a certain way. The bent light can be gathered into an image of an object or scene. Some lenses make objects look bigger. Such lenses are used to make distant objects appear closer in binoculars and telescopes. Other lenses are used in eyeglasses and cameras. Most lenses are made of glass or plastic.

Many people wear eyeglasses to help them see better. People who are *nearsighted* have trouble seeing objects that are far away. They wear eyeglasses with lenses that are thicker at the edges than at the center. Such lenses are *concave.* People who are *farsighted* have difficulty seeing objects that are close. They wear eyeglasses with lenses that are thicker at the center than at the edges. Such lenses are *convex.*

Other articles to read include: **Binoculars; Camera; Contact lens; Glass; Microscope; Telescope.**

Convex and concave lenses

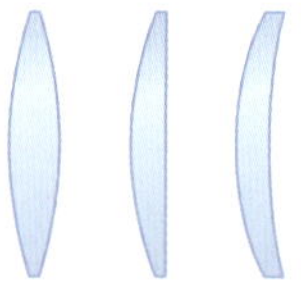

Convex lenses are thicker at the center than at the edge.

Concave lenses are thicker at the edge than at the center.

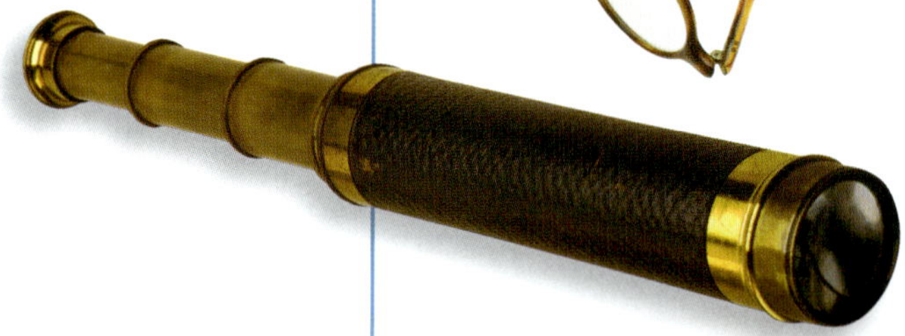

The lenses in eyeglasses correct for defects in vision. A telescope's lenses makes distant objects appear closer.

In a video camera, lenses gather and focus light.

Leonardo da Vinci

Leonardo da Vinci *(lee uh NAHR doh duh VIHN chee)* (1452–1519), was a great artist and scientist. He lived in Italy during the *Renaissance (REN uh sons).* The Renaissance was a time of great improvements in art and science.

During the late 1460's, Leonardo became an apprentice to Andrea del Verrocchio, a leading painter and sculptor in Florence. He remained with Verrocchio as an assistant for several years after completing his apprenticeship. Leonardo painted two of the world's most famous paintings—*Mona Lisa* and *The Last Supper.* He made many drawings to plan his paintings. He also used drawings to work out his scientific ideas. In addition, he was an architect and engineer, helping in several large construction projects. For example, he designed improvements to the canals in the city of Milan.

Leonardo da Vinci was a great artist and scientist.

Leonardo studied many areas of science. He made designs for hundreds of inventions. Many of his ideas were way ahead of his time. For example, Leonardo was the first person to make a scientific study of how birds fly. He then drew plans for a helicopter and a parachute centuries before flying machines were invented. He produced designs for a variety of war machines, among them tanks, machine guns, and movable bridges. He was also an early pioneer in the study of human *anatomy* (body structure).

Leonardo was born on April 15, 1452, probably outside the village of Vinci, near Florence in central Italy. The name *da Vinci* simply means *from Vinci.* He spent most of his life in Florence and Milan. He died on May 2, 1519.

Other articles to read include: **Engineering; Invention.**

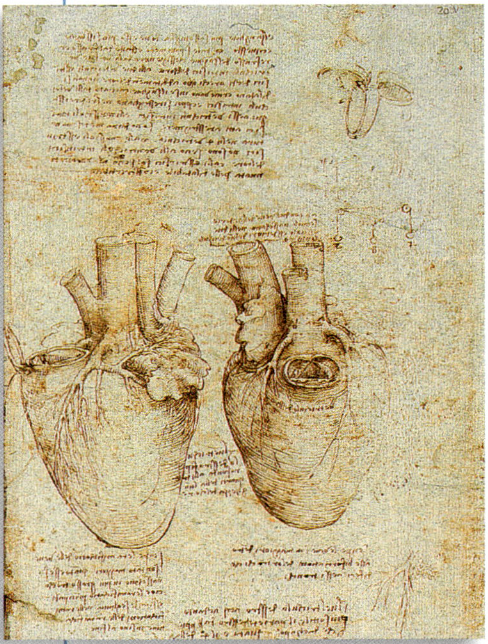

Leonardo da Vinci made these sketches of the human heart in the early 1500's. His work helped people learn more about the organ's structure.

Lever

A lever *(LEHV uhr* or *LEE vuhr)* is one of the six simple machines. A lever has a rod or bar. The rod or bar turns on a support called a *fulcrum (FUHL kruhm).* A force is used on one part of the rod. This moves a load on another part.

There are different kinds of levers. One simple kind of lever is a seesaw. The fulcrum is in the middle of the seesaw. A downward force at one end moves a person up at the other end.

In other levers, the fulcrum is closer to the load. Less force is needed to lift the load on such levers. But the force must be applied over a greater distance. Lifting a wheelbarrow by its handles makes use of this principle.

Crowbars, brooms, and balance scales are levers. Other tools, such as scissors, consist of two or more levers.

Other articles to read include: **Machine; Tool.**

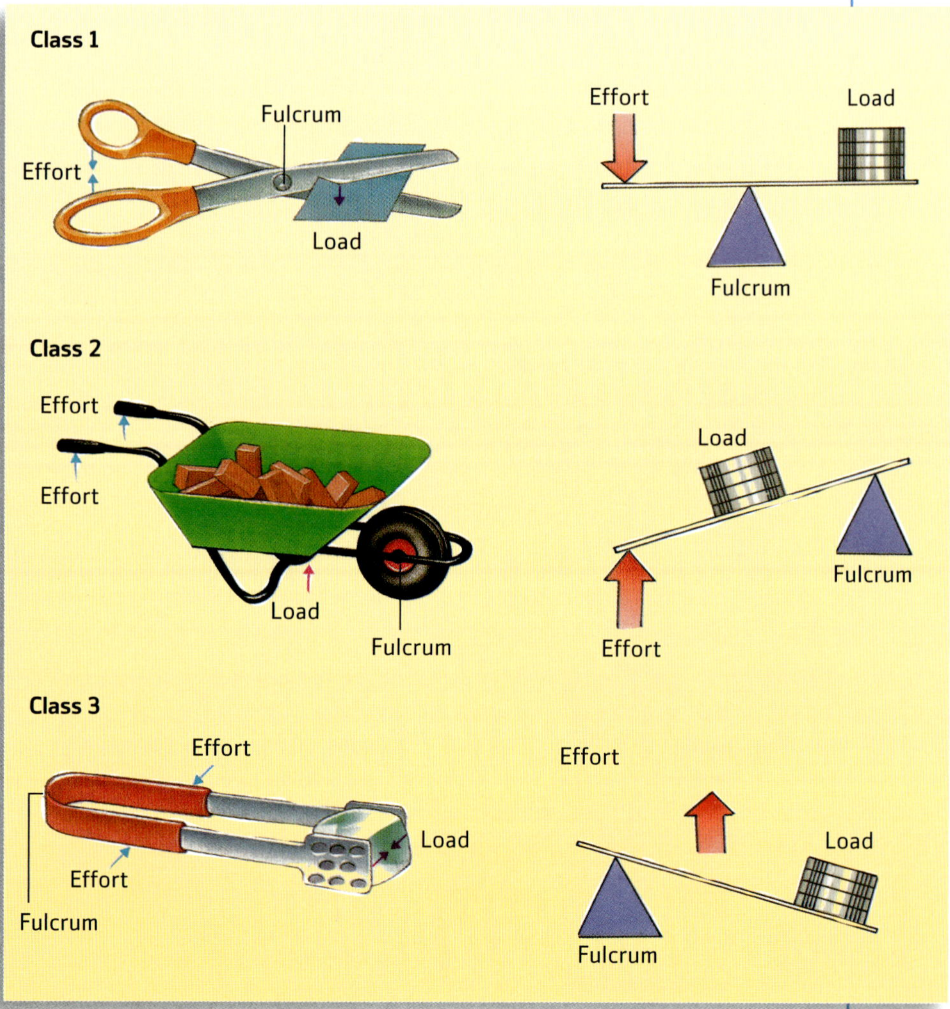

Levers come in many shapes and sizes, but there are three main classes. Each class features a different arrangement of the force applied or *effort,* the fulcrum, and the load.

Light bulb

A light bulb is a device that changes electric energy into light. Light bulbs are used in home lighting, car headlights, and flashlights. One kind of light bulb is an *incandescent bulb.* It passes electricity through a wire called a *filament.* The filament heats up and glows. It sits inside a glass bulb. *Fluorescent bulbs* pass electricity through special gases in a glass tube. The gas gives off energy. The energy is invisible. But it makes a coating on the glass glow brightly.

Humphry Davy, a British chemist, demonstrated the idea of an incandescent light bulb in 1802. He ran electricity through strips of platinum. The strips glowed. But his device was expensive. It never caught on.

In the late 1870's, the English scientist Joseph Swan invented a cheaper light bulb. It used a cotton-based carbon filament. Around the same time, the American inventor Thomas Edison began experimenting with light bulb design. His assistants took all the air out of glass bulbs. Without air, filaments inside the bulbs lasted longer.

Other articles to read include: **Edison, Thomas Alva; Electric light; Fluorescent lamp; Swan, Joseph Wilson.**

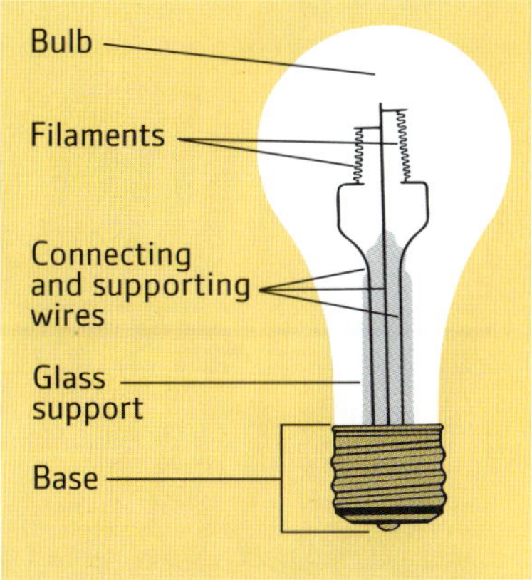

Incandescent light bulbs use wires called *filaments* that glow brightly when electric current runs through them.

Light pollution

Light pollution is caused by *artificial* (human-made) lighting. At night, city lights create a glow across the sky. People cannot see the stars as a result. Astronomers cannot do their work. Lights may shine in unwanted places. Such lights waste energy. Also, artificial lights can harm wildlife. The light can change animals' natural behavior and movements.

Lights can be shielded to not shine up into the sky. Such lights only shine on the ground. Shielded lights help reduce light pollution. Some communities work to fight light pollution. They limit the type and position of lighting fixtures.

Other articles to read include: **Electric light.**

Light pollution from a city creates a glow across the sky. The glow makes it impossible to see the stars.

A lighthouse can signal to sailors that land is near.

Lighthouse

A lighthouse is a tower with a strong light. Sailors can see the light from far offshore. The light signals that land is near. Lighthouses may also warn of dangerous rocks and reefs.

People build lighthouses on land that sticks out into the ocean. They also build them on rocks that stick up out of the sea. Some lighthouses stand in the sea itself. They are built on rocks beneath the water.

Lighthouses give off different patterns of light. Some have a steady light. Others have patterns of long or short flashes. The patterns help sailors identify a particular lighthouse. Sailors can then figure out where they are on a map.

Sailors can also recognize a particular lighthouse in daytime. Lighthouses are sometimes painted with different patterns, such as checks or stripes. The patterns help sailors tell them apart.

The lamps in a lighthouse shine through lenses. The lenses gather the light into a strong beam, so that it can be seen for many miles. Many lighthouses also use foghorns or bells to signal ships in bad weather, when the light is hard to see.

Lighthouses were probably first used by the ancient Phoenicians and Egyptians. They lit fires on hilltops or tall structures. The ancient Romans built lighthouses in many places. The first lighthouse in North America was Boston Lighthouse. It was built in 1716.

Lighthouses used to have *keepers.* A keeper was a person in charge of cleaning and maintaining the light source. The keeper also rescued shipwrecked sailors. Today, almost all lighthouses are automatic. They do not need people to run them.

Other articles to read include: **Electric light; Navigation; Ship.**

Many lighthouses feature lights with unique colors or patterns.

Lightning rod

A lightning rod protects homes and other buildings from damage by lightning. A common type is a simple metal rod placed on top of a building. A wire leads from the rod to another rod called the *ground rod.* The ground rod is buried about 10 feet (3 meters) in the ground. If lightning strikes the building, the electric charge is safely carried away to the ground rod.

Other articles to read include: **Electric current; Franklin, Benjamin.**

Lightning rods protect many buildings. A lightning bolt's charge travels from the rod through a wire and safely into the ground.

Lilienthal, Otto

Otto Lilienthal *(LIHL ee uhn THAWL)* (1848–1896) was a German inventor. He worked in *aviation (AY vee AY shuhn).* Aviation is the building and flying of aircraft. He made the first successful flight in a piloted *glider.* A glider is a winged aircraft with no engine. Lilienthal's work inspired the Wright brothers. The Wright brothers built the first working airplane.

Lilienthal developed many different models of gliders. From 1891 to 1896, he made thousands of glider flights.

In August 1896, Lilienthal crashed one of his gliders. He died from his injuries on Aug. 10, 1896.

Other articles to read include: **Airplane; Glider; Wright brothers.**

Otto Lilienthal became the first person to pilot a glider, in 1891. But his gliders were difficult to control.

Lippershey, Hans

Hans Lippershey was the first person to patent a telescope.

Hans Lippershey (1570–1619) was a Dutch *optician (op TIHSH uhn).* An optician makes eyeglasses. Lippershey is often given credit for making the first telescope, in 1608. He mounted two glass lenses in a narrow tube. Lippershey was born in Germany. He moved to the Netherlands as an adult.

Other people claim the invention of the telescope. However, Lippershey's *patent* application is the earliest record of a telescope that was actually built. A patent is a legal document. It allows a person to make, use, or sell an invention. A description of Lippershey's instrument quickly reached the famous scientist Galileo Galilei. Galileo built his own telescope in 1609.

Other articles to read include: **Lens; Telescope.**

Liquid crystal

Electric charges can change the appearance of a liquid crystal, forming numbers or other images in a liquid crystal display.

A liquid crystal is a fluid that forms orderly patterns. Liquid crystals are used in television and computer screens and other displays. Such screens are called *liquid crystal displays* or LCD's.

A liquid crystal can flow like a liquid. But it has some characteristics of a solid crystal. A solid crystal's matter is arranged in regular, repeating patterns. Matter in liquid crystal also forms patterns. The patterns can be changed by an electric charge, a magnet, or a change in temperature. A clear liquid crystal may become cloudy. A colored liquid crystal may change color.

An LCD is made of a grid of tiny *pixels.* Each pixel is made up of liquid crystals. The liquid crystals are normally clear. Electric charges are applied to certain pixels to make them darken. The pattern of clear and darkened pixels forms an image. Special filters can make the image appear in color.

Other articles to read include: **Computer; Television.**

Lock

A lock is a device that prevents something from opening. Many locks prevent doors from being opened. Locks may also stop devices from being used. The simplest locks are *mechanical.* Their moving parts work without electricity.

Most mechanical locks have metal parts called *tumblers.* When the right key is put into the lock, it pushes the tumblers back. Then the key can turn part of the lock. As the part turns, it moves the *bolt*—the piece that keeps the door or other object shut. The bolt slides out of the way, and the door opens.

Some kinds of locks are electric. One kind is opened with a special plastic card. The lock reads a code on the card. It sends the information to a computer. If the code on the card matches a code in the computer, the lock opens.

Another kind of electric lock opens with a combination of letters or numbers. People punch or dial the combination. If the combination matches one in a computer, the lock opens.

Some electric locks recognize people's fingerprints, eyes, voices, or other features. A scanner compares the feature with information in a computer. If they match, the lock opens.

Other articles to read include: **Machine.**

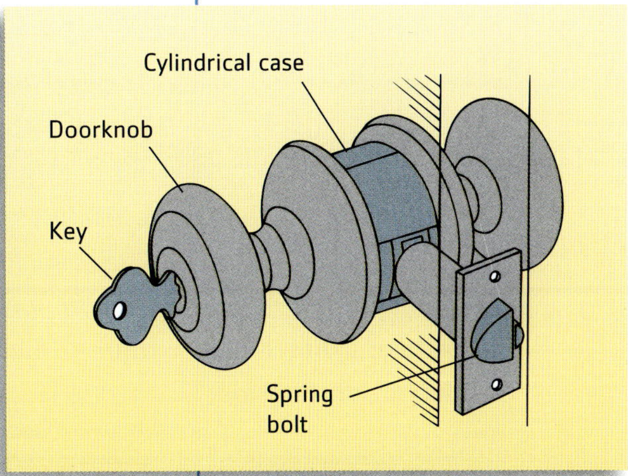

Many doors have a locking mechanism that is part of the doorknob.

Locomotive

A *locomotive (LOH kuh MOH tihv)* is the engine that moves a train. Locomotives pull trains on railroad tracks. Sometimes locomotives push trains instead of pulling them.

There are three main kinds of locomotives. The oldest kind is the *steam locomotive.* It heats water to make steam. The steam powers the engine. Steam locomotives are still used in parts of the world today.

Continued on the next page

A steam locomotive

Locomotive *Continued from the previous page*

Diesel locomotives burn diesel fuel. Some of them use the energy of burning fuel to turn the wheels. But most of them use this energy to make electric power. They are called *diesel-electric locomotives.* The electric power is used to turn the train's wheels.

Electric locomotives do not produce their own power. Wires or rails bring electric power to them. Many high-speed passenger trains use electric locomotives.

Other articles to read include: **Diesel engine; Electric motor; Engine; Piston; Steam engine; Train.**

Parts of a diesel-electric locomotive

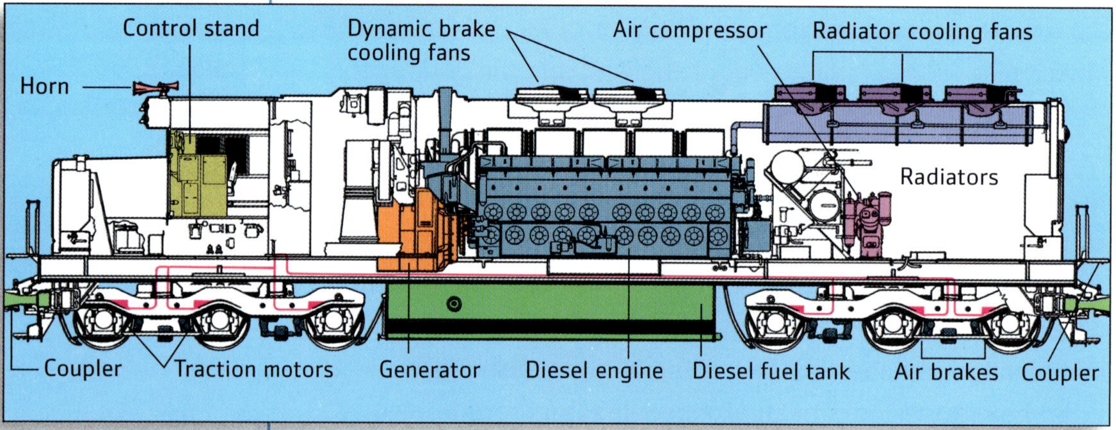

Ada Lovelace

Lovelace, Ada

Ada Lovelace (1815–1852) was an English noble who wrote the first published computer program. She was also one of the first people to predict the power of computers.

Augusta Ada Byron was born on Dec. 10, 1815, in London. She was the daughter of the famous poet Lord Byron. In 1835, she married William King. King was made Earl of Lovelace in 1838.

Ada Lovelace was educated in mathematics. She became interested in the work of the English mathematician Charles Babbage. Babbage had built early computing machines. Lovelace worked for Babbage for a number of years. In 1843, she published an article about the machines. It showed how the machines could be programmed to perform different calculations. These were some of the first computer programs.

Continued on the next page

Lovelace suffered from poor health by her 20's. She turned to gambling on horse races. Her losses put her deeply in debt. Lovelace died of cancer on Nov. 27, 1852, in London. In 1979, a computer programming language, called *Ada,* was named in her honor.

Other articles to read include: **Computer.**

Lucid, Shannon Wells

Shannon Wells Lucid *(LOO sihd)* (1943–) is a United States astronaut. She set the world record for time in space by a woman. In 1996, she spent 188 days in space, mostly aboard the Russian space station Mir *(meer).* It was also a world record for time spent in space by anyone, man or woman, from the United States.

Lucid traveled to and from the space station on the space shuttle Atlantis. On Mir, she conducted science experiments. She studied the effects of *weightlessness* (the absence of weight), a common condition in space travel. She studied its effects on living tissue and the growth of protein crystals.

Shannon Wells was born on Jan. 14, 1943, in China. She grew up in Oklahoma. She married Michael F. Lucid, a businessman, in 1968. From 2002 to 2003, Lucid was chief scientist of the National Aeronautics and Space Administration (NASA). She continued to work at NASA until her retirement in 2012.

Other articles to read include: **Astronaut; Space exploration.**

Shannon Wells Lucid

Mm

Machine

Machines *(muh SHEENZ)* are devices that make doing things easier. They can do work that could not be done without them. Some machines help lift heavy furniture. Others carry big boxes for long distances. Factories use many kinds of machines, such as drills and saws. Businesses use typewriters, computers, and other office machines. Automobiles, buses, and airplanes are machines. Trucks, trains, and ships are machines, too. Without machines, modern life would be impossible.

People have made many different kinds of machines to satisfy their needs. Early people made axes of stone. They used the axes as weapons and tools. Over time, people made wagons and carriages and then, much later, motors and cars. They made printing presses that printed books. Machines gave people more and more control over the world around them. To make these machines

Continued on the next page

Six kinds of simple machines

The *lever* is one of the earliest and simplest machines. It is a long bar or rod that turns on a *fulcrum.* A crowbar is one kind of lever. A force or *effort* applied at one end of the lever lifts a load on the other.

The *wheel and axle* has two connected parts: a large wheel and a smaller axle. Turning the wheel requires less force than turning the axle. Thus, a load connected to the axle is easier to lift or move by turning the wheel.

The *pulley* consists of a wheel with a grooved rim over which a rope is passed. It is used to change the direction of the force applied to the rope. A block and tackle uses two or more pulleys to reduce the amount of effort needed to lift a load.

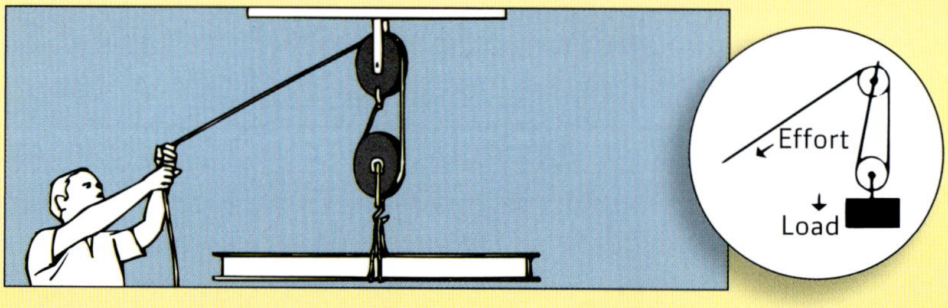

work, people learned how to use the power of falling water and such fuels as coal and oil.

Some machines have just a few parts. Other machines have many parts. But all machines with moving parts make use of one or more of the *simple machines.* The six simple machines are (1) the lever, (2) the wheel and axle, (3) the pulley, (4) the inclined plane, (5) the wedge, and (6) the screw.

The simplest kind of lever is a rod or bar. It rests and turns on a support called a *fulcrum (FUL kruhm).* A force or *effort* is applied at one part of the lever. This force lifts a load, or weight, at another part. There are several kinds of levers. A seesaw, a wheelbarrow, and the human arm are all levers.

A wheel and axle works with spinning forces. A large wheel is connected to a smaller shaft called the *axle.* Spinning the wheel causes the axle to spin, and vice versa. Using the wheel to turn

Continued on the next page

A car consists of many different simple machines working together.

Sliding or skidding a load up an *inclined plane* is easier than lifting it directly. The longer the slope, the smaller the force required. But the load must travel a longer distance.

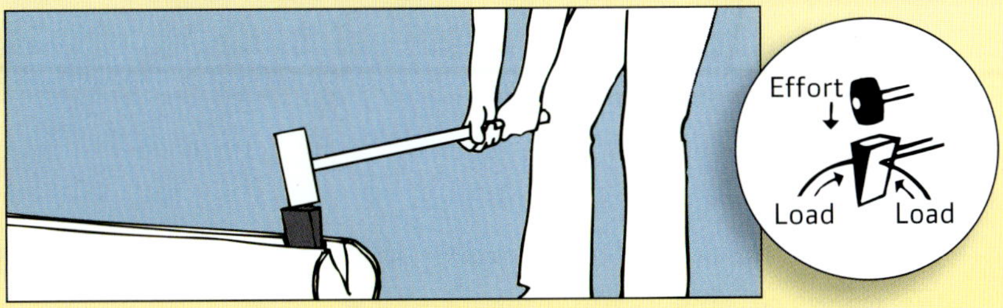

The *wedge,* when struck with a hammer or mallet, changes a downward effort into sideways forces. A thin wedge is more effective than a thick one.

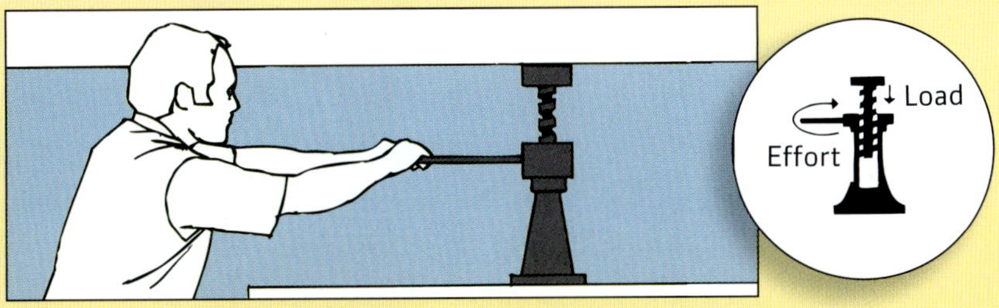

The *screw* is a spiral inclined plane. The *jackscrew* is a combination of the lever and the screw. It can lift a heavy load with small effort.

Pulleys attached to a crane help lift heavy loads.

Machine *Continued from the previous page*

the axle takes less force than turning the axle itself. But the wheel must be turned farther. One kind of wheel and axle is called a *windlass.* It is used to lift a bucket of water from a well. The bucket is tied with a rope to the axle. The axle connects to a crank that is easy to spin. As the crank spins, the axle winds the rope, pulling the bucket up.

A pulley is similar to a wheel and axle. It is basically a wheel with a rope wound around it. Pulling one end of the rope causes the other end to rise. Pulleys make it easier to lift heavy loads.

The inclined plane is a ramp. It may not seem like a machine, but it helps people do work. For example, a person may not be able to lift a heavy box into the back of a truck. But an inclined plane makes this work easier. The person can slide the box up a ramp and into the truck. Pushing the box up the ramp takes less force. But the box has to move a greater distance.

A wedge is thick at one end and narrows to a thin edge. An ax is an example of a wedge. To split a log, you pound the ax down. The shape of the wedge changes the downward force to sideways forces. The sideways forces split the log apart.

A screw is basically a twisted inclined plane. It has a *thread* that winds around a central rod. The thread sticks out from the body of the screw. Twisting the screw drives it downward or upward. Small screws help hold the pieces of objects together.

Continued on the next page

A knife is a wedge. It changes a downward force into sideways forces that split apart carrots.

Machines make life easier. But no machine can create energy out of nothing. There is always some sort of tradeoff. For example, pushing a box up an inclined plane takes less force than lifting the box. But the box has to move a greater distance. Cars are made of many simple machines put together. But a car cannot move on its own. The car needs to use fuel or a battery to spin its wheels.

Other articles to read include: **Factory; Inclined plane; Lever; Pulley; Screw; Tool; Wedge; Wheel and axle.**

Many everyday objects are actually simple machines. For example, a broom is a type of lever.

Machine tool

A machine tool is a powered machine for cutting and forming. Machine tools can cut metals and other materials into useful shapes. They can also bend, drill, grind, hammer, and squeeze such materials. Machine tools are much more exact than hand tools. People who use machine tools are called *machinists.* Many machine tools are controlled by computers.

Machine tools are used to make parts for automobiles, computers, televisions, and thousands of other products. Factory machines are also made with machine tools.

Machine tools come in a wide range of sizes. There are hundreds of kinds of machine tools. Some do one task, such as grinding or drilling. Others, called *machining centers,* carry out several kinds of tasks.

Other articles to read include: **Factory; Machine; Tool.**

Machine tools cut, grind, or form metals and other materials into useful shapes.

The mineral magnetite, also called lodestone, is a natural magnet that attracts iron and certain other metals.

Magnet

A magnet is an object that can draw in or push away certain other objects. A magnet works with a noticeable, invisible force. The force is most obvious in certain metals. Magnets are used as fasteners and clasps. Tiny magnets are used in electronic devices, including audio players, computers, phones, and televisions.

Magnets have many different shapes. The most common are bars, disks, squares, cylinders, and rectangles. A *horseshoe magnet* is a bar magnet bent into a U shape. No matter the shape, all magnets have two regions called *poles.* One side is called the *north* pole, and the other is the *south* pole. If two magnets are brought together, like poles will *repel* (push away) each other. For example, the two north poles will force each other away. If the poles are opposite, the magnets will attract each other. A north pole and a south pole will pull together.

There are three basic types of magnet. They are (1) permanent magnets, (2) temporary magnets, and (3) electromagnets.

Permanent magnets are common. They are the kind used in many magnetic toys. They are used to hold or pick up pins and paper clips. They are also used to hang notes on refrigerators.

Temporary magnets are usually pieces of metal that are not magnets on their own. They become magnetized when they touch a magnet. For example, if you hold a permanent magnet above a pile of paper clips, the pile will attach to the magnet. But not all of the paper clips need to touch the permanent magnet to be lifted. The paper clips that touch the magnet become temporary magnets. These in turn will attract more paper clips. When

Continued on the next page

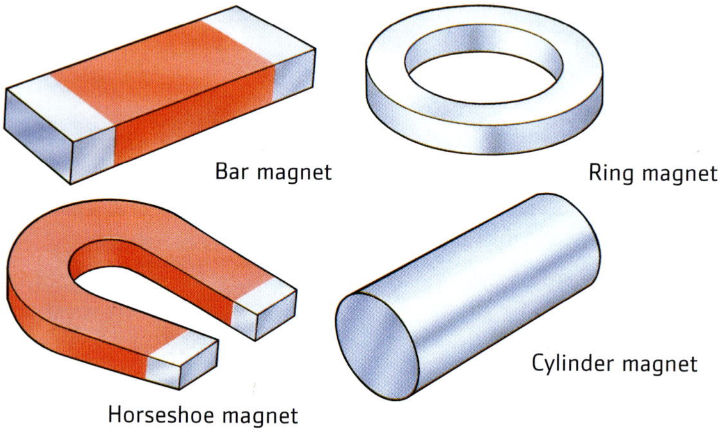

Magnets take many different shapes.

the magnet is pulled away from the pile, the paper clips stop attracting one another.

Electromagnets get their magnetism from *electric current* (the flow of electricity). The simplest electromagnets pass a current through a coil of wire. One end of the coil becomes the north pole of the electromagnet. The other end becomes the south pole. The poles switch position if the direction of the current is reversed. If the current is stopped, the coil loses its magnetism. This characteristic of electromagnets makes them useful as switches and in electric motors.

Some rocks, minerals, and meteorites are natural magnets. Earth, the sun, and many other objects in space are giant magnets. The most powerful magnets in the universe are *neutron stars,* the remains of exploded stars.

Other articles to read include: **Compass; Electric motor; Electromagnet; Magnetic levitation train.**

Magnetic levitation train

A magnetic levitation train floats above a track without touching it. The track is called a *guideway.* The train, called a *maglev* train for short, floats because of magnetic forces. Maglev trains are not slowed by friction—that is, the rubbing of wheels against a track. They are thus fast and quiet. The fastest maglev trains can travel well over 300 miles (480 kilometers) per hour.

There are two main kinds of maglev trains. They rely on two features of magnetic forces: *repulsion* (pushing away) and *attraction* (pulling toward).

Electrodynamic maglev trains use magnetic repulsion. Such trains are magnetically pushed away from guideways.

Electromagnetic maglev trains use magnetic attraction. Such trains are pulled upward from the ground.

Other articles to read include: **Electromagnet; Train.**

Magnetic repulsion holds an *electrodynamic maglev train* away from the *guideway* (track).

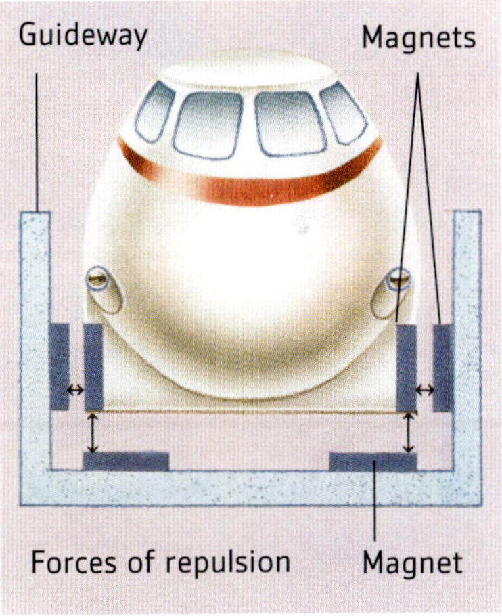

The world's first commercial maglev rail system began service in Shanghai, China, in 2004.

Magnifying glass

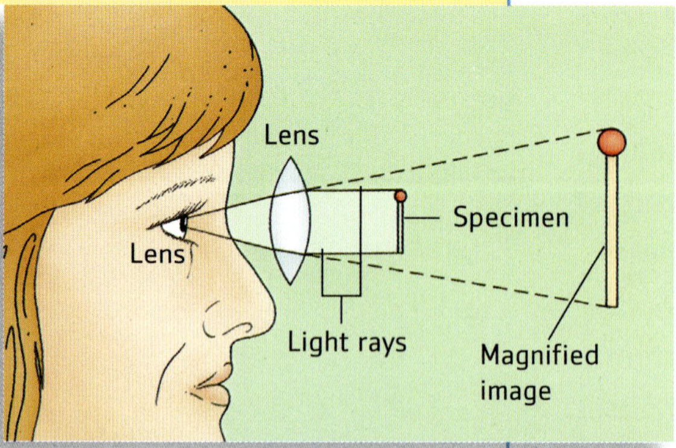

The lens of a magnifying glass bends light rays, making small objects look bigger.

A magnifying glass is a curved piece of clear glass or plastic. Looking through it can make small objects appear bigger. A magnifying glass is usually round. The glass or plastic is thin at the edge and thicker toward the middle. These variations in thickness change the way light passes through.

We see an object because light rays bounce off the object and enter our eyes. The light rays generally travel straight into our eyes. When the rays pass through a magnifying glass, the light rays are bent. The bending can make distant objects look bigger.

Other articles to read include: **Lens; Microscope.**

Map

A map is a drawing of an area or region. Maps may show countries, cities, streets, mountains, oceans, rivers, and many other parts of Earth. Maps have also been made of Earth's moon; of the planets Mars, Mercury, and Venus; and even of the night sky. People use maps to measure distances, plan trips, and find their way. Because Earth is round,

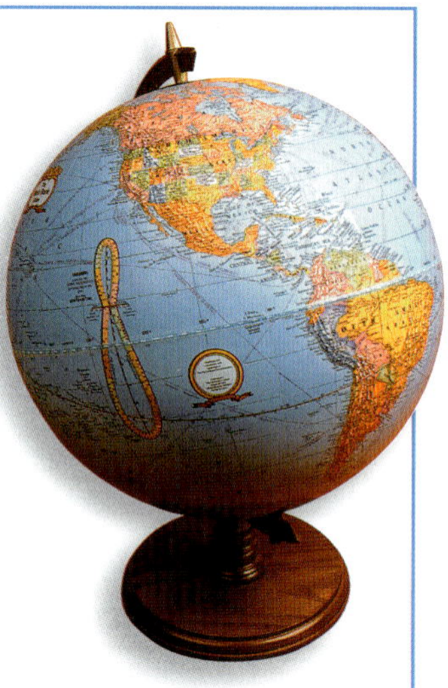

A *globe* is a round map. It shows the place and shape of areas precisely as they are on Earth.

Most maps that people use are flat. Certain areas must be stretched or shrunk on a flat map.

Continued on the next page

the most accurate way to show it is on a round map called a *globe.* But most maps are flat because flat maps are easy to carry, to print in books, and to display on computer screens.

There are many different kinds of maps. Each kind shows different things about an area. *General reference maps* help people find and describe places. They show mountains, prairies, lakes, rivers, roads, and cities. *Navigation maps,* also called *mobility maps,* show people how to find their way from one place to another on land, on water, or in the air. Road maps, street maps, and public transportation maps are navigation maps. A navigation map of a building is often called a *floor plan.* For example, an indoor mall will often have a floor plan near every entrance. This tells shoppers where the different stores are in the mall.

Thematic maps show how something is spread over an area. For example, a rainfall map shows which areas get much rain and which areas are dry. A *population map* shows where people live in an area.

Inventory maps show the exact place of a special feature. For example, they might show every school in a district, every campsite in a park, or every gold mine in a country.

Other articles to read include: **Global Positioning System; Globe; Navigation.**

1. A *general reference map* helps people find and identify many different features. This example includes land features as well as cities and countries.

2. A *mobility map,* such as a road map, helps people find their way from one place to another.

3. A *thematic map* shows a pattern for a particular feature. This population density map shows darker colors where more people live.

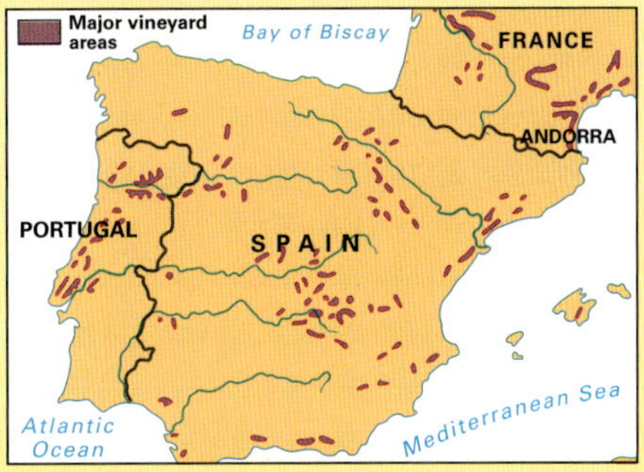

4. An *inventory map* shows the exact location of specific features. This map locates vineyards, where grapes are grown.

Guglielmo Marconi (standing) is shown with his assistant, G. S. Kemp, in the laboratory.

Marconi, Guglielmo

Guglielmo Marconi *(goo LYEHL moh mahr KOH nee)* (1874–1937) was an Italian inventor. He became famous for developing wireless telegraphy, today called radio.

Marconi was born in Bologna, Italy. He became interested in telegraph signals as a young man. At that time, the signals were sent through electric wires. Marconi wondered if he could send telegraph signals in waves through the air, without wires. After experimenting indoors and outdoors, he succeeded in 1895.

In 1901, Marconi sent the first wireless signals across the Atlantic Ocean, from England to Canada. He shared the 1909 Nobel Prize in physics with Karl Ferdinand Braun of Germany. Their work helped develop radio broadcasting.

In 1912, the crew of the sinking ship *Titanic* used Marconi's equipment to signal for help. The ship *Carpathia* heard the *Titanic*'s signal and came to the rescue. The *Carpathia* picked up 705 people and saved many lives.

Other articles to read include: **Radio; Telegraph.**

The Spirit rover explored the surface of Mars from 2004 to 2009, when it became stuck in loose dirt.

Mars Exploration Rover Mission

The Mars Exploration Rover Mission is a project to study Mars. It consists of two robotic *rovers* named Spirit and Opportunity. A rover is a vehicle that rolls around. The two rovers carry and use scientific instruments. These instruments were created by American and European scientists and engineers.

The mission's main goal is to gather evidence of ancient water on Mars. The surface of Mars appears dry and cold today. But orbiting spacecraft have found clues that Mars once might have been wetter and warmer. Scientists designed Spirit and Opportunity to identify and analyze dirt and rock on Mars for evidence of past water.

Continued on the next page

The rover Opportunity explored on the side of Mars opposite that explored by the Spirit rover.

The National Aeronautics and Space Administration (NASA) launched Spirit on June 10, 2003. Opportunity followed on July 7. Spirit landed on Jan. 4, 2004, in Gusev Crater. Opportunity landed three weeks later in Meridiani Planum, a broad plain on the planet's opposite side.

Spirit and Opportunity each have rolled over 4 miles (6 kilometers) on their investigations. They have found convincing evidence that the planet's surface and underground once held water.

The rovers were sent for a 90-day mission. But both Spirit and Opportunity continued to gather information for more than five years. In 2009, Spirit became trapped forever in a bed of loose dirt. Spirit continued to gather information for about two more years. Opportunity continued to move well and gather information from different areas.

Other articles to read include: **Space exploration.**

Mars Pathfinder

The Mars Pathfinder was a United States spacecraft. It sent images and other data from the surface of Mars for nearly three months in 1997. On July 4, 1997, Pathfinder "bounced-down" on the Ares Vallis flood plain of Mars. It bounced because part of its mission was to test a new landing system that used parachutes and airbags. Just before landing, the airbags inflated to completely enclose the spacecraft. This cushioning enabled

Continued on the next page

The Sojourner Rover, carried to Mars by the Pathfinder spacecraft, examined a Martian rock in 1997.

The Pathfinder mission tested a parachute and airbag landing system. The craft bounced to a successful landing.

Mars Pathfinder

Continued from the previous page

Pathfinder to land in a rocky valley filled with boulders.

After landing, Pathfinder released the Mars Sojourner Rover. The rover is a small, six-wheeled robot that analyzed the rocks and soil on Mars. The rover circled Pathfinder, roaming as far as 35 feet (12 meters) from the craft. The Pathfinder mission returned more than 16,500 images to scientists on Earth, about 550 of them from the rover. The photos included spectacular color pictures of the planet's surface and views of the planet's moons and the sun.

Pathfinder identified volcanic rocks that scientists had not expected to find on Mars. It also found that a cloud layer covered the Martian sky in the morning.

Other articles to read include: **Space exploration.**

Match

A match is a thin piece of cardboard or wood used to start fires. A match has a tip made of a special chemical mixture. This mixture burns easily. When the tip is rubbed against a special surface, the match bursts into flame. Some matches burn when rubbed against any rough surface. *Safety matches* must be rubbed against a special surface. The surface is often on the matchbox. The careless use of matches has caused many fires. All kinds of matches should be stored where children cannot reach them.

In 1827, an English pharmacist named John Walker invented a kind of match. Rubbing it against sandpaper caused a series of small explosions. The Swedish chemist Gustave E. Pasch invented the first safety matches in 1844. Joshua Pusey, a Philadelphia attorney, created the first book matches in 1892. In 1943, Raymond D. Cady, a chemist with the Diamond Match Company, produced a waterproof match. It could light after eight hours under water.

Other articles to read include: **Explosive.**

Safety matches light on fire when rubbed against a special surface, often part of the matchbox.

Materials

Materials are useful solid substances. Some materials are *natural materials*. They are found in nature and are not changed much when used. Such materials include stone and wood. Other materials, such as plastic, are not natural. They are *synthetic (sihn THEHT ihk) materials*. People make them by combining or changing natural materials. Rubber is a material that can be both natural and synthetic. Natural rubber comes from a tree. Synthetic rubber is produced from oil. Scientists who study and develop materials are called *materials scientists*.

Materials have many different qualities. Some materials are strong and heavy. Such materials include steel and concrete. Strength and weight make steel and concrete useful in building skyscrapers. Other projects require materials that are both strong and lightweight. Cars and airplanes are built with lighter metals and plastics, for example.

Glass is an important material, in part because light passes through it. Glass is made from sand and other minerals. Many kinds of plastics also let light pass through. Plastics are made from petroleum. They can be shaped into almost any form.

Continued on the next page

Wood from trees has long been used to build houses, ships, and furniture.

Leather and fur come from animals. These materials are used to make warm clothing.

Strong stone, such as marble, is often used in buildings, statues, and monuments.

Materials *Continued from the previous page*

Some materials, including many metals, carry electricity. These materials are called *conductors.* Wires are made of such conductors as copper. Other materials, such as plastic or rubber, block electricity. They are called *insulators.* Wires are often wrapped in insulators for protection. Some materials have qualities of both conductors and insulators. They are called *semiconductors.* Computer chips are made out of semiconductors.

Several kinds of synthetic materials are sometimes combined to make a new material. Glass fibers can be added to plastic to make *fiberglass,* for example. Fiberglass is a stiff, lightweight material. This material is used to make car parts, fishing rods, and boats.

All materials consist of extremely tiny particles called *atoms* and *molecules.* The atoms and molecules determine the material's qualities. They are like building blocks. To fit together, they form *chemical bonds* with one another. Materials scientists divide materials by the three kinds of chemical bonds they form. Metals form one kind of bond. *Ceramics*—like brick, cement, and glass—form another kind. Plastics form a third kind.

Other articles to read include: **Building construction; Cement and concrete; Glass; Metal; Plastics; Synthetics; Textile; Wood.**

Metals, such as iron, have many useful properties for modern buildings and technology.

Ceramics, such as bricks, are often strong and resistant to heat, but brittle.

Plastics are made from chemicals in petroleum. They can take on many shapes.

EXPERIMENT

Testing the properties of materials

! Make sure you ask a teacher or other adult to check that your tests are safe and to help you with your activities.

Materials are all around us. Some materials are natural. Others are synthetic (made by people). Some materials come from living things. Others come from minerals or are made from chemicals. People have relied on the amazing variety of materials to create all sorts of inventions, from ancient farm tools to skyscrapers to advanced computers.

Before we can use materials, we have to know their qualities (properties). Otherwise, we could make something from the wrong material, and it would not work properly. A good way to understand materials and their uses is to test their properties. Simple tests include heating, bending, hammering, scratching, and placing in water.

Try collecting 20 or more materials from in and around your home. It is best to start with simple materials like a piece of wood, a spoonful of salt, or a rock. Try not to collect things that are made up of more than one material.

What you need:

- 20 or more samples of different materials (wood, salt, a rock, a leaf, aluminum foil)
- a baking tray
- an oven
- a piece of cloth
- a hammer
- a bowl
- water
- pen or pencil
- paper

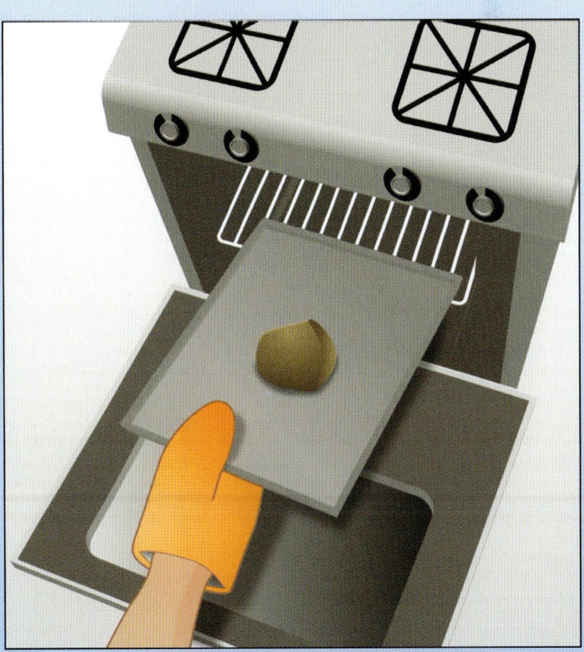

1. Place a small sample on a baking tray and place it in a cold oven. Heat up the oven, then switch it off and wait until it is cool before removing the sample. Do this with adult supervision.

Continued on the next page

EXPERIMENT

Testing the properties of materials *Continued from the previous page*

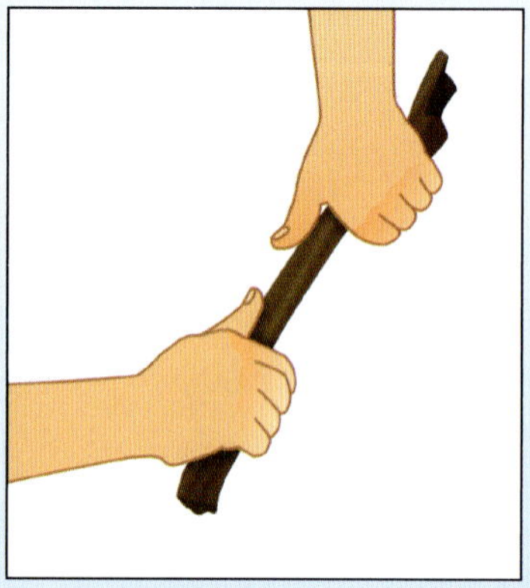

2. Try bending a larger sample with your hands.

3. Wrap each sample in a cloth and hit it with a hammer. Does it shatter? Do this with adult supervision.

4. Leave each sample in a bowl of water. Does it float or sink? Does it change if you leave it there for a few days?

5. When you have tested your materials, fill in the results on your data sheet. Your list of results will show the different properties of the materials.

	Material	Heating not burning	Bending	Hammering	Adding water	Natural, artificial, or both	Metallic, non-metallic, or both
1.	wood	burns	splinters	dents	floats	natural	non-metallic
2.	salt	nothing	—	powders	dissolves	natural	metallic
3.	rock						
4.	leaf						
5.	twig						
6.	aluminum foil						
7.							
8.							

The data sheet will help you to organize your collection and to discover the properties of each material. Some materials have already been written down and described on the sheet to show you how. Draw up your own data sheet using these ideas as a starting point. With practice, you can invent your own tests to suit the types of materials in your collection. If you do invent your own test, always check with an adult first, to make sure it is safe to do.

http://bit.ly/UKZyq6

McAuliffe, Christa

Christa McAuliffe *(muh KAW lihf)* (1948–1986) was chosen to become the first schoolteacher to travel in space. McAuliffe was selected by the National Aeronautics and Space Administration (NASA). She was chosen from more than 11,000 teachers who had asked for the job. She planned to record her thoughts and experiences before, during, and after her space flight. McAuliffe flew aboard the space shuttle Challenger on Jan. 28, 1986. The shuttle was destroyed in an accident shortly after take-off. The accident killed McAuliffe and the six other crew members.

Sharon Christa Corrigan was born on Sept. 2, 1948, in Boston. She married Steven McAuliffe in 1970. They had two children. McAuliffe earned a bachelor's degree from Framingham State College in 1970. She received a master's degree in education from Bowie State College in 1978. From 1982 until her death, McAuliffe taught social studies at Concord High School in Concord, New Hampshire.

Other articles to read include: **Astronaut; Space exploration.**

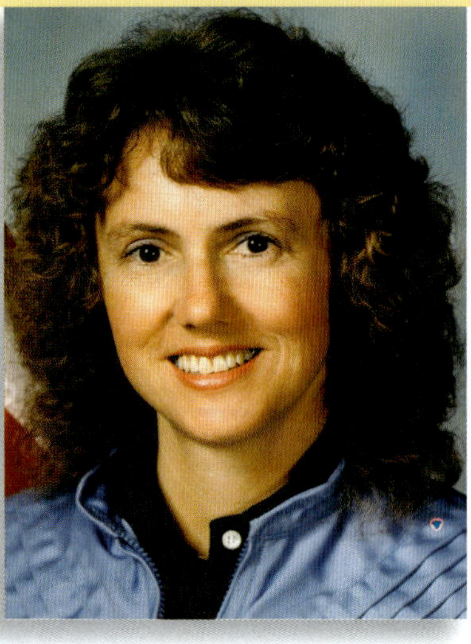

Christa McAuliffe

Mechanical drawing

A *mechanical drawing* shows the exact measurements of an object from different angles.

A mechanical drawing is a precise picture of a structure or object. Buildings and bridges are built using mechanical drawings. The same is true for every automobile and refrigerator.

A mechanical drawing shows how an object should look, much as might a sketch. But mechanical drawings are more exact than sketches. They include measurements. They also show objects from different views—such as from the top and sides.

People used to draw mechanical drawings on paper. They used such tools as compasses, protractors, and T squares. Today, much mechanical drawing is done on computers. Making mechanical drawings on a computer is called *computer-aided design* (CAD). CAD provides many advantages over traditional design methods. For example, an architect can use CAD to "walk through" a model of a building before construction begins.

Other articles to read include: **Building construction; Computer; Engineering.**

Metal

Metals are the most numerous kind of *chemical element.* A chemical element is a material made up of one kind of atom. Metals make up a large part of Earth.

Metals and *alloys* (mixtures of metals) are some of the most important materials in modern life. Strong steel frames hold up skyscrapers and other buildings. Automobiles, ships, and airplanes are made from metals and alloys. So are computers, electronics, batteries, and even some medicines. People have long made weapons and armor out of metal. Plants and animals both need small amounts of certain metals to stay healthy.

Many metals are shiny. They reflect light. Metals are also good *conductors* (carriers) of electricity and heat. Most metals can be hammered into thin sheets or stretched out into wires.

Other articles to read include: **Alloy; Bronze; Materials; Mining; Steel; Welding; Wire.**

At a *foundry,* metal is melted and poured into molds to form certain shapes.

Steel, like many metals and alloys, can be rolled and squeezed into thin sheets.

Metals are used to make automobiles as well as the machines that build them.

EXPERIMENT

Testing for metal

Do not use a high-power battery for this experiment—it will make the wires very hot.

Look around your home. How many different metals can you find? The most common metals are aluminum and iron. You may also find some copper or gold. Other materials are *alloys*—that is, mixtures of metals. Alloys include brass, steel, and bronze.

Metals have several properties that make them different from nonmetals. You can sort metal materials from nonmetal materials by testing them. For example, many kinds of metals can bend easily. Metals also typically get hot quickly. And metals are conductors—that is, electricity passes through them. Some nonmetal materials may have one or two of these properties. For example, certain plastics bend easily. But plastics do not get hot easily or carry electricity. Only metals have all three of these properties.

Here is a test that you can do to see how well an electric current passes through different elements.

1. Cut three pieces of wire about 6 inches (15 centimeters) long. Attach the end of one piece to the battery. Fix the other end to the bulb with the tape.

http://bit.ly/14HZqZO

What you need:

- scissors
- some plastic-coated copper wire
- tape
- a 1.5-volt (D) battery
- a 1.5-volt light bulb in a light bulb holder
- a steel spoon
- some iron nails
- some nickel coins
- a piece of charcoal

2. Attach another piece of wire to the other side of the battery. Fix the third piece of wire to the other side of the bulb with the tape. Wind the two free ends of the wire around two iron nails.

3. Check that the electric circuit is wired correctly by touching the tips of the nails together. The bulb should light up. Now test your spoon, nails, coins, and charcoal by placing the tips of the nails at each end of the substance.

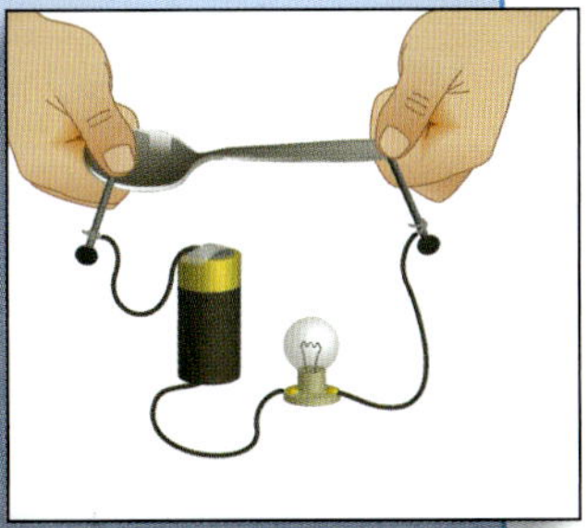

What's going on:

When you have finished testing the items, you should notice that some of the results are the same. All the metals light up the bulb. They are good electrical conductors. One substance is a nonmetal. It will not light up the bulb.

A metal detector gives off a sound or other signal when it is brought near metal.

Metal detector

A metal detector *(dih TEHK tuhr)* is used to find hidden or lost metal. It is an electronic device. A metal detector gives off a sound, a visual signal, or a vibration when it finds metal.

Police officers and airport security people use metal detectors to check for hidden weapons. Treasure hunters use metal detectors to find lost coins and other valuable metals. Metal detectors are also used by *archaeologists (AHR kee OL uh jihsts),* scientists who study objects left behind by people long ago.

Metal detectors have different sizes and shapes. They may be small enough to hold in the hand. Or, they may be large enough for a person to walk through.

Other articles to read include: **Metal.**

Microphone

A microphone changes sound into electrical signals. The signals travel over wires or through the air. The signals may travel to a recording device. The signals can also be played through a *loudspeaker.* The loudspeaker changes the signals back to sound. A telephone has both a microphone and a loudspeaker, for example.

Some entertainers and speakers hold microphones in their hands. Some people prefer to use microphones on stands. An electrical cord connects such a microphone to an electrical outlet. Many performers use cordless microphones. Such microphones enable them to move around on a stage without getting tangled in wires. People on television often use tiny microphones that attach to clothing.

The first microphone was a telephone developed by Alexander Graham Bell in 1876. Today, microphones are widely used. Microphones pick up sound from bands at concerts. They are used to record television shows and motion pictures. Many computers and other electronic devices have built-in microphones.

Other articles to read include: **Bell, Alexander Graham; Telephone.**

Microphones change sound waves into electrical signals. The waves vibrate a *diaphragm.* These vibrations are converted to patterns of electric current.

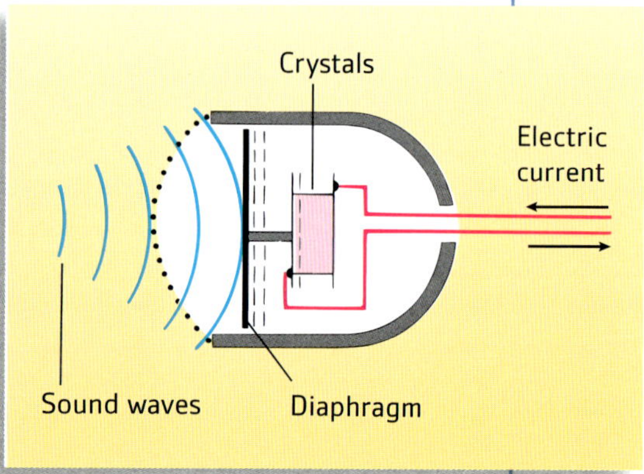

Microscope

Microscopes are devices that make tiny things look bigger. Microscopes are one of the most important tools of science. They are used by many kinds of scientists. For example, a doctor may use a microscope to look at a cell. Computer chips have structures that can only be seen with microscopes.

Optical microscopes use one or more lenses, or curved pieces of glass. The lenses bend the light rays that pass through the microscope. The bending of the light rays makes the object appear large enough for study.

Other kinds of microscopes use beams of *electrons.* Electrons are tiny bits of matter. Electron microscopes can show far smaller objects than can optical microscopes.

Other articles to read include: **Electron microscope; Lens; Magnifying glass.**

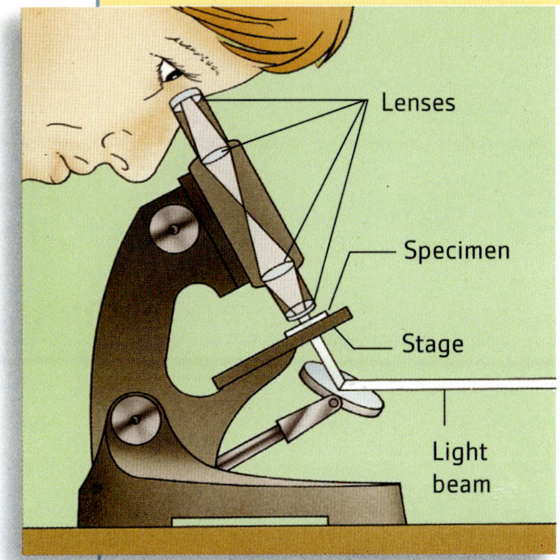

An *optical microscope* bends light rays that pass through a specimen. The bent light makes the specimen appear much bigger.

Microsoft Corporation

Microsoft Corporation is a company that makes computer *software.* Software is the programs or instructions used by a computer. Microsoft is one of the largest software makers. It also makes a popular video game system called the Xbox. Microsoft's headquarters are in Redmond, Washington.

Microsoft was started by Bill Gates and Paul Allen. In 1975, they began to design programs for personal computers (PC's). At the time, PC's had just become available. Gates and Allen founded Microsoft that year. In 1980, International Business Machines Corporation (IBM) chose Microsoft to develop the *operating system* for its first personal computer. An operating system is the main program for controlling a computer's functions.

In 1985, Microsoft introduced an operating system called Windows. Windows enabled people to control a computer by pointing and clicking with a computer mouse. Older operating systems relied on complicated typed instructions. Windows also let people perform multiple tasks, each in a different "window" on the computer screen. Microsoft also makes other software products. Excel is a Microsoft program used to organize numerical and financial information. Word is a program used to type, edit, and print documents. PowerPoint helps people to create presentations.

Other articles to read include: **Computer; Electronic game; Gates, Bill; International Business Machines Corporation.**

Microwave oven

Microwave ovens are devices that heat food quickly. Microwave ovens produce a form of energy called *microwaves.* This energy causes tiny bits of matter in food to move quickly. The bits of matter move and rub together, producing heat. The heat cooks the food.

Water absorbs microwaves easily. Most food, even solid food, contains large amounts of water. Unlike conventional ovens or stoves, microwaves do not cook food from the outside in. Microwaves, however, cannot pass all the way into thick pieces of food.

Microwaves can pass through glass, paper, and most kinds of plates and plastics. But metal objects should never be used in a microwave, because they cause sparking.

Microwave ovens heat food using an invisible form of energy.

Mining

Mining is the taking of minerals and other substances from the ground. People mine iron for use in buildings, cars, refrigerators, and many other things. People mine salt for food and coal for fuel. Gold, silver, and diamonds come from mines. People mine stone for buildings and gravel for roads, too.

There are many ways of mining. Some minerals lie at or near the planet's surface. They include gold, tin, and copper. Limestone, *gypsum (JIHP suhm),* and mica come from surface mines called *quarries.* Sand, gravel, and large stones also are mined in quarries.

Some minerals are deeper underground. They include lead, potash, salt, and *uranium (yu RAY nee uhm).* Coal is also mined underground. Some minerals are dissolved in oceans and seas. They include salt, *magnesium (mag NEE zee uhm),* and sulfur. Other minerals are found scattered among rocks and gravel. Still others are found in large masses.

Continued on the next page

Most miners today use machines and heavy equipment in their work. High-power drills dig holes to reach *ore* (rock that contains desirable minerals). Other machines dig out the ore. Power shovels load the ore into trucks and trains. In underground mines, elevators called *skips* carry ore to the surface. Miners use pumps to take minerals from seas and oceans. They sometimes use explosives to break up large masses of hard rock that contain ore.

It takes many people to operate a mine. Among the workers in mines are geologists, chemists, engineers, computer specialists, electricians, truck drivers, and inspectors.

Other articles to read include: **Alloy; Materials; Metal.**

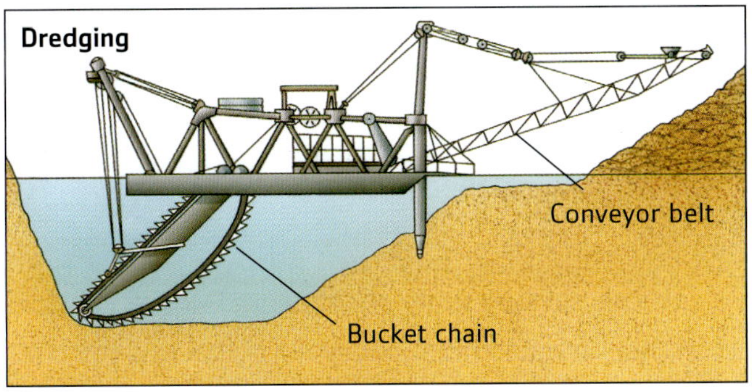

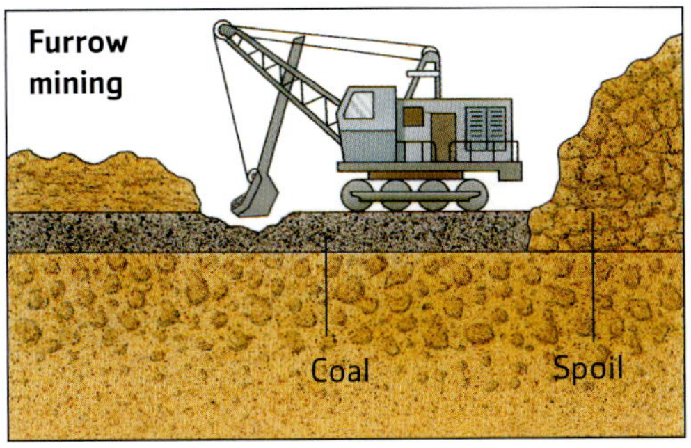

Surface mining removes materials that are close to Earth's surface. In *dredging* (top), machines scoop loose sand or gravel from a lake or pond. They separate useful minerals from the sand or gravel. In *furrow mining* (above), workers dig up a shallow layer of flat ground to reach coal or other minerals below. They pile up the *spoil* (waste) behind.

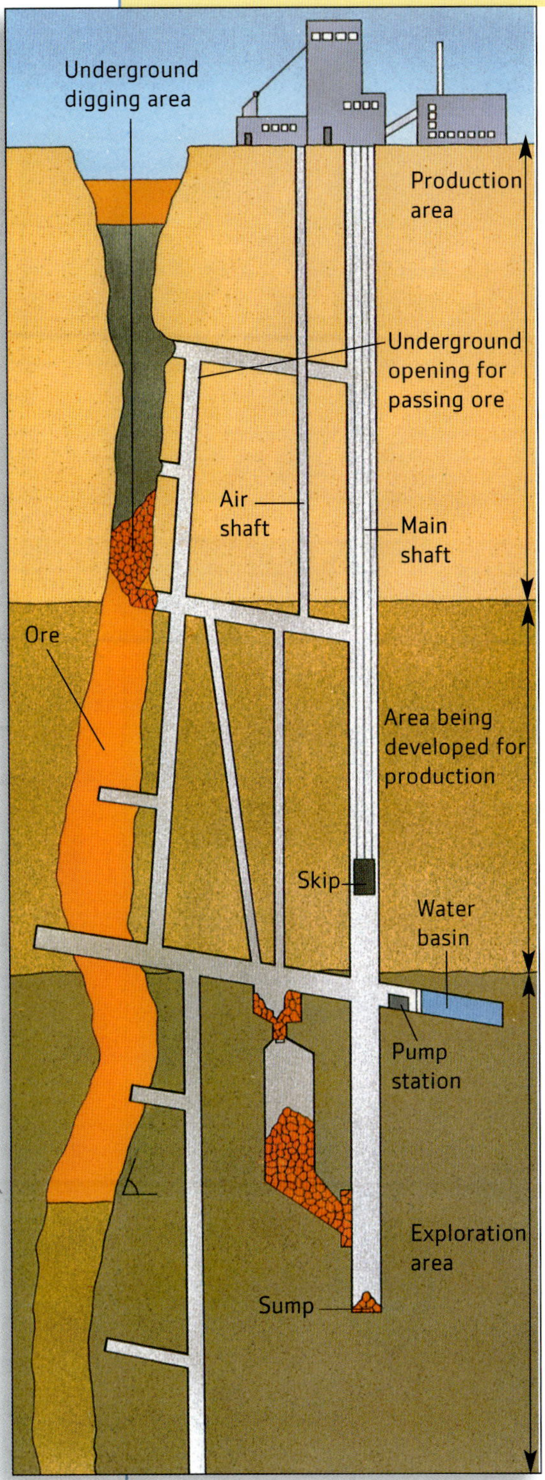

A *shaft mine* is a system of horizontal and vertical passages through which ore is removed and hauled to the surface.

In 1995, the space shuttle Atlantis became the first United States spacecraft to link up with Russia's Mir space station.

Mir

Mir *(meer)* was a long-running space station built by the Soviet Union. Mir was made up of several units, called *modules*. The modules were launched separately. The first module went up in 1986. The space station was destroyed in 2001. *Mir* is the Russian word for *peace*.

The Soviet Union began to put Mir together during its "space race" with the United States. The Soviets wanted to operate Mir for five years. But the country collapsed in 1991. The Russians decided to leave Mir in space longer. During one period, the station was occupied by at least one person for almost 10 straight years.

Russia ended the Mir program in March 2001. It sent Mir into Earth's atmosphere, causing it to burn up.

Other articles to read include: **Satellite, Artificial; Space exploration.**

Mirror

A mirror is a smooth surface that reflects light. When you look into a mirror, the light bounces back into your eyes. You see the light as an image in the mirror.

Mirrors create sharp, clear reflections because they are both smooth and shiny. Shiny surfaces reflect light well. Smooth surfaces reflect light in a uniform direction. The uniform lines produce a clear reflection. Rough surfaces, such as shiny rocks, also reflect light. But they scatter light in all directions. No reflection is formed. The moon, for example, shines at night because it reflects sunlight. But it is too rough to be a mirror.

Many mirrors are made of smooth glass backed with shiny silver or aluminum. The glass supports the metal and protects its shiny surface. Many mirrors in scientific instruments have the metal coating in front of the glass. A polished sheet of metal—without glass—can also serve as a mirror. A flat sheet of water, such as a calm, clear lake on a sunny day, can also act like a mirror.

Other articles to read include: **Lens; Microscope; Telescope.**

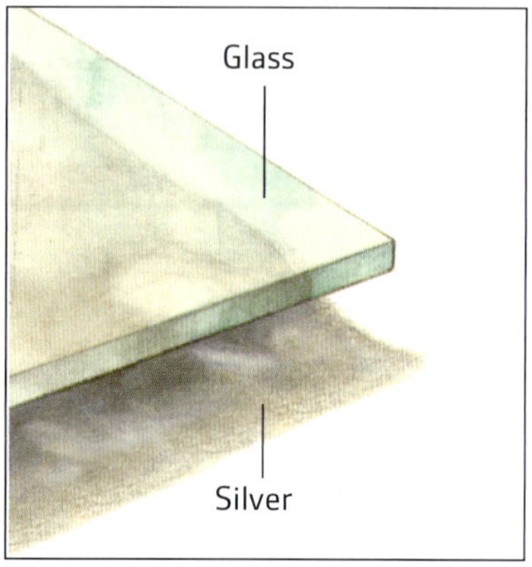

A mirror has a thin layer of shiny silver or aluminum behind a sheet of smooth glass. The shininess and smoothness contribute to a clear reflection.

Modem

Modems are small machines that send data from one computer to another computer. People use modems to connect to the Internet.

Some modems work through telephone lines. They change data into sounds. Other modems send data through cable television lines. Certain modems are *wireless.* They can send data over radio waves. People can buy or rent modems from *Internet service providers* (ISP's).

Other articles to read include: **Computer; Internet; Telephone; Wireless communication.**

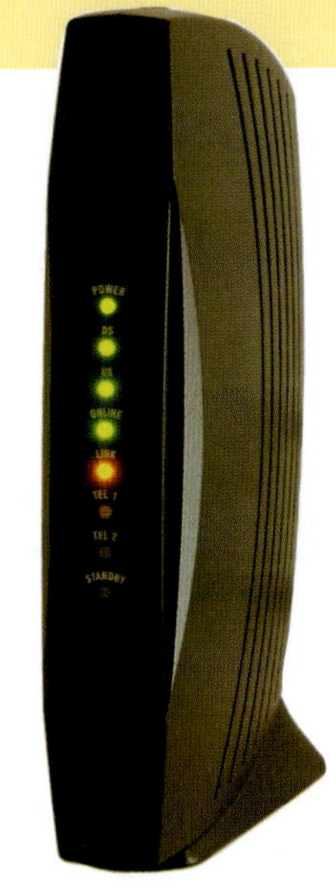

A *cable modem* can connect computers to the Internet via cable television lines.

Montgolfier brothers

The Montgolfier *(mont GAHL fee uhr* or *mawn gawl FYAY)* brothers built the first hot-air balloons. The brothers were French papermakers. Joseph Michel Montgolfier was born on Aug. 26, 1740. Jacques Étienne Montgolfier was born on Jan. 7, 1745.

The brothers experimented with large bags filled with hot gases. The gases came from burning wool and moist straw. Because hot air is lighter than cold air, the cloth bags rose.

The brothers first launched a balloon in 1782. In September 1783, they launched a balloon carrying a sheep, a duck, and a rooster. King Louis XVI watched the balloon float up into the air. In November, a French scientist and a French nobleman flew for about 25 minutes above Paris in one of the Montgolfiers' balloons. It marked the first human flight through the air in history.

Other articles to read include: **Airship; Balloon.**

The Montgolfier brothers built one of the first hot-air balloons. It was launched at a public gathering in Annonay, France, on June 4, 1783.

Garrett Augustus Morgan (above) patented a gas mask in 1912. It had an airtight canvas hood worn over the head (right).

Morgan, Garrett Augustus

Garrett Augustus Morgan (1877–1963) was an African American inventor. He developed a number of devices that improved safety. They include versions of the gas mask and the traffic light.

Morgan was born on March 4, 1877, in Paris, Kentucky. He moved to Cleveland in 1895. In 1912, Morgan developed a new gas mask. It had an airtight canvas hood that was worn over the head. The hood was connected to a special breathing tube. Many police departments and fire departments throughout the United States used Morgan's gas mask. In 1916, Morgan used his device to rescue more than 20 trapped workers. They were stuck in a smoke-filled water tunnel in Cleveland.

In 1923, Morgan patented his version of the traffic light. The light was different from those in use today. But it did use red, yellow, and green lights.

Other articles to read include: **Gas mask; Invention.**

Morse, Samuel Finley Breese

Samuel Finley Breese Morse (1791–1872) was an American inventor and painter. He and his partners built the first practical *telegraph.* Their machine used electric signals to send messages across great distances over wires. Before that time, some of the fastest messages were delivered by messengers on horseback. Morse also invented a code that used dots and dashes to spell out the messages. It is called Morse code.

Morse was born in Charlestown, Massachusetts. He studied science in college, but his love was art. He became a respected portrait painter. But he did not make enough

Continued on the next page

money to earn a living. In the mid-1830's, he began to experiment with the telegraph. Morse hoped to develop a whole system of telegraphs that would stretch across the United States.

In 1843, Congress paid Morse and his partners to build a test telegraph wire between Baltimore, Maryland, and Washington, D.C. On May 24, 1844, Morse successfully sent the message "What hath God wrought!" Although the telegraph worked, the government would not pay to build more telegraph lines. Morse and his business partners developed a telegraph network themselves.

Other articles to read include: **Invention; Morse code; Telegraph.**

Samuel Finley Breese Morse received a patent for the first successful electric telegraph in the United States. He also invented Morse code.

Morse code

Morse code is a system for sending messages. It was developed by the American inventor Samuel Finley Breese Morse.

Morse wanted to find a way to send messages over wires. The wires could carry electric signals. He needed a code so that the person receiving the signals could understand the message.

Morse's code used short and long pulses to stand for letters, numbers, and other characters. The short and long pulses were written on paper as dots and dashes. For example, one of the most famous messages in Morse code is *SOS*. *SOS* is a signal that the person sending the message is in danger. *SOS* is written ● ● ● ▬ ▬ ▬ ● ● ● in Morse code.

Morse built a machine called a *telegraph* to send messages across wires. He sent the first telegraph message in 1844.

Other articles to read include: **Morse, Samuel Finley Breese; Telegraph.**

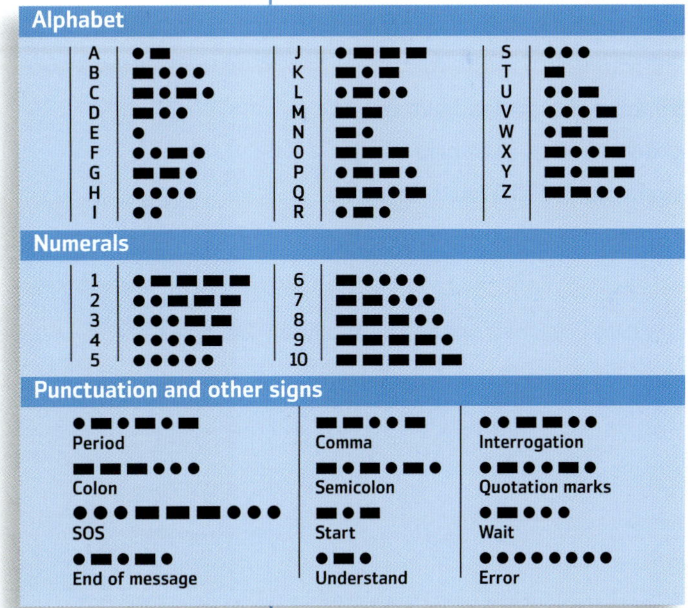

International Morse code consists of short and long pulses, which are written out as dots and dashes.

This motorcycle is made for traveling on streets and roads.

Motorcycle

A motorcycle *(MOH tuhr SY kuhl)* is an engine-powered vehicle with two or three wheels. The engine is between the front and back wheels. It runs on gasoline. People ride motorcycles for fun, for sport, and to get around. Many people call motorcycles "bikes."

There are two main kinds of motorcycles. One kind is made for riding on streets and roads. This kind includes street bikes, touring bikes, and motor scooters. The other kind is made for riding on rougher surfaces. *Trail bikes,* for example, can travel on rough roads, climb hills, and cross streams. Their tires have deep grooves that grip rough surfaces. *Mopeds* are small motorcycles that are started by pedaling.

Motorcycles have tires that are somewhat like automobile tires. The tires have grooves that help keep them from slipping when going around turns. Motorcycles have front and rear brakes. The rider controls the motorcycle with hand controls and foot pedals.

The gasoline-powered motorcycle was invented by Gottlieb Daimler, a German engineer, in 1885. He attached an engine to a bicycle frame.

Other articles to read include: **Bicycle; Daimler, Gottlieb; Gasoline engine; Tire.**

Some motorcycles have deeply grooved tires that grip rough surfaces for off-road riding.

Nanotechnology

Nanotechnology *(NAN oh tehk NOL uh jee)* is the making and use of extremely small structures. Such structures are only slightly larger than atoms and molecules—the basic building blocks of matter. The name *nanotechnology* comes from a measurement called the *nanometer.* A nanometer is 0.000000001 meter ($\frac{1}{25,400,000}$ inch), about $\frac{1}{100,000}$ the width of a human hair.

Nanotechnology includes the production of useful items called *nanoparticles.* Nanoparticles are 1 to 100 nanometers across. They have many uses. For example, they are used in sunscreen to scatter harmful rays from the sun. They are also used in paints and food packaging. *Nanocomposites* may combine nanoparticles and other materials, such as plastics. They can be stronger and lighter than the original materials. *Nanodevices* are extremely tiny machines.

Richard Feynman, an American physicist, first described the concept of nanotechnology. He gave a lecture about it in 1959, called "There's Plenty of Room at the Bottom." Practical demonstrations of nanotechnology began appearing in the 1980's and 1990's. By the 2010's, some computer chips contained parts built with nanotechnology.

Other articles to read include: **Computer chip; Engineering.**

National Aeronautics and Space Administration (NASA)

The National Aeronautics and Space Administration (NASA) is a United States government agency. It researches flight within and beyond Earth's atmosphere. NASA has thousands of scientists, engineers, and technicians. One of NASA's major facilities is the John F. Kennedy Space Center on Merritt Island, in Florida. Another is the Lyndon B. Johnson Space Center in Houston.

In 1957, President Dwight D. Eisenhower gave responsibility for a United States space program to the National Advisory Committee for Aeronautics (NACA). NACA had been founded in 1915. NACA became NASA in 1958. Its headquarters are in Washington, D.C. NASA has launched many space flights. Some have carried

Continued on the next page

National Aeronautics and Space Administration (NASA) *Continued from the previous page*

astronauts and some have not. The flights without astronauts have included artificial satellites and space probes. These craft are used for scientific research and for such things as communication systems and weather forecasting.

In 1969, NASA's Apollo 11 spacecraft became the first craft to land human beings on the moon. In 1981, NASA launched Columbia, the first space shuttle. In 1986, however, NASA suffered one of the worst accidents in its history. The shuttle Challenger broke apart shortly after launch. All seven crew members were killed.

In 1993, the United States and Russia agreed to work toward the construction of a space station. It became known as the International Space Station (ISS).

In 2003, the shuttle Columbia broke apart as it reentered Earth's atmosphere. All seven crew members were killed. NASA introduced new safety measures after the accident.

NASA's space exploration goals include more missions to the moon, possibly to an asteroid, and, eventually, to Mars. NASA is working on several new space vehicles. It is working with private companies to achieve many of its goals.

Over the years, NASA has started and supported many science programs. These programs do not only involve space flight. They also involve astronomy, aviation, *meteorology* (the study of weather), oceanography, and many other fields.

Other articles to read include: **Astronaut; Challenger disaster; Columbia disaster; Kennedy Space Center; Satellite, Artificial; Space exploration.**

A NASA astronaut works in space on the International Space Station (ISS). NASA helped build the ISS.

Thousands of scientists, technicians, and engineers work for NASA.

National Air and Space Museum

Historic aircraft are displayed at the National Air and Space Museum's Steven F. Udvar-Hazy Center at Washington Dulles International Airport in Virginia.

The National Air and Space Museum, in Washington, D.C., features exhibits on *aviation* (flying) and space flight. It is part of the Smithsonian Institution. The museum holds the largest collection of historic aircraft and spacecraft in the world. It has more than 20 galleries, a theater, and a planetarium. Its displays include the Wright brothers' 1903 *Flyer;* Charles A. Lindbergh's *Spirit of St. Louis;* X-1 and X-15 aircraft; and Mercury, Gemini, and Apollo spacecraft. Museum visitors can touch a rock from the moon and walk through a space station.

The museum sponsors and conducts research into the history, science, and technology of aviation and space flight. Further museum research includes planetary science, geology, and geophysics.

Congress created the National Air Museum in 1946. The museum was given its present name in 1966. The museum's main building opened in 1976. In 2003, the museum opened the Steven F. Udvar-Hazy Center at Washington Dulles International Airport in Virginia. The center displays many more artifacts. These artifacts include the Lockheed SR-71 Blackbird, the Boeing B-29 Superfortress *Enola Gay,* and the space shuttle Discovery. The museum pieces are maintained and restored at the Paul E. Garber Preservation, Restoration, and Storage Facility in Suitland, Maryland.

Other articles to read include: **Airplane; Space exploration.**

Navigation

Navigation *(NAV uh GAY shuhn)* is the practice of finding and guiding people or objects. Captains must navigate ships and airplanes. Spacecraft have complex navigation equipment. People also use navigation to drive cars or to walk around cities. The person who does the navigating is called a *navigator (NAV uh GAY tuhr)*. Today, computers and satellites help people navigate easily.

The word *navigate* comes from two Latin words meaning *ship* and *to drive.* Ships at sea once relied on expert navigators. Otherwise, they might easily become lost. Basic navigation tools include a chart and a compass. A compass is used to find north, south, east, and west.

An early navigation method was called *dead reckoning.* To use dead reckoning, the navigator must know exactly where a ship was at a certain time. The navigator then figures out how fast and which way the ship has gone since then. The navigator can then use the time difference to figure out where the ship has gone.

Continued on the next page

A device called a *sextant* measures the angle between the horizon and objects in the sky. This angle helps a navigator to determine position.

Global Positioning System (GPS) devices are used by automobile drivers to track their location. The devices use radio signals from satellites to determine position.

Airplane pilots use many radio and computerized devices to keep track of a plane's position and direction.

Another method is called *piloting.* In piloting, the navigator uses a landmark, such as a floating marker called a *buoy (BOO ee),* to find out where a ship is. The buoy is marked on a special map called a *chart.* The navigator figures out how far the ship is from the buoy and in which direction. Using a chart and other tools, the navigator can then see exactly where the ship is.

Navigators can also use the sky. The position of the stars, sun, and moon in the sky can help the navigator figure out where a ship is on Earth.

Modern navigators use radio signals. The Global Positioning System (GPS) helps people navigate easily. It is a system of satellites that orbit Earth. The satellites beam down radio signals. These signals can be picked up by devices on ships, cars, and even phones. The device uses the signals to tell its location.

Other articles to read include: **Airplane; Compass; Global Positioning System; Map; Radar; Satellite, Artificial; Ship; Sonar.**

Nitroglycerin

Nitroglycerin is used as both an explosive and as a medicine. This spray bottle of nitroglycerin can help treat chest pain.

Nitroglycerin *(NY truh GLIHS uhr ihn)* is a powerful explosive. It is used in dynamite. It is also used as heart medicine.

Nitroglycerin was discovered in 1846 by Ascanio Sobrero, an Italian chemist. But nitroglycerin was not reliable as an explosive. Almost 20 years later, the Swedish chemist Alfred Nobel found a way to use nitroglycerin safely. Nobel called his invention *dynamite.* It became the most widely used explosive until the 1950's.

Sobrero also tasted nitroglycerin. It gave him a terrible headache. Doctors knew of another substance called *amyl nitrite.* It also caused bad headaches. But it helped people with chest pains. This led them to try nitroglycerin as a medicine. Today, doctors treat chest pain with nitroglycerin.

Other articles to read include: **Dynamite; Explosive.**

Nuclear reactor

A nuclear *(NOO klee uhr)* reactor is a device that maintains controlled *nuclear reactions.* Such reactions involving splitting or combining the *nuclei* (cores) of atoms. Nuclear reactions give off tremendous energy, which can be used to make electric power.

In most reactors, rods of uranium are held close together. The nucleus of a uranium atom is large and easy to split. This splitting process is called *nuclear fission.* When one uranium nucleus splits, the pieces fly off and split other atoms nearby.

Nuclear reactors in a power plant split atoms to generate electric power.

The energy from fission creates a great deal of heat. The heat boils water in the reactor, creating steam. The hot steam, in turn, spins machines called *turbines.* The spinning turbines generate electric power.

In a nuclear reactor, the fission is highly controlled. It happens at a steady pace. Special *control rods* can also quickly stop the fission. Reactors differ from nuclear weapons, which release all their energy at once.

Other articles to read include: **Electric power; Nuclear waste; Turbine.**

Nuclear waste

Nuclear *(NOO klee uhr)* waste is leftover material from a nuclear power plant. Most nuclear power plants start with the element uranium as a fuel. The *nuclei* (cores) of uranium atoms are split in a device called a *nuclear reactor.* The splitting releases energy. The energy is used to make electric power.

When uranium atoms split apart, the pieces form *radioactive* elements. Radioactive elements release dangerous energy for a long time—sometimes thousands of years. They can cause cancer and other deadly health problems.

Nuclear wastes are hard to get rid of safely. The radioactive materials continue to give off heat. Most nuclear power plants store their wastes in pools of water not far from the plant. The water helps keep the waste cool. After several years, the waste can be moved to air-cooled concrete containers. But it still remains dangerous.

Hazardous wastes; Nuclear reactor.

Nuclear weapon

A nuclear *(NOO klee uhr)* weapon is the most dangerous and destructive kind of weapon. Its energy comes from changes in the *nuclei* (cores) of atoms. Atoms are the basic building blocks of matter. A single nuclear weapon could kill millions of people. A large nuclear war could ruin Earth's climate.

Only two nuclear weapons have ever been used in war. They were dropped on Japan by the United States at the end of World War II (1939–1945). The bombs killed tens of thousands of people. After the war, the United States and the Soviet Union built thousands more nuclear weapons. Many were far more powerful than the weapons used against Japan.

There are two main kinds of nuclear weapons. *Fission weapons* split apart nuclei. They are also called *atomic bombs.* When a nucleus splits, it releases a huge amount of energy. The two bombs dropped on Japan were fission weapons.

Thermonuclear weapons are far more powerful than fission weapons. They make energy by *fusing* (combining) hydrogen nuclei. The great heat and light from the sun comes from the same kind of reaction. Thermonuclear weapons are also called *fusion weapons* or *hydrogen bombs.*

A nuclear explosion causes several effects. The explosion creates a huge fireball. A *blast wave,* also called a *shock wave,* shoots out in all directions. The wave's pressure collapses buildings. The explosion also sends out rays of light and heat. The rays can burn skin and start fires. These effects depend on the weapon's power, the weather, and the terrain. The blast and heat from a medium-sized weapon could largely destroy several miles or kilometers around the explosion.

Other effects are deadly long after the explosion. The fireball expands to a mushroom-shaped cloud. The cloud contains *radioactive* dust and debris. Such material gives off dangerous energy for a long time. The radioactive material eventually falls to the ground. This *fallout* can spread far and wide. It can cause cancer.

The United States and Russia have most of the world's nuclear weapons. China, France, India, Israel, Pakistan, and the United Kingdom also have nuclear weapons. South Africa once devel-

Continued on the next page

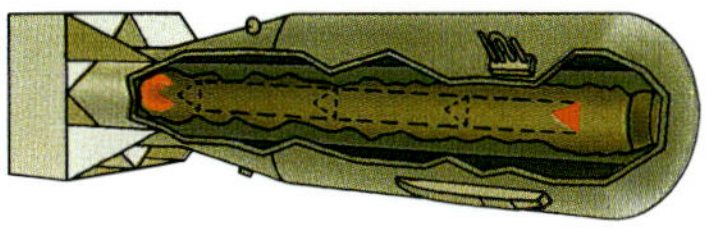

Gun-type fission weapon

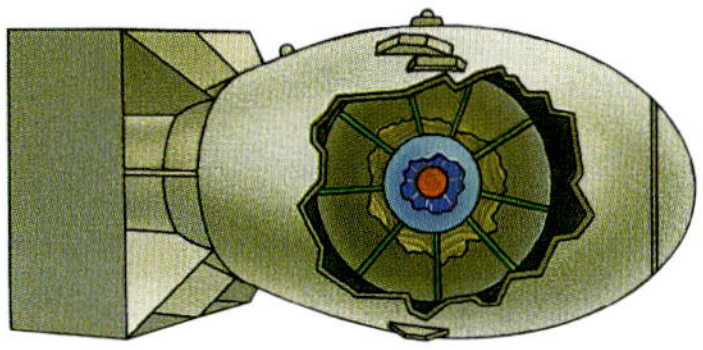

Implosion-type fission weapon

Fission weapons split apart the *nuclei* (cores) of atoms. *Gun-type* weapons start the fission reaction by violently combining two samples of nuclear material. *Implosion-type* weapons compress their nuclear material using conventional explosives.

The explosion of a nuclear weapon creates a huge mushroom-shaped cloud.

Nuclear weapon *Continued from the previous page*

oped nuclear weapons. But the country destroyed them in the early 1990's. North Korea has exploded several nuclear devices in tests. Iran has developed nuclear weapon material, but the country says it is only for peaceful purposes.

Other articles to read include: **Bomb; Explosive.**

Nylon products are strong and smooth. Nylon can be molded into shapes, such as this nylon gear.

Nylon

Nylon is a very strong *synthetic material.* Synthetic materials do not come from nature. They are made by people.

Nylon is made of chemicals from other materials, including coal, water, oil, and natural gas. Products made from nylon are strong and smooth. They do not shrink. They dry quickly. They are not harmed by most kinds of oil or grease.

Nylon was first made in 1935 by Wallace H. Carothers, an American chemist at the DuPont Company. Carothers then led a team of scientists to study nylon. His team did not learn how to make nylon in large quantities until 1938. The company introduced the first nylon products the next year.

Women's stockings were some of the first nylon products. Nylon is also used in fabrics, gears, bearings, hardware, brush bristles, electrical appliances, carpeting, tires, and fishing line. Surgeons even use nylon thread to sew up wounds.

Other articles to read include: **Materials; Plastics; Synthetics.**

Nylon fibers have a smooth surface that makes them resistant to wear.

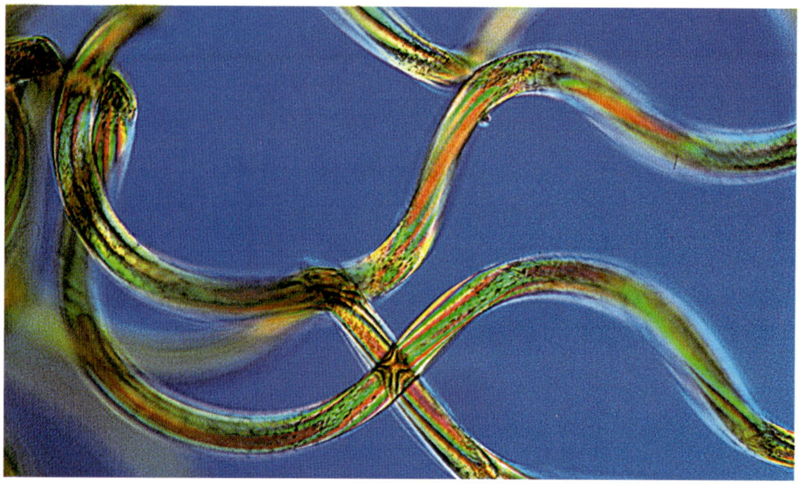

Observatory

An observatory *(uhb ZUR vuh TAWR ee)* is a place where scientists can study planets, stars, galaxies, and other objects in space. An observatory has at least one telescope or similar device. Most observatories are built on the ground. But observatory equipment is also used underground, in the atmosphere, and in space. The word *observatory* can also mean an old structure that people once used to note important days of the year.

Earth's atmosphere helps determine where telescopes are placed. The atmosphere distorts light passing through it. Observatories on Earth are usually placed high on a mountain, above most clouds, where the atmosphere is thin. Many telescopes work with visible light. Some other types of light arriving from space are invisible to the human eye. Telescopes have been made to detect these invisible forms of light. These include telescopes that detect infrared light, radio waves, and ultraviolet light. The light detected by these telescopes is often changed into images people can see.

Continued on the next page

Most observatories are built on the ground. The W. M. Keck Observatory in Hawaii has two of the largest optical telescopes in the world.

Some observatories orbit Earth in space. The Hubble Space Telescope takes sharper images of celestial objects than can ground-based telescopes of comparable size.

Observatory *Continued from the previous page*

The staff of an observatory includes engineers, astronomers, telescope operators, and others. Astronomers who are not on the staff do most of the research. There are many scientists and only a few large telescopes. Therefore, scientists often must schedule a time to use them.

Other articles to read include: **Chandra X-ray Observatory; Keck Observatory; Telescope.**

The Very Large Array radio observatory in Socorro, New Mexico, consists of 27 huge, movable dish antennas.

Elisha Graves Otis

Otis, Elisha Graves

Elisha Graves Otis (1811–1861) was an American inventor. He built the first elevator with an automatic safety device. Elevators in Otis's day were held up by ropes. If the rope broke, the elevator would fall. Otis's device stopped the elevator from falling.

Otis was born in Halifax, Vermont. He worked as a mechanic. In 1852, he invented his safety elevator. In 1854, Otis demonstrated the invention in New York. He raised himself on the elevator and cut the rope. Otis did not fall. His invention became very popular with the development of the skyscraper in the late 1800's.

Other articles to read include: **Elevator; Invention.**

Panama Canal

The Panama Canal is a waterway that cuts across Panama in Central America. It connects the Atlantic Ocean and the Pacific Ocean.

A system of devices called *locks* raises and lowers water levels in the Panama Canal.

The Panama Canal has changed the way people and goods travel from place to place. Before the canal, ships traveling between New York and San Francisco had to sail around the tip of South America. By sailing through the Panama Canal, ships travel less than half as far.

The canal has several sections. The main section is a lake that lies about 85 feet (26 meters) above sea level. To reach this lake, ships from the Atlantic Ocean travel through sections called the Gatun Locks. A *lock* has steel gates at each end. When closed, the gate at one end acts like a dam. It holds back the high water in front of a ship. The gate at the other end closes behind the ship. Water flows into the lock. It raises the water in the lock, lifting the ship to the high-water level. The front gate then opens, and the ship moves forward.

From the locks, the ship sails into Gatun Lake. Then the ship sails through the Gaillard *(GIHL yahrd)* Cut, a long channel. At the end, it passes through locks that lower it to another channel. From there, the ship sails to the Pacific Ocean. Ships coming from the Pacific pass through the locks in the opposite direction to reach the Atlantic Ocean.

The United States built the Panama Canal. For 10 years, thousands of people worked on it. It was finished in 1914. The canal was run by the United States. In 1977, the United States and Panama agreed that Panama would take control of the canal in 1999. At the end of 1999, Panama took over control of the canal. In 2007, Panama began expanding the canal to handle larger ships.

Other articles to read include: **Canal; Ship.**

A paper mill produces giant rolls of paper that can be cut into smaller sizes.

Paper

Paper is an important industrial product. Books, magazines, and newspapers are printed on paper. People use paper towels and tissues in the home. Paper is also used to make boxes and packages.

Paper is made from a material called *cellulose (SEHL yuh lohs).* Cellulose comes from plant fibers. These fibers are tiny, hairlike threads. The fibers are mixed with water and strained through a screen. As the paper dries, the fibers stick to one another to make paper.

Fibers for paper come from different plants. Some of the plants used are bamboo, cotton, hemp, jute, sugar cane, wheat, and rice straws. Wood is the major source of paper fiber in North America.

Other articles to read include: **Printing; Wood.**

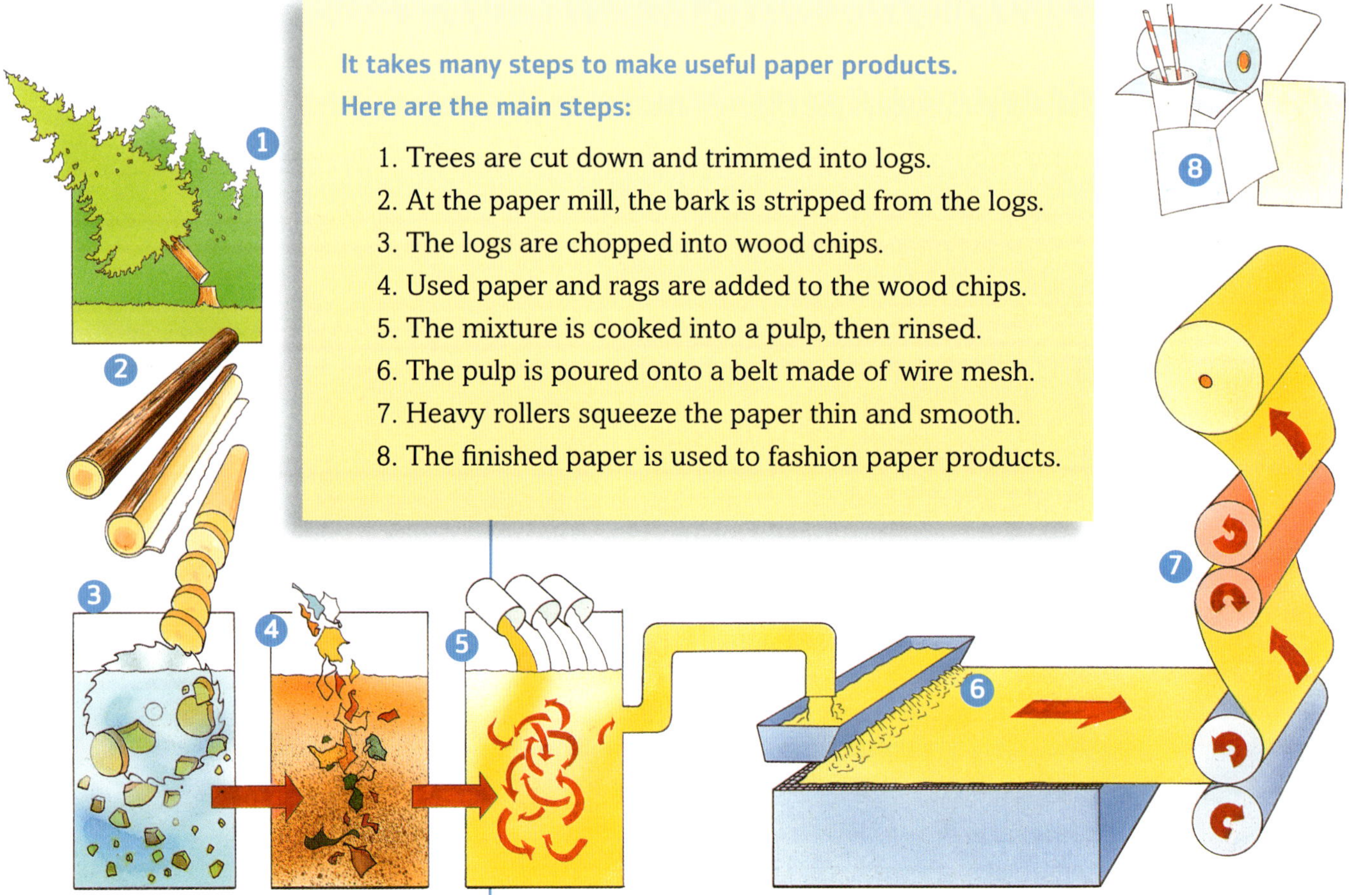

It takes many steps to make useful paper products. Here are the main steps:

1. Trees are cut down and trimmed into logs.
2. At the paper mill, the bark is stripped from the logs.
3. The logs are chopped into wood chips.
4. Used paper and rags are added to the wood chips.
5. The mixture is cooked into a pulp, then rinsed.
6. The pulp is poured onto a belt made of wire mesh.
7. Heavy rollers squeeze the paper thin and smooth.
8. The finished paper is used to fashion paper products.

Parachute

A parachute is a large piece of fabric that slows a falling person or object. When something falls, a force of gravity pulls it toward Earth. However, air pushes against the falling object or body. This *air resistance* works against gravity. A parachute has a large surface. It spreads out so that much more air pushes against it. The parachute thus increases air resistance. Parachutes can also slow objects moving along the ground.

People use parachutes to jump from airplanes or to drop supplies. The part that spreads out is called the *canopy (KAN uh pee)*. For many years, parachutes had round canopies. Today, most have canopies shaped like rectangles. Such parachutes are easier to control than round-canopied parachutes. Modern parachutes are usually made from a material called nylon.

A person may wear the canopy folded in a pack. When a cord is pulled, a tiny parachute opens. It pulls the pack open. Then the larger canopy spreads out.

Other articles to read include: **Airplane.**

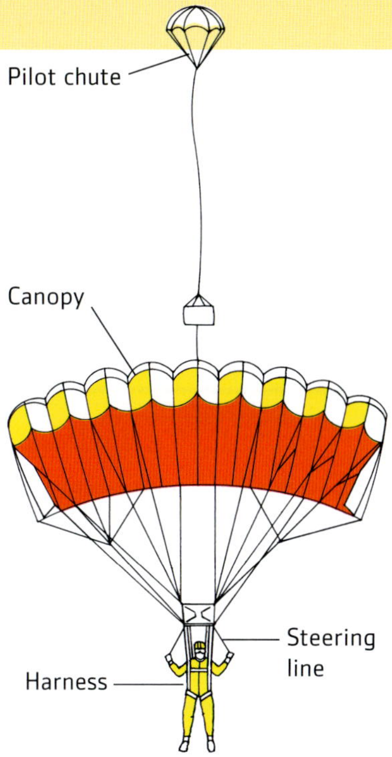

A tiny *pilot chute* helps the main canopy of a parachute open and quickly spread out.

Pen and pencil

Pens and pencils are tools used for writing or drawing. Pens are one of the most popular writing tools. They write or draw with ink. There are several different kinds of pens. A *ballpoint pen* uses a tiny ball as its tip. The ball rolls around, spreading ink from inside the pen. A *fountain pen* uses a triangular tip instead of a ball. Early pens were made of straws, reeds, or feathers.

Pencils are the most widely used writing and drawing tools in the world. Pencils make marks using a thin stick of *graphite*. Graphite is a powdery form of carbon. It is dark gray in color. There are many kinds of pencils. For example, doctors use a special pencil to mark a person's skin before an operation.

Other articles to read include: **Paper.**

Pencils and pens are important writing tools.

Pendulum

A pendulum *(PEHN juh luhm)* is a hanging object that swings freely. A simple pendulum is a weight hanging from a string or wire. If the other end of the string or wire is held steady, the weight can swing back and forth. As the weight moves, it follows a path. This path is called the *arc of the pendulum*. The time the weight takes to swing once is the pendulum's *period*.

In the 1600's, the Italian scientist Galileo *(GAL uh LAY oh)* discovered that a pendulum's period is the same whether its arc is small or large. He thought of the idea that a pendulum might serve as the basis for a clock that kept steady time. The Dutch scientist Christiaan Huygens *(HOY gehns)* developed a pendulum clock in 1657.

Pendulums also have other uses. A *metronome* is a pendulum device that keeps time for musicians. In 1851, the French scientist Jean Foucault *(foo KOH)* used a pendulum to prove that Earth spins.

Other articles to read include: **Clock.**

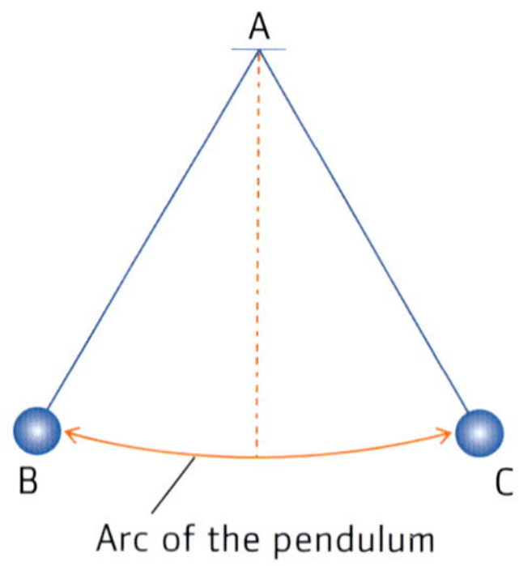

A simple pendulum swings from a fixed point (A), forming a path called an *arc* between two points (B and C).

A *metronome* is a ticking, clocklike device with a pendulum that can be adjusted to swing at different speeds.

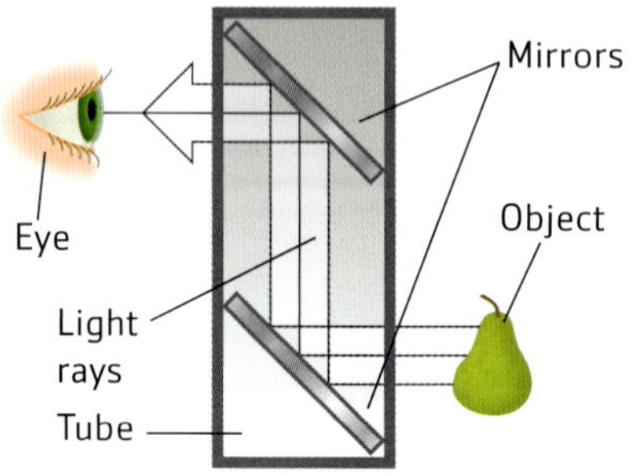

Mirrors in the tube of a periscope bounce the light from one end to the other.

Periscope

A periscope *(PEHR uh skohp)* is a tool for seeing when ordinary vision is blocked. A simple periscope is a tube with a mirror at each end. The mirrors are angled. They bounce a reflection from one mirror to the other and into the viewer's eye. Looking in one end of the periscope gives the view from the periscope's other end.

Periscopes are used in tanks and submarines. Submarine crews use periscopes to see above water. Tank crews use periscopes to see outside the tank from safely inside. Scientists can use periscopes in laboratories. They can observe dangerous reactions in this way without the risk of harm.

Other articles to read include: **Mirror; Submarine; Tank.**

Phonograph

A phonograph has a needle that runs along grooves in a record. The device converts the pattern of the grooves into sounds.

A phonograph is a device that plays sounds from records. Phonographs are also called *record players* or *gramophones*. Until the mid-1980's, they were the most common device for listening to music and other sound recordings. Today, most people listen to music that has been recorded *digitally*—that is, in computer files or on compact discs (CD's).

A phonograph record stores sounds as grooves in its surface. The grooves have jagged waves. These waves match up with the sounds. The record is spun on a phonograph as a needle called a *stylus* rides along the groove. The waves in the groove cause the stylus to vibrate. The vibrations are changed into electric signals. The signals travel to speakers. The speakers change them back into sound. In a *stereophonic* phonograph, the stylus responds to two separate sets of waves—one on either side of the groove. One wave goes to the left speaker. The other wave goes to the right speaker.

The American inventor Thomas Edison invented the first practical phonograph in 1877. It could record sound on tinfoil wrapped around a cylinder. Emile Berliner, a German immigrant to the United States, invented the gramophone in 1887. The gramophone was a phonograph that used discs instead of cylinders. The discs were cheaper and had better sound.

In 1948, the plastic 33 ⅓-rpm LP record appeared on the market. The letters *rpm* stand for *revolutions per minute*. This number tells how fast the record spins. *LP* stands for *long-playing*. This record held more sound and was stronger than older kinds of records. In 1949, the 45-rpm disc was introduced. Stereophonic phonographs and discs appeared in 1958. Digital CD's were introduced in the 1980's. Phonograph and record sales fell sharply. By the 2000's, many people owned computers, cell phones, and devices called *portable media players* that could store thousands of digital songs. Some hobbyists still collect and play records.

Other articles to read include: **Compact disc; Edison, Thomas Alva; Portable media player.**

In the studio, a photographer can carefully control the way a subject is lit.

Photography

Photography *(fuh TOG ruh fee)* is a way of making pictures with light. These pictures are called *photographs,* or *photos.* Photographs are made with a device called a *camera.* Light rays that are reflected from a scene pass into the camera through the *lens.* The lens is a curved piece of glass at the front of the camera. The lens bends the light to form a clear picture of the scene at the back of the camera. There, the image is recorded. People who take photographs are called *photographers.*

Photography is important for many reasons. Photographs of people far away help us learn about the people, their customs, and their countries. Photography lets us see important news events all over the world. Photography also records important events in the past.

Cameras can go where people cannot go. They let us see images from the surface of Mars and inside the human body. Cameras can also record clear images of objects or actions that are hard to see normally. For example, special cameras can show an insect flapping its wings faster than the eye can track. Many photographers today create photographs that are among the finest art produced. These photographs are often displayed in art galleries and museums.

There are also simpler reasons that photography is important. Many people enjoy photography as a way to remember fun vacations, special celebrations, beloved family members, and good friends.

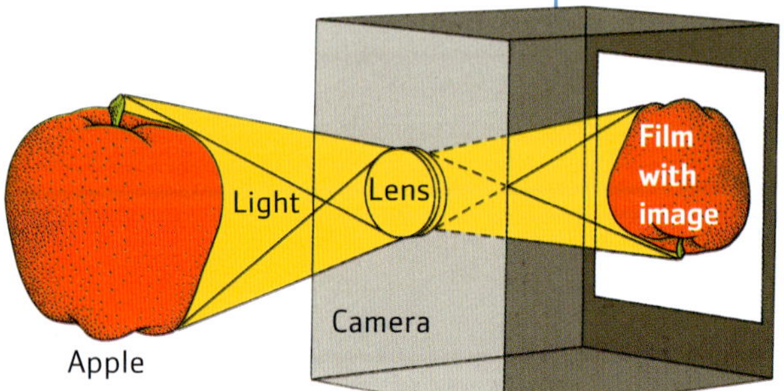

A camera lens takes in light from an object or scene. The light forms an upside-down image within the camera.

The process of photography works in various ways, depending on the kind of camera used. Digital cameras record images using a *charge-coupled device* (CCD). Light reflected from an object shines on the CCD. The CCD changes the light into electronic signals. These signals are recorded as a computer file. Digital

Continued on the next page

Older cameras recorded images on rolls of film (above). Newer cameras (right) record images as digital files. The files can quickly be transferred to a computer.

photographs can be saved on computers. They can be shared with others over the Internet.

Film cameras use a thin, flexible sheet of paper or plastic called *film*. The film contains special chemicals that change when exposed to light. The chemicals "record" the light, producing an image called a *negative*. This image has the light and dark parts reversed. The negative is then transferred to paper. In the process, the image is reversed again to resemble the original scene.

Photography was invented in the early 1800's. The first photograph was taken in 1826 in France. Early photographers needed a great deal of equipment. They also needed some knowledge of chemistry. In one early form of photography, the picture was produced on a sheet of silver-coated copper. These pictures were known as *daguerreotypes (duh GEHR uh typs)*. They were the first popular photographs. Photographic paper was invented in 1839. In 1888, the American manufacturer George Eastman introduced the Kodak box camera. It was the first camera that was easy for non-experts to use.

During the 1900's, cameras became smaller. Photographs became sharper. Color film began to be produced in the 1930's. Digital photography was introduced in the 1950's and 60's. At first, digital photography was mostly used by scientists. By the 1990's, digital photography had become widely popular. In the 2000's, many companies stopped producing film and film

Continued on the next page

The *daguerreotype* was an early form of photograph. This daguerreotype shows a California gold miner from the 1840's.

Photography *Continued from the previous page*

cameras. By the 2000's and 2010's, many phones worked as digital cameras. People could easily share huge photo collections on the Internet.

Other articles to read include: **Camera; Cellular telephone; Eastman Kodak Company; Holography; Lens.**

Cell phones and other small devices often have built-in cameras. Ordinary people can use them to record historic events, such as this anti-government protest in Thailand.

Pigment

Pigment is a colorful powder. Paints are made from pigments mixed with a fluid. People sometimes mix pigments with other materials. Other times, they cover a material with pigment. Pigments give other materials color.

Some pigments provide color for plastics, paint, and ink. Different pigments have different colors. The pigment *iron oxide* can be for yellow or red, for example. A blue or green pigment is *phthalocyanine (*THAL *uh SY uh neen).*

Pigments are powders that can give color to a wide variety of objects.

Pigments can be mixed to make other colors. Red and yellow pigments are mixed to make orange. Red and blue are mixed to make purple.

People's skin has a pigment called *melanin.* People with more melanin have darker skin than others. Melanin also gives color to freckles.

Other articles to read include: **Dye.**

Pilâtre de Rozier, Jean-François

Jean-François Pilâtre de Rozier *(zhahn frahn swah pee laht ruh duh roh zyay)* (1756–1785) was a French scientist. He was the first person to rise into the air on a hot-air balloon. On Oct. 15, 1783, Pilâtre de Rozier's balloon lifted him about 80 feet (24 meters) into the air. This balloon was anchored to the ground with a cable.

Pilâtre de Rozier made a second balloon flight on Nov. 21, 1783. He took along a French army officer. This time, the balloon floated free. They stayed in the air about 25 minutes and drifted over Paris.

Pilâtre de Rozier was born on March 30, 1757, in Metz, France. He was killed in a balloon accident on June 15, 1785. He was trying to fly across the English Channel.

Other articles to read include: **Balloon.**

Jean-François Pilâtre de Rozier

Piston

A piston is a device in many machines. It is a solid rod that moves back and forth inside a tube. This tube is often called the *cylinder.* Pistons are used in engines and pumps. They are also used in *compressors* (machines that squeeze air and other gases) and in some kinds of musical instruments.

Most engines use pistons to change the energy of burning fuel into mechanical energy. One example is the gasoline engine in a car. The engine contains several cylinders. Each cylinder fills with a mixture of air and fuel. A piston pushes down on this mixture, compressing it. A spark ignites the mixture. This creates an explosion. The explosion pushes the piston back up. The piston's down-and-up motion turns a long rod called a *crankshaft.* The crankshaft turns the car's wheels.

Other articles to read include: **Automobile; Engine; Gasoline engine; Machine.**

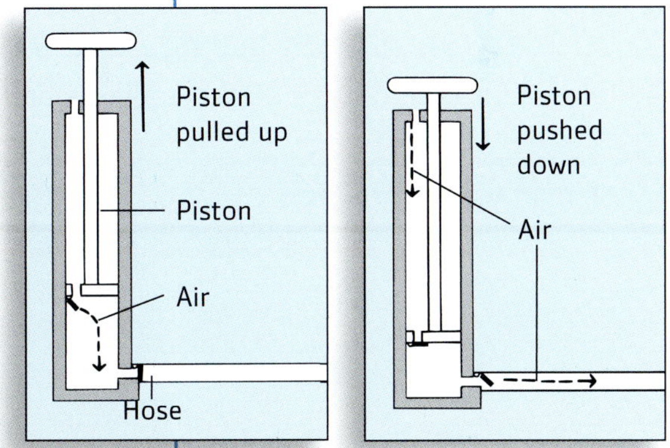

A bicycle pump has a piston that moves up and down, squeezing air through the hose and into a bicycle tire.

Plastics

Plastic can be formed into many useful products, such as these clear water bottles and their rigid caps.

Plastics are materials that can be shaped into almost any form. They are among the most useful materials ever made. Plastics can be as stiff as steel. They can also be as soft as cotton. They can be any color—or clear as crystal. There are hundreds of kinds of plastics. They are used in a huge variety of products.

Plastics are made of special *molecules* (combinations of atoms) called *polymers.* Polymers form long chains. In some plastics, the polymers line up like logs in an orderly stack. In others, the polymer chains are tangled like cooked spaghetti. The properties of a plastic depend on the structure of its polymers.

Plastics are used in many ways. They are often used in cars and airplanes. Builders may use plastics instead of wood, stone, glass, and metal. Doctors can mend bones with plastic parts. Plastic fibers, or threads, may be used instead of cotton, silk, or wool to make cloth. Tough plastic fibers are used in seat belts, carpeting, and furniture. Plastics are sometimes used instead of paper for packing and wrapping and instead of glass in bottles and jars.

The chemicals in plastics come from largely from *petroleum,* such as oil or natural gas. Other materials are added to give plastics colors or added strength or softness.

Plastics are formed in many ways. In some cases, plastic powder is poured into a hollow form called a *mold.* The plastic is heated and pressed into shape. Other plastics are formed by melting plastic beads. The resulting liquid is squirted into a mold. The plastic hardens in seconds.

Bottles are made by putting a hollow tube of plastic into a mold. When hot air or steam is blown into the tube, it blows up like a balloon and fills the mold. Plastic foam is made by putting

Making plastic products

Continued on the next page

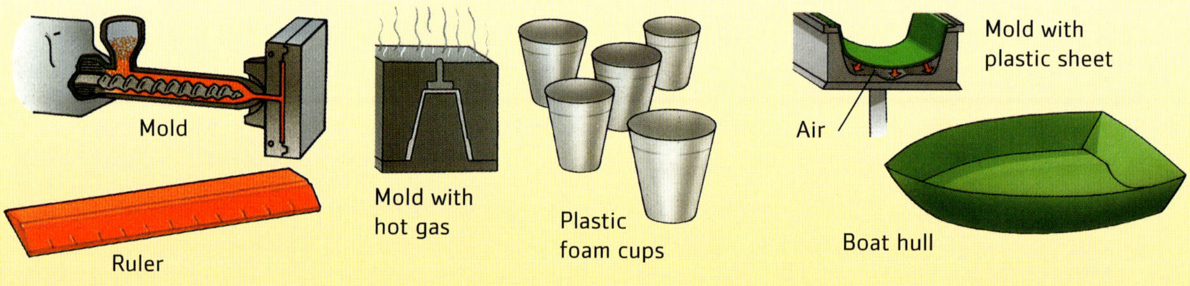

In *injection molding,* plastic material under high pressure is shot into a *mold.* The material fills the mold, which is shaped like the final product—in this case, a ruler.

In *foaming,* a gas is added to a heated plastic material. As the gas expands in the material, bubbles are created. The resulting product, such as a foam cup, is lightweight.

In *thermoforming,* a sheet of plastic is clamped down on a mold and heated until it becomes soft. Then, air is sucked out through holes in the mold, drawing the plastic sheet into the mold. Boat hulls can be shaped using this method.

a gas into heated plastic and letting it bubble. Foam cups, packing materials, and cushions are made in this way.

For thousands of years, people made objects out of *resins.* Resins are sticky or oily natural substances, such as tree sap. They are similar to plastics but not as useful or as cheap.

In the 1860's, two brothers made a plastic called *celluloid (SEHL yuh loyd)* from cotton and chemicals. In the early 1900's, a chemist named Leo Baekeland made the first *thermosetting plastic.* After melting, the plastic set into a hard, durable form. He called it Bakelite. Inventors have since developed many kinds of plastics.

Paper and other natural materials break down. But most plastic waste does not. Plastics can pollute the air, water, and soil. Some plastics can be *recycled.* They are collected, cleaned, melted down, and made into new products. Some plastics are *biodegradable (BY oh dee GRAYD uh buhl).* Sunlight or tiny living things called bacteria break them down into harmless chemicals.

Many children's toys, such as this truck, are assembled from pieces made by squirting liquid plastic into a mold and letting it become solid.

Other articles to read include: **Biodegradable material; Landfill; Materials; Nylon; Recycling; Synthetics.**

Plow

A plow is a tool that prepares soil for planting. A plow digs into the ground. It pushes, cuts, and lifts the soil to break it up.

Farmers *till* (turn up with a plow) the soil for many reasons. Plowing softens the ground and makes it easier to plant seeds, for example. Tilling covers up the remains of the last crop. It also kills weeds and insects. In addition, air moves through the loose soil more easily. Living things in the soil, including plant roots, depend on oxygen in the air to grow.

A mechanical plow pulled by a tractor can quickly turn up huge areas of soil for planting.

People have long known that plants grow better in loose soil. Early plows were probably forked branches worked by hand. People later used oxen to pull plows. They made plows out of iron or steel. They designed special plows for thick soil. The term *plow* is also used to describe other types of equipment, such as vehicles used to clear snow and machines that dig trenches.

Other articles to read include: **Crop; Farm and farming; Soil; Tool; Tractor.**

Plumbing

Plumbing is the use of pipes to carry water into and out of buildings and other structures. A building's plumbing system has two sets of pipes. One set brings in clean water. The other set takes out dirty water and solid wastes.

Cities and towns get water from rivers and lakes or from wells. The water first goes to a *treatment plant,* where it is cleaned. Then the clean water flows to a *pumping station.* It is pumped into large pipes called *water mains.*

The pipes that bring water into buildings from the water mains are called *service lines.* The water that comes into a building is cold. One pipe brings water to a *hot-water heater.* That water is heated in a tank. Hot water flows from the heater through pipes to bathtubs, sinks, washing machines, or dishwashers. Cold water flows through another set of pipes to all those places and to toilets. When people turn on a faucet, flush a toilet, or use a washing machine or dishwasher, a valve opens and lets the water flow in.

After water is used, it is emptied out through the *drainage system.* The drainage system has large pipes. Materials do not get stuck easily in these pipes. The pipes carry used water and solid wastes to a large pipe called the *soil stack.* The soil stack empties into a drain under the building. In most places, the drain empties into a sewer that carries the used water away. In other places, the drain is connected to a *septic tank.* Waste is stored in the tank until it breaks down.

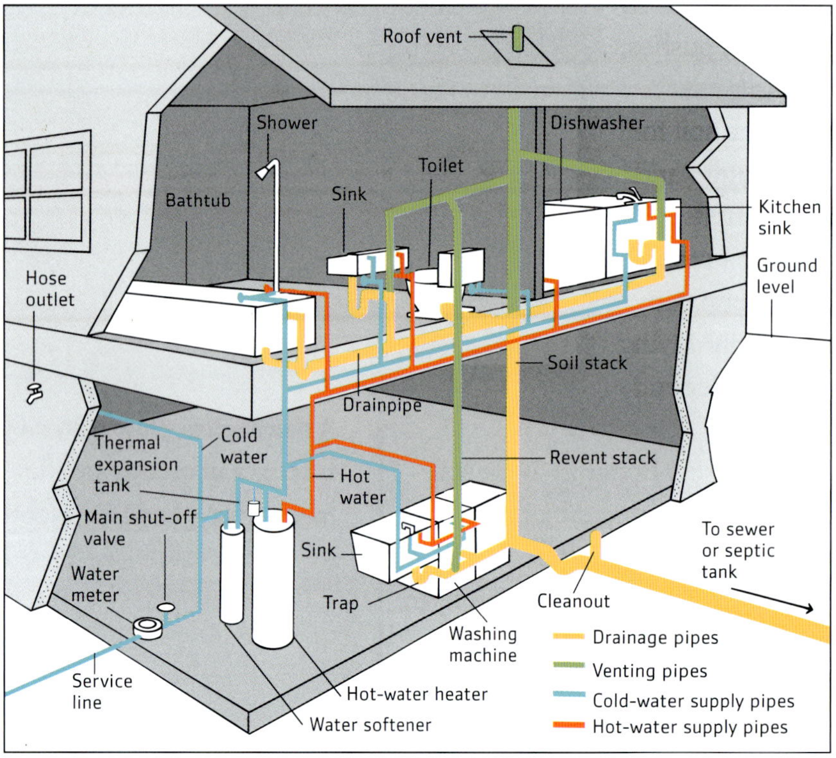

A house's plumbing system includes several kinds of pipes. A *service line* supplies clean water to the home. *Drainage pipes* carry dirty water and waste out of the home. A *hot-water heater* and connected pipes supply hot water to sinks, showers, and other appliances. *Venting pipes* keep air flowing through the system.

Continued on the next page

Most toilets have two parts—a bowl and a tank. The bowl and the tank are connected. A rubber stopper covers the opening from the tank to the bowl. It keeps the water from running into the bowl until the toilet is flushed.

When the toilet is flushed, the stopper lifts. Water rushes from the tank into the toilet bowl. As the water goes down, a float attached to a valve inside the tank sinks. It makes the valve open. Water starts flowing in.

The stopper drops back into place, and the tank fills. As it fills, the float rises. It makes the inlet valve shut. Then the tank stops filling.

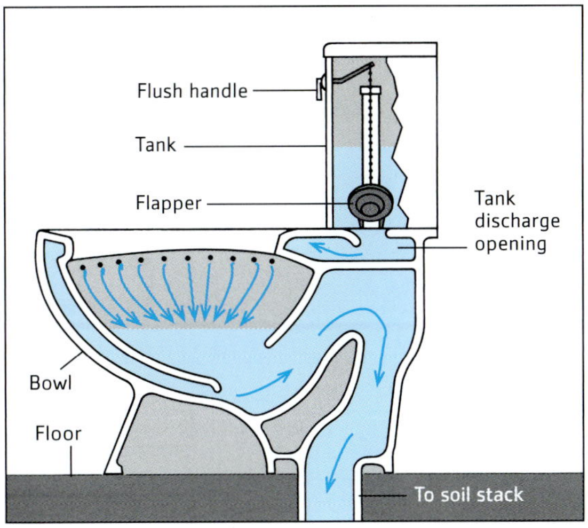

Flushing a toilet lifts a *flapper,* allowing water to rush into the toilet bowl. When the tank is nearly empty, the flapper drops back down.

The Indus Valley civilization used plumbing by about 2500 B.C. This civilization was located in what are now Pakistan and western India. Its homes had drains. The ancient Romans built complex plumbing systems. They used lead pipes. The word *plumbing* comes from the Roman word for lead.

The Roman Empire went into decline around 400 B.C. Knowledge of plumbing was lost for centuries. A type of flush toilet was developed in the 1500's. In 1778, Joseph Bramah, an English cabinetmaker, developed an improved flush toilet. Septic tanks were invented in the mid-1800's. A modern sewerage system began working in London in the 1860's.

Other articles to read include: **Building construction; Sewage.**

Polyester

Polyesters *(POL ee EHS tuhrs)* are widely used plastic materials. Polyesters can be spun into fibers. They can be squeezed into films. They can be combined with other materials and shaped into plastic parts.

Polyesters, like other plastics, are made of tiny bits of matter called *polymers.* Polymers form long chains. Each polymer chain is a pattern of smaller pieces. In polyesters, these pieces connect to each other by *esters.* An ester is made of one carbon atom and two oxygen atoms.

Continued on the next page

Polyester *Continued from the previous page*

Polyester fibers are used in tires and clothing. They are strong and flexible. Polyester film is used to make such things as shrink wrap, magnetic tape, and plastic bottles. Some kinds of polyesters are combined with materials such as *fiberglass* (glass threads). The combination makes strong, stiff material used in cars and boats.

Other articles to read include: **Plastics; Textile; Tire.**

Porcelain vases are valued for their delicate beauty.

Porcelain

Porcelain *(PAWR suh lihn)* is a material valued for its beauty and strength. Porcelain is a type of *ceramic.* Like other ceramics, porcelain is made from clay baked at high temperatures. Porcelain is white, delicate, and *translucent.* A translucent material lets light through. Porcelain is often called *china,* or *chinaware,* because it was first made in China. Porcelain is the hardest ceramic product. For this reason, it is used to make some electrical and laboratory equipment. Porcelain is most famously used in fancy vases and dishes. It is also used in decorative objects.

Porcelain is made from a mixture of two ingredients: kaolin and petuntse. Kaolin is a pure white clay. Petuntse is a mineral found only in China. It is ground to a fine powder and mixed with kaolin. This mixture is *fired* (baked) at temperatures from about 2280 °F (1250 °C) to 2640 °F (1450 °C). At these high temperatures, the petuntse melts together. It forms a kind of natural glass. The kaolin does not melt and so allows the item to hold its shape. The process is complete when the petuntse joins itself to the kaolin.

Other articles to read include: **Materials; Pottery.**

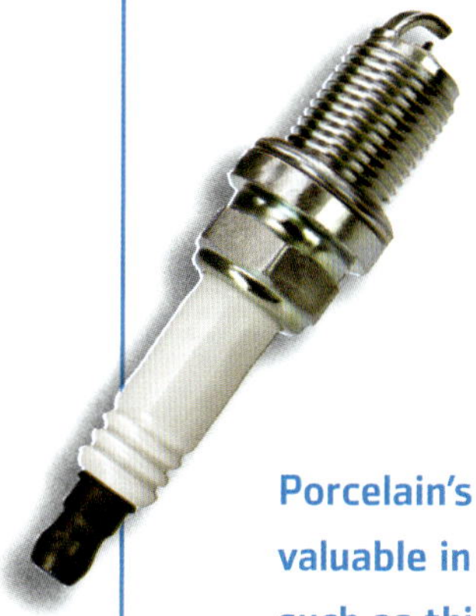

Porcelain's durability makes it valuable in electrical devices, such as this spark plug.

Porco, Carolyn C.

Carolyn C. Porco (1953–...) is an astronomer. She studies planets and moons in the *solar system.* The solar system is the sun and everything that revolves around it, including Earth. Porco has worked on several *space probe* missions. Space probes are machines launched into space to study planets up close. They send pictures and other information back to scientists.

Voyager 1 and Voyager 2 were the first probes Porco worked on. The probes were launched in the late 1970's. They photographed Jupiter, Saturn, Uranus, and Neptune. They found dark "spokes" in Saturn's rings, among other discoveries. Porco helped explain the spokes. The spokes may result from fine dust being raised above the main ring by electrical and magnetic forces.

In the early 1990's, Porco began working on the Cassini probe to Saturn and its moons. She was named leader of the imaging team. The team is in charge of taking photographs with the probe's cameras. Porco's team made many discoveries. For example, they found *geysers* (jets) spewing water and ice on Saturn's moon Enceladus.

Porco was born on March 6, 1953, in New York City. She completed her doctorate degree at the California Institute of Technology in 1983. The same year, she began working on the Voyager probes. Porco has taught at the University of Arizona and the University of Colorado. She has also done scientific research at the Space Science Institute in Boulder, Colorado.

Other articles to read include: **Space exploration.**

Portable media player

A portable media player is a small device that plays songs or videos. It is sometimes called a PMP. People can read text on some PMP's. Many mobile phones also work as PMP's.

The first portable media player was Sony's Walkman, which was introduced in 1979. It played audio cassette tapes. Later PMP's played compact discs (CD's).

Modern PMP's use *digital* (computer) files. Such files may hold songs, videos, or text. These files are easy to download from the Internet. Apple Inc.'s iPod plays digital files. The popular device was introduced in 2001.

Other articles to read include: **Compact disc; Digital video recorder; Tape recorder.**

A portable media player can play songs and videos.

Pottery (above) is made from baked clay. A potter spins clay on a wheel, shaping it by hand (below). The clay is then baked in a hot oven called a *kiln* (below right).

Pottery

Pottery is a solid material made of baked clay. Pottery is used to make plates, vases, and other household objects. Some works of art are made of pottery.

Pottery is a kind of *ceramics.* Ceramic products also include bricks, cement, pipes, and other materials used in making things. The three main types of pottery are (1) earthenware, (2) stoneware, and (3) porcelain *(PAWR suh lihn).*

Earthenware is baked at relatively low temperatures. It may have a colorful *glaze.* A glaze is a glassy coating. Glazed earthenware is more colorful than other kinds of pottery. But earthenware breaks and chips easily.

Stoneware is a hard, heavy kind of pottery. It is baked at relatively high temperatures. Stoneware is not often glazed. The high heat turns the surface glossy. Stoneware is stronger and heavier than earthenware.

Porcelain is the most delicate type of pottery. Potters make porcelain from a fine white clay. Another material in porcelain turns glassy when baked. Light can shine through a thin piece of porcelain.

There are four basic steps in making pottery. They are (1) preparing the clay, (2) shaping the clay, (3) decorating and glazing, and (4) firing.

Potters prepare clay by pressing and squeezing it with their hands or with a machine. This makes the clay soft and smooth.

There are several methods of shaping clay. Some potters shape the clay with their hands.

Continued on the next page

They may roll the clay into strips and *coil* (wrap) them around. Potters also use special equipment. A *potter's wheel* has a round, flat surface that spins. The potter shapes a mound of clay as it spins on the wheel.

Potters can decorate their pottery by pressing their fingers into the soft clay or by scratching lines into it. Other designs can be drawn on pottery using colored substances. Glazing adds color and makes pottery smooth and waterproof.

After a piece of pottery is glazed, it is *fired* (baked). The potter puts it in an oven called a *kiln*. Firing makes pottery hard and strong. It also hardens the glaze and makes the glaze stick to the clay.

Other articles to read include: **Materials; Porcelain.**

Power plant

The Itaipú Dam power plant, on the Paraná River in Brazil, is one of the world's largest *hydroelectric* plants. It uses the energy of water flowing from a dam to make electric power.

A power plant is a place where electric power is produced. Most power plants burn coal, oil, or natural gas. The burning gives off heat. The heat turns water into steam. The steam pushes against a huge, fanlike device called a *turbine*. The pushing causes the turbine to spin. The spinning motion is used to make electric power. Wires carry the electric power to cities and other places.

Some kinds of power plants use steam made with other heat sources. *Nuclear power plants* use the heat from splitting atoms to make steam, for example. *Geothermal power plants* use steam from heat below Earth's surface.

Other power plants do not use steam at all. *Hydroelectric* (*HY droh ih LEHK trihk*) *power plants* use falling water to spin turbines. Windmills use blowing wind to spin turbines.

Other articles to read include: **Dam; Engine; Electric power; Nuclear reactor; Solar energy; Turbine; Water power; Windmill.**

Offset lithography

Relief printing

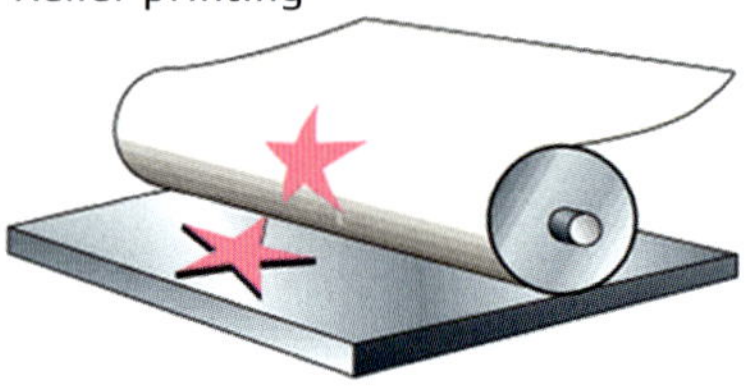

Recess printing

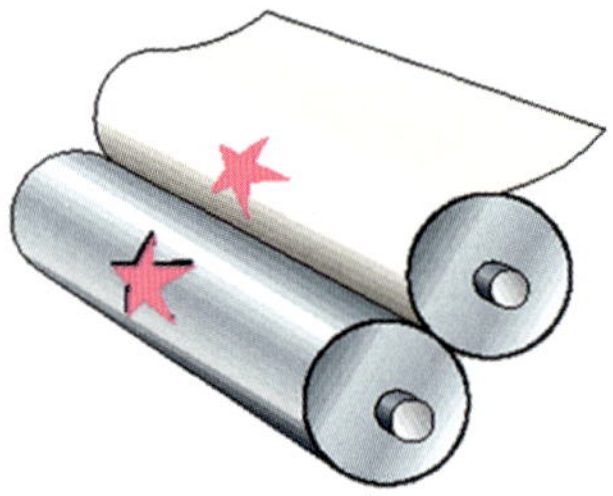

Printers transfer ink to paper in three main ways. In *offset lithography,* the design is first transferred to a rubber-coated cylinder and then to the paper. In *relief printing,* ink is transferred to the paper from a raised surface. It is transferred from a sunken surface in *recess printing.*

Printing

Printing is the use of machines to put words and images on paper or other items. Printing is an important form of communication. Books, newspapers, and magazines are available in print. Artwork is often printed. School tests and business documents may also be printed. Such materials as cans, bottles, T-shirts, and wallpaper often have printed designs on them.

The printing industry is important in many countries. It is one of the largest industries in both the United States and Canada. Printing differs from *publishing.* Publishing involves making and selling the material to be printed. Some publishers, such as newspaper companies, own printing equipment. But many publishers must work with separate printing companies.

Printing relies on machines called *printing presses.* Modern printing presses are huge, electric-powered devices. They can quickly print thousands of pages, all alike, in full color. The most common printing process is called *offset lithography (lih THOG ruh fee).* In offset lithography, metal plates are treated so that ink will only stick to certain areas. The plates are then covered with a layer of ink. The inked plates are then stamped onto a round, rubber-coated roller called a *cylinder (SIL uhn duhr).* Large sheets or rolls of paper are fed into the printing press. The cylinder then prints the words and pictures onto the paper.

To print a color picture, printers usually make four printing plates. Each plate is inked with one color—yellow, *magenta* (purple-red), *cyan* (light blue), and black. Each color is printed separately. These four colors can combine to form almost any color.

Before printing, people had to copy written text by hand. Copying books was expensive. It took much time and skill. By the 700's, the Chinese, Japanese, and Koreans were using block printing. They carved symbols and pictures on wood blocks. They inked the raised images. Then they transferred the ink to paper. By 1045, a Chinese printer named Bi Sheng (also spelled *Pi Sheng*) made the first *movable type.* Movable type consists of small blocks that can be rearranged to print different pages. Bi Sheng used a separate piece of clay for each symbol in Chinese writing.

Continued on the next page

Movable type worked much better in Europe than in China. The Chinese language makes use of thousands of symbols. European languages, on the other hand, use only the letters in an alphabet. European printers made pieces for each letter. They rearranged the letters to make a book's words and sentences and then inked them. In 1440, the German inventor Johannes Gutenberg developed the first European printing press. It could produce many copies rapidly. Gutenberg's invention soon changed Europe. Books spread far and wide. More people learned how to read and write.

Other articles to read include: **Camera; Communication; Gutenberg, Johannes; Paper.**

To print in color, printers use four plates, each inked with a different color—yellow, magenta, cyan, or black. The combination of these four inks can make almost any color.

Prism

A prism *(PRIHZ uhm)* is a solid object with two faces of the same size and shape. These faces, called *bases,* are also *parallel* to each other. *Parallel* means that they are the same distance apart everywhere. The two bases are joined to each other by three or more sides.

One kind of prism has bases shaped like triangles. It is often made of glass or some other clear material. This kind of prism can bend light as it passes through the glass. As the light bends, it splits up to form a rainbow of colors called a *spectrum (SPEHK truhm).* Such prisms are used in optical instruments to change the direction of light.

Other articles to read include: **Binoculars; Periscope.**

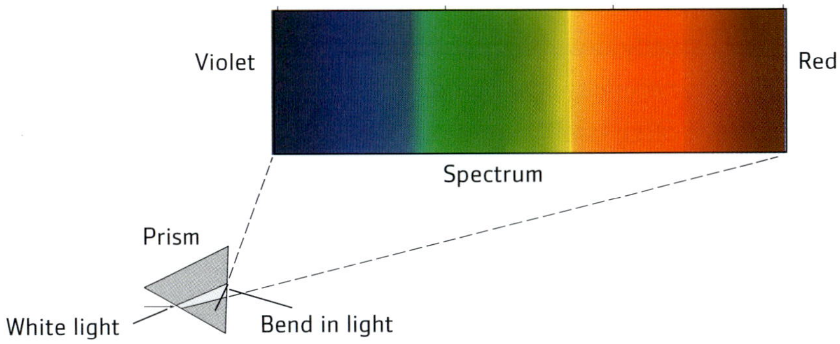

A prism bends light, splitting white light into a rainbowlike band called a *spectrum.*

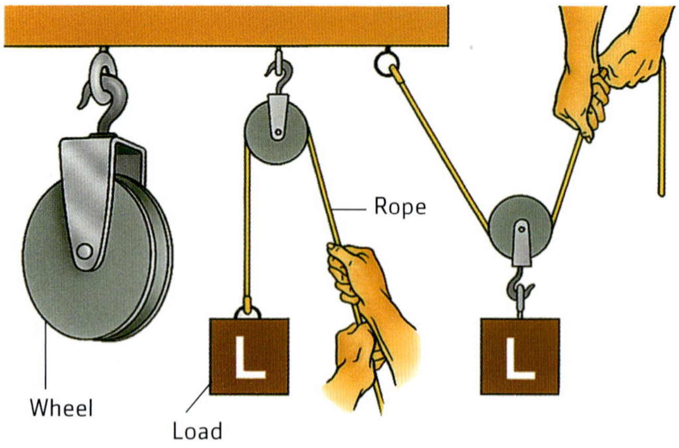

Pulley

The pulley *(PUL ee)* is a simple machine used to lift things. It is made up of a wheel and a rope. In the simplest pulley, the wheel is attached overhead. A rope goes up around the wheel, then back down. One end of the rope holds a load. Pulling down on the other end of the rope lifts the load. Pulling down on a rope is often easier than lifting a load directly.

In another kind of pulley, the wheel—not the rope—is attached to the load. A rope goes through the pulley. One end is tied to a fixed structure overhead. Pulling on the other end of the rope raises the pulley wheel and the load. The pulley reduces the force needed to lift the load. But the rope must be pulled twice as far to lift the load the same distance. Other pulley systems use two or more wheels.

A pulley has a wheel over which a rope is pulled. The load to be lifted may be attached to the rope or to the pulley itself.

Other articles to read include: **Machine; Wheel and axle.**

Pump

A pump is a device that moves liquids or gases. Pumps are used in many other kinds of machines. They are used in home heating systems, refrigerators, wells, and jet and automobile engines. Pumps do many kinds of jobs. Some put the air into bicycle tires. Others push cooling chemicals into nuclear power plants. Most pumps are made of steel, but some are made of glass or plastic.

There are two main kinds of pumps. *Dynamic pumps* move fluid in a steady flow. They are used in jet engines and in factories. *Positive displacement pumps* move fluid bit by bit. These pumps are often used to move sticky or thick fluids.

People have used pumps for thousands of years. The ancient Egyptians used water wheels with buckets attached to them to move water to their crops. The ancient Greek mathematician

Continued on the next page

Archimedes invented a screw pump. It was a screw that turned in a hollow tube. Turning the screw pulled up water from underground.

Other articles to read include: **Engine; Machine; Piston.**

A *lift pump* may be used to draw water from a well. The pump works through the action of a *piston,* which moves up and down.

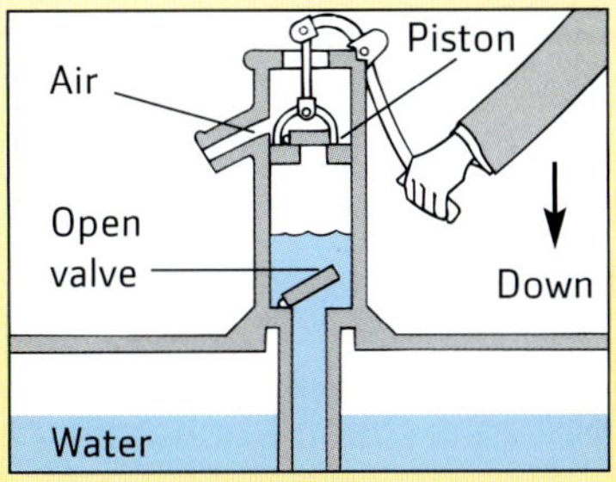

When the handle is pushed down, the piston moves up, forcing out air. Water moves in through a valve at the bottom of the pump to replace the air.

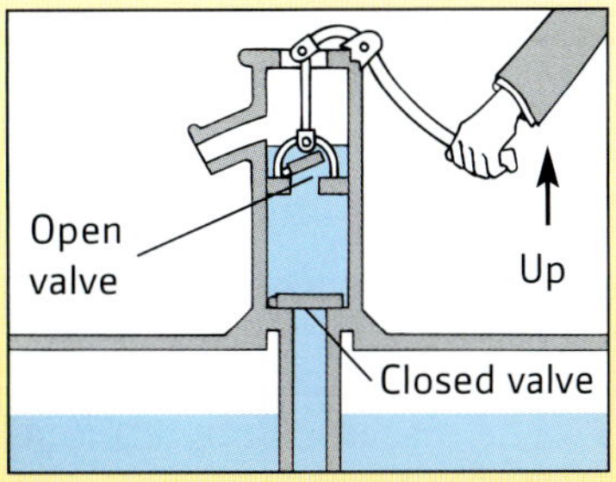

When the handle is pulled up, the piston moves down through the water. A valve on the piston opens, while the valve at the bottom of the pump closes.

Pushing down again on the handle causes the piston to move up. This forces the water above the piston to pour out of the spout.

Pyramid

A pyramid *(PIHR uh mihd)* is a kind of structure with four sides shaped like triangles. The sides come to a point at the top. Ancient people built huge pyramids as places of burial or worship. The most famous pyramids—the Pyramids of Giza—were built about 4,500 years ago. They were tombs for Egyptian kings. These Egyptian pyramids are among the *Seven Wonders of the Ancient World,* a list of famous structures built between 2500 B.C. and 250 B.C.

The Pyramids of Giza have stood on the west bank of the Nile River in Egypt for at least 4,500 years.

There are about 35 large, ancient pyramids still standing in Egypt. The largest of these is the pyramid of Khufu *(KOO foo),* also called the Great Pyramid. This pyramid is made of more than 2 million stone blocks. Each of the blocks weighs about 2.5 tons (2.3 metric tons). The Great Pyramid originally stood 481

Continued on the next page

Pyramid *Continued from the previous page*

feet (147 meters) high. It is slightly shorter now because some of the top stones have fallen away.

The ancient Egyptians placed *mummies* (preserved dead bodies) of rulers and other important people in the pyramids. The Egyptians believed that a person's body should be kept from decay so that the soul could live forever. They made a mummy by taking out a dead person's organs and drying the body. They then wrapped the body in cloth. These mummies were hidden in secret rooms inside or underneath the pyramids. The secret rooms were also filled with treasures.

The ancient Babylonians built pyramid-shaped buildings called *ziggurats.* The Babylonians lived in what is now Iraq. The native people of Central and South America also built large pyramids many hundreds of years ago. These pyramids typically had giant steps on the sides. The tops of the pyramids were flat. The people built places of worship called *temples* on the tops of the pyramids. Two of the best surviving examples of ancient Indian pyramids can be seen in Mexico, at Teotihuacán *(tay oh tee wah KAHN).* These are the Pyramid of the Sun and the Pyramid of the Moon.

Other articles to read include: **Building construction; Engineering.**

The Pyramid of the Sun, in Teotihuacán, Mexico, was built hundreds of years ago by the Toltec Indians.

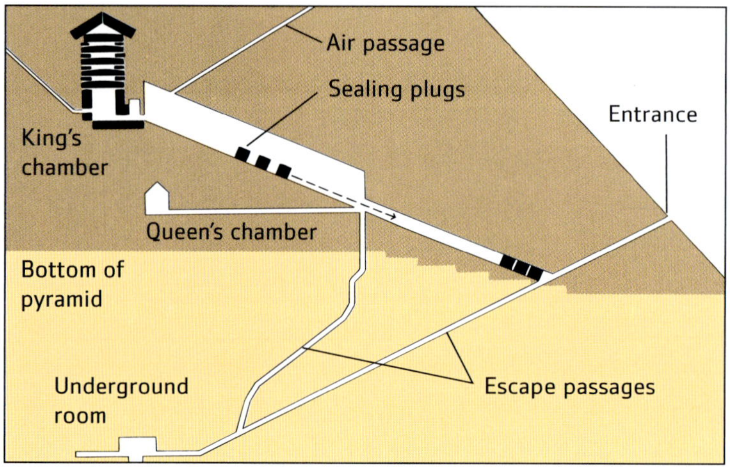

The inside of the Great Pyramid in Egypt holds tombs for the king and queen. After the burial, workers slid huge blocks called *sealing plugs* down a passage to block entrance to the tombs. The workers left the pyramid through escape passages.

Radar

Radar is a device that uses *radio waves* to locate objects. Radio waves are an invisible form of energy. By bouncing these waves off an object, a radar device can tell how far away the object is. A radar device can also tell how big an object is and how fast it is moving. Radar can work in the dark and in heavy fog, rain, or snow.

Radar has many uses. Pilots use radar to land airplanes safely at busy airports. In bad weather at sea, ship captains use radar to find their way. Military forces use radar to watch for surprise attacks from enemy airplanes or missiles. Weather forecasters use radar to keep track of storms. Scientists use radar to study the other planets and their moons.

Radar devices are called *sets.* Most radar sets send out radio waves. The waves bounce off objects. The reflected waves, called *echoes,* return to the radar set. The time it takes for the echoes to return indicates how far away the object is. The direction that the echoes come from tells where the object is.

A radar set's *transmitter* produces radar waves. A radar set's *antenna* sends the waves out. The antenna can also collect the echo waves from an object. A *receiver* makes the echoes easy to see on a screen. The screen shows the echoes as spots of light. It may also show the object's shape.

Other articles to read include: **Airplane; Navigation; Radio; Ship.**

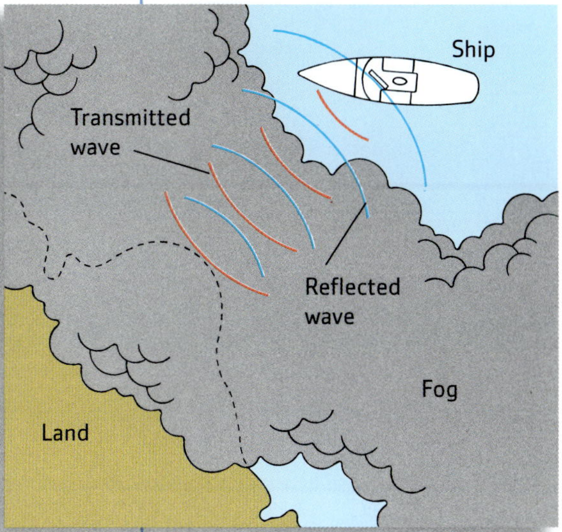

Radar works using radio waves, which can travel through fog and clouds. In this illustration, a ship sends out radio waves (red) to detect land. The waves bounce off nearby land, and their echoes (blue) travel back to the ship.

A ship's radar set includes devices for both transmitting and receiving radio waves.

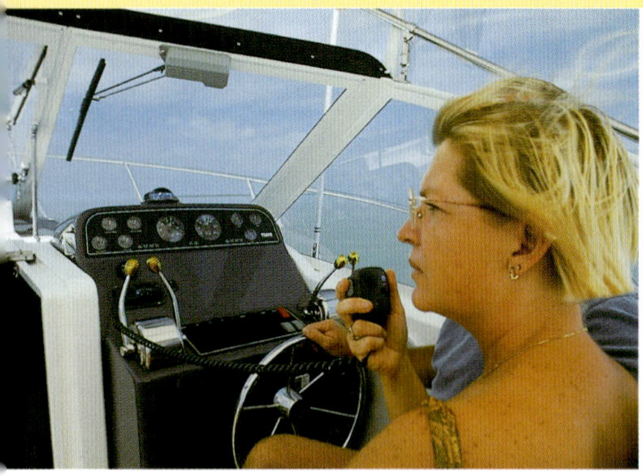

A woman on a boat uses a two-way radio to send messages to people on land and to receive messages back from them.

Radio

A radio is a device that sends or receives signals over a long distance. The signals are patterns of *radio waves.* Radio waves are a form of light, but they are invisible to human eyes. They travel through the air and through space, somewhat like waves on the ocean. Radio waves also can go through solid objects, such as walls.

Many people listen to radios for entertainment or information. The signals picked up by such radios are broadcast by *radio stations.* A person at the radio station may talk into a *microphone.* A microphone changes sounds into electrical signals. These signals travel to a nearby transmitter. The transmitter strengthens the signals. Then it changes them into radio waves. The waves are broadcast by an *antenna* on the transmitter. The two main kinds of radio signals are referred to as *amplitude modulation* (AM) and *frequency modulation* (FM). AM forms signals by changing the "height" of a radio wave. FM works by changing the waves' *frequency*—that is, the space between a wave's peaks and valleys.

A radio picks up the broadcast waves. It changes the signal patterns in the waves into an electrical signal. The main parts of a radio are the antenna, *tuner,* and speaker. The antenna receives the broadcast radio waves. The speaker changes the electrical signal into sounds. The tuner allows the listener to select a *frequency* (channel) to listen to.

People use radios every day to listen to music, news, and other programs. However, radio has many additional uses. People on ships and in airplanes use radio to talk to other people on land. This kind of radio is called a *two-way radio.* Firefighters and police officers also use two-way radios to send and receive information quickly. Radio is used to send directions to computers on spacecraft. Cellular telephones work with radio waves. In addition, wireless Internet connections, such as Wi-Fi, send many kinds of data over radio waves.

Many people contributed to the invention of radio. An Italian inventor named Guglielmo Marconi *(goo LYEHL moh mahr KOH nee)* was the first person to send a radio signal through the air. He did this in 1895. Most historians credit Reginald A. Fessenden, a Canadian scientist, with the first radio broadcast of the human

Continued on the next page

voice, in 1906. In the 1990's, *satellite radio* became popular. Satellite radio systems use satellites circling high above Earth to send high-quality radio signals. Wireless Internet connections became widespread in the 2000's.

Other articles to read include: **Airplane; Cellular telephone; Marconi, Guglielmo; Microphone; Radar; Remote control; Satellite, Artificial.**

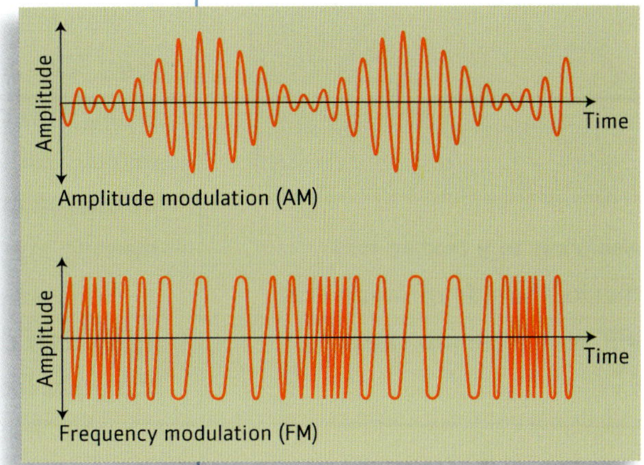

In *amplitude modulation* (AM), the *amplitude* (strength) of a radio wave is varied to carry a signal. The *frequency* (rate of vibration) is varied in *frequency modulation* (FM).

Radiosonde

A radiosonde *(RAY dee oh sond)* is a package of instruments that measure weather. The instruments are in a small, lightweight box. Radiosondes are carried high up into the sky on balloons. Such weather balloons are used by *meteorologists (MEE tee uh ROL uh jihsts).* A meteorologist is a scientist who studies weather.

A radiosonde has devices that measure temperature, air pressure, and *relative humidity (hyoo MIHD uh tee).* Relative humidity tells how much moisture is in the air. The devices on a radiosonde work with a *radio transmitter.* The transmitter sends the measurements to stations on the ground. A *radio direction finder* at the ground station tracks the radiosonde. Tracking helps find out the speed and direction of the wind at different levels in the air.

Other articles to read include: **Balloon; Radio; Weather forecasting.**

A *radiosonde* is a tiny package of weather instruments that is carried high into the sky by a balloon.

A worker in a textile mill checks threads of rayon that will be woven into cloth.

Rayon

Rayon is a fiber made from wood or cotton. People use rayon to make industrial materials. It is also used in clothing and fabrics. Some rayon fabrics are used in spacecraft parts.

Rayon is made from plant material called *cellulose (SEHL yuh lohs).* The cellulose is treated with chemicals to turn it into a liquid. It is pushed through small holes in machines called *spinnerets.* The liquid forms thin threads. The threads flow into a bath of chemicals. The chemicals make the threads harden. The threads are then twisted together to make rayon yarn.

Some rayon loses strength when it gets wet. It gets strong again as it dries. Rayon is easily dyed. It can be made into fabrics that look like cotton, wool, or silk.

Other articles to read include: **Materials; Textile; Wood.**

Recycling

Recycling *(ree SY klihng)* is the habit of using materials again instead of throwing them away. Recycling helps people save materials and energy. It keeps materials from filling up *landfills* (garbage dumps). Recycling also helps protect the environment by cutting *pollution.*

Many kinds of materials can be recycled. Cans, glass, paper, and some plastics can be recycled. Aluminum can be reused to make such items as beverage cans and chewing gum wrappers. Paper is recycled to make new paper and cardboard. Glass can be reused to make new kinds of glass, including glass bottles. It can also be used in place of sand in the making of *concrete.* Concrete is a hard material used to build houses and many other objects. Some plastic can be melted down and used to make new plastic products.

Some people recycle lawn clippings and other yard waste. Such materials can be broken down into *compost.* Compost is a substance that makes soil healthier and helps plants grow.

Recyclable materials are most useful if they are kept separate from garbage. The separation keeps the material from becoming

Continued on the next page

too dirty. Many cities collect material to be recycled. In other places, people must drop off materials at special locations. Some companies buy waste material that is later recycled.

Other articles to read include: **Compost; Conservation; Glass; Landfill; Materials; Metal; Paper; Plastics.**

Workers at a recycling plant sort through discarded items. The workers separate paper, plastic, metal, and other recyclable materials.

Workers sort glass containers by hand according to color. Once sorted, the glass can be smashed into small pieces, melted, and made into new containers.

Crushed aluminum cans are wrapped and stacked. They will be melted down and made into large blocks, which can be used to make new aluminum products.

Shredded paper is moved at a recycling center before being turned into a watery pulp. The pulp can then be dried and reformed into new paper products.

Refrigeration

Refrigeration is the process of removing heat. Refrigerators keep food and beverages cold. They prevent food and medicines from spoiling. Air conditioners work much like refrigerators. They keep buildings cool. For thousands of years, people have used some kind of refrigeration. Modern refrigerators are powered machines.

Heat only flows from warmer substances to cooler ones. Refrigeration works by moving heat into a *refrigerant.* A refrigerant is a substance that can quickly absorb much heat. Ice can be a refrigerant. Because it is cold, ice absorbs heat from air or warm objects that it touches. Ice can absorb a large amount of heat before melting. Adding salt or other chemicals to ice can make it absorb even more heat.

Dry ice is another kind of refrigerant. Dry ice is not made of water. It is the solid form of carbon dioxide gas. Dry ice does not melt into a liquid. Instead, it turns directly into a gas. Food processing companies sometimes use dry ice to keep food frozen.

Refrigerators in home kitchens are called *mechanical refrigerators.* They work through a process called the *refrigeration cycle.* They change liquids into gases and then back to liquids. The refrigeration cycle works because liquids absorb much heat when they turn to gas. This effect explains why sweat cools your skin. The liquid sweat turns to water vapor, taking heat with it.

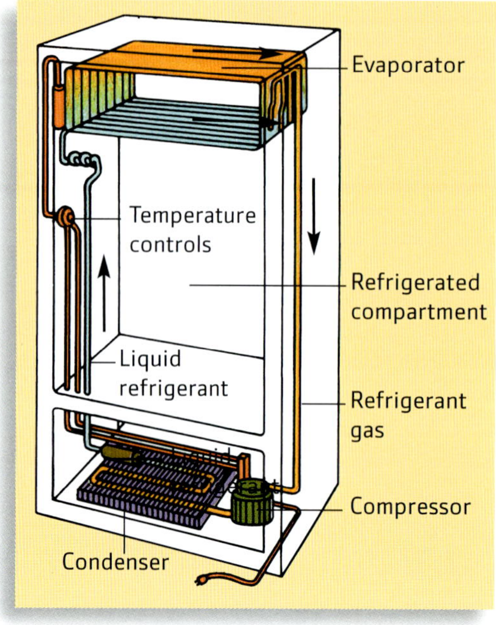

In an electric refrigerator, an *evaporator* turns a liquid refrigerant into a gas. In the process, the refrigerant absorbs much heat. The area around the evaporator becomes colder. An electrically powered compressor pumps the gas into a *condenser,* where it turns back into a liquid.

Continued on the next page

In common refrigerators, liquid refrigerant is held in a storage tank. It is put under high pressure. It moves through pipes to a place called the *evaporator.* The evaporator is the coldest part of the refrigerator or freezer. At the evaporator, pressure is reduced. With a lower pressure, the liquid can expand and turn into gas. In the process, it absorbs a large amount of heat. An electric-powered *compressor* pumps the gas away and raises its pressure. The gas flows into a *condenser.* There, it loses its heat to the outside air. It is squeezed back into a high-pressure liquid. The liquid flows back into the storage tank, and the cycle continues.

Other articles to read include: **Air conditioning; Electric motor; Pump.**

Refrigeration keeps foods and beverages cold and prevents them from spoiling.

Remote control

A remote control is a device that controls a machine or device from a distance. Remote controls can operate television sets, DVD players, automatic garage doors, guided missiles, model aircraft, robots, and spacecraft. Some remote controls operate machines that are a few feet or meters away. Others operate machines that are millions of miles or kilometers in the distance.

An example of a remote control system is a radio-controlled model airplane. The remote control has a *transmitter* that sends signals to a *receiver* in the plane. The receiver decodes the signals. The signals direct electric motors that control the plane's movements.

Remote controls make it easier to operate objects. They also help people do tasks that otherwise would be too difficult or dangerous.

Other articles to read include: **Machine; Radio; Robot.**

A remote-controlled robot helps military personnel to find and disarm bombs from a safe distance.

Sally Kristen Ride

Ride, Sally Kristen

Sally Kristen Ride (1951–2012) was the first woman United States astronaut to travel in space. In June 1983, she and four other astronauts made a six-day flight on the space shuttle Challenger. During the flight, Ride helped launch satellites and do experiments. Ride made her second shuttle flight in October 1984, also aboard Challenger. On that mission, she helped launch another satellite.

Ride was born in Los Angeles on May 26, 1951. She earned a doctorate degree in physics in 1978. That same year, she was selected to become an astronaut.

Ride was scheduled to fly a third flight in 1986. However, the Challenger was destroyed in an accident that year. Ride's mission was canceled. Ride was assigned to a special group to investigate the accident.

Ride began to teach at Stanford University in California in 1987. In 1989, she became a professor at the University of California at San Diego and director of the California Space Institute. In 2003, the shuttle Columbia broke apart as it returned to Earth. Ride again served in a special group to investigate the accident. Ride died on July 23, 2012.

Other articles to read include: **Astronaut; Columbia disaster; Space exploration.**

Rifle

A rifle is a gun with spiral grooves inside its long barrel. The grooves make the bullet spin. Without spin, a bullet would not stay pointed forward in flight. It would tumble over and over. The spinning motion increases the accuracy of the bullet. The rifle was invented in Europe about 1500. It was more accurate than any previous firearm.

Rifles are usually held against the shoulder when firing. Soldiers use rifles in battle. People also use rifles to hunt animals and to compete in shooting matches.

Military rifles and sporting rifles differ greatly. Military rifles are designed to work under the harshest conditions. Most military rifles are *automatic* or *semiautomatic.* An automatic rifle can fire bullets quickly one after another with one squeeze of the trigger. A semiautomatic rifle fires and reloads one bullet with each squeeze of the trigg hunting and target rifles take longer to reload.

Other articles to read include: **Firearm; Gun.**

Road

Roads are strips of land used for travel, generally by wheeled vehicles. Roads are important to all kinds of people. Farmers use roads to move their crops to stores. Truck drivers move goods from place to place on roads. People drive to work on roads. Millions of cars, buses, bikes, and trucks travel along roads every day.

Roads within towns and cities are often called *streets.* Streets carry vehicles within a small area. They also connect small communities to one another. Streets have names or numbers to help people find them.

A *highway* is a road that carries a large number of vehicles. People can drive faster on highways. Highways connect large cities and towns.

Highways are large roads that carry many vehicles every day.

Roads are often divided into *lanes.* Each lane carries a single line of traffic. Small roads may have only one lane in each direction. Some highways have four or more traffic lanes.

Most road work involves improving roads. Roads wear out over time. Roads in cold regions must be cleared of ice and snow.

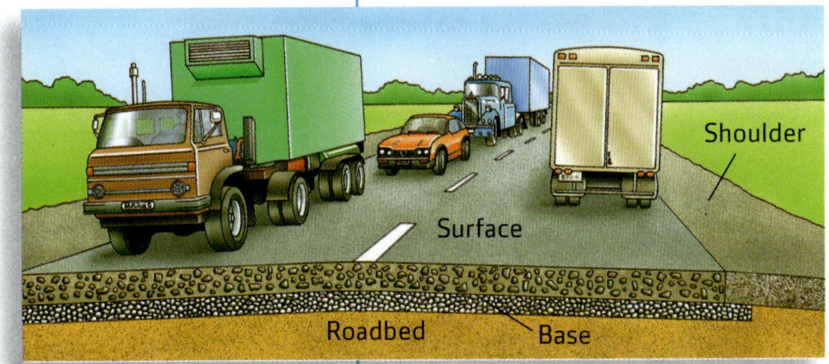

Roads are built in layers. The bottom layer, the *roadbed,* is natural soil. It is covered with a *base* of sand, stone, or other material. The *surface* is laid on top of the base. Many roads have *shoulders* for stopping in emergencies.

Sometimes, new roads are needed. Highway planners must figure out how people will use the new road. They must plan for future changes to the area around the new road.

The first job in building a new highway is to clear a path for the road. Next, the path must be prepared by shaping the lanes and smoothing the soil. Ditches are dug alongside the path, and pipes are placed to carry away rain water. Then paving begins. The pavement is made of soil or crushed rock. This mixture is bound together with bitumen or cement. In busy areas, workers put up lights alongside the road.

The ancient Egyptians, Chinese, and other civilizations built roads thousands of years ago. The first great road builders were the ancient Romans. Roman roads drained water into ditches. The Romans built more than 50,000 miles (80,000 kilometers) of roads in their empire. Some of these roads still are in use.

Other articles to read include: **Automobile; Cement and concrete; Transportation.**

The robotic "hand" of the Mars Exploration Rover Spirit is shown in this 2004 photograph. Robots are sometimes used to explore places—such as Mars—that human explorers cannot reach.

Robot

A robot is a machine that works *automatically*—meaning that it moves by itself. Robots are usually controlled by computers. Factories often use robots. Robots weld, drill, or paint car parts. They wrap foods and put together electronics. Many of the jobs that robots do are too dangerous, hard, or boring for people to do. The term *robot* comes from the Czech word *robota,* meaning *drudgery* (hard, dull work).

There are many kinds of robots. But few resemble humans, as do the robots of science fiction. Most robots are bulky machines that stay in one place. They use a single arm to lift objects and operate tools. However, some robots can move from place to place. These robots often have cameras. The cameras send images and videos to people controlling the robots. Such robots have been used to explore places that humans cannot easily visit. Such places include the ocean floor and the surface of Mars. Advanced robots can move around without direct human control. They can sense objects that block their way and avoid them.

The science that deals with robots is called *robotics.* Robotics relies on computers. With advanced computers, robots can perform more complicated tasks. They can move and react without depending on human controllers. Some robotics researchers work in the field of *artificial intelligence.* This field involves making computers that can "think" or "behave" like humans.

Other articles to read include: **Artificial intelligence; Computer; Machine; Remote control.**

Robotic arms assemble automobiles at a factory.

Rocket

A rocket is the most powerful kind of engine—and the only kind of engine that works in outer space.

A rocket is a device that pushes itself forward by shooting gases in the opposite direction. A rocket is a kind of *engine.* Like car engines and jet engines, rockets produce motion. Rockets are the only kind of engine that works in outer space. They are also the most powerful kind of engine.

Most rockets produce motion by burning a fuel. These rockets are called *chemical rockets.* In addition to fuel, rockets carry a substance called an *oxidizer.* Burning fuel requires oxygen, which the oxidizer supplies. Jet engines work much like rockets, but they do not have an oxidizer. They get oxygen from the air. Because rockets do not need oxygen from the air, they can burn fuel in outer space. A rocket's mixture of fuel and oxidizer is called *propellant.*

A chemical rocket burns fuel inside a *combustion (kuhm BUHS chuhn)* (burning) chamber. The burning creates hot gas. The gas rapidly *expands* (spreads out) in all directions. An opening in the back of the rocket called the *nozzle* lets the gas out. As the gas moves out from the nozzle, the rocket is pushed in the opposite direction. This movement can be explained by the laws of motion discovered by the English scientist Isaac Newton. Newton's laws say that for every action, there is an equal and opposite reaction.

Continued on the next page

Rockets power many kinds of fast-flying guided missiles, such as the Patriot missile shown here.

ACTIVITY

Rocket power

A rocket engine works in space because the force that shoots out of the back of a rocket creates a thrust that drives the rocket forward. You can see how this works by making a model rocket from a balloon, a plastic or paper soda straw, some string, and some heavy paper. You will also need a scissors.

What you need:

- a balloon
- a plastic or paper soda straw
- string
- heavy paper
- scissors

1. Cut off about one-third of the soda straw. Slide this section of the soda straw about halfway into the open end of the balloon.
2. With the string, tie the end of the balloon firmly around the soda straw. Do not tie it so tightly that the straw is pinched shut, however.
3. Cut a small rectangle of paper about two inches by four inches (5 centimeters by 10 centimeters) in size. Fold this in half, then open it up. In the center, right on the creased line, poke a small hole with the scissors.
4. Then slide the hole over the end of the straw sticking out of the balloon. Press the two folds of the paper together again, slightly. This is the tail of your rocket.
5. Fill the balloon full of air by blowing into the soda straw. Press your thumb over the end of the straw to keep the air from escaping, and point the balloon in the direction you want it to go. Take your thumb off the end of the straw. The air will rush out of the balloon, creating a thrust that will make the balloon shoot forward. This is much like how a real rocket works.

http://bit.ly/11uXW6N

Rocket *Continued from the previous page*

Most space rockets have two or three sections, called *stages.* Such rockets are called *multi-stage (MUHL tih* STAYJ*)* rockets. Each stage has a rocket engine, propellant, and oxidizer. The first stage, the lowest, launches the rocket. After the first stage has burned its propellant, the rocket drops that section. The second stage then fires. The rocket uses one stage after another in this way.

People use rockets mostly for scientific research, space travel, and war. Rockets are used to launch satellites into a circular path, called an *orbit,* around Earth.

Other articles to read include: **Engine; Goddard, Robert Hutchings; Guided missile; Space exploration.**

Chinese warriors fired rockets in battle during the A.D. 1200's. The use of rockets as weapons and fireworks spread from China throughout much of Asia and Europe.

Rotary engine

A rotary engine is a kind of engine that makes use of a *rotor* (spinning part). Other kinds of engine use a *piston,* not a rotor. The piston moves up and down, not around. The rotor in a rotary

Continued on the next page

A rotary engine uses the energy of burning fuel to spin a rotor, turning an *output shaft.* Other kinds of engine, by contrast, burn fuel to move a device called a *piston* back and forth.

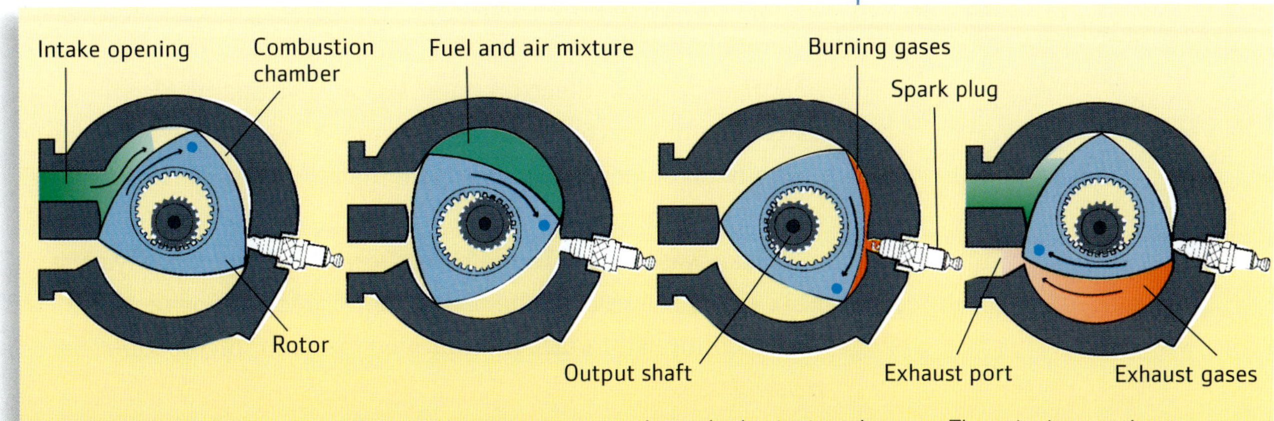

The spinning *rotor* draws a mixture of fuel and air into the *combustion chamber.*

The rotor continues to spin, compressing the mixture of fuel and air against the chamber.

A *spark plug* ignites the fuel. The burning gases expand, driving the rotor to spin an *output shaft.*

The spinning continues. The burned gases leave through the exhaust, and the cycle begins again.

Rotary engine *Continued from the previous page*

engine is mounted inside a chamber. A mixture of fuel and air burns inside the chamber. The burning fuel produces hot gases that expand against the rotor and cause it to turn. With a piston engine, the up-and-down movement of the pistons must be changed into *rotary* (circular) motion for a car's wheels to turn. A rotary engine, however, produces rotary motion directly.

The first practical rotary engine was developed during the 1950's. Early rotary engines were smaller and lighter than piston engines. At high speeds, they worked more quietly than piston engines. But at low speeds, rotary engines shake around and make more noise than do piston engines. People developed piston engines that worked better than rotary engines. Today, few manufacturers make cars with rotary engines.

Other articles to read include: **Automobile; Gasoline engine; Piston.**

Ernst Ruska

Ruska, Ernst

Ernst Ruska (1906–1988) was a German engineer. He invented a kind of microscope called the *electron microscope.* For this work, he was awarded the 1986 Nobel Prize in physics.

An electron microscope can show tiny things in great detail. It is much more powerful than a regular microscope, called an *optical microscope.* Electron microscopes use beams of extremely tiny particles called *electrons.* They use the beams to magnify an object's image. Optical microscopes use visible light for the same purpose.

Ruska was born in Heidelberg, Germany. With the physicist Max Knoll, Ruska built the first electron microscope in 1931. Ruska continued to design improved electron microscopes for many years.

Other articles to read include: **Electron microscope.**

Satellite, Artificial

An artificial satellite is an object made by people that *orbits* (travels around) a body in space. Most artificial satellites orbit Earth. Artificial satellites differ from *natural satellites*—that is, natural objects that orbit a planet. Earth's moon is a natural satellite.

People use artificial satellites to study the universe and forecast the weather. Satellites relay Internet and telephone signals around the world. People use satellites to help steer ships and airplanes, to monitor crops and other resources, and to support military activities. Artificial satellites also have orbited the moon, the sun, asteroids, and the planets Venus, Mars, Jupiter, and Saturn. Such satellites gather detailed information about the bodies they orbit.

This satellite is part of the Global Positioning System. It sends signals to Earth that help people find their location.

Spacecraft with people on board in orbit also are considered to be artificial satellites. These objects include space capsules and space stations. Pieces of space debris or space junk are also considered artificial satellites. Space debris includes burned-out rocket boosters and empty fuel tanks that have not fallen to Earth.

The Soviet Union launched the first artificial satellite in 1957. It was called Sputnik 1. Since then, dozens of countries have developed, launched, and operated satellites. Today, thousands of working satellites orbit Earth.

Other articles to read include: **Earth observing satellite; Global Positioning System; Space debris; Space exploration; Sputnik; Weather satellite.**

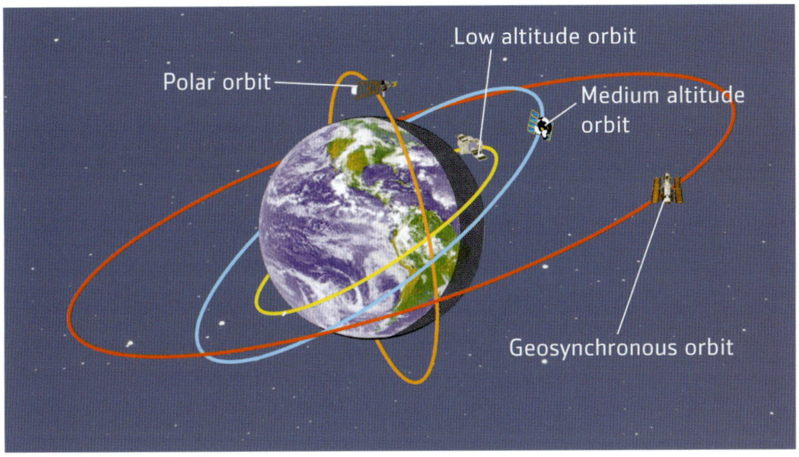

Satellites orbit Earth at various *altitudes* (heights). The lower the altitude, the faster the satellite circles the planet. *Geosynchronous* satellites orbit at the same rate that the planet spins, so they stay above the same spot on Earth. A polar orbit passes over the North and South poles.

A saw has sharp, slanted teeth that can cut through many materials. This photograph shows a *circular saw.*

Saw

A saw is a cutting tool. It has a metal blade with sharply pointed teeth along one edge. Saws are used to cut almost any material.

A saw's teeth are slanted. Every other tooth slants to the left. The rest slant to the right. The slanting teeth help the saw move through the material being cut. As a saw cuts, the teeth remove some of the material as sawdust. The cut made by the saw is wider than the blade, so the blade slides through the material without sticking.

The smoothness of the cut depends on the size of the saw's teeth. A saw with many small teeth can make smoother cuts.

The two main kinds of saws are handsaws and power saws. Handsaws are pulled and pushed with a back-and-forth motion. Some make only straight cuts. Others make both straight and curved cuts. Power saws are run by an electric motor or a gasoline engine. Some power saws are attached to a special table. Others are held by hand. Most power saws can be fitted with different types of blades to cut different materials. The blades of power saws move at fast speeds and the saws must be handled with great care. The most commonly used type of power saw is the *circular saw.* Its blade is shaped like a circle, with teeth all around.

Other articles to read include: **Electric motor; Gasoline engine; Machine tool; Tool.**

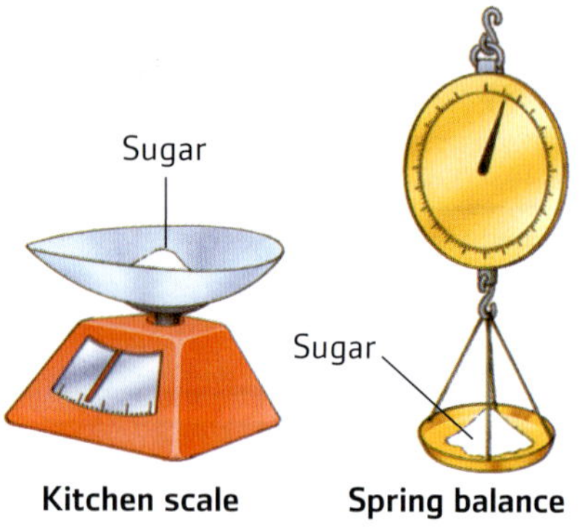

Scales are used to measure the weight or mass of something, such as a spoonful of sugar. Two kinds of mechanical scales are shown here.

Scale

A scale is a device used to measure weight or *mass* (amount of matter). Scales can measure very light substances, such as chemicals. Or they can weigh heavy objects, such as automobiles.

The oldest type of scale is the *balance.* A balance is a horizontal bar with a pan on each end. Balances were first used in Egypt in 2500 B.C. To weigh an object, a person puts it on one of the balance's pans. The person puts objects with known weights on the other pan. When the two pans balance, the person can figure out how much the first object weighs. *Mechanical scales* were invented in the 1700's. Some mechanical scales have built-in weights that can be adjusted. Other scales use springs instead of weights. Some scales measure weight electronically.

Other articles to read include: **Balance.**

Schooner

A schooner's sails run along the ship's length, from front to back.

A schooner is a kind of sailing ship. It has two or more *masts* (poles) that hold up the sails. A schooner's sails run along the ship from front to back.

The first American schooner launched in 1713. People thought it seemed to skim over the water. The ship's name comes from the word *scoon,* which means *skim.*

Schooners were popular during the 1700's and 1800's. A small crew could easily sail a schooner. For this reason, schooners were used by fishing crews, merchants, smugglers, and slave traders.

One famous schooner was called the *Amistad.* It was sailed by Spanish slavers. In 1839, its slaves rebelled and sailed the ship to the United States.

The largest pure sailing ship ever built was a schooner called the *Thomas W. Lawson.* It was made in 1902. It had seven masts.

Other articles to read include: **Ship.**

Screws come in different sizes and shapes (below).

Screw

Kinds of screws

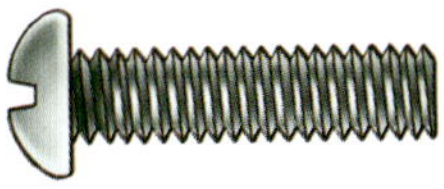

Round head machine screw

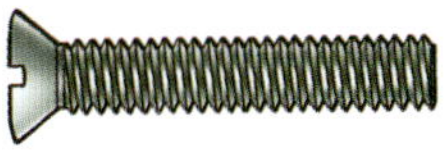

Flat head machine screw

Round head wood screw

Flat head wood screw

A screw is basically a ramp that spirals around a central shaft. It is one of the six *simple machines* discussed in physics. Most screws are small. They hold materials together, such as pieces of wood or metal. Screws are also used to open and close clamplike tools called *vises.* Some screws are much larger. Ship and airplane propellers, for example, are screws.

A screw has a long central shaft. The shaft is topped by a wider, flat part called the *head.* A screw's *thread* is the twisting ramp or ridge that wraps around the shaft. When screws are turned, their threads pull them into or push them out of an object. Most screws have a slot in the head. A screwdriver is placed into this slot in order to turn the screw.

Screws come in different sizes and shapes. They are usually made of steel, copper, aluminum, or other metals.

Other articles to read include: **Machine; Tool.**

Search engine

A search engine is a computer program used to find information. Many search engines work on the Internet. The Internet contains information on practically every subject. Much of that information is found on websites. But unlike the information in a reference book, information is not readily organized across the Internet. Search engines help Internet users easily find particular websites or information.

A person uses an Internet search engine by entering *keywords* or *search terms.* The search engine then shows a list of *links.* The links lead to websites that have something to do with the keywords. The list of links is called the *search results.* The first search results listed are often those the search engine considers most useful. Modern search engines let users narrow their searches. Users can also search for pictures, maps, videos, news articles, and other kinds of information.

Other articles to read include: **Computer; Google Inc.; Internet; Website.**

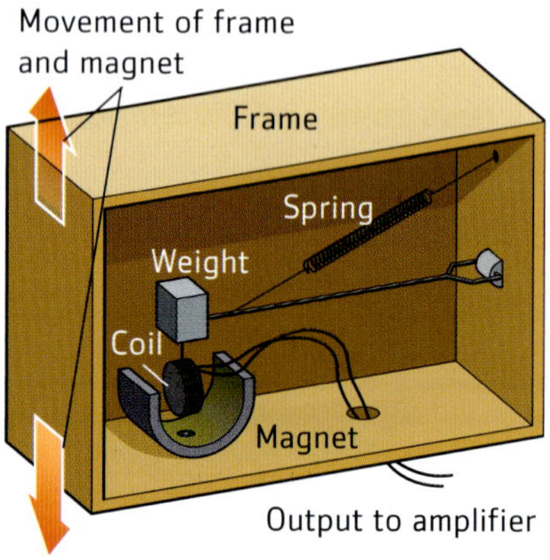

Shaking ground causes the frame of a seismograph to move. A weight tends to remain still. A magnet helps to measure the difference in movement between the frame and the weight.

Seismograph

A seismograph *(SYZ muh graf)* is a device that measures small movements of the ground. It is used to find the location and strength of earthquakes. Scientists also use seismographs in the hunt for oil and the study of Earth's insides.

A seismograph includes a weight. The weight hangs from a frame by a delicate spring. The frame moves with the ground, but the weight tends to stay still. The seismograph measures differences in movement between the weight and the frame. Some seismographs magnify ground movements by as much as 10 million times. More than one seismograph is needed to pinpoint the location of an earthquake.

Some seismographs are *portable* (easily moved). Scientists place them in areas that show recent *seismic* (ground-shaking) activity. Scientists also use them to learn what the Earth is like underground in a certain area. To do this, the scientists put them around the area to be studied. Then, the scientists set off explosives. The explosives create waves of vibration. The waves travel differently through different materials. The seismographs measure the waves. In this way, scientists can figure out what is under the surface.

Other articles to read include: **Machine.**

Semaphore

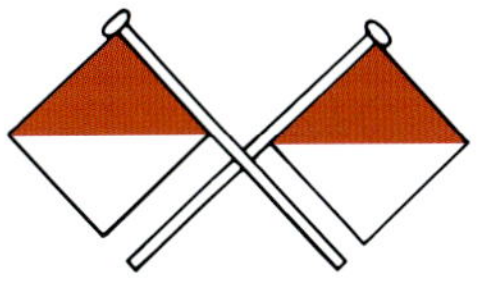

Semaphore *(SEHM uh fawr)* is a way of sending messages with flags. The messages can be sent between ships or between ship and shore. People on ships use red-and-yellow striped flags for semaphore. Red-and-white striped flags are used on land.

The message sender holds one flag in each hand. The flags are held in different positions. Each position stands for a letter of the alphabet or a certain phrase. People trained in semaphore can understand the messages.

A semaphore system was invented in the 1790's by Claude Chappe of France. The messages were sent from special towers. The towers used tall posts with moving arms, rather than flags. Messages could be sent from tower to tower over long distances.

Other articles to read include: **Chappe, Claude; Communication; Ship.**

Semaphore flags are used to send messages between ships or between a ship and the shore. Red-and-yellow flags, (above left) are used at sea. Red-and-white ones (below left) are used on land.

The semaphore code makes use of two flags for sending messages. Flag positions represent letters and special words.

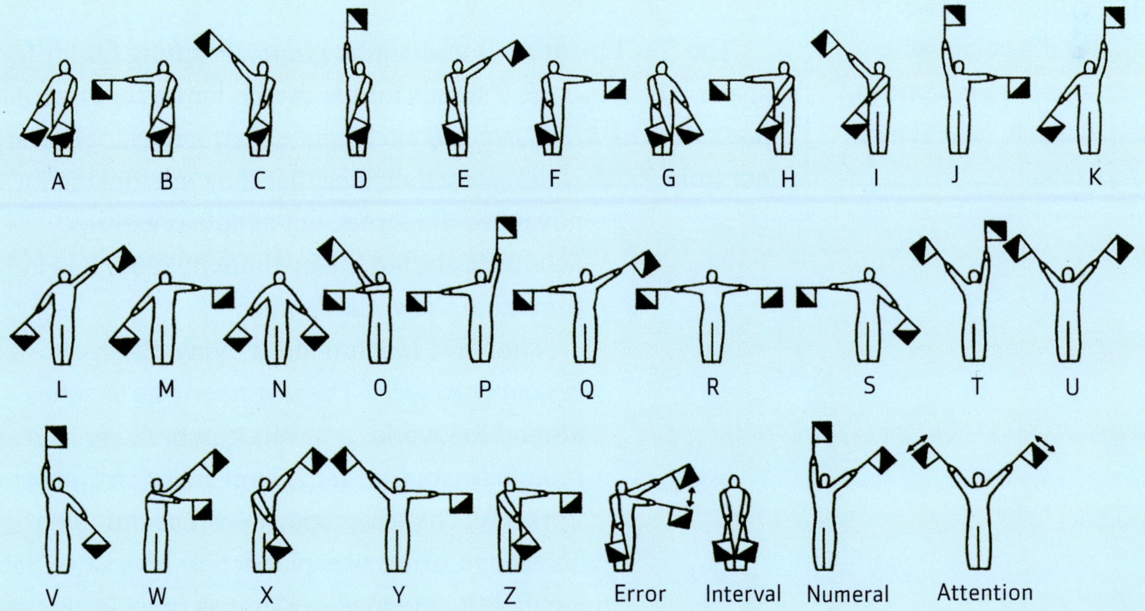

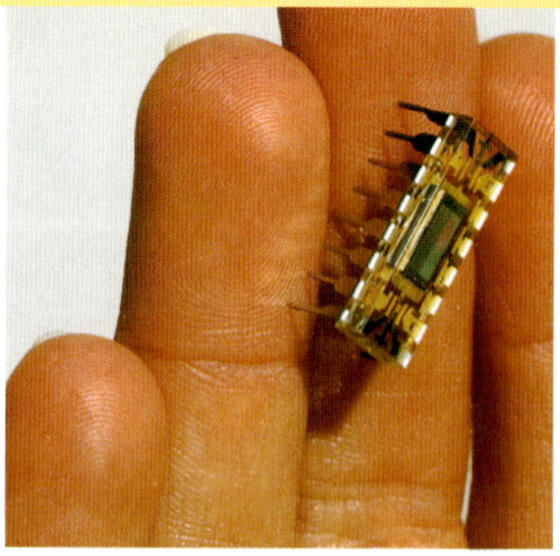

Semiconductors are used in many kinds of electronic devices, such as this computer chip.

Semiconductor

Semiconductors *(SEHM ee kuhn DUHK tuhrz)* are materials used to make parts for radios, computers, and other electronic equipment. The element *silicon (SIHL uh kuhn)* is an important semiconductor. Computer chips are made of silicon.

Semiconductors are named for the special way they *conduct* (carry) electricity. They conduct electricity better than *insulators,* such as rubber. But they conduct less easily than conductors, such as copper.

Semiconductors are useful because they can precisely control the flow of electricity. They have many uses in modern technology. Lights called *light-emitting diodes* (LED's) make use of semiconductors. LED's are used in computer and television screens. *Solar cells* use semiconductors to convert the sun's light into electric energy. Some lasers use semiconductors.

Other articles to read include: **Computer chip; Electric current; Electronics; Insulator, Electric; Transistor.**

The SETI Institute searches for signs of alien life using radio telescopes around the world—such as this one in New South Wales, Australia.

SETI Institute

The SETI Institute is a scientific group searching for life in space. The word *SETI* stands for the *s*earch for *e*xtra*t*errestrial *(EHKS truh tuh REHS tree uhl) i*ntelligence. Extraterrestrial means not from Earth. *Intelligence* indicates that they are looking for advanced life forms, not simple creatures. Scientists started the institute in 1984. It is in Mountain View, California.

The SETI Institute does many different research projects. The institute uses facilities around the world. It also began building its own radio telescope with the University of California at Berkeley. The telescope, known as the Allen Telescope Array, was planned to consist of 350 small dish antennas working as one big antenna.

Other articles to read include: **Space exploration; Telescope.**

Sewage

Sewage *(SOO ihj)* is water that contains waste material. The waste comes from human activities. Sewage is also called *wastewater.*

Sewage comes from the sinks and toilets of homes, restaurants, office buildings, and factories. Sewage contains bits of human waste. It also contains other solid matter, such as ground-up garbage. In addition, most sewage contains harmful chemicals and bacteria. Some of the bacteria can cause disease.

Most sewage eventually flows into lakes, oceans, rivers, or streams. In many countries, special treatment plants treat almost all sewage in some way. These plants remove harmful materials. The rest of the wastewater can be safely returned to the environment.

Untreated sewage looks and smells bad. It can cause illness. It also pollutes the water, killing fish and other living things.

Other articles to read include: **Hazardous wastes; Water pollution.**

A sewage treatment plant removes harmful materials from wastewater.

Sewing machine

A sewing machine uses a needle to bind materials with thread. Before sewing machines, people had to sew clothes by hand. Sewing machines made it much easier to make clothes. Factories with sewing machines can make clothing quickly and cheaply.

Thomas Saint, an Englishman, developed the first sewing machine in 1790. But his machine was not practical. The American Elias Howe is considered the inventor of the modern sewing machine. He developed his machine in 1846. It sewed an upper and lower thread through cloth. The same kind of thread pattern is used in modern sewing machines. In 1851, Isaac Singer patented the foot-operated *treadle,* a kind of pedal. His company first put an electric motor on a sewing machine in 1889.

Other articles to read include: **Machine; Textile.**

A sewing machine uses a needle to bind materials together with thread.

Shannon, Claude Elwood

Claude Elwood Shannon (1916–2001) was an American mathematician and computer scientist. His ideas are widely used in modern computers. Shannon determined how computers could work using a *binary code.* Binary code uses only two symbols, for example *1* and *0.*

Claude Elwood Shannon

Shannon also worked in the field of *artificial intelligence.* Artificial intelligence is the effort to design computers that work much like a person thinks. During the 1950's and 1960's, he developed machines that played chess against human opponents.

Shannon was born in Petoskey, Michigan, on April 30, 1916. He studied mathematics and electrical engineering at the Massachusetts Institute of Technology (MIT). In 1941, Shannon began working at Bell Laboratories in New Jersey. In 1957, he joined the faculty at MIT. He taught there until he retired, in 1978. Shannon died Feb. 24, 2001.

Other articles to read include: **Artificial intelligence; Binary number; Computer.**

Alan Bartlett Shepard, Jr.

Shepard, Alan Bartlett, Jr.

Alan Bartlett Shepard, Jr. (1923–1998), was the first American to travel in space. He was also the fifth astronaut on the moon.

Shepard was born in East Derry, New Hampshire. He served in World War II (1939–1945) and became a Navy test pilot. In 1959, he was chosen as one of the first astronauts.

In April 1961, Yuri Gagarin *(YOOR ee gah GAHR ihn)* of the Soviet Union became the first person to travel in space. On May 5, 1961, less than a month later, Shepard rocketed 117 miles (188 kilometers) into space from Cape Canaveral, Florida. He landed 15 minutes later, 302 miles (486 kilometers) out in the Atlantic Ocean. In 1971, he commanded Apollo 14, the third mission that landed astronauts on the moon.

Other articles to read include: **Astronaut; Gagarin, Yuri Alekseyevich; Space exploration.**

Ship

A ship is a large, seagoing vessel. Ships are among the oldest and most important forms of transportation. Every day, thousands of ships cross the oceans. They also sail along seacoasts and travel on inland waterways.

Some ships are simple wooden vessels. Other ships rank among the largest moving structures ever built. These huge cargo ships crisscross the oceans. They form a network of trade among countries. Military forces move troops and equipment on ships. The largest military ships are the *aircraft carriers*. They are floating military bases that launch warplanes.

The difference between a ship and a boat is mostly size. A ship is a large vessel. It carries everything it needs to cross oceans. A large ship is almost like a floating city. It makes its own power, heat, and electricity. A boat, on the other hand, is a smaller craft. Boats usually stay close to shore.

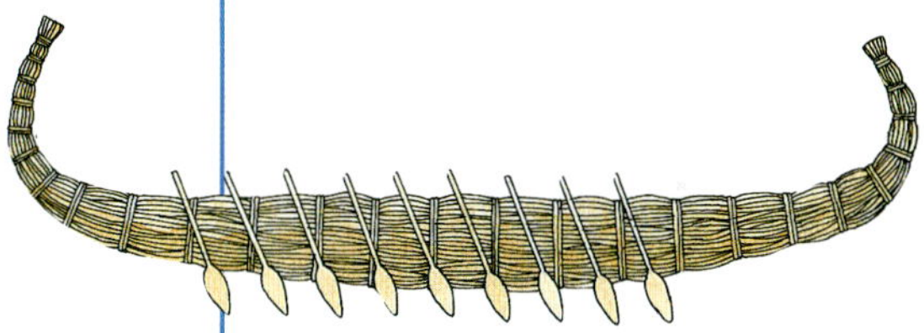

Egyptians traveled along the Nile River in reed riverboats about 3500 B.C.

Every ship has a watertight shell called a *hull*. The hull is shaped to cut through water. The *keel* is often called a ship's backbone. It is a long fin or blade along the bottom of the hull. The keel helps keep the ship stable. Ships often carry extra weight called *ballast*. Without ballast, a ship might tip over.

The earliest ships were powered by human muscle. People moved them by paddling or rowing. Sailing ships are powered by wind. Most modern ships burn fuel for power. Their engines spin propellers beneath the water. The propellers push the ship forward. *Nuclear energy* powers a small number of large ships. Nuclear energy is produced by altering atoms. Almost all nuclear-powered ships are military vessels.

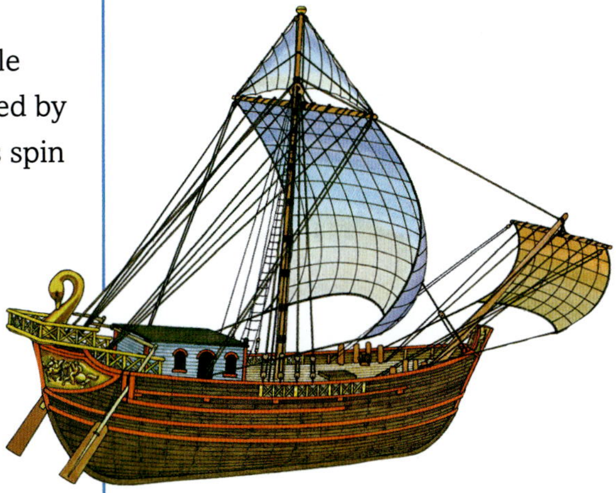

Around 200 A.D., Roman grain ships carried farm products across the Mediterranean Sea.

Most ships today are cargo ships. They carry raw materials or manufactured goods. There are several kinds of cargo ships. *Container ships* are designed to carry giant boxes. The boxes can be filled with many kinds of cargo. It is easy to load and unload the boxes, because they are all the same shape and size. *Tankers* carry liquid cargo, usually oil. *Dry bulk carriers* transport such raw materials as grain or metal ore.

Other ships do not carry cargo. They perform other tasks. Some ships are made to break through icy waterways. Certain

Continued on the next page

The Vikings sailed long, narrow, speedy ships on the Atlantic Ocean between the 700's and 1000's.

The *cog* was a one-masted ship with a square sail. It was developed in northern Europe during the 1200's.

Ship *Continued from the previous page*

ships are designed to tow other ships. Passenger ships carry people. People take vacations on *cruise ships.*

Ships are designed by experts called *naval architects.* A ship is almost always built near water. Some are built in *dry docks.* The dry dock is a bay that can be flooded when the ship is ready.

Life on a ship can be quite different from life on land. Wind, currents, and waves cause a ship to move constantly. This motion can make people seasick. A ship must carry enough food, medicine, and fuel for its voyage. Many modern ships have automated equipment. But even a high-tech ship needs a team of officers and crew. A ship's captain is responsible for everyone and everything on board.

Ships must obey *maritime law.* They must pass safety tests. Each ship must fly the flag of a certain country. A country's *merchant marine* includes all of the commercial ships that fly its flag.

Ships can cause pollution and other forms of environmental damage. Oil spills from tankers rank among the worst environmental accidents. Ships can also bring plants and animals to new places. These living things can multiply out of control, becoming *invasive species.*

Some of the earliest sailors crossed the Mediterranean Sea almost 130,000 years ago. They settled on the island of Crete. Many of the world's great civilizations relied on ships. They used ships for trade, exploration, and warfare. By 3000 B.C., the ancient Egyptians learned how to build sailing ships. Egyptian ships carried huge stones on the Nile River. The ancient Phoenicians, Greeks, and Romans improved ship technology.

Between the 700's and 1000's, Viking ships sailed around Europe. Some Vikings reached Greenland and North America. In the early 1400's, the Chinese mariner Zheng He commanded a huge fleet of ships. He sailed around the Indian Ocean.

Over time, ships used more sails and *masts,* the poles that hold up sails. Beginning in the 1400's, European sailors crossed the Atlantic Ocean on ships. They came to the "New World" of

Continued on the next page

The *Great Eastern,* launched in the United Kingdom in 1858, combined sails with steam power.

North and South America. Their voyages forever changed ways of life in the Americas and in Europe.

During the mid-1800's, steam-powered ships began to replace sailing vessels. Steamships could cross the seas much more quickly. Distant places became more connected. During the 1800's and early 1900's, many people crossed the seas on huge passenger ships. But passenger ships declined after the 1940's. More people began traveling on airplanes instead.

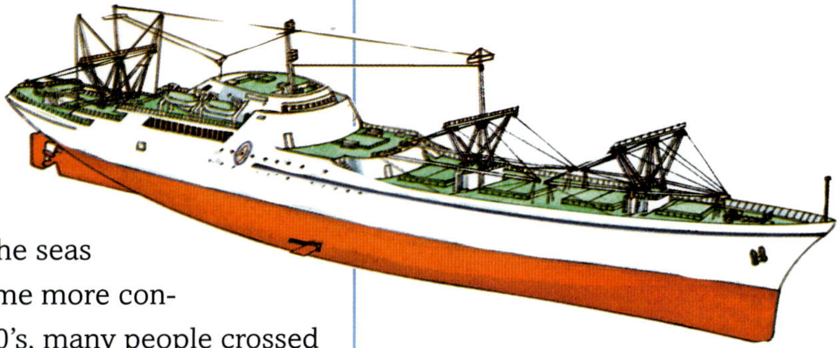

The *Savannah,* launched in the United States in 1959, was the world's first nuclear-powered merchant ship.

During the 1900's, cargo ships became larger. They took on specialized shapes. Today, container ships transport food and electronics from factories to consumers. Tankers carry oil across the oceans. Modern society could not exist without ships.

Other articles to read include: **Navigation; Schooner; Steam engine; Submarine; Transportation.**

A modern container ship carries a huge amount of goods. The goods are packed in large, identical boxes called *containers.*

Short circuit

A short circuit *(SUR kit)* is a problem that can occur with electric devices. It happens when electric current accidentally leaves or skips part of its intended *circuit* (looping path). It can happen when two bare wires touch. Water can also cause a short circuit. Sometimes short circuits are dangerous. They may cause a fire by heating wires or making sparks. They can also pose a danger of electrocution.

There are two basic types of short circuits. The first type involves two circuits. If two bare wires from two different circuits come in contact, a short circuit occurs. The second type of short circuit involves a circuit and a *grounded* object. An object that can drain off electricity from a circuit is said to be grounded. It is called *grounded* because any circuit that touches the ground will drain electricity. For example, you can place a metal bar on a bare live wire. As long as nothing is touching the bar, the bar is not grounded. The electricity in the wire acts as if the bar is not there. However, if the bar were to touch the ground or any grounded object, a short circuit occurs. A short circuit usually blows a *fuse (fyooz)*. A fuse is a device that protects an electric circuit against damage. Devices called *circuit breakers* serve a similar function.

Water is dangerous around electricity. Water by itself does not conduct electricity. But no water is perfectly pure. It has other things in it, such as a small amount of dissolved metal. Such things conduct electricity. Pouring water over two circuits will cause them to short circuit. Water is especially dangerous because a small amount can spread over a large area.

Other articles to read include: **Electric circuit; Electric current.**

Devices called *circuit breakers* can help prevent damage from short circuits by switching off current. Large buildings may have several boxes, each containing many circuit breakers.

ACTIVITY

Make a short circuit

If the plastic covering that insulates a wire wears through, allowing two bare wires to touch, the electric current can pass directly from one wire to another. This causes what is known as a *short circuit*. Learn how a short circuit occurs in the following experiment.

! Ask a teacher or other adult to help you with this experiment. Never touch bare electric wires with current running through them. Remember to use a low-power battery for this experiment.

What you need:

- a 1.5-volt penlight bulb and bulb holder
- a 1.5-volt battery
- three pieces of bare wire, each about 10 inches (25 cm) long
- a screwdriver
- masking tape

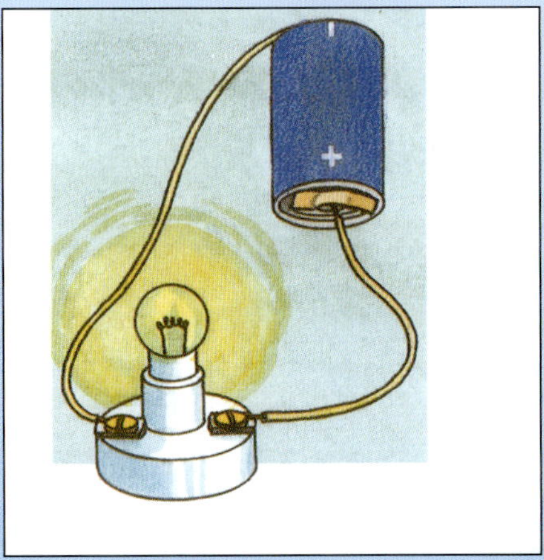

1. Fasten the ends of 2 wires to the bulb holder using the screwdriver. Tape the other ends of the wires to the top and bottom of the battery. The bulb will shine brightly.

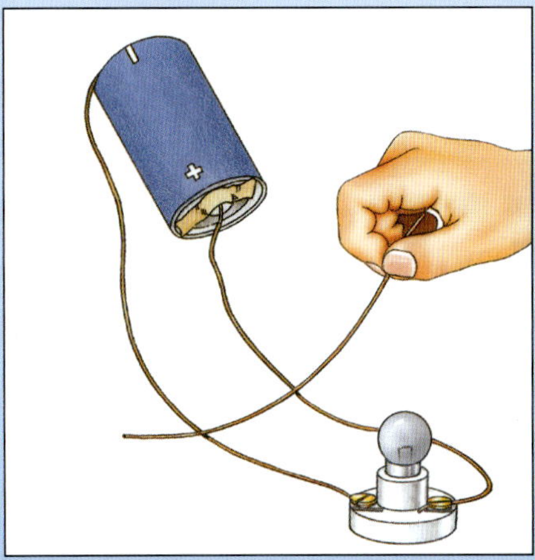

2. Drop the third piece of wire across the wires connecting the bulb and battery. What happens?

What's going on:

The extra wire has caused a short circuit. The current is flowing through this wire rather than through the bulb. The current flows more easily through the thick wire, which has less resistance than the thin filament of the bulb.

http://bit.ly/WzcyOS

A siphon draws liquid from a higher container to a lower one.

Siphon

A siphon *(SY fuhn)* is an arrangement used to draw liquid from a container. The siphon takes the liquid over the edge of the container. The liquid is drained to a lower level. Most siphons are bent tubes or hoses. They move liquid from a higher container to a lower container.

One common way to make a siphon is by putting one end of a tube into a container of liquid. Then put the other end at a level lower than the container. Next, use suction to pull liquid from the first container into the tube. Once the liquid has started flowing, the suction can be removed. The liquid will continue to flow.

A siphon works because of *gravity.* Gravity pulls the liquid in the tube down. As it falls, this liquid pulls more liquid up into the tube. The liquid will keep moving through the tube until the liquid in both containers is at the same height or until the top container is empty.

Siphons have many uses. For example, they are used in plumbing and in *irrigation* (the watering of crops).

Other articles to read include: **Pump.**

A scuba diver uses air tanks to stay underwater for long periods.

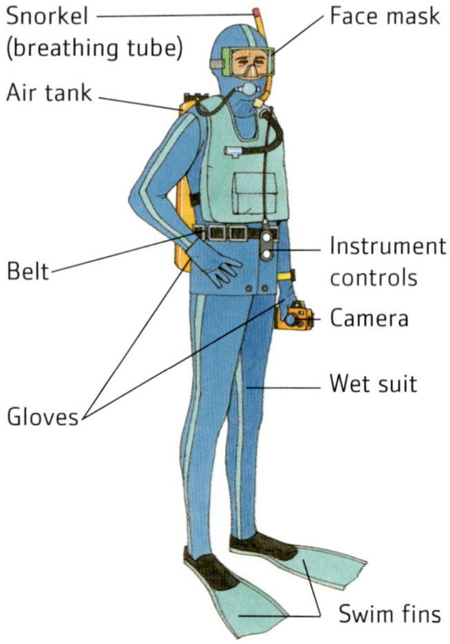

Skin diving

Skin diving is a form of diving underwater. The term often refers to simply diving while holding one's breath. It can also refer to *scuba diving*—that is, diving with air tanks. The air supply allows scuba divers to stay deep underwater for long periods.

Some divers wear *wet suits.* The rubbery suit covers the body tightly. It keeps the diver warm in cold water.

Scientists and hobbyists use scuba diving equipment. They may catch fish or collect shells, rocks, or other objects. They also may take underwater photographs and record sounds that underwater creatures make. Military forces also use scuba diving equipment.

Skyscraper

Skyscrapers are the world's tallest buildings. These giant structures were first built during the late 1800's in Chicago and New York City. Skyscrapers provide space for offices, stores, hotels, restaurants, sports clubs, and other businesses. People live in skyscrapers, too. Some skyscrapers have so much space and offer so many activities and services that they are like small cities.

Much planning goes into building a skyscraper. These buildings have two main parts. The part below ground is the *foundation*. The part above ground is the *superstructure*. Both parts help support the weight of the building. Skyscrapers must also be supported against high winds.

The world's tallest skyscrapers include the Burj Khalifa in Dubai, United Arab Emirates; the Abraj Royal Clock Tower Hotel in Mecca, Saudi Arabia; the Petronas Twin Towers in Kuala Lumpur, Malaysia; and One World Trade Center in New York City, United States.

Other articles to read include: **Building construction.**

The world's tallest skyscraper is the Burj Khalifa, in Dubai, United Arab Emirates.

Sled

A sled is a vehicle used to move over snow or ice. A sled has *runners,* or rails, instead of wheels. The runners slide easily over snow or ice. Sleds help people to get around in areas with much snow and ice. People in parts of Alaska and Canada's Yukon travel on sleds. The sleds are pulled by strong dogs called huskies.

Sleds are used for fun and recreation, too. *Bobsleds* are special racing sleds.

Sleds have different names in different parts of the world. A sled may be called a *sledge,* a *sleigh,* a *toboggan,* or a *troika.* Horses or reindeer are sometimes used to pull sleds.

In early times, people made sleds from logs tied together. Such sleds were used to haul things over snow and bare ground. Later, people found that a sled would move more easily with runners under the logs.

Other articles to read include: **Transportation.**

A sled has rails called *runners* that slide over snow and ice.

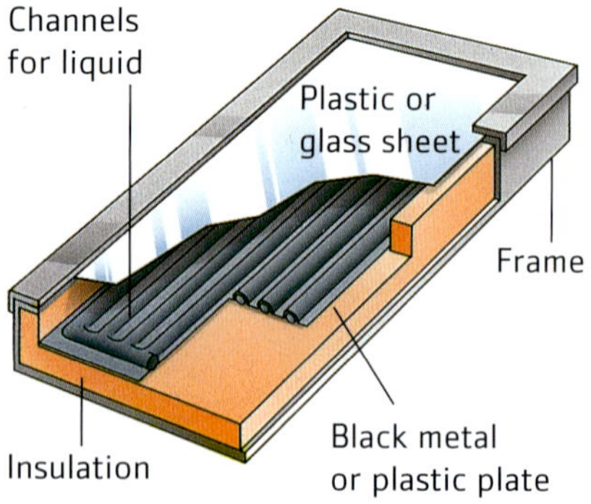

This solar collector has a black plate that absorbs sunlight, heating a liquid. Insulation keeps the liquid hot as it flows through the channels. The hot liquid can be used to heat a home.

Solar energy

Solar energy is energy from sunlight. Sunlight is used for heat and to make electric power. Earth gets a huge amount of energy from the sun. But this energy is spread out over large areas. Solar energy devices collect the sun's energy. Devices called *solar cells* change this energy into electric power. Other devices focus the sun's energy to make heat.

Solar cells use sunlight to make an *electric current*. An electric current is a flow of electricity. Such a current can provide power for electronic devices. Solar cells, like computer chips, are often made from materials called *semiconductors*. Some wristwatches and calculators get power from solar cells. Spacecraft and satellites get power from solar cells, too. Large solar cells can provide electric power for homes and other buildings.

A *solar thermal conversion system* does not directly make electric current. Instead, it gathers heat. The system uses large mirrors to catch and concentrate sunlight. The sunlight's great heat can boil water, creating steam. The steam, in turn, can run machines that make electric power.

Other articles to read include: **Electric power; Semiconductor; Solenoid.**

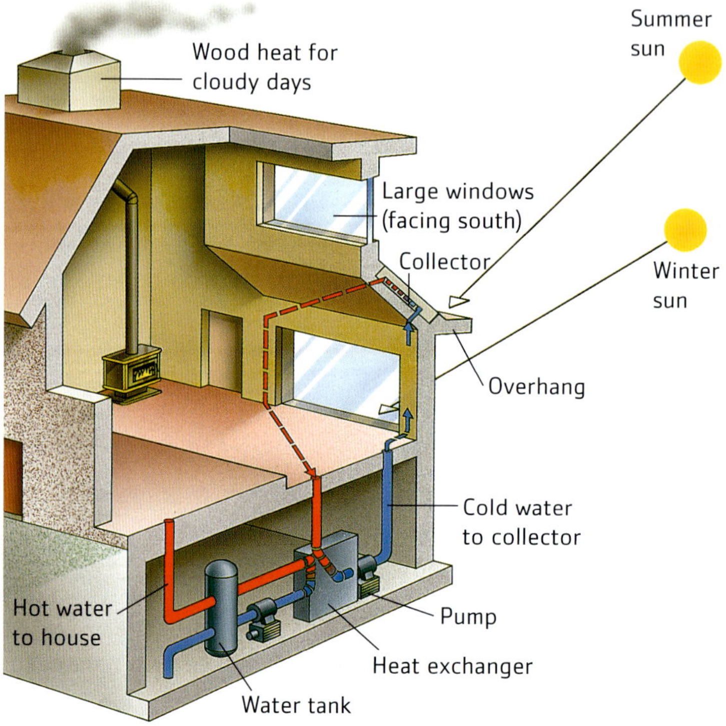

Hot liquid from collectors flows through a solar-heated home, heating water that is used throughout the house. The home also has large windows that let in heat from the sun.

ACTIVITY

Make a solar collector

On a sunny day you can feel the heat coming off the ground, once the energy of the sun has warmed it. The sun supplies enough energy to each square yard or square meter of Earth's surface to power several electric light bulbs. If we could trap and use just a fraction of this energy, we would no longer need to burn polluting fuels, such as coal and oil. Make this simple solar heater and learn more about how solar energy works.

What you need:

- 2 large aluminum foil pie pans
- scissors
- ping-pong balls
- a paintbrush
- an awl
- cardboard
- tape
- clay flowerpots
- wooden dowels
- two thermometers
- a pen or pencil
- paper or notebook

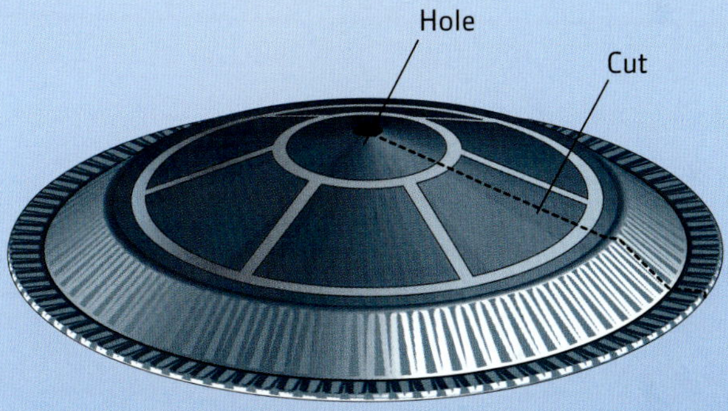

1. Make a hole in the center of a pie pan. Cut from the edge of the pan to the hole. Overlap the cut edges so that the base of the pan curves like a satellite dish.

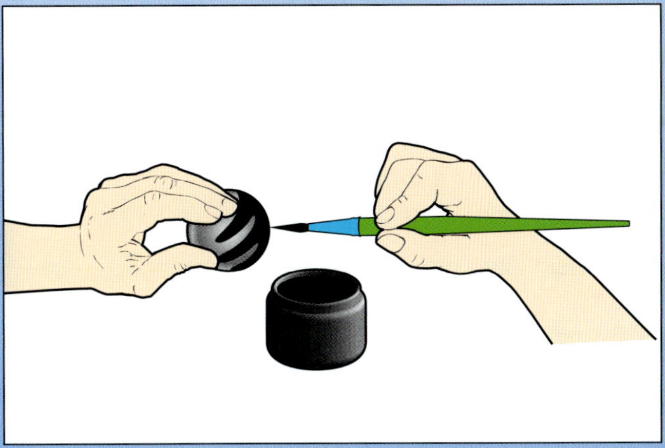

2. Paint a ping-pong ball black. Ask a teacher or other adult to use the awl to make two holes in it at a 90° angle to each other.

3. Use cardboard and tape to fix the pan at an angle on top of the flowerpot.

Continued on the next page

ACTIVITY

Make a solar collector *Continued from the previous page*

4. Push a dowel through the hole in the pan. Mount the black ball on top of the dowel. Place your solar heater in the sun. Adjust the angle of the pan and the height of the ball until sunlight is reflected on the ball.

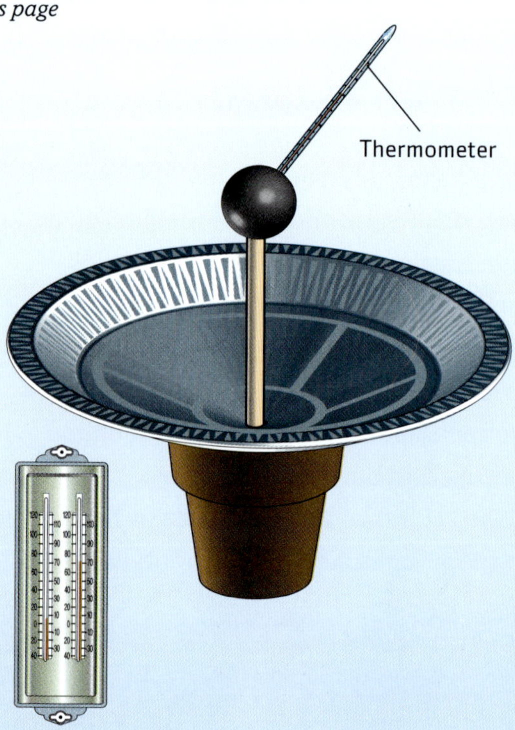

Now you are ready to test your solar heater. Use the thermometers to compare the temperature of the surrounding air to the temperature inside the ball. Because Earth is constantly spinning, you will need to move the reflector dish to keep the sun focused on the ball. In real solar power stations, large reflectors are moved automatically by computer, so that they track the sun as it crosses the sky.

Experimenting with your solar heater

Make a note of the temperature inside the black ball after a few minutes. Record the temperature every hour for several hours. Create a solar heater with a white ping-pong ball and repeat the experiment. How do you think the results will compare? When are the temperatures highest? Lowest? Note the temperature at the same time of day every day for a month. Note the weather conditions at the time of your readings. How does weather affect the amount of the sun's energy absorbed by the ball? If you could keep records over several seasons, how do you think the temperature would change in summer? In winter? Would your results be the same if you used a ball painted a different color? What if you used colored cloth instead of a ball? What if you didn't change the angle of the pan?

What's going on:

This solar heater uses a curved reflector to concentrate sunlight and heat the air inside a ball. Solar power stations in the United States and elsewhere use the same method. Large reflectors focus sunlight on water pipes or boilers. Steam from the boilers turns turbines to make electric power.

http://bit.ly/Xtbg34

Solenoid

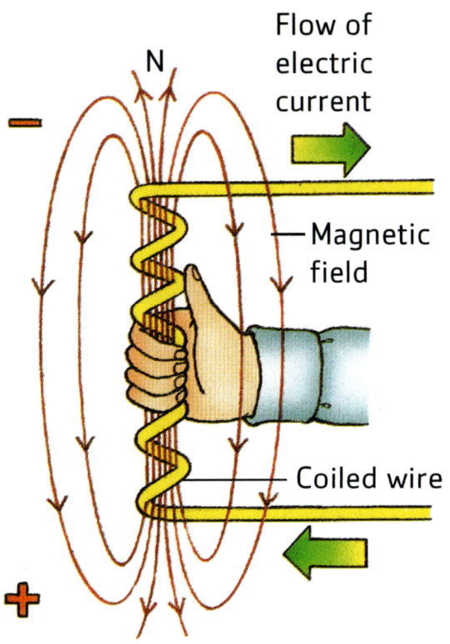

A solenoid *(SOH luh noyd)* is a coil of wire. It becomes a magnet when electricity flows through it. One of the solenoid's ends becomes a north magnetic pole. The other end becomes a south pole. Many electromagnets use solenoids.

Solenoids are used in electric door locks. They can move the bolt back and forth to lock and unlock the door. They are also used in loudspeakers, automobile turn signals, mechanical sorting devices, and *circuit breakers* (switches that turn off an electric current if it becomes too strong).

Other articles to read include: **Electric current; Electric circuit; Electromagnet; Lock; Wire.**

A *solenoid* is a coiled wire that can create or strengthen a magnetic field. If you hold the coil as shown here, your thumb points to the north magnetic pole.

Sonar

Sonar is the use of sound energy to spot objects. Sonar devices can measure how far away an object is. They can also tell how fast an object is moving and in which direction. A sonar device can even produce a picture of an object, such as an

Continued on the next page

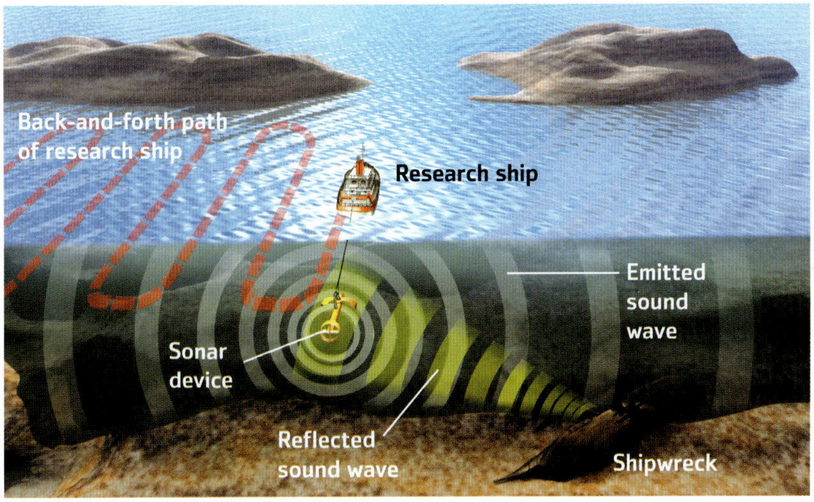

Sound waves from a sonar device bounce off objects underwater. The device can find the objects by measuring the reflected waves.

Sonar *Continued from the previous page*

unborn baby. The word *sonar* comes from *so*und *n*avigation *a*nd *r*anging.

Sonar works well underwater. Sound travels better through water than do radio waves or light. People use sonar to find submarines and other underwater objects. Sonar can also work in the air. Some animals use a form of sonar called *echolocation.* Such animals include dolphins and certain kinds of bats and whales.

There are two kinds of sonar: *active sonar* and *passive sonar.* Active sonar equipment sends out sound waves from a machine called a *transmitter.* Underwater transmitters make a sharp pinging sound. The sound waves travel through the water until they hit an object. Then the sound waves bounce back to the sonar device. The device figures out the distance by measuring how long it takes for the sound to return. Sound travels about 1 mile (1.6 kilometers) per second through water.

Passive sonar makes use of sound waves given off by another source. It does not have a transmitter to send out sounds.

Other articles to read include: **Navigation; Ship.**

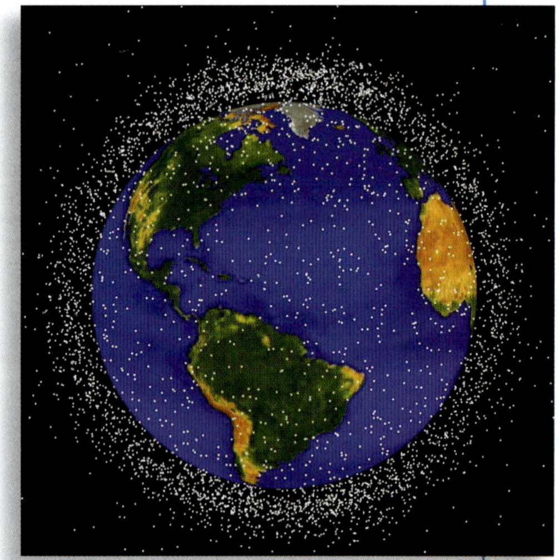

Scientists have identified thousands of pieces of space debris around Earth.

Space debris

Space debris is an object made by people that remains in orbit around Earth but serves no purpose. It is sometimes called *space junk.* Space junk ranges from used rocket *stages* (sections) to tiny paint chips that have come off spacecraft. Space debris does not include working satellites. It also does not include natural chunks of matter called *meteoroids.*

Scientists have identified thousands of pieces of space debris. Space experts worry about space debris. Collisions with space debris can damage spacecraft or injure astronauts.

Many space missions leave in orbit such objects as bolts, tools, and protective covers for scientific instruments. Sometimes a satellite breaks apart in orbit. The explosion of an old rocket stage can produce hundreds of pieces of debris.

Other articles to read include: **Satellite, Artificial; Space exploration.**

Space exploration

Space exploration is traveling into space to gather information about the universe beyond Earth. Space exploration can help people discover how the sun, the planets, and the stars were formed. People might also learn whether life exists on other planets. Some space exploration is done by spacecraft that carry people. Other exploration is done by robotic spacecraft. With each mission, scientists gain knowledge that will help plan future missions.

The first U.S. astronaut to "walk" in space was Edward H. White II, on June 3, 1965.

Earth is surrounded by air, which makes up the atmosphere. Beyond the atmosphere is outer space. There is no clear boundary between the atmosphere and outer space. However, most scientists say that space begins somewhere beyond 60 miles (95 kilometers) above Earth. Satellites orbit Earth above the atmosphere. Satellites perform many tasks. They beam television programs and telephone calls all around the globe, track weather patterns, and aid in navigation.

To reach space, a craft must overcome Earth's gravitational pull. Gravity gives everything on Earth its weight. It keeps us from floating away into space. The larger and heavier an object is, the harder it is to get it off the ground.

Large, heavy spacecraft need a powerful *booster rocket* to launch them. Boosters burn fuel. The burning gives off gases that push the spacecraft off the ground and into the air. Once in space, a spacecraft fires rockets to change its speed or direction.

To return to Earth, a spacecraft must slow down. Once in the atmosphere, the spacecraft loses much of its speed. It begins falling toward Earth. Parachutes slow it down even more. Some spacecraft parachute to the ground. The early United States space capsules "splashed down" into the ocean. The space shuttle landed on a runway.

Spacecraft that carry astronauts must provide everything people need to survive. They must provide the astronauts with air to breathe and water to drink. They also have heating and cooling controls to keep the temperature comfortable. Special toilets on board suck body wastes into collection containers. Meals on spacecraft must be easy to make and store. Some of these meals are frozen foods that can be warmed up on board. Trash is kept in unused places on the space vehicle. It is brought back to Earth.

Continued on the next page

Space exploration *Continued from the previous page*

Astronauts wash themselves with wet towels. Some *space stations* have showers. A space station is a spacecraft where astronauts live and work for a long time. Space travelers have special sleeping bags strapped to a cushion and a pillow. However, most astronauts like to sleep floating in the air. They just wear a few straps to keep them from bouncing around the cabin. Some astronauts wear blindfolds to block the sunlight that streams in the windows.

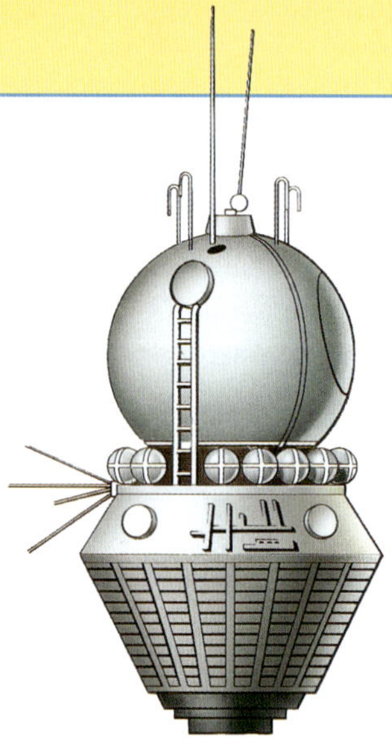

The Soviet Vostok spacecraft in 1961 carried Yuri A. Gagarin into space on the first human space flight.

Astronauts must eat good food in space to stay healthy. During long missions on a space station, they ride exercise bikes, use treadmills, and perform other kinds of exercise. The activity keeps their muscles, bones, and hearts from growing weak. Some astronauts take medicine that makes them feel better in the weightless environment.

Astronauts can enjoy the magnificent view of space from the spacecraft window. Space stations also have books, tapes, and computer games for the astronauts. Astronauts sometimes use entertainment to help them deal with feelings of homesickness, loneliness, and other emotional problems.

The Apollo-Soyuz Test Project, in 1975, was the first mission that united American astronauts with Soviet cosmonauts in space.

Once in space, the crew members carry out the goals of their mission. They gather information about Earth, the stars, and the sun. They experiment with the effects of weightlessness on various materials, plants, animals, and themselves. They also repair, replace, or build equipment. Some spacecraft bring supplies to space stations.

Astronauts use radio, television, computers, and other equipment to communicate with mission control on Earth. Computers tell the astronauts and mission control where the spacecraft is and where it is going.

An astronaut wears a special space suit to work outside the spacecraft. A space suit can keep an astronaut alive for six to eight hours. The suit has many layers of material.

Continued on the next page

Apollo 11 blasted off on July 16, 1969 (above), carrying astronauts to the moon. Only powerful rockets can lift a spacecraft beyond Earth's gravity.

The Apollo spacecraft carried several stages. Each stage contained a rocket engine that separated from the craft once it burned its fuel.

China's first *taikonaut* (astronaut) was launched into space aboard a Long March rocket in 2003.

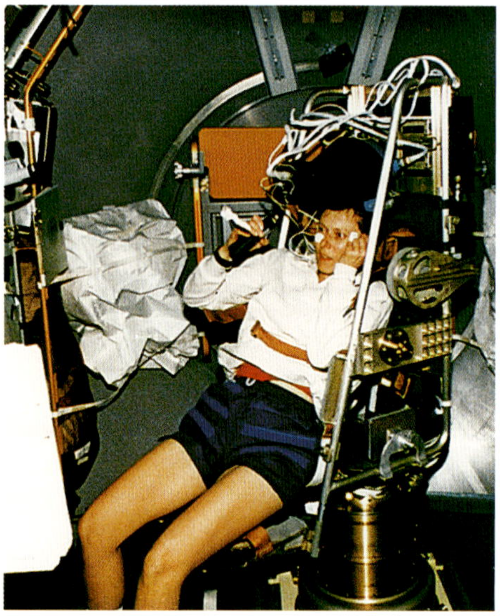

An astronaut studies the effects of weightlessness in space. The chair tests the astronaut's sense of direction.

Space exploration *Continued from the previous page*

It keeps the astronaut from getting too hot or cold and protects against impacts. Equipment in a backpack supplies the astronaut with air to breathe. A helmet blocks out strong, harmful rays from the sun. Thin, flexible gloves allow the astronaut to feel small objects and handle tools. The astronaut communicates with the crew and mission control through a radio.

Space exploration began on October 4, 1957. On that day, the Soviet Union launched Sputnik 1, the first artificial satellite to orbit Earth. Yuri A. Gagarin *(gah GAHR ihn),* a Soviet cosmonaut, was the first human being to travel in space. He made his space flight on April 12, 1961.

Many space launches and developments in space exploration followed. The first human voyage to the moon was in December 1968, when the United States launched the Apollo 8 spacecraft. It *orbited* (circled) the moon 10 times and returned safely to Earth. In July 1969, U.S. astronaut Neil A. Armstrong became the first person to set foot on the moon. During the 1970's, astronauts and cosmonauts developed skills for living on space stations.

In April 1981, the U.S. space shuttle Columbia blasted off. The shuttle was the first reusable spaceship. It was also the first spacecraft able to land at an ordinary airfield. The U.S. space shuttle program ended in 2011.

Many *space probes* have also been launched into space. Space probes do not carry people. They have studied every planet. Two space probes, Voyager 1 and 2, will be the first spacecraft to leave the solar system. Both were launched in 1977. They are predicted to leave the solar system sometime in the mid-2010's.

Other articles to read include: **Astronaut; Challenger disaster; Columbia disaster; European Space Agency; Hubble Space Telescope; International Space Station; Mars Exploration Rover; Mars Pathfinder; National Aeronautics and Space Administration; Observatory; Rocket; Satellite, Artificial; Space debris; Spitzer Space Telescope; Sputnik.**

Speedometer

A speedometer *(spee DOM uh tuhr)* is a device that tells the speed of an automobile or other vehicle. A speedometer may show the speed in miles per hour, kilometers per hour, or both. Vehicles have speedometers on their dashboards, the area behind the steering wheel.

Some speedometers are electronic. They pick up signals from a part of the car called the *transmission*. The signals travel to a display on the dashboard. The display shows the car's speed.

A *mechanical speedometer* uses a dial display. The dial is connected to a magnet near gears in the car. The faster the gears turn, the harder the magnet pulls. This causes the dial to swing toward the actual speed.

An instrument called an *odometer (oh DOM uh tuhr)* measures the total distance that a vehicle travels. It also has a readout on the dashboard.

Other articles to read include: **Automobile.**

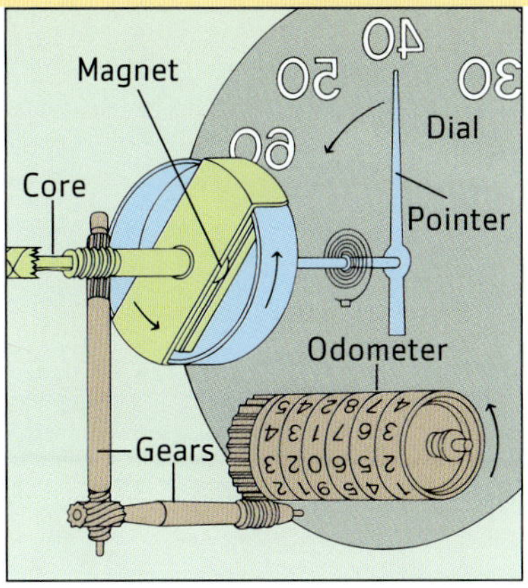

A mechanical speedometer measures speed with a magnet connected to a dial. The faster the gears spin, the harder the magnet pulls. An *odometer* shows the total distance traveled.

Spitzer Space Telescope

The Spitzer Space Telescope is a spacecraft that gathers *infrared rays* (heat rays) from distant objects. From some objects, heat reaches Earth, but little visible light does. Spitzer can view these objects more clearly than can many other telescopes.

The Spitzer Space Telescope follows Earth in its *orbit* (path) around the sun. Because it is in space, Spitzer can study objects that telescopes on the ground cannot see. Scientists use the telescope to study the formation of stars and planets. They also use it to study asteroids and other objects near Earth as well as faraway galaxies.

The Spitzer telescope was launched by the National Aeronautics and Space Administration (NASA). They named it after the American astronomer Lyman Spitzer, Jr. He was the first to suggest launching large telescopes into space.

Other articles to read include: **National Aeronautics and Space Administration; Satellite, Artificial; Space exploration; Telescope.**

NASA scientists work on the Spitzer Space Telescope before launch.

Sputnik

Sputnik *(SPUHT nihk)* is the name of several *artificial satellites.* An artificial satellite is a craft made to circle the Earth or another body. Sputnik 1 was the first artificial satellite ever launched. The Sputniks were launched by the Soviet Union. They circled Earth. They did not carry a human crew.

Sputnik 1 was launched Oct. 4, 1957. It circled Earth once every 96 minutes at a speed of 18,000 miles (29,000 kilometers) per hour. It fell to Earth on Jan. 4, 1958.

Sputnik 2 was launched Nov. 3, 1957. It carried the first space traveler, a dog named Laika.

The Soviet Union launched several other Sputniks. The last one launched in March 1961.

Other articles to read include: **Satellite, Artificial; Space exploration.**

Sputnik 1, the first artificial satellite, was launched by the Soviet Union in 1957. It transmitted radio signals that were received on Earth.

Steam engine

A steam engine is a device that turns the energy of expanding steam into motion. The steam may be used to spin a device called a *turbine (TUR bihn).* Steam-powered turbines are used on large ships. Power plants use steam-powered turbines to make electric power. Steam can also push metal rods called *pistons (PIHS tuhnz)* up and down. The up-and-down motion of pistons can spin a vehicle's wheels. But few steam-powered piston engines are in use today.

The development of the steam engine in the 1700's made modern industry possible. Before then, people had to depend on their own muscles or on animal, wind, or water power. A steam engine could do the work of many horses. It could supply the power needed to run all the machines in a factory.

A steam engine uses heat energy to boil water, making steam. The hot steam expands, pushing outward. This pushing force can spin turbines or push pistons. Most steam engines have an area in which coal, oil, or some other fuel is burned to produce heat energy.

Steam locomotives hauled nearly all trains before the invention of the diesel engine. Today, steam engines still provide train service in some parts of the world.

Continued on the next page

Hero, a scientist who lived in Egypt, described the first known steam engine about A.D. 60. The device was a small, hollow globe on a pipe that ran to a steam kettle. But the device was without use. In 1698, Thomas Savery, an Englishman, developed the first practical steam engine. It was a pump that drained water from mines. In 1712, an Englishman named Thomas Newcomen invented a steam-powered piston engine. Beginning in 1763, the Scottish engineer James Watt greatly improved Newcomen's steam engine design. Watt's steam engines were widely used in industry.

Other articles to read include: **Engine; Locomotive; Piston; Steamboat; Train; Turbine; Watt, James.**

How a steam engine works

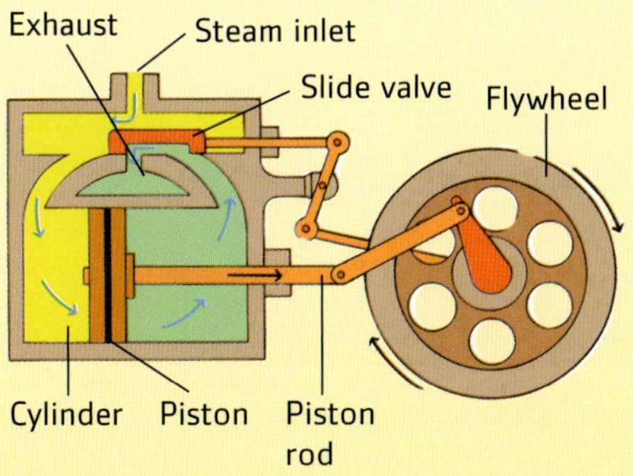

Steam, shown in yellow, pushes a piston back and forth in a cylinder. A *slide valve* directs the steam to one side or the other. In this illustration, steam enters the cylinder's left side. The steam's energy pushes the piston to the right. As the piston moves, the *piston rod* turns the *flywheel* half a turn.

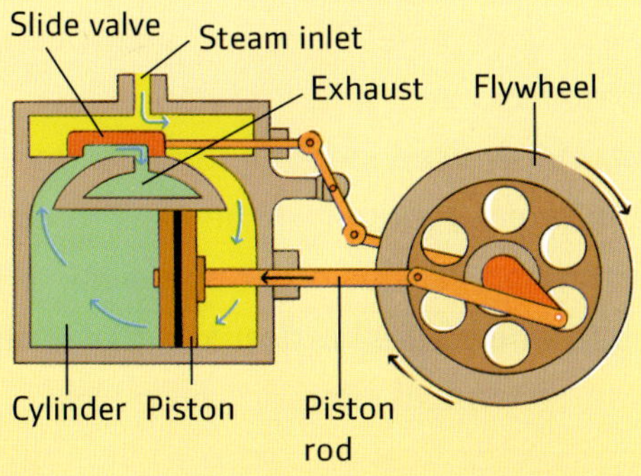

When the piston reaches the right side of the cylinder, the slide valve moves. Now the steam flows into the right side of the cylinder. It pushes the piston back to the left. The piston rod then pulls the flywheel around to complete one turn. The *exhaust* lets the steam out.

Steamboat

A steamboat is a steam-driven vessel that travels on rivers and lakes or near the seacoast. Steamboats are smaller than *steamships.* A steamship can cross the open sea.

In 1787, John Fitch demonstrated the first workable steamboat in the United States. The first successful steamboat was Robert Fulton's *Clermont.* In 1807, it steamed 150 miles (241 kilometers) up the Hudson River from New York City to Albany. The journey took about 30 hours. Steamboats were once an important means of transportation. They carried people along rivers before the development of airplanes, automobiles, and railroads. Some steamships are still used throughout the world.

Other articles to read include: **Fulton, Robert; Ship; Steam engine.**

The steamboat was once an important means of transportation.

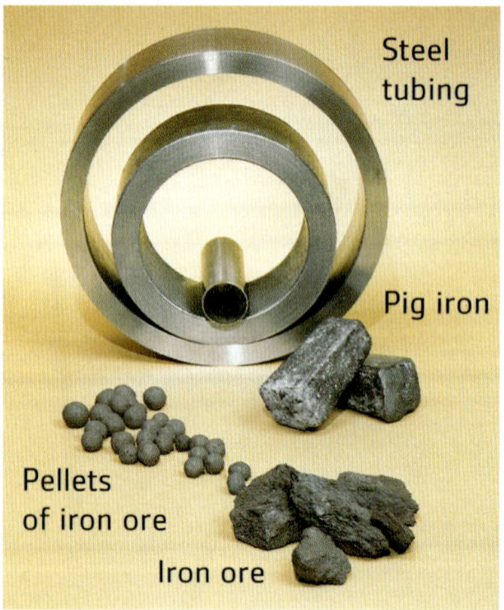

Steel is made from iron and carbon. Some kinds of steel contain other elements as well.

Steel

Steel is iron with carbon added to it. Iron is a metal. Carbon is a nonmetallic chemical element. Steel may also contain other elements. Steel can be used to make many different things, from paper clips to large machines.

There are thousands of kinds of steel. They can be grouped into *carbon steel, alloy steel, stainless steel,* and *tool steel.*

Carbon steel is the most widely used steel. It contains iron and carbon. It is used to make different products, from cans to cars.

Alloy steel contains carbon and various other chemical elements. It can be made into one of the hardest kinds of steel.

Stainless steel contains the chemical element *chromium.* Stainless steel resists *corrosion* (chemical breakdown). It is used to make items such as pots and pans.

Tool steel contains a mix of many different elements. It is used to make very hard metalworking tools.

Other articles to read include: **Alloy; Metal; Tool.**

Submarine

Scientists use small submarines to study the ocean.

A submarine is a type of ship that travels underwater. Most submarines are built to be used in war. These submarines can attack enemy ships. They can also launch missiles at targets on land. The most advanced submarines are powered by devices called *nuclear reactors.* A nuclear reactor generates power from the breakdown of atoms. More than 150 crew members can live aboard a nuclear submarine for months at a time.

Some submarines are used by scientists to explore the ocean. These submarines are used to study objects and living things underwater and gather scientific information. They are smaller than the submarines used for war. They carry only a few crew members.

A submarine's tube-shaped body allows it to move quickly underwater. The outer surface of a submarine is made of strong metal. This metal keeps the submarine from being crushed by the high pressure of the water around it.

The *Turtle,* an early submarine, was designed by a college student at Yale College during the Revolutionary War (1775–1783). It launched a failed attack against a British warship in New York Harbor. But submarines had little use in warfare until World War I (1914–1918). In that war, German submarines called *Unterseeboote* or *U-boats* sank many ships. In 1954, the United States Navy developed the first nuclear-powered submarine, the *Nautilus.*

Other articles to read include: **Holland, John Philip; Nuclear reactor; Periscope; Ship.**

A nuclear submarine is powered by a nuclear reactor instead of fuel-burning engines. Such a submarine can stay underwater for months.

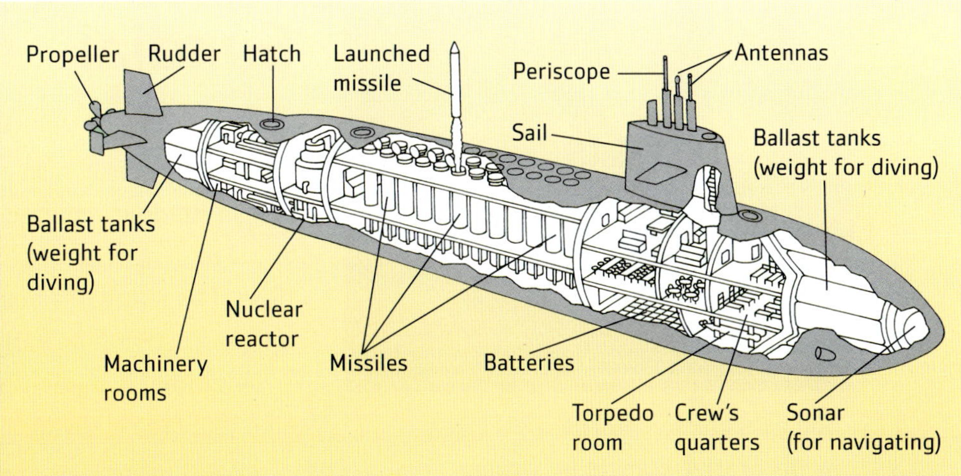

Subway

A subway is an underground railway. Crowded cities often have subways. Subway trains can quickly transport huge numbers of city dwellers. Modern subway trains run on electric power. Some parts of a subway system may be above ground.

London was the first city to have a subway. Its first underground passenger train opened in 1863. London's subway system, often called the *tube,* is now the longest in the world. New York City's subway system is the longest in the United States.

Other articles to read include: **Electric motor; Train.**

Electric-powered subway trains provide transportation for many city dwellers.

Sundial

Sundials are sometimes used today as decorative objects in gardens.

The sundial is the oldest known tool for measuring time. It makes use of shadows cast by the sun. These shadows change as the sun moves across the sky. The length or angle of the shadow tells the time. The sundial is believed to have been used in ancient Babylon as early as 4,000 years ago.

A sundial is made up of a *dial face* and a *pointer.* The dial face is divided into hours. The pointer is a

Continued on the next page

flat piece set in the center of the dial. It points toward the North Pole in the Northern Hemisphere. It points toward the South Pole in the Southern Hemisphere.

Other articles to read include: **Clock.**

Superconductor

A superconductor *(SOO puhr kuhn DUHK tuhr)* is a material that can *conduct* (carry) electricity without loss of energy. Many common materials are conductors of *electric current.* An electric current is a flow of electricity. A copper wire, for example, conducts electric current well. But some of the energy in the current changes to heat as it moves through a wire. In a superconductor, an electric current loses no energy at all.

Electricity and magnetism are closely related. For this reason, some superconductors are used to make extremely powerful magnets.

Many metals can become superconductors. But they must be cooled to extremely low temperatures. Such low temperatures are difficult to produce on Earth. For this reason, superconductors are not widely used. Certain *ceramic* materials become superconductors at higher temperatures than metals do. But they still must be cooled to temperatures far below freezing.

Other articles to read include: **Electric current; Metal; Wire.**

Superconductors have several amazing properties. For example, a superconductor will expel a magnetic field, causing a magnet to hover above it without touching.

Joseph Wilson Swan

Swan, Joseph Wilson

Joseph Wilson Swan (1828–1914) was an English chemist, electrical engineer, and inventor. In 1860, he developed an electric light. The light in Swan's bulb did not last long. The inventor Thomas Edison developed an improved electric light about 20 years later.

In 1883, Swan experimented with new types of *filaments (FIHL uh muhnts).* A filament is the thin wire in a light bulb. It is the part that gives off light. Swan also helped to produce a type of photographic plate. In 1879, he received a license to produce a type of photographic paper. His many other projects included the invention of artificial silk.

Other articles to read include: **Electric light; Invention; Photography.**

Nylon is a *synthetic* material, a substance invented by human beings. Nylon forms long, thin threads called *fibers.*

Synthetics

Synthetics *(sihn THEHT ihks)* are substances or materials made by people. Synthetics combine two or more chemicals to make a new substance. Some synthetics take the form of long, thin threads, called *fibers.* Others are thin sheets or liquids that can be molded into different shapes.

Many products are made with synthetic materials. All plastics are synthetics. Synthetic fibers are used in such products as tires, brushes, and clothing.

Some synthetics are strong and hard. Others can be stretched. Tough plastics are used in furniture, machinery parts, and packaging. Many synthetics are not greatly harmed by chemicals, insects, or sunlight.

Other articles to read include: **Materials; Plastics; Textile.**

Tank

A tank is an armored vehicle built for war. It is covered with a thick layer of steel or other strong material. Its wheels roll along inside a loop of metal track. Tanks can travel over many kinds of rough ground, including some hills. Three or four soldiers usually operate the tank.

Tanks carry such weapons as cannons, machine guns, and missile launchers. In most tanks, the weapons stick out from inside a kind of tower called a *turret.* The turret can swing around to point the weapons in any direction. Tanks were first used by the British during World War I (1914–1918). During World War II, all the warring nations used tanks. Over 6,000 tanks were used in the Arab-Israeli War of 1973. Nearly half were destroyed. Tanks also played an important role in Iraq during the Persian Gulf War of 1991 and the Iraq War (2003–2011).

Other articles to read include: **Cannon; Gun.**

A tank is a heavily armed and armored war vehicle that can travel over rough ground.

Tape recorder

The tape recorder is a machine once widely used for storing sound, pictures, and other kinds of information. A tape recorder stores information on magnetic tape. The tape may be held in a cartridge called a *cassette.* A tape recorder can also play back recordings.

Magnetic tape is a thin plastic ribbon. During recording, sounds are changed into electric signals. These signals cause magnetic changes. The changes create magnetic patterns on the tape. When the tape is played, the magnetic patterns are changed back into electric signals. The electric signals then travel to a speaker, which changes them back into sound. Most cassette tapes have two wheels called *reels.* As the tape recorder runs, the tape gradually winds from one reel to the other.

Continued on the next page

The tape recorder was once widely used for voice and music recordings. This handheld model has a microphone for recording spoken statements.

Tape recorder *Continued from the previous page*

Valdemar Poulsen, a Danish inventor, made the first magnetic recording device in 1898. During World War II (1939–1945), German engineers made plastic magnetic tape. By the 1950's, tape recorders were widely used in the music industry. In the mid-1960's, consumers could buy cassette tapes. These tapes were popular for many years. But in the 1990's, compact discs (CD's) and *digital* (computerized) music files became popular. By the 2010's, few consumers listened to music on cassette tapes. But magnetic tape remained in use. Some backup computer storage devices record data to magnetic tape.

Other articles to read include: **Compact disc; Digital video recorder; Magnet; Videotape recorder.**

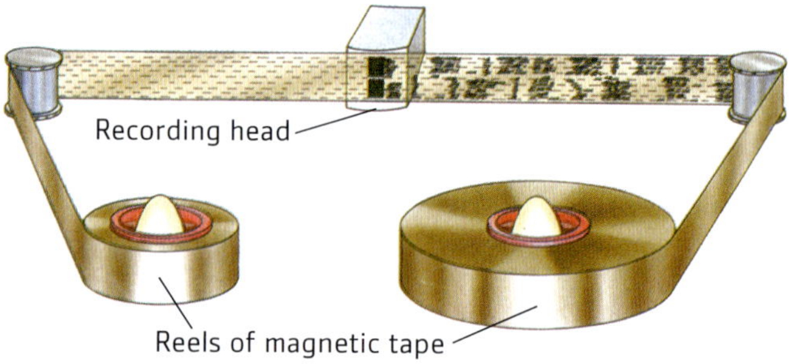

A cassette has two reels of magnetic tape. As the tape moves from one reel to the other, it passes a *recording head.* The head records information in magnetic patterns on the tape.

A Taser shoots electrified wires at people, stunning them.

Taser

The Taser is a stunning weapon. It shoots out electrified wires. Tasers are considered *nonlethal* or *less-lethal* weapons. They are not used to kill. Police officers use Tasers. They stun suspects who fight or run away. Soldiers, security guards, and private citizens may also use Tasers. The name Taser is a trademark of Taser International.

Tasers can hit targets up to 35 feet (11 meters) away. They shoot wires with darts. The darts stick in a target's clothing. The wires carry electric current. This current dazes the target. It may also cause pain and muscle spasms. In rare cases, Tasers have caused deadly heart attacks and breathing problems.

Other articles to read include: **Electric current.**

Technology

Technology *(tek NOL uh jee)* is the use of tools, machines, and materials. Technology is all around us. People use technology to grow food and produce clothing. They share ideas using such technologies as books, telephones, and computers. They build cities and light up the night with technology. People have used technology to explore our world and to travel to other worlds. People have also used technology to conquer and destroy one another in wars.

Technology is closely related to science. Scientists use such technologies as microscopes, telescopes, and computers. These technologies help scientists learn more about the world. Scientific knowledge, in turn, helps people build better technology.

Even so, people used technology long before they knew much about science. Millions of years ago, the ancestors of modern human beings made simple tools out of wood, stone, or animal bones. About 600,000 years ago, people discovered how to make fire.

Farming was a major advance in technology. People first learned to farm about 8000 B.C. Farming allowed people to settle in one place. Settled people developed civilizations. These civilizations developed such technologies as canals, sailing ships, and writing.

Over history, traders have spread new technologies from place to place. For example, the Chinese began using gunpowder by 900 A.D. By the 1200's, traders brought knowledge of gunpowder to Europe. Gunpowder soon reshaped warfare in Europe. Armor and castle walls were no match for firearms and cannons.

Traders also brought knowledge of the printing press from China to Europe. The Chinese had used printing as early as 600 A.D. But printing was better suited for European languages. By the 1400's, Europeans began printing huge numbers of books. More people learned how to read and write.

Technology can provide a powerful advantage in war. In the 1500's, steel armor and advanced weapons helped Spanish warriors conquer the Aztec Empire.

Continued on the next page

Much modern technology relies on electric power to work. Wind turbines are a clean source of electric power.

Modern technology, such as this tiny portable media player, would have been unimaginable to people living hundreds of years ago.

Technology *Continued from the previous page*

And the books themselves helped spread technology and scientific knowledge far and wide.

Much of modern technology has its roots in the Industrial Revolution. The Industrial Revolution began in Great Britain during the late 1700's. During this period, people learned how to build steam engines. The first factories appeared. New machines and chemicals made it much easier to farm.

By the late 1800's, people learned to use electric power. Cities soon glowed with electric lights. Many people abandoned old ways of life. They moved out of the countryside and worked in city factories. These factories could produce goods quickly and cheaply. By the early 1900's, factories turned out such complex products as automobiles. Governments built new roads and railways. Distant places became much easier to reach. By the 1940's, a passenger could quickly travel around the world on an airplane. Such a journey would have taken weeks on a ship.

New electronic communication also joined distant places together. The telegraph was invented in the mid-1800's. People could instantly send coded messages over long wires, from one city to another. Telephones and radios enabled voices to be carried over great distances. These technologies, like the printing press before, brought about major social changes.

During the 1940's, people in the United States and the United Kingdom invented the first electronic computers. Afterward, computer technology developed very quickly. Computers became both smaller and more powerful. Other technologies soon came to depend on computers. For example, modern cars, ships, airplanes, and missiles rely on tiny computers. In the 1960's, the United States government linked together a large number of computers. This network eventually became the Internet. By the 2010's, nearly a third of the world's population could get on the Internet.

Technology has made it easier for people to work. Before the Industrial Revolution, farmers could barely grow enough food to feed their own families. In the 2000's, a single farmer could grow enough food for more than 100 people. Medical technology helps people survive diseases. And such technologies as television and

Continued on the next page

electronic games entertain millions of people around the world.

But the great power of modern technology can also create great harm. Factories, farms, and cars cause pollution, dirtying Earth's air, water, and soil. Technology uses up such natural resources. Some resources, such as trees, can be regrown. Others, such as oil, coal, and natural gas, cannot be replaced.

Modern weapon technologies can make wars much more deadly. World War II (1939-1945), the most destructive war in history, was fought with modern weapons. Between 50 million and 60 million people died. Nuclear weapons were invented at the end of World War II. A large nuclear war could destroy Earth's ability to support life. As technology becomes ever more advanced and powerful, people must make sure it does not threaten our survival.

Other articles to read include: **Communication; Computer; Electronics; Factory; Farm and farming; Invention; Machine; Materials; Printing; Tool.**

New technologies often bring about major changes in the way people work. Many people, such as this stock broker, use computers all day at their jobs.

Telegraph

The telegraph was once an important way to send messages. It could send electric signals over long wires. People used telegraphs from the mid-1800's to the mid-1900's. They laid telegraph wires around the world. The wires let distant people send messages to one another in seconds. Before the telegraph, most messages only traveled as fast as horses could carry them. The telephone and other technologies eventually took the telegraph's place.

The telegraph had a sending device and a receiving device. The sending device was a small metal arm with a button at the end. People tapped the key to send a message. The taps sent electric signals in Morse code. The code was a system of dots and dashes. A dot was a short tap. A dash was a long tap. The dots and dashes stood for letters of the alphabet. For example, a dot followed by a dash stood for the letter *A*. The signals went along wires to the

Continued on the next page

A telegraph operator taps out a message in Morse code.

Telegraph *Continued from the previous page*

telegraph's receiving device. The receiving device sounded out the dots and dashes with clicking sounds. A person who knew Morse code listened to the clicks. The person wrote down each letter so that the message could be read.

Many people worked on the ideas that made the telegraph possible. Samuel F. B. Morse was one of the main inventors, and Morse code was named after him. He made the first working telegraph in 1837. Later telegraphs had receiving parts that could type out messages. Morse code messages could eventually be sent by radio instead of through wires.

Other articles to read include: **Morse, Samuel Finley Breese; Morse code.**

Telephone

The telephone is a device that sends and receives voice signals. These signals may travel over wires or over radio waves. *Landline* phones transmit signals over wires. *Cellular* telephones, also called *cell phones* or *mobile phones,* make use of radio waves. The word *telephone* comes from two Greek words meaning *far* and *sound*.

A huge system called the *telephone network* connects all the world's telephones. It includes cables that crisscross the continents and oceans. It includes radio towers and satellites high above Earth. The telephone network works closely with the Internet, the global network of computers. Many cellular phones can connect to the Internet.

Telephones work by changing sound into electric signals. In a landline phone, these signals travel over wires. The wires connect directly to the phone. When a person calls from a cell phone, the signals are changed into radio waves. A nearby radio tower picks up the waves. It changes the waves back into electric signals. Then it sends the signals over the telephone network. The signals reach another person's phone almost instantly. A speaker on that phone changes the signals back to sound.

Every phone has its own number. The telephone network links one telephone number to another. When two people are talking on telephones, the network must keep their connection open.

Many phones—especially cellular phones—have other features. They can send text messages over the telephone network. Some cellular phones have cameras. *Smartphones* are cell phones that work much like small computers. They can play music, videos, and games. They can also connect to the Internet and display websites.

Continued on the next page

Alexander Graham Bell, a Scottish-born teacher, invented the telephone. He began working with his idea for a telephone in 1874. In 1876, he showed his telephone at the Centennial Exposition in Philadelphia.

The earliest telephones had to connect directly to one another. A pair of iron wires connected each pair of phones. *Switchboards* made these connections more practical. A switchboard brought together all the telephone connections in an area. It could switch signals from one connection to another. The first switchboard began operating in 1877 in Boston. In 1891, the first international connection went into operation. It ran from London to Paris.

During the 1900's, the telephone network grew rapidly. The Internet was developed in the 1960's. It originally used the telephone network's lines. In the late 1970's and early 1980's, many countries started developing cellular systems. By the early 2000's, more people used cell phones than landline phones.

Other articles to read include: **Bell, Alexander Graham; Cellular telephone; Fax machine; Internet; Modem; Telegraph.**

The telephone has gone through many changes since it was invented.

First telephone (1876)

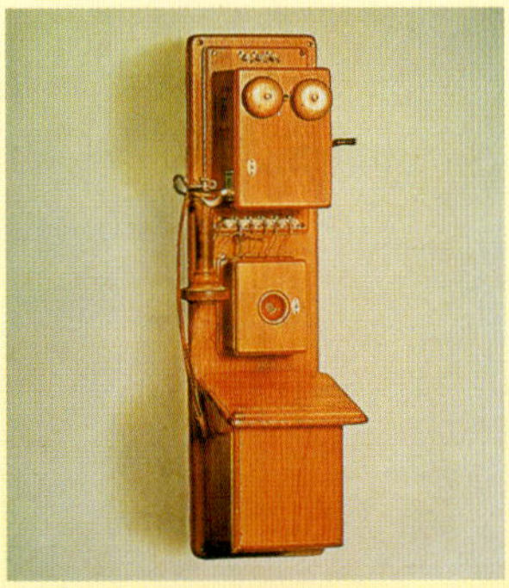

Wall phone (1882)

Dial phone (1919)

Desk phone (1928)

Desk phone (1937)

Princess phone (1959)

Trimline phone (1968)

Smartphone (2012)

The William Herschel Telescope, in Spain, is named after the British astronomer who discovered the planet Uranus in 1781.

Telescope

The telescope is a device for seeing faraway things. A telescope can give a closer view of objects in the distance. In addition, people can see many things with telescopes that cannot be seen with human eyes alone. A common telescope looks like a long tube. One end of the tube is smaller than the other. A person puts the small end up to one eye and looks through the tube. Seen through the tube, things appear closer than they really are.

Two small telescopes can be joined side by side to make *binoculars.* A person can look through binoculars with both eyes. People sometimes use binoculars to get a closer look at sporting events.

Scientists called *astronomers* use large telescopes to study the planets, stars, and other things in space. Without telescopes, people would know little about such things.

The most common kind of telescope is an *optical telescope.* Such a telescope is designed to "see" in visible light, just as human eyes do. Other kinds of telescopes can detect waves of other kinds of light that are invisible to human eyes. Such waves include radio waves and X rays. Astronomers use these telescopes to study objects in space that give off the different types of invisible rays.

The dish antennas of the Very Large Array, in New Mexico, can detect radio waves with great accuracy.

Telescopes have different sizes and shapes. Some telescopes are small enough to hold in one hand. Huge bowl-shaped radio telescopes may measure up to 1,000 feet (300 meters) across. This distance is almost as long as three football fields.

Some telescopes are carried by spacecraft. The Hubble Space Telescope, launched in 1990, views the sky while it circles Earth. The Hubble was launched into space to get the telescope above the air that surrounds Earth. Although air seems clear, it can make stars and other sky objects look blurry. For example, stars seem to twinkle because their light comes to our eyes through moving layers of air. The Hubble Space Telescope thus gets a sharper image than many telescopes on the ground. Some telescopes on the ground have special equipment to overcome the effects of the atmosphere.

Continued on the next page

People can see objects because the objects reflect or give off light that then enters the eyes. Optical telescopes work by bending this light. One kind of optical telescope has a curved piece of glass called a *lens* at its large end. This lens is the *objective lens.* It bends light from the object to form an image of the object inside the telescope. The light from this image then goes through another lens, called the *eyepiece,* at the small end of the telescope. The eyepiece bends the light again, making the object look bigger. The bending of light by a lens is called *refraction.* Telescopes with such lenses are called *refracting telescopes.*

Another kind of optical telescope uses a mirror instead of an objective lens. The mirror is bowl-shaped. Light from an object bounces off the mirror, forming an image inside the telescope. Light from the image then goes through an eyepiece, making the object look bigger. A mirror is said to reflect light. Such telescopes are thus called *reflecting telescopes.* A reflecting telescope can generally produce a better image than can a refracting telescope. All the largest modern telescopes are reflecting telescopes.

Continued on the next page

The three main kinds of optical telescopes are refracting, reflecting, and refracting-reflecting telescopes.

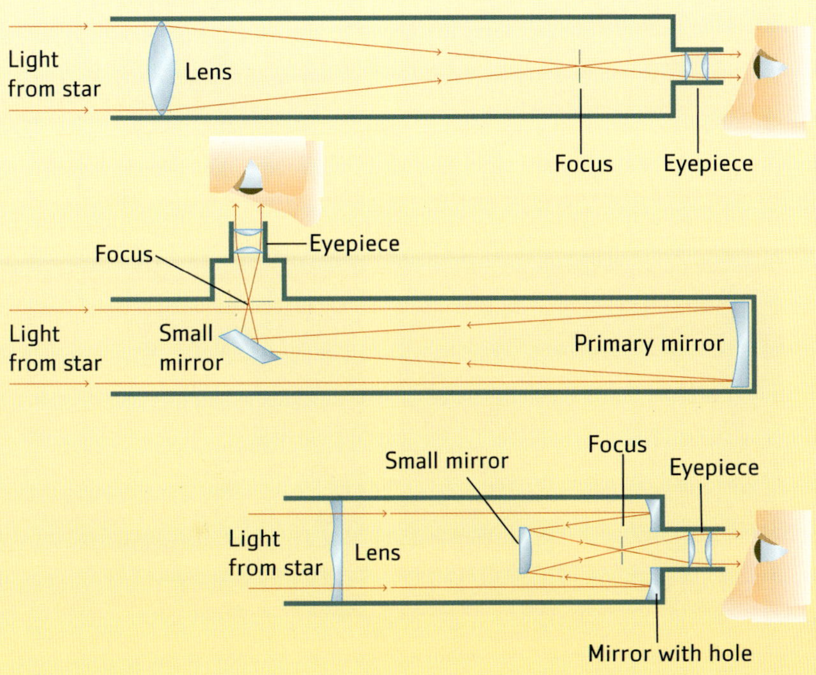

A refracting telescope has a large lens that bends light rays to meet at a point called the *focus.* There, an image of the star is formed. The image can be seen through the eyepiece.

A reflecting telescope has a large primary mirror that reflects starlight to a smaller mirror. The light then travels to the focus at the side of the telescope, where it can be viewed.

A refracting-reflecting telescope has a large lens and a large mirror with a hole in the middle. Light from a star reflects from this mirror to a smaller mirror. The light then travels to the focus, where it can be viewed.

Telescope *Continued from the previous page*

Many telescopes can be made to work like a giant camera, taking a picture of faraway objects. Astronomers can then study the picture.

Objects in space often look dim, even through a telescope. To make them look bright, astronomers use a telescope with a very large lens or mirror. A larger lens gathers more light into the telescope. So objects seen through the telescope look much brighter.

Radio telescopes pick up faint radio waves from objects in space. Most radio telescopes capture these waves with a large, bowl-shaped *dish antenna,* or dish. The dish reflects radio waves the same way a mirror reflects light waves. But radio waves are much longer than light waves. For this reason, a radio telescope's dish has to be much larger than the mirror of an optical telescope.

Continued on the next page

Different kinds of telescopes can be used to study different forms of energy given off by cosmic objects such as the Crab Nebula, a huge cloud of gas and dust.

The Hubble Space Telescope can photograph objects in visible light.

The Chandra X-ray Observatory can photograph the X-ray energy given off by objects.

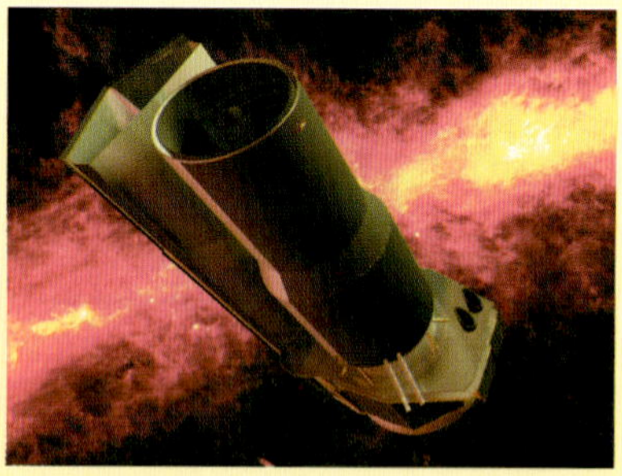

The Spitzer Space Telescope can photograph objects in infrared light.

This image of the Crab Nebula, photographed by the Hubble Space Telescope, shows the nebula's appearance in visible light.

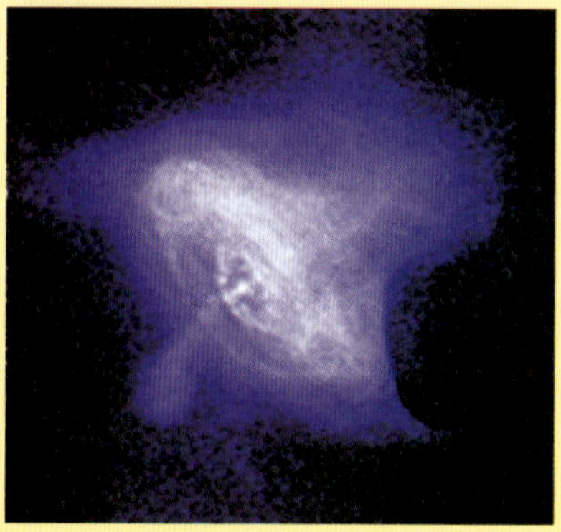

This X-ray image of the Crab Nebula, from the Chandra X-ray Observatory, shows high-energy radiation flowing from an object in its center.

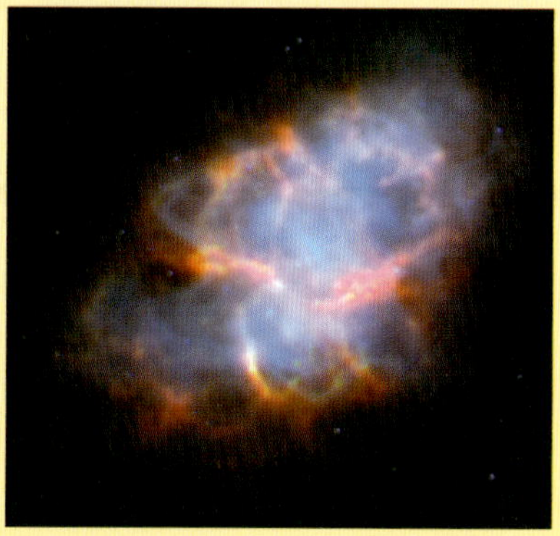

Other features of the Crab Nebula are revealed in this infrared view captured by the Spitzer Space Telescope.

The dish sends the radio waves to another part of the telescope. This part changes the waves into electric signals. A radio receiver strengthens the signals. It also keeps track of the point in space that the signals came from. This information goes to a computer. The computer may draw a diagram of the source of the radio waves or give other information about the source.

Microwaves are generally thought of as shorter radio waves. Telescopes that detect microwaves use a dish antenna as do other radio telescopes. But the dishes for microwaves do not need to be as large.

Ultraviolet light has waves just a bit shorter than those of visible light. *Infrared light* has waves just a bit longer than those of visible light. Both of these forms of light are collected by reflecting telescopes similar to optical telescopes. However, these telescopes have special sensors. The sensors can detect the different types of light.

The shortest waves are *X rays* and *gamma rays.* They can pass through most materials used to make mirrors. The telescopes that detect these waves thus do not use a mirror or a dish. Instead, they use special sensors that can "see" the waves and turn them into images.

The Dutch scientist Hans Lippershey is often given credit for making the first telescope, in 1608. It was made of two glass lenses in a narrow tube. Within a year, the Italian astronomer Galileo built a telescope like Lippershey's. Galileo was the first person to use a telescope to study the planets. Galileo discovered some surprising things with his telescope. For example, he found that there were moons going around the planet Jupiter. In 1668, the English astronomer Isaac Newton built a telescope that used a mirror.

In the late 1930's, Grote Reber, an American engineer, built the first radio telescope and operated it in his backyard. Scientists who used early radio telescopes found strong radio waves coming from the sun. Later, astronomers found that radio waves also came from what was left of exploded stars in some dark parts of the sky. Later, scientists found rapidly spinning stars called *pulsars* that send out radio waves in even pulses.

Other articles to read include: **Chandra X-ray Observatory; Hubble Space Telescope; Keck Observatory; Lens; Lippershey, Hans; Radio; Space exploration; Spitzer Space Telescope; Very Large Telescope.**

Amateur astronomers use telescopes to view many kinds of objects in the night sky.

Television

Television, or TV, is a device people use to get information and entertainment. TV brings moving pictures and sound from around the world into millions of homes.

People with TV sets can watch events that happen far away. They can see sporting events, such as the Olympic Games. They can see historic events, such as battles in distant lands. TV also helps viewers see and learn about people and places in other countries. TV can even take people out of this world, as when astronauts send videos back from space.

People use TV for fun, too. Many people enjoy such TV entertainment as adventure stories, comedy shows, cartoons, game shows, and movies.

Television works because of *electronic signals,* electric currents that are modified to carry information. A TV signal begins when a TV camera takes a picture of a scene. Light from the scene enters the TV camera. The TV camera changes the light into electronic signals. At the same time, a microphone picks up the sounds from the scene. The microphone changes the sounds into electronic signals, too.

A TV set picks up these signals. The TV changes the electronic signals back into pictures and sounds. A television screen is made of a grid of tiny squares called *pixels.* Electronic signals can make each pixel change color. The pattern of pixels forms pictures on the screen. Changing patterns produce the appear-

Continued on the next page

A plasma television displays images through the use of a *plasma* (electrically charged gas). The plasma gives off *ultraviolet light* when excited. Such light is invisible, but it causes *phosphors* in the screen to glow. The pattern of glowing phosphors creates an image.

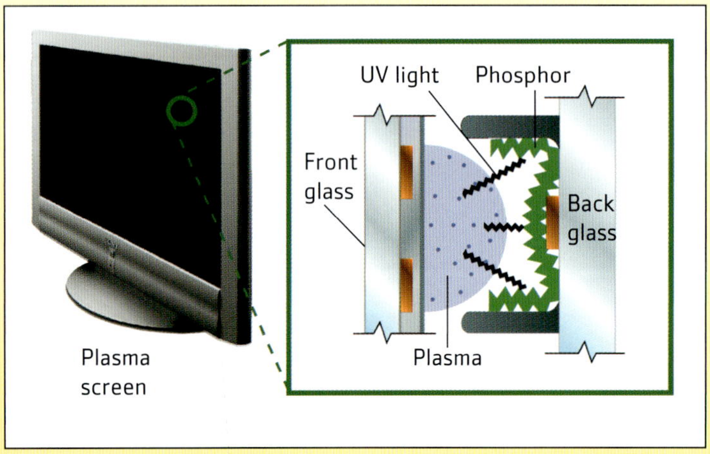

A plasma television produces a wide-screen, high-resolution image that appears sharp even when viewed up close.

ance of motion. In addition, most TV's have speakers. The speakers change electronic signals into sounds.

TV shows come from different kinds of TV stations. Most TV stations in the United States are commercial stations. The rest are public stations. Commercial stations make money by selling time on TV to companies. These companies run commercial advertisements during TV programs. These commercials show the company's products. Public stations depend mostly on money given to them by the government and donated by viewers.

Both commercial stations and public stations offer programming though *over-the-air broadcasting.* They send their TV signals over the airwaves to people's homes.

However, many people pay a monthly fee to receive TV signals through *cable television systems* or *direct-broadcast satellite* (DBS) systems. Cable television systems receive TV signals through thick wires called *cables.* DBS systems use dish-shaped antennas to receive TV signals from satellites high above Earth. Both cable and DBS systems offer viewers a variety of programming greater than that available by over-the-air broadcasting.

Many people record TV programs to watch later. Devices called *digital video recorders* (DVR's) can store hundreds of hours of TV programs. In addition, many TV shows are available over the Internet.

Televisions can be used for other purposes besides watching and recording programs. For example, many people use their TV sets to play video games.

Many scientists helped make television possible. Experiments that led to television began in the 1800's, but TV did not come about until the 1920's. The first television broadcast was made in 1936 by the British Broadcasting Corporation (BBC) in the United Kingdom. In 1939, the National Broadcasting Company (NBC) made the first TV broadcast in the United States. In the early days of television, all programs were in black and white. Color television programs became common during the 1960's.

Beginning in the 1990's, TV's began using *digital technology.* In these kinds of TV's, the electronic signals are changed into a series of 1's and 0's—the same kind of code used by computers. Digital signals are clearer than older *analog signals.* Around the same time, *high-definition* televisions (HDTV's) became popular.

Continued on the next page

Analog signals

Digital signals

Television programming can be transmitted through either analog or digital signals. In older analog signals, images and sounds were encoded in the shape of invisible waves. Newer TV signals are digital. They use a precise numerical code for images and sounds, much as do computers.

Television *Continued from the previous page*

HDTV's have more pixels than older TV's, so they produce sharper pictures. By 2010, televisions with three-dimensional (3-D) displays became more common. Such televisions send separate images to the right and left eyes, often through special glasses. The two images combine to give the illusion of depth.

Other articles to read include: **Camera; DVD; Electronic game; Microphone; Satellite, Artificial; Videotape recorder.**

Closed-circuit televisions display views captured by cameras. Such televisions are used to monitor certain areas remotely, rather than to view programs.

Edward Teller

Teller, Edward

Edward Teller (1908–2003) was an American scientist. He is known as the father of the *hydrogen (HY druh juhn)* bomb, a type of nuclear weapon. His work in *nuclear physics* helped lead to the development of the hydrogen bomb in 1952. In nuclear physics, scientists study the behavior of the *nuclei* (cores) of tiny particles called *atoms.*

Teller was born in 1908 in Hungary. He earned a doctor's degree from the University of *Leipzig (LYP sihg)* in Germany. Teller moved to the United States in 1935. During World War II (1939–1945), he joined the effort to build a nuclear weapon. He worked at a laboratory in Los Alamos, New Mexico, where people built the first atomic bomb. In 1952, he started a laboratory in California that designed nuclear weapons.

Other articles to read include: **Bomb; Nuclear weapon.**

Tereshkova, Valentina Vladimirovna

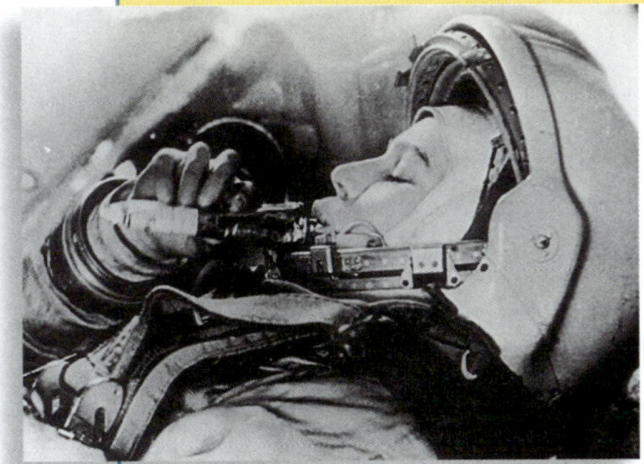
Valentina Tereshkova

Valentina Vladimirovna Tereshkova *(VAH lehn TEE nah vlah DEE mih RAWV nuh teh rehsh KAW vah)* (1937–) became the first woman to travel in space. Tereshkova was a *cosmonaut,* a Russian astronaut.

Tereshkova made her flight from June 16 to June 19, 1963, in the spacecraft Vostok 6. She traveled around Earth 45 times. She operated the spacecraft by hand. When the space flight was over, she piloted the capsule toward Earth. She jumped from the falling capsule and landed with a parachute.

Tereshkova was the first space traveler who had not been a test pilot earlier. Instead, she was a parachute jumper. She started parachuting as a hobby. She made over 125 jumps before entering space-flight training school.

Other articles to read include: **Astronaut; Space exploration.**

Tesla, Nikola

Nikola Tesla

Nikola Tesla (1856–1943) was an inventor of electrical technology. He is most famous for inventing a system for *alternating current.* An *electric current* is the movement of electric charges. Some currents flow in only one direction. This kind of current is called *direct current.* Alternating current, on the other hand, changes direction many times each second. Alternating current can transport electric power over long distances much better than can direct current. Today, alternating current systems are used all over the world. Most homes use alternating current.

Tesla was born in 1856 in what is now Croatia *(kroh AY shuh).* He studied engineering in school. Tesla saw a generator with a motor that ran on direct current. He then got an idea to build alternating current motors. He built his first one in 1883. In 1884, Tesla began working for the American inventor Thomas Edison. Tesla quit after one year. In 1887, Tesla started the Tesla Electric Company in New York City.

Other articles to read include: **Alternating current; Direct current; Edison, Thomas Alva; Electric current; Electric motor; Electric power; Westinghouse, George.**

People use textiles to make clothing, such as these dresses on display in Thailand.

Textile

A textile is a fabric or a cloth. The word *textile* once meant only cloth that was made by weaving yarn on a loom. Today, the word is used for many different kinds of fabric. The *fibers* (long pieces of thread) and yarns used to make fabrics are called textiles, too.

Some fibers in textiles come from plants. For example, cotton comes from the cotton plant. Animal fibers, such as wool, are also used in many textiles. Sheep supply most of the wool used.

Other kinds of textile fibers are made from chemicals in oil or in natural gas. Such fibers include nylon and polyester. Still other types of textile fibers are made from glass or metals.

Manufacturers make most textiles by *weaving* or *knitting*. Weaving is a method that involves two sets of yarns. The yarns are crossed over and under one another. Knitting involves a single yarn or set of yarns. In knitting, yarn is tied in loops. The loops are connected to one another using needles.

Textiles are used in clothing and in thousands of other products. Some of these products include basketball nets, boat sails, book covers, fire hoses, flags, mailbags, parachutes, and umbrellas. Parts of tires and seat belts are also made from textiles. So are some kinds of tape and bandages.

Continued on the next page

Different fabrics are made using different techniques.

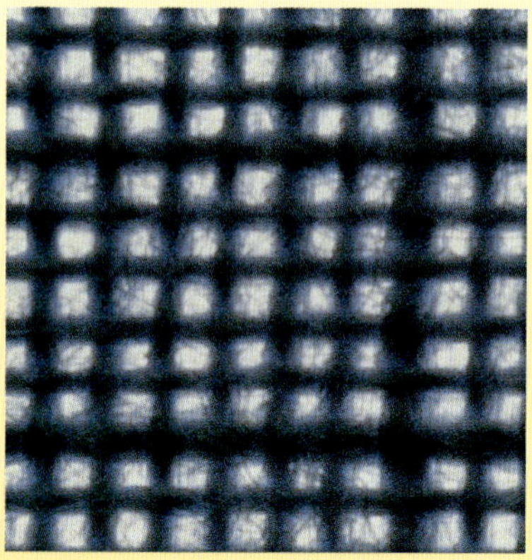

A *woven* fabric is made of two sets of yarns that are crossed over and under each other.

A *knitted* fabric has a single yarn or set of yarns in the form of loops that are linked together.

A *nonwoven* fabric is made of one or more sheets of fibers joined together.

A worker at a textile mill operates an automatic weaving machine.

A quality control inspector at the mill checks rolls of fiber.

No one knows when the first textiles were made. But markings on ancient pottery show that people made textiles at least 27,000 years ago.

Other articles to read include: **Dye; Synthetics; Tire; Weaving.**

Thermometer

A thermometer is a tool that measures temperature. Temperature tells people how hot or cold something is. Many substances *expand* (grow larger) as they get warmer. They *contract* (get smaller) as they get cooler. A thermometer works by measuring these kinds of changes. It will show the size of the change by displaying a number. A thermometer can measure the temperature of a gas, a liquid, or a solid.

Scientists first used thermometers during the 1500's and 1600's. The earliest kind of thermometer was called an *air thermometer.* It was made of an opened glass tube and a dish of water. As the temperature changed, the water would move up or down in the tube. Scientists could tell the temperature based on how much water was inside the tube.

There are many other kinds of thermometers that people use today. One popular kind is the *liquid-in-glass thermometer.* It has a

Continued on the next page

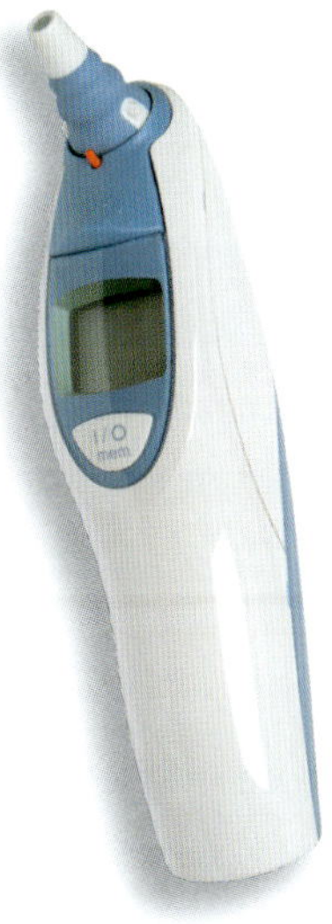

This digital thermometer measures the temperature inside a person's ear. It senses *infrared rays* (heat rays) that the inner ear gives off.

Thermometer *Continued from the previous page*

thin, closed glass tube. Inside the tube is a liquid. When the temperature of the liquid goes up, the liquid takes up more space. The liquid then rises in the tube. Mercury, a liquid metal, is often used in such a thermometer. Alcohol is also commonly used.

Most *digital thermometers* take temperature readings with slender metal devices called *probes.* These thermometers display numbers for the temperature on small screens.

Other articles to read include: **Barometer; Weather forecasting.**

Thermostat

This thermostat has a dial that can be set to the desired temperature. Another dial tracks the actual temperature.

A thermostat *(THUR muh stat)* controls the temperature inside a machine or a room. Many home appliances use thermostats. These appliances include air conditioners, heaters, and refrigerators.

Thermostats measure changes in temperature. They can turn a machine on or off. If the air in a refrigerator becomes too warm, for example, it will trigger the refrigerator's thermostat. The thermostat will turn on the cooling unit. When the temperature becomes cool enough, the thermostat will shut off the cooling unit.

Many thermostats are made from two strips of different metals bonded together. Different metals *expand* (grow) and *contract*

Continued on the next page

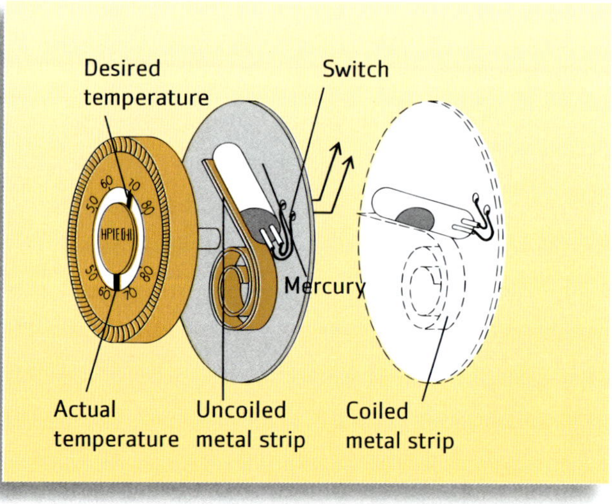

If the temperature in the room becomes too cold, a metal strip inside the thermostat uncoils. This causes a drop of mercury to close a switch and start the heating system. After the temperature reaches the desired level, the metal strip coils up and the mercury opens the switch, shutting off the heat.

(shrink) differently in response to changes in temperature. This causes the bonded strips to bend or stretch with temperature changes. The bending or stretching closes or opens a switch. The switch turns a machine on or off.

Other articles to read include: **Air conditioning; Refrigeration; Thermometer.**

Tire

A tire is a covering for the outside of a wheel. Tires are used on airplanes, bicycles, buses, motorcycles, tractors, trucks, and many other vehicles.

Most tires are made of rubber. Some tires are made of solid rubber. But most tires are filled with air. The air is held under pressure. The air supports the weight of a vehicle. It also cushions the vehicle when the tire rolls over bumps. Most tires have grooved patterns called *treads* on their outside surface. The tread helps the tire grip the road.

A Scottish engineer named Robert W. Thomson invented the air-filled tire in 1845. This kind of tire began to be used on automobiles in 1895.

Other articles to read include: **Automobile; Bicycle; Motorcycle; Tractor; Truck; Wheel and axle.**

The face of a tire, called the *tread,* has many grooves. The tread provides *traction* (grip), preventing the tire from slipping on the road.

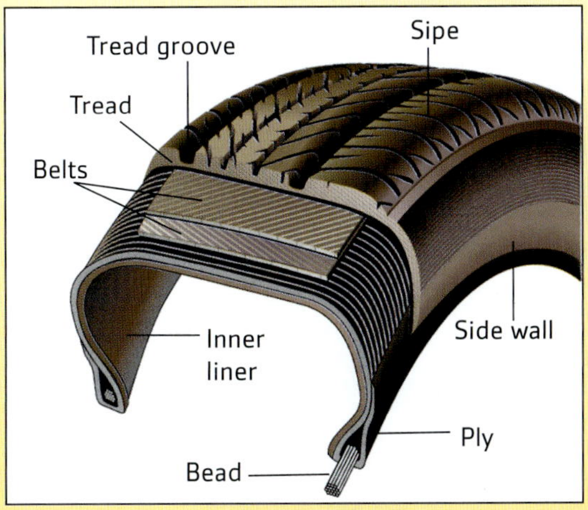

Grooves and many smaller slits called *sipes* make up a tire's tread pattern. Tire *belts* push as much of the tread against the road as possible. Doing so improves traction and reduces wear. Rubber *side walls* cover and protect the rest of the tire from the outside. Inside a tire, the *inner liner* helps keep in the air. The body of a tire is made of layers. Each layer is called a *ply.* The plies wrap around two strong bundles of wires called *beads.* The beads rest against the tire rim.

Tool

A tool is a device used to do a job. Tools are used to measure, hold, shape, and cut. Tools that workers use with their hands are called *hand tools.* Tools that do the work on a machine are called *machine tools.*

Carpenters and cabinetmakers use *woodworking tools.* A *rule* is used for measuring length. The *square* and *protractor* measure angles. *Compasses* mark circles and arcs. The carpenter's *levels* and *plumb lines* help make sure the work will be straight.

Other kinds of woodworking tools include *vises* and *clamps.* These tools hold materials in place while they are being shaped. Shaping tools include saws, chisels, planes, files, and boring bits. Woodworkers also use hammers to pound nails into wood. Screwdrivers are used with screws to join sections of wood.

Metalworking tools are used to make machines and other metal items. These tools must be more exact than woodworking tools.

Continued on the next page

Common hand tools include hammers, screwdrivers, and wrenches.

Handheld power tools, such as this drill, may be used to work with either wood or metal.

Machine tools, such as this metal lathe, are power-driven machines used to shape metal.

They can measure very small distances. Tools called *micrometers (my KROM uh tuhrz)* and *calipers (KAL ih puhrz)* can measure lengths as small as $\frac{1}{10,000}$ inch (0.0025 millimeter). A *hacksaw* is a tool that cuts metal. *Taps* and *dies* cut the grooves into machine parts.

Machine tools are power-driven machines that are used to shape metal. A *lathe* is used for cutting metal into round shapes. A *milling tool* cuts flat surfaces or special shapes. A *grinding wheel* rubs against a metal surface to make it smooth.

People began using tools hundreds of thousands of years ago. They learned that rocks and sticks of certain shapes could be used for cutting, grinding, and other tasks. When people learned to work with iron and steel, they started making stronger, sharper tools. In the 1700's, people learned how to run machines with steam power. Steam engines, gasoline engines and electric power made machine tools possible.

Other articles to read include:
Factory; Hammer; Iron Age; Machine; Machine tool; Plow; Saw; Technology.

Some of the first tools made by humans were sharp-edged stones.

At the dawn of the Iron Age, about 1500 B.C., people began to make strong farm tools and weapons out of iron.

A *tracklayer tractor,* also called a *crawler,* has tracks that go around the wheels. Such tractors are used for construction and other heavy jobs.

Tractor

A tractor *(TRAK tuhr)* is a vehicle that pushes or pulls tools or machines over the land. Tractors are very important in agriculture. They are used on almost every farm to pull plows, combines, and other large, heavy machines. Tractors are used in other jobs, too. People use tractors to carry logs from place to place, to help build highways, and to clear snow from roads.

There are two major kinds of tractors. They are the *wheel tractor* and the *tracklayer tractor,* also called a *crawler.*

Most farm tractors are wheel tractors. They have two or four high rear wheels. These large wheels keep the tractor steady. Wheel tractors also have one or two smaller front wheels. These small wheels make the tractor easy to steer.

Crawler tractors are used for such heavy jobs as removing large numbers of trees from an area. They have tracks that go around the wheels.

Tractors pull things using three main parts. The *drawbar* is a device used to attach equipment to the tractor for pulling. The *hydraulic (hy DRAW lihk) system* controls the position of tools that are connected to the tractor. The *power take-off* gives power to machines that are pulled by the tractor.

Tractors were first used in the 1870's. These tractors were powered by steam. Later, tractors with gasoline engines were invented. Modern tractors have both speed and power. Many tractors also have a closed-in *cab,* the place where the driver sits. The cab can be heated or air-conditioned.

Other articles to read include: **Farm and farming; Machine; Wheel and axle.**

A *wheel tractor* pulls a plow across a farm field. The small front wheels are easy to steer. The large back wheels keep the tractor steady.

Train

A train carries goods across the barren interior of Australia.

Trains are an important means of transportation. Some trains carry passengers. Fast passenger trains can travel at speeds well over 200 miles (320 kilometers) per hour. Other trains haul coal, grain, lumber, machinery, and other freight. A long freight train with many cars can haul thousands of tons.

Unlike airplanes, automobiles, and ships, trains are not steered. Instead, they move along a *railroad track.* The track has two rails. The rails guide the train's wheels. Powerful machines called *locomotives* move most trains along the track.

Many passenger trains have electric locomotives. They draw electric power from lines connected to a power station.

Other locomotives have *diesel-electric engines.* Such a locomotive is like a moving power station. It burns fuel to create electric power. The electric power moves the train.

Trains began running in the United Kingdom in the 1820's. These trains had steam engines. They hauled wagons of freight or coaches with passengers.

During the late 1800's and early 1900's, thousands of steam trains traveled across the United States. They carried most of the nation's freight and long-distance passengers. The first railroad across western North America was completed in 1869. This railroad helped open the American West to settlers.

During the mid-1900's, airplanes became more popular than trains for passengers. However, large numbers of people still travel by train. High-speed trains began running in the late 1900's in a number of countries. In 2011, the world's longest high-speed railroad opened in China.

Some high-speed trains are *magnetic levitation trains,* often called *maglev trains.* Maglev trains do not have wheels. Instead, they use magnets to float just above a track.

Other articles to read include: **Diesel engine; Locomotive; Magnetic levitation train; Steam engine.**

An engineer works at the controls of a high-speed passenger train in Russia.

Transformer

A transformer *(trans FAWR muhr)* is a device that changes the *voltage* of an electric current. An electric current is a flow of electricity. Voltage is something like the "strength" of an electric current. Transformers work with the type of current known as *alternating (AWL tuhr NAY tihng) current.* Alternating current continually reverses its direction of flow.

Power plants make alternating current with very high voltage. The high-voltage current can travel long distances over power lines. But such high voltage would overwhelm most household devices. A transformer lowers the voltage of current entering a home or office. The current can then be used to power computers, televisions, and other devices.

Most transformers consist of two coils of wire. The coils are wound around a hollow iron core. One coil is connected to the source of current. The current comes out through the other coil with its voltage changed. The number of twists in the coils determines the change in voltage.

Other articles to read include: **Alternating current; Electric current; Electric power; Power plant; Volt; Wire.**

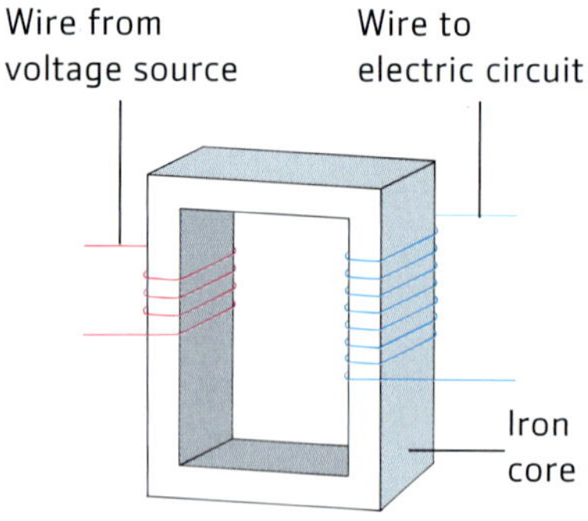

A transformer often has two coils of wire with different numbers of twists. When a current passes from one coil to the other, the voltage changes.

Transistor

The transistor *(tran ZIHS tuhr)* is a small device used widely in computers and electronics. A transistor controls the flow of electric current. It can switch current on and off, like a light switch. Or it can strengthen an electric signal. Scientists at the Bell Telephone Laboratories in New Jersey invented transistors in 1947.

Transistors are the main parts of *computer chips.* A computer stores information—such as words, sounds, or videos—in a code of 1's and 0's. By switching on or off, a transistor can switch between a 1 and a 0. Transistors can thus *process* (work with) computerized information. A fingernail-sized computer chip may contain billions of transistors.

Continued on the next page

A transistor is switched on when tiny charged particles called *electrons* move across it. They flow from a region called the *source* to another region, the *drain.* The *gate region* controls their flow.

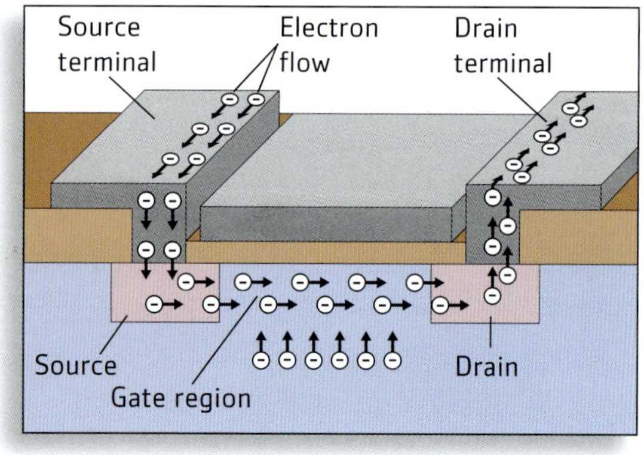

Another kind of transistor does not just switch on or off. It can make an electric signal stronger. Radios use these kinds of transistors. Radio waves generate weak electric signals. Transistors make these signals stronger. The radio can then change the pattern of current into sounds that people can hear.

Other articles to read include: **Computer chip; Electric current; Electronics; Semiconductor.**

Transportation

Transportation is the movement of people and objects from one place to another. Transportation takes people where they want to go. It also brings people the products they want.

Millions of automobiles transport people across the land.

Ships, such as this oil tanker, carry huge amounts of cargo across oceans.

In early times, transportation was slow and difficult. Prehistoric people traveled mainly on foot. They carried loads on their backs or on their heads. Sometimes they had to drag heavy loads along the ground. Later, they began to use animals to haul loads. Then wagons and sailing ships were invented. The use of animals, wagons, and sailing ships helped people travel farther and more easily. But transportation was still quite slow.

Inventors made the first vehicles with engines during the late 1700's and early 1800's. With engine-powered vehicles, people began to travel faster and more easily than ever before.

Today, airplanes fly across continents in hours. Trains, trucks, and giant cargo ships carry products around the world. Millions of people use cars to get around. Buses take students back and forth to school.

Vehicles with engines, such as cars and airplanes, have made life easier for all of us. But they have caused problems, too.

Continued on the next page

The bicycle ranks among the most popular forms of engineless transportation.

Transportation *Continued from the previous page*

Engines need huge amounts of fuel. They use up much of Earth's energy supply. Cars and trucks crowd many streets and highways. The fumes that come out of them dirty the air.

Land transportation is the most common kind of transportation. Cars, buses, motorcycles, and trucks are land vehicles that get their power from engines. They all ride on wheels. Trains are also an important form of land transportation. Unlike other kinds of vehicles, trains cannot be steered. But some trains can safely travel much faster than cars. The fastest passenger trains can move well over 200 miles (320 kilometers) per hour.

Some kinds of land transportation use no engines. People use their own muscle power to walk or to ride bicycles. Some people ride animals or use them to carry loads. Such animals include camels, donkeys, elephants, horses, llamas, and oxen.

Water transportation includes boats, ships, and rafts. People use boats mostly on rivers, canals, and lakes. A ship is larger than a boat and can travel across oceans. Ships carry many kinds of products, called *cargo.* Almost all ships and many boats are powered by engines. Canoes, rowboats, sailboats, and rafts do not have engines.

Air transportation includes airplanes and helicopters. Both airplanes and helicopters are powered by engines. Airplanes are a fast way to carry people and products from one place to another. Helicopters are slower and smaller than airplanes. But unlike airplanes, helicopters can hover in one place. Some people also travel through the air in gliders or balloons, which have no engine.

Other articles to read include: **Air cushion vehicle; Airplane; Airship; Automobile; Balloon; Bicycle; Cable car; Engine; Gasoline engine; Glider; Helicopter; Jet; Locomotive; Magnetic levitation train; Motorcycle; Road; Rocket; Ship; Steam engine; Steamboat; Submarine; Tank; Tire; Train; Truck; Wheel and axle.**

Airplanes are among the fastest means of transport.

Truck

Many kinds of trucks perform specialized work. This photograph shows a heavy dump truck.

A truck is a large motor vehicle. A truck is designed to carry heavy loads. Trucks carry almost everything we eat, wear, and use.

Trucks have large, powerful engines. The biggest trucks are called *triple trailers.* These huge trucks are made up of three trailers pulled by a *tractor.* Trailers are like large boxes on wheels. The tractor contains the engine and the cab, where the driver sits.

Trucks have many uses. They haul materials to factories. They carry products to stores and warehouses. Trucks are used in agriculture, too. They haul fruits, vegetables, and animals from farms to markets.

Many people use trucks to move to a new home. Trucks carry people's furniture and household goods. Some large trucks even move houses. Trucks called *bookmobiles* serve as traveling libraries. Some trucks carry medical equipment and workers. The workers use the equipment to collect blood or take X rays. Some trucks are used as *ambulances (AM byoo luhn sihz).* They serve as moving emergency rooms.

Governments use trucks in many ways. The U.S. Army carries soldiers and weapons on trucks. State governments use trucks to help build bridges, roads, and parks. City police and fire departments need trucks, too. Trucks are also used to sweep streets, clear away snow, and collect garbage.

Some types of trucks are used as mobile homes. Some people use such trucks while camping or traveling. These trucks are called *recreational (REHK ree AY shuhn uhl) vehicles.*

There are three main types of truck: (1) light, (2) medium, and (3) heavy. These types are based on the *gross vehicle weight.* This measure includes the weight of the truck plus the load it carries. Most trucks in the United States are light. These trucks include pickup trucks and tow trucks. Most light trucks have gasoline engines, as do most cars.

Medium trucks are wider and higher than light trucks. They are used to deliver packages and bottled goods, such as water and soft drinks. In a medium truck, the driver can stand behind

Continued on the next page

There are three main types of truck: (1) light trucks, (2) medium trucks, and (3) heavy trucks. Light trucks include pickup trucks and tow trucks. Medium trucks are often used for deliveries. Heavy trucks include dump trucks, cement trucks, and tractor-trailers.

Truck *Continued from the previous page*

the steering wheel and step on and off the truck easily. Most medium trucks run on diesel fuel rather than gasoline.

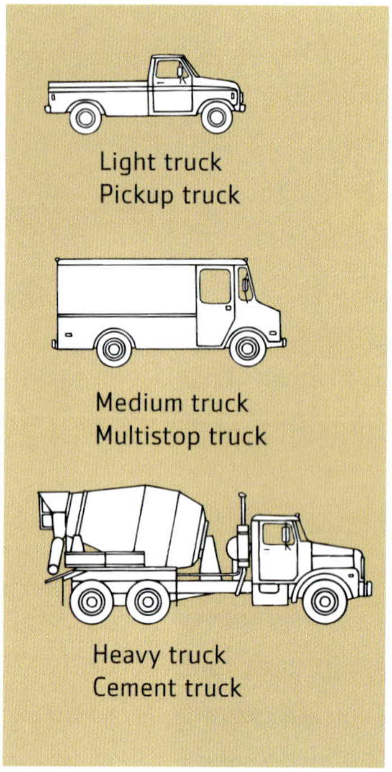

Heavy trucks, such as dump trucks and tractor-trailers, do all kinds of hard work. The rear of a dump truck tilts for easy unloading. Tractor-trailers have a type of powerful tractor in front. This tractor pulls a separate trailer with a full set of wheels. Almost all heavy trucks have diesel engines. Diesel engines are heavy. But they change fuel to energy better than do gasoline engines. Trucks with diesel engines can haul heavier loads than can trucks with gasoline engines.

Other articles to read include: **Automobile; Engine; Tractor.**

Motor-traffic tunnels, used by cars and trucks traveling on roads, are among the most familiar kinds of tunnels.

Tunnel

A tunnel is an underground passage. Many tunnels are dug through hills and mountains. Others lie under cities and waterways. Tunnels provide an easy way past mountains and bodies of water. The four main types of tunnels are (1) railroad tunnels, (2) motor-traffic tunnels, (3) water tunnels, and (4) mine tunnels.

Railroad tunnels are often cut through the rocks of mountains. Railroad tunnels shorten travel times. Trains use less energy traveling straight through a tunnel than they do climbing up a slope. The world's longest railroad tunnel is the Seikan Tunnel in Japan. It is 33 ½ miles (53.9 kilometers) long.

Motor-traffic tunnels are used by cars and trucks. These tunnels have big fans. The fans blow away the fumes that come out of motor vehicles. Many tunnels also have signal lights and

Continued on the next page

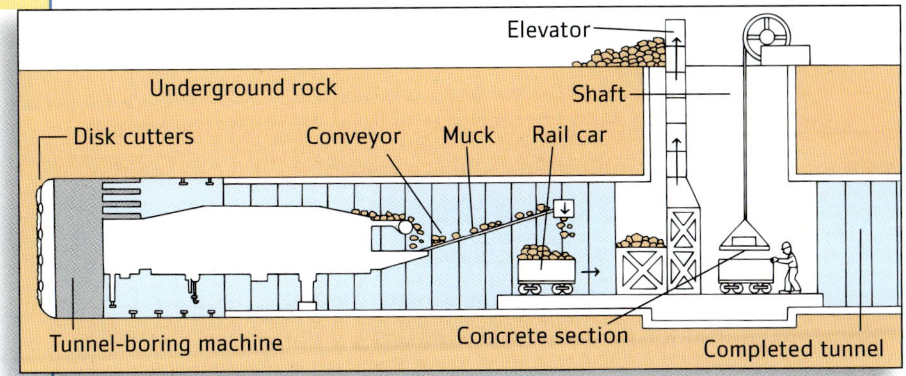

To make a tunnel, a *tunnel-boring machine* digs through rock. It uses attachments called *disk cutters.* The broken rock, called *muck,* is removed by conveyor and rail car. The muck is then brought to the surface in an elevator. Concrete sections for lining the new tunnel are lowered through a shaft.

special equipment to prevent traffic jams. The Laerdal Tunnel in Norway is the world's longest motor-traffic tunnel. It is 15.2 miles (24.5 kilometers) long.

Water tunnels carry water to cities and power plants. They are also used on farms to bring water to crops. Tunnels also carry waste through sewer systems.

Mine tunnels are used to reach valuable minerals. These minerals often lie deep underground.

Other articles to read include: **Automobile; Mining; Road; Train.**

Turbine

A turbine *(TUR bihn* or *TUR byn)* is a device turned by the movement of a fluid. The fluid may be water, gas, wind, or steam.

A *windmill* is a type of turbine. It has a wheel of propellerlike blades on a shaft. The wind pushes against the blades, turning the shaft. The shaft's spinning motion has energy. This motion can be used to make electric power.

Other turbines are turned by the movement of steam, other gases, or water. Steam turbines are often used in power plants. Water turbines in dams are turned by falling water. They are also used to generate electric power. Jet engines use turbines turned by hot gases.

Other articles to read include: **Electric generator; Electric power; Engine; Water power; Wind power; Windmill.**

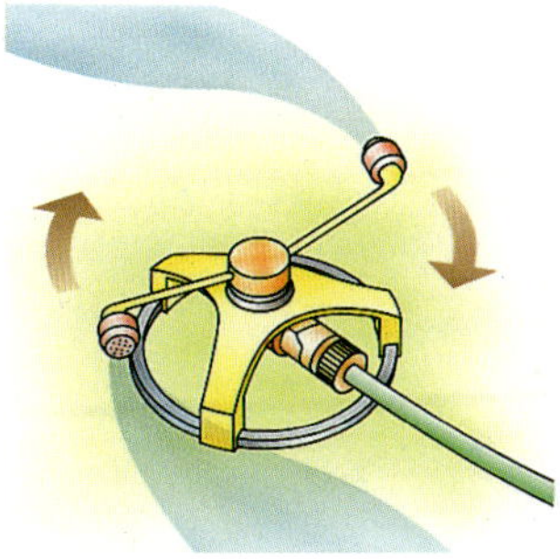

Turbine wheels include pinwheels (above left), which turn when air is blown against their blades. A sprinkler (above) is another kind of turbine that spins as water squirts out.

Alan Mathison Turing

Turing, Alan Mathison

Alan Mathison Turing (1912–1954) was an English mathematician and computer pioneer. In 1936, he described how to build a computer that could perform any calculation. This device is now called the *Turing machine.* The computer did not actually exist. It was a thought experiment. But the Turing machine became an important model for figuring out what tasks a computer could perform.

Turing was born on June 23, 1912, in London. He studied mathematics at Cambridge and Princeton universities. During World War II (1939–1945), he helped crack German communication codes. After the war, he worked on a project to build the first British electronic computer. In 1950, he proposed a test for figuring out if machines can "think" like humans. This test is now called the *Turing test.* It is often discussed in the field of artificial intelligence. Turing died on June 7, 1954.

Other articles to read include: **Artificial intelligence; Computer.**

The typewriter was once a common tool in homes and offices.

Typewriter

A typewriter is a machine that makes printed letters and figures on paper. The typewriter was invented in 1867 by an American inventor named Christopher Latham Sholes. For more than 100 years, people in homes and offices wrote on typewriters. But few people use typewriters today. Computers have taken the place of typewriters.

Each key on a typewriter has a letter or number on it. When pressed, the key hits an inked ribbon or a thin strip of carbon tape. The ribbon or tape is in front of the paper. The force of the key hitting the ribbon or tape makes a mark on the paper.

Other articles to read include: **Computer; Paper; Printing.**

Vacuum cleaner

A vacuum cleaner is a machine that sucks up dirt and dust. People use vacuum cleaners to remove dirt from floors, carpets, furniture, curtains, and other objects.

A vacuum cleaner sucks up air through a fan. As the fan spins, it pushes air away from it. Air from the outside then rushes in to fill the space. As the air flows in, it pulls dirt along with it. A bag or filter catches the dirt. The cleaned air is blown out of the machine. The bag must be emptied or changed regularly.

Other articles to read include: **Air cleaner; Machine.**

Two kinds of vacuum cleaner are the *canister vacuum* and the *upright vacuum.* In the canister vacuum (below left), a fan pulls dirt through a hose and into a bag. In an upright vacuum (below), the fan draws in dirt that has been loosened by an *agitator,* a rotating cylinder with bristles.

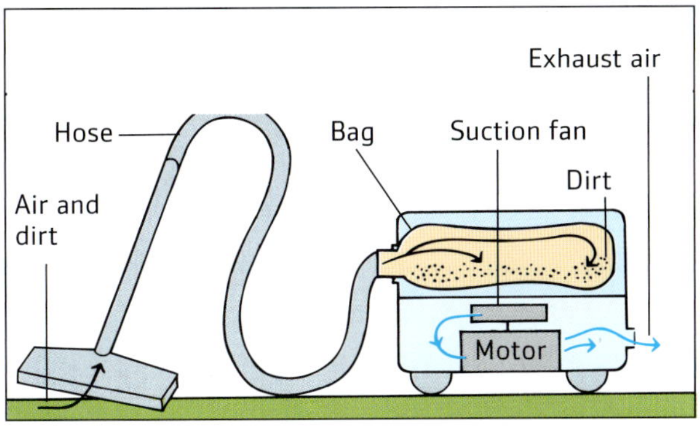

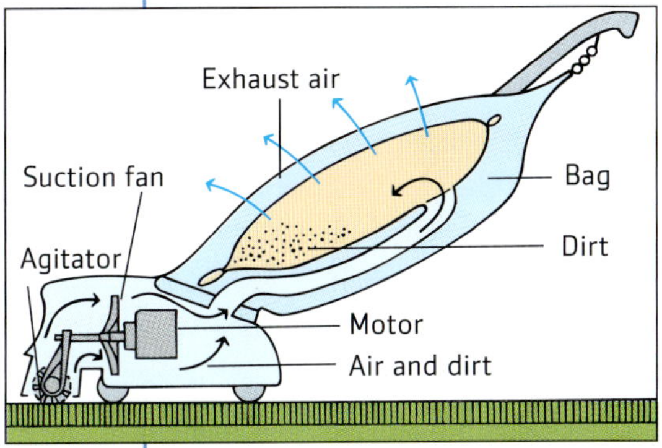

Vacuum tube

A vacuum tube is a device used in early computers and electronics. Many vacuum tubes look like light bulbs. Some have metal coverings, instead of glass.

There is almost no air inside a vacuum tube. This lack of air is a partial *vacuum.* Vacuum tubes also have *electrodes* inside them. Electric signals travel between electrodes.

Microwave ovens and older televisions use vacuum tubes. Otherwise, vacuum tubes are rarely used today. Tiny devices called *transistors* have taken their place.

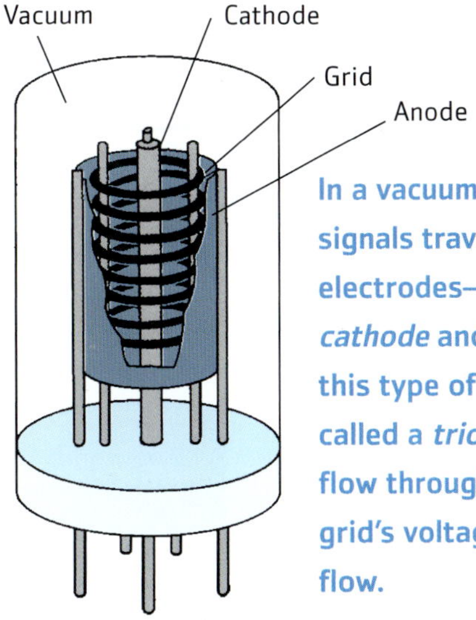

In a vacuum tube, electric signals travel between two electrodes—called the *cathode* and the *anode.* In this type of vacuum tube, called a *triode,* the signals flow through a grid. The grid's voltage controls the flow.

Other articles to read include: **Computer; Electrode; Electronics; Television; Transistor.**

A Velcro fastener consists of two strips. One strip (above left) is covered in tiny hooks. The other (above right) is covered in tiny loops.

Velcro

Velcro is a fastener made of tiny hooks and loops. It is used in clothing, shoes, and sports and medical equipment. It is also used inside automobiles and airplanes. A Swiss engineer named Georges de Mestral got the idea for Velcro in the 1940's. He was pulling burs from his dog's fur. Burs are prickly seed coverings that stick to fur or cloth. Mestral helped found Velcro Industries.

A Velcro fastener is made up of two strips. The strips are glued or sewn onto fabrics or other objects. Tiny hooks cover one of the strips. The hooks are made of strong thread. A fuzzy mat of thin loops covers the other strip. When the strips are pressed together, the hooks attach to the loops. The two strips stick together. The strips can be pulled apart and used again and again.

Other articles to read include: **Textile.**

Very Large Telescope

The Very Large Telescope (VLT) is one of the most powerful telescopes in the world. It actually consists of eight separate telescopes. Astronomers can use these telescopes in combination, as if they were a single telescope. They can also use them separately. The VLT is at Paranal Observatory on Paranal Mountain in Chile.

Continued on the next page

The Very Large Telescope, in the Atacama Desert of northern Chile, actually includes eight separate telescopes.

The four largest telescopes of the VLT are called *unit telescopes.* The mirrors of these telescopes are each 27 feet (8.2 meters) wide. Four *auxiliary (awg ZIHL yuhr ee) telescopes* have mirrors that are 71 inches (1.8 meters) wide.

Scientists made the first observations through a unit telescope in May 1998. Construction of the VLT was completed in 2006.

Other articles to read include: **Mirror; Space exploration; Telescope.**

Each of the VLT's eight telescopes can be used separately or in combination with the others.

Videotape recorder

A videocassette recorder (VCR) can play and record videotapes.

A videotape recorder is a machine once widely used to record pictures and sound. It is also known as a VTR or video recorder. Videotape recordings are made on special magnetic tape called *videotape.* This tape can be played on machines called *videocassette recorders* or VCR's. A VCR connects to a television.

Most videotape recorders use *tape cassettes.* The tape is a long plastic strip. It is coated with a thin layer of material called iron oxide. This material holds pictures and sounds in special magnetic patterns. VCR's record television programs by changing the pictures and sounds into magnetic patterns. These patterns are recorded on the tape. When the tape is played, the VCR changes the magnetic patterns back into pictures and sounds.

Videotape recorders were popular in the 1980's and 1990's. Television studios recorded shows with them. People used videotape recorders to record home movies. But in the late 1990's and early 2000's, *digital* recording devices became more popular. These devices could record videos on discs or as computer files. Videotape recorders are rarely used today.

Other articles to read include: **Digital video recorder; Tape recorder; Television.**

This children's toy works by overlaying real-world objects with a virtual reality of computer effects. This combination of the virtual and real is called *augmented reality.*

Virtual reality

Virtual reality, abbreviated VR, is a computerized environment that seems similar to a real-world experience. VR is often experienced by wearing a special headset. The headset has two small screens, one for each eye. The screens show a virtual—rather than physical—place, similar to the world of an electronic game. The headset may also have speakers that play sounds. Wearing the headset makes it feel as if you are actually inside the virtual world, rather than viewing it on a screen.

Virtual reality systems can track a person's head and body movements. When the VR user turns his head or walks forward, the screens change their views to match. Some VR systems have special gloves. The gloves can sense a person's hand movements. They send these motions to the VR computer program. Then the headset screens show virtual hands moving in the same way. Other equipment makes users feel as if the objects have weight. It can also make the users feel as if they could move around in the electronic world.

Research into VR equipment began in the early 1960's. VR games appeared in stores and video game rooms in the early 1990's. Some people, such as astronauts, used VR systems for training. In the late 2000's and 2010's, some advanced cell phones

Continued on the next page

A virtual reality system gives the user the sense of actually being inside an electronic world. In this photograph, an engineer uses a VR headset and handheld controller. They enable him to study the design for a new car as if he were already inside the factory.

and other electronics could display a related experience called *augmented reality.* In augmented reality, a person might point a phone's camera at a real-world place, such as a famous building. The phone's screen then shows useful information or images about the place. In this way, the system overlays the real world with a layer of virtual reality.

Other articles to read include: **Cellular telephone; Computer; Computer graphics.**

Volt

The volt is a unit of electrical measurement. A volt is a single unit of *voltage.* The term *voltage* describes the *electric potential* of a circuit or wire that carries electricity. Electric potential is defined as the work done in moving a unit of charge over a certain distance. Electric potential can also be thought of as the force that drives electric current through a circuit or wire. The volt was named for Alessandro Volta, an Italian scientist.

A simple comparison can be helpful in describing voltage. A wire that carries electricity can be thought of as a pipe filled with water. The electric potential, or voltage, is the force exerted by a pump that pushes the water through the pipe. The amount of pressure exerted by the pump is like the voltage in a wire. The volt is a unit that measures the pressure, also called *tension*.

The voltage of a battery is printed on its side. It is usually 1.5, 6.0, or 9.0 volts. The voltage of a power line to your home is much higher. The voltage of the electric current going through the wires in most homes is at least 110 volts. Sometimes, the voltage may be as high as 220 volts. Electric current that must travel over great distances is best moved with a very high voltage. The type of wire that carries this high voltage can be seen on the tallest electrical towers. They are sometimes called *high-tension wires.* They carry electricity that can be as high as 400,000 volts. As the electricity gets nearer to homes and businesses, the voltage is lowered in several steps.

Other articles to read include: **Battery; Electric current; Volta, Alessandro.**

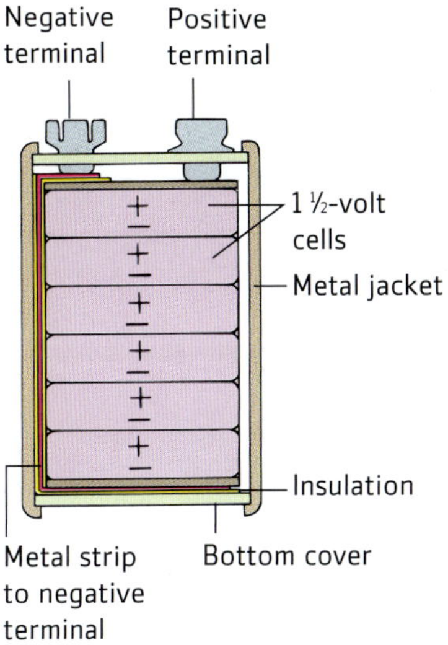

A 9-volt battery has six individual chambers called *cells.* Each cell produces 1 ½ volts of electricity. The cells are connected together so that their total voltage equals 9 volts.

Alessandro Volta

Volta, Alessandro

Alessandro Volta *(VOL tah* or *VOHL tah)* (1745–1827) was an Italian chemist and inventor. He is known for inventing the *voltaic pile.* The voltaic pile was an early kind of battery. A battery is a device that uses chemicals to make electric current.

Volta built a *stack,* or pile, of many pairs of disks. Each pair was made of the metals zinc and silver. Between each pair, he placed a disk of cloth or heavy paper soaked with an acid solution. The acid solution conducted electricity between the metal disks. Finally, Volta connected the pile to an *electric circuit.* An electric circuit is a path through which an electric current can flow. The voltaic pile caused electric current to flow through the circuit.

The *volt* is named in Volta's honor. The volt is a unit used to measure electricity.

Other articles to read include: **Battery; Electric circuit; Electric current; Volt.**

This photograph shows a model of one of the twin Voyager spacecrafts.

Voyager

Voyager is the name of two robotic *space probes.* A space probe is a kind of spacecraft. It gathers information using scientific equipment. It sends the information back to Earth.

The Voyagers were launched by NASA, the United States space agency. The probes studied the outer planets of the *solar*

Continued on the next page

system. The solar system is the group of objects that includes Earth, the seven other planets, and the sun they orbit.

Voyager 1 was launched on Sept. 5, 1977. It passed Jupiter on March 5, 1979. It passed Saturn on Nov. 12, 1980. Then, it continued toward the edge of the solar system.

Voyager 2 was launched on Aug. 20, 1977. It visited Jupiter on July 9, 1979, and Saturn on Aug. 25, 1981. Voyager 2 went on to pass Uranus on Jan. 24, 1986, and Neptune on Aug. 25, 1989.

The Voyagers gathered information about Jupiter, Saturn, Uranus, and Neptune. They also studied these planets' rings and moons. The probes found proof of volcanoes on Jupiter's moon Io *(EYE oh)*. They detected icy fountains on Neptune's moon Triton *(TRY tuhn)*. They also sent back information about the atmosphere of Saturn's moon Titan.

Each Voyager probe carried the same set of scientific instruments. One instrument measured the strength, shape, and

Continued on the next page

Voyager 2 captured this image of the Great Red Spot on Jupiter, a long-lived storm that is larger than Earth.

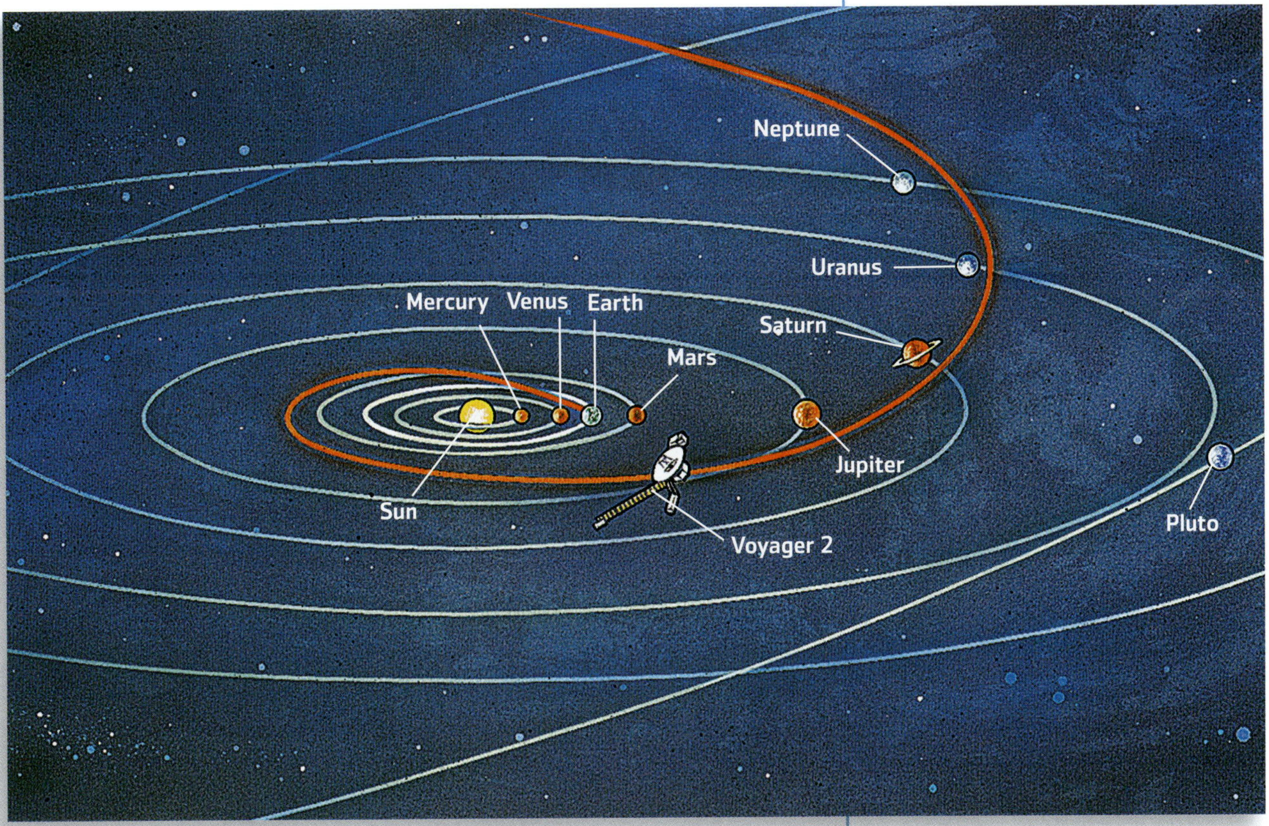

Voyager 2 launched Aug. 20, 1977. Its path through the solar system is shown in red.

Voyager *Continued from the previous page*

direction of the planets' and moons' *magnetic fields.* A magnetic field is the influence of a magnetic object, such as a planet or moon. Other instruments measured light from the planets, their rings, and their moons.

The two Voyagers kept going to the far reaches of the solar system. They continued to send back valuable information into the 2010's. They are expected to be the first space probes to leave the solar system.

Other articles to read include: **National Aeronautics and Space Administration; Space exploration.**

Bright spots cover the surface of Jupiter's moon Callisto in this image taken by Voyager 2. The spots result from meteor strikes that exposed brighter material beneath the dark surface.

Voyager 2 took this enhanced image of the planet Neptune. The image shows a large dark storm, similar to Jupiter's Great Red Spot.

Saturn's atmosphere, shown in this colorized image taken by Voyager 2, has separate bands of clouds.

Washing machine

A washing machine is a device that cleans clothes, linens, and other items. Modern washing machines work automatically. A person puts laundry and detergent into the machine and sets the controls. The machine then fills with water. An electric motor stirs or tumbles the soaked laundry, helping to remove dirt. Finally, a *spin cycle* removes extra water from the laundry by spinning it very quickly.

Before the washing machine was invented, people had to wash clothes by hand. People beat wet clothes or rubbed them with a scrubbing board and a brush. Some people still wash clothes this way. Early washing machines had a washtub topped by two rollers. The rollers were turned by hand. The rollers squeezed the water out of wet clothes.

The first washing machine powered by an engine was made in the early 1900's. It used a gasoline engine. In 1911, an electric-powered model became available. Later models added water pumps and drains, spin cycles, timers, and water temperature controls.

Other articles to read include: **Electric motor; Machine; Textile.**

A *tumbler* washing machine is loaded through a front door. Inside, a basket spins like a rolling barrel, tumbling the clothes around.

Water pollution

Water pollution *(puh LOO shuhn)* is the dirtying of water. Water can be polluted with garbage, sewage, metals, or other chemical materials. These substances can leak into underground water supplies and rivers, lakes, or oceans. Water pollution can harm or kill fish, frogs, birds, and other animals. It can also spread disease among people. It can make water supplies unsafe to drink.

Water pollution can come from several activities. Factories and farms release harmful chemicals into water supplies. Burning fuel in cars and in power plants can lead to *acid rain*. When the rain falls, it pollutes water supplies. Some cities release sewage into rivers, lakes, and seacoasts.

Laws and regulations help protect the public water supply from pollution. In many countries, sewage must be *treated* before being released. Most of its harmful chemicals must be removed. Other laws protect certain water supplies. They prevent industries from polluting drinking water or certain bodies of water.

Other articles to read include: **Landfill; Sewage.**

Crude oil from a damaged storage facility washes ashore in Beirut, Lebanon.

Continued on the next page

Water pollution by farm chemicals can cause algae to grow out of control, as it has in this lake in China.

Water power

Water power is an important source of energy. The motion of flowing water can be used to make electric power. Such power is called *hydroelectric (HY droh ih LEHK trihk) power.* It can be used again and again. Other ways of making electric power include burning coal, oil, and natural gas. But these fuels cannot be reused.

Continued on the next page

Many hydroelectric power plants are built in dams. Water falling through the dam has energy that can be used to make electric power.

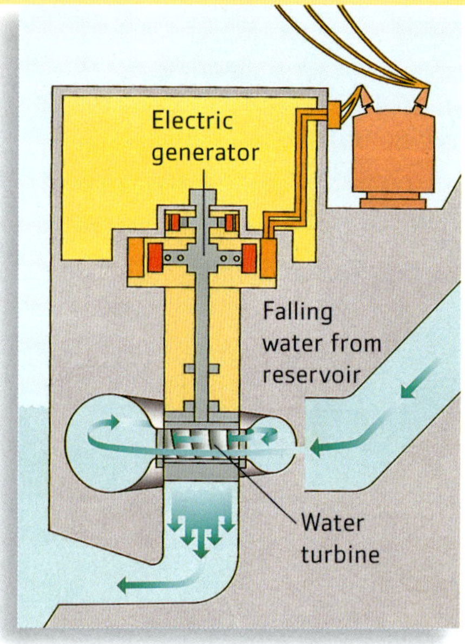

A *hydroelectric* power plant uses the force of falling water from a reservoir to spin a *turbine.* The turbine's motion powers an electric generator.

Water power *Continued from the previous page*

Many hydroelectric power plants are built on dammed-up rivers. Water is kept behind a dam in a storage pool called a *reservoir (REHZ uhr vwahr).* Some of the water is allowed to flow through the power plant. This water pushes and spins wheellike machines called *turbines.* The turbines are connected to *generators.* The generators change the spinning motion of the turbines into electric power. After it spins the turbines, the water flows out to the river.

Hydroelectric power plants cost less to run than do other kinds of power plants. They also do not *pollute* (dirty) the air. But hydroelectric power cannot be used everywhere.

People have long used flowing water to spin machines. The ancient Romans used water wheels to grind grain.The first hydroelectric power plant was built in Appleton, Wisconsin, in 1882.

Other articles to read include: **Dam; Electric generator; Electric power; Turbine.**

Waterproofing

Waterproofing is a treatment that keeps water out of cloth, leather, wood, or other materials. Many different chemicals are used in waterproofing. Most form a coating over the material.

Waterproofing is widely used in the *textile industry.* Textiles are fabrics and fibers. Cloth fibers may be waterproofed either before or after weaving.

Waterproofing treatments are sold in spray containers. They can be sprayed on clothes and furniture.

In 1823, the Scottish chemist Charles Macintosh invented a water-resistant fabric. It was a mixture of cloth and rubber. A raincoat of this material is sometimes called a *mackintosh.*

Other articles to read include: **Textile; Wax.**

Waterproof fabric resists becoming soaked, causing water to bead on its surface.

Watson-Watt, Sir Robert

Sir Robert Watson-Watt (1892–1973) was a Scottish engineer and inventor. He helped develop a system called *radar (RAY dahr).* Radar is used to locate distant objects.

In 1919, Watson-Watt made an early type of radio direction finder. The device helped locate the direction of an incoming radio signal. At the time, Watson-Watt worked with a British weather department.

In 1935, Watson-Watt began working on ways to find aircraft with radio waves. By 1940, he had helped build dependable radar stations along British shores. These stations helped detect enemy airplanes in the Battle of Britain during World War II (1939–1945).

Watson-Watt was knighted in 1942 for his effort in developing radar. After the war, he lived in Canada and the United States before returning to England.

Other articles to read include: **Invention; Radar; Radio.**

Sir Robert Watson-Watt

Watt

The watt is a unit of electric power. The symbol for the watt is *W.* Electric power is the amount of electric energy used over a certain time. The watt was named for the Scottish engineer and inventor James Watt.

The number on an electric light shows its *wattage* (need for power in watts). For example, a light bulb operating at 100 *volts* and using 2 *amperes (AM pihrz)* consumes 200 watts (100 volts × 2 amperes). The volt is a unit for measuring the force of electric energy. The ampere measures the strength of an electric current.

The watt also is used to measure mechanical power. A machine needs a power of 1 watt if it uses 1 *joule (jool)* of energy in 1 second. The joule is a unit of work done by a machine or person.

Other articles to read include: **Electric power; Volt; Watt, James.**

Lights of similar brightness can have different *wattages,* the need for power measured in watts. Incandescent bulbs (above left) have a higher wattage than fluorescent lights and light-emitting diode (LED) bulbs (above middle and right).

James Watt's steam engine, developed during the late 1700's, led to the widespread use of steam power in industry.

Watt, James

James Watt (1736–1819) was a Scottish engineer and inventor. He is best known for improving the steam engine. The *watt,* a unit of power, is named for him.

Thomas Newcomen, an English inventor, built the first commercial steam engine in 1712. In the 1760's, James Watt noticed a flaw in the design of Newcomen's engine. A part called the *cylinder* was first heated by steam and then cooled by water. Watt realized that this process wasted a lot of steam and fuel.

Watt invented a new steam engine. The cylinder stayed hot. A separate part called the *condenser* changed steam back into water by cooling. This device saved a large amount of steam and fuel.

Other articles to read include: **Invention; Steam engine; Watt.**

This candle burns a kind of mineral wax called *paraffin.*

Wax

Wax is a fatty material. It is widely used to protect surfaces. Wax resists air, water, and chemical change. Most wax is solid at room temperature. It becomes soft when heated. Manufacturers make three kinds of wax: *mineral, animal,* and *vegetable.*

Most mineral wax comes from *petroleum (puh TROH lee uhm).* Petroleum comes from rocks far beneath the ground. Liquid petroleum is used to make oil. Petroleum wax resists moisture and chemicals. It has no odor or taste. It is used to waterproof such paper products as milk cartons and waxed paper. Petroleum wax also is used to make polishes for cars, floors, and furniture.

Animal wax is used alone or with petroleum wax in candles and other products. *Beeswax* is a type of animal wax. Bees make beeswax when they build honeycombs. *Wool wax* comes from a greasy coating on unprocessed wool.

Vegetable wax comes from the natural coatings of plants. One important type comes from the leaves of palm trees.

Other articles to read include: **Textile; Waterproofing.**

Weather balloon

A weather balloon is a special type of balloon used by *meteorologists (MEE tee uh ROL uh jihsts).* Meteorologists are scientists who study and predict the weather.

Weather balloons are launched from hundreds of places around the world. Many of the balloons carry a device called a *radiosonde (RAY dee oh sond).* A radiosonde is a package of scientific instruments. The instruments measure the temperature, *humidity* (wetness), and pressure of the air at various heights. A radiosonde also includes a radio. The radio sends the measurements to weather stations on the ground.

The weather balloon lifts the radiosonde about 19 miles (30 kilometers) into the air. Eventually, the balloon pops or deflates. The radiosonde floats back to the ground by parachute.

Other articles to read include: **Balloon; Radiosonde; Weather forecasting.**

Weather balloons are launched from around the world.

Weather forecasting

Weather forecasting is the process of predicting the weather in the near future. Scientists who study and predict the weather are called *meteorologists (MEE tee uh ROL uh jihsts).* They gather information about Earth's atmosphere from the surface, the air, and even outer space.

Meteorologists try to predict the development and movement of future weather systems, such as storms. They use weather maps and computer models of the atmosphere to do this. They also use a variety of instruments. These include *barometers (buh ROM uh tuhrz), thermometers (thuhr MOM uh tuhrz),* and *hygrometers (hy GROM uh tuhrz).*

Continued on the next page

Meteorologists study a map that shows the different levels of air pressure in an area.

Weather forecasting

Continued from the previous page

Barometers measure air pressure. Hygrometers measure *humidity* (wetness in the air).

Meteorologists also use *radar systems* and *weather satellites* to track storms. Radar systems send out waves of energy called *microwaves.* The waves bounce off water droplets or ice in clouds. Computers analyze the returning microwaves. A weather satellite orbits above Earth. A satellite can view storms and weather patterns from above. Both radar and satellites can help determine the path and *severity* (seriousness) of a storm.

Other articles to read include: **Barometer; Hygrometer; Radar; Radiosonde; Thermometer; Weather balloon; Weather satellite; Weather Service, National; Weather vane.**

Weather satellite

A weather satellite *(SAT uh lyt)* is a spacecraft that studies Earth's weather and climate. Weather satellites *orbit* (travel around) Earth in space.

Weather satellites help scientists find storms. They also provide information about the air. Such information may include air temperature and wind speed.

Continued on the next page

An image from the U.S. weather satellite GOES 8 shows a tropical storm reaching the coasts of Louisiana and Texas.

Some weather satellites measure the total energy entering and leaving Earth's atmosphere. This data helps scientists track changes in climate.

Most weather satellites pass over the North and South poles in their orbits. Other weather satellites orbit above a single spot on the equator.

Other articles to read include: **Satellite, Artificial; Weather forecasting.**

A weather satellite called a Geostationary Operational Environmental Satellite (GOES) orbits Earth above the equator.

Weather Service, National

The National Weather Service is a United States government organization. It monitors the weather in the United States and its territories. At the National Weather Service, scientists called *meteorologists (MEE tee uh ROL uh jihsts)* study weather patterns. The National Weather Service makes forecasts of weather events. It also issues warnings in cases of dangerous weather, such as hurricanes and tornadoes.

The National Weather Service is part of the National Oceanic and Atmospheric Administration (NOAA). NOAA is part of the U.S. Department of Commerce.

Other articles to read include: **Weather forecasting.**

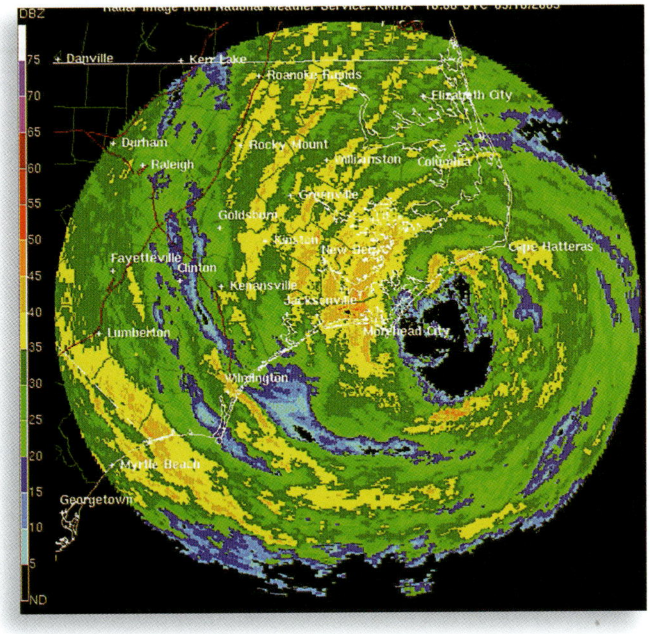

A Doppler radar image from the National Weather Service shows the eye of a hurricane approaching the North Carolina coast.

A rooster decorates this weather vane.

Weather vane

A weather vane shows the direction of the wind. Part of the weather vane is a pointer. The pointer turns freely on an upright rod. The pointer is usually shaped like an arrow. Sometimes it has a decoration on top.

One end of the pointer is wide. A breeze will force it to turn. It turns until the wind is blowing on both sides evenly. When this happens, the pointer is facing the wind.

Most weather vanes have a circular plate underneath the pointer. This plate has the directions of the compass on it. People look at it to tell what direction the wind is coming from.

Other articles to read include: **Weather forecasting.**

Weaving

Weaving is a way of making cloth. In weaving, threads are crossed over and under one another. Many kinds of fabric are woven. Most blankets, clothing, and rugs are woven. Weavers use different types of thread. They may even use grasses, thin strips of wood or metal, and other materials.

All woven materials have two sets of threads. One set of threads runs lengthwise. These threads are called the *warp.* Another set of threads runs the width of the warp,

Continued on the next page

Weaving involves crossing threads over and under one another. Machines called power looms can quickly weave huge amounts of cloth.

turning over and under the warp threads. These other threads are called the *weft.*

There are different types of weaves. In *plain weaves,* the weft goes over one warp thread and under the next one, over and over. Other types of weaves have more complex patterns. Different patterns have different textures. In *satin weaves,* for example, a weft may cross over 12 warp threads. Satin weaves have a very soft texture. In *pile weaves,* weft yarns have loops that stay above the fabric's surface. These loops give carpets, towels, and corduroy a fuzzy texture.

Some people weave by hand. But weavers often use a machine called a *loom* to help them. Some looms are operated by hand levers or by foot pedals. Power looms are used in factories.

Almost all looms weave cloth in much the same way. Frames hold the warp threads in position. Strings or wires stop the threads from tangling. A device called a *shuttle* holds the weft thread. The shuttle acts somewhat like a sewing needle. It draws the weft thread over and under the stretched-out warp threads. As the cloth is woven, it is wound around and tightened. It comes out along a metal or wooden frame at the bottom of the loom.

Other articles to read include: **Textile.**

Website

A website is a presentation of information on the Internet. Many companies, schools, and other organizations have websites. Some people have their own websites, too. Websites may include words, pictures, sounds, and videos. People can also play games or buy products on websites.

A website generally includes a number of web pages. For example, World Book's Student website includes web pages for thousands of articles.

A website often contains a number of web pages. Each web page has its own address, called a *uniform resource locator* (URL). Computers use the URL to find a web page on the Internet.

Web pages contain *hyperlinks* to other pages. Hyperlinks are special words or images. When a person clicks on a hyperlink, the computer shows the linked page. The *World Wide Web* refers to all of the Internet's web pages. They are connected together with hyperlinks.

Other articles to read include: **Internet; Wiki.**

Wedge

A wedge is a tool with two or more sloping sides. The sides come together at a sharp edge or a point. Wedges are used to split or pierce different materials. They can also move or support a heavy object. Knives, chisels, axes, doorstops, pins, needles, and nails are all wedges. The wedge is one of six *simple machines* studied in physics.

A person may hammer a wedge into an object. The greater the angle between the wedge surfaces, the greater the force needed to hammer it. If the wedge angle is too great, it is impossible to drive the wedge into the object.

Other articles to read include: **Hammer; Machine; Tool.**

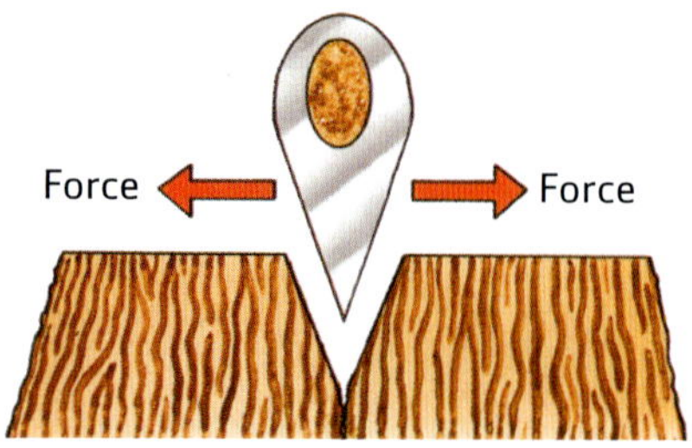

A wedge is a simple machine. It changes a downward *effort* (applied force) into sideways forces that can split objects.

Welding

Welding is the use of intense heat or pressure to bond pieces of metal together. Factories weld parts together to make cars, refrigerators, and other products. Builders weld metal pieces of buildings and bridges. Other workers weld tiny parts of computer chips.

One way of welding is to fasten two pieces of metal together and heat them until they are partly melted. They stick together when the metal cools. In *arc welding,* the heat comes from a powerful electric spark. The heat may otherwise come from burning gases or a laser.

Another form of welding squeezes two pieces of metal together. The great pressure causes the pieces to join without melting them. Coins of different metals are made this way.

Other articles to read include: **Electric current; Electrode; Metal.**

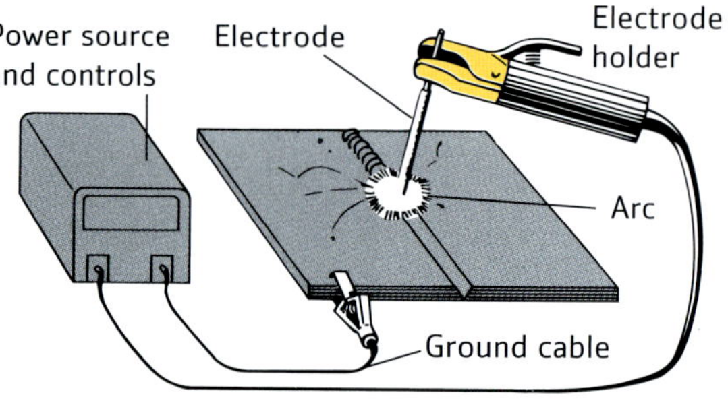

Arc welding uses a powerful electric spark to join two pieces of metal. The spark runs from a device called an *electrode* to the metal, heating the metal to form a weld.

Well

A well is a hole in the ground from which a fluid is taken. Water wells are the most common wells. They supply drinking water. There are also many oil and natural gas wells. Some wells are used to get salt and sulfur from deep in the ground.

The underground water that flows into wells is called *ground water.* Most of this water comes from rain that soaks into the ground. The water slowly moves downward into a zone of soil and rock filled with water. The top of this zone is the *water table.* It is the level at which water stands in a well.

Other articles to read include: **Mining; Pump; Soil.**

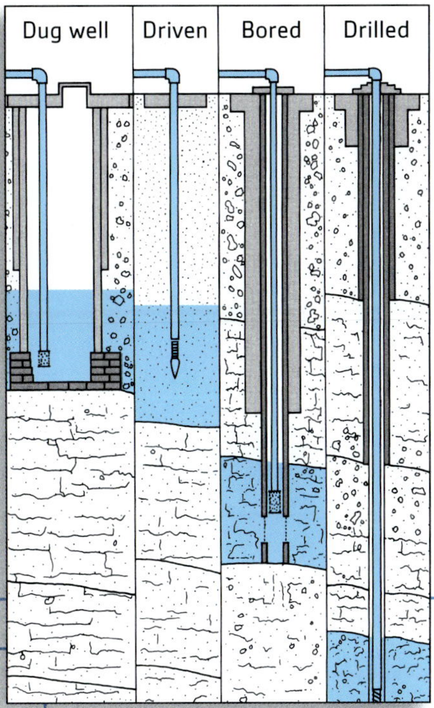

Different methods are used to create wells of different depths. The shallowest wells are dug or are driven into the ground with a sharp point. Such wells may reach 15 meters (50 feet) deep. A tool called an *auger* is used to create a bored well, which can reach 30 meters (100 feet) in depth. Wells can be drilled to 300 meters (1000 feet) and beyond.

Westinghouse, George

George Westinghouse (1846–1914) was an American inventor and manufacturer. He produced *air brakes* for railroad cars. These brakes helped stop trains more quickly and safely. He also perfected inventions that helped trains stay on, and switch between, tracks. Westinghouse invented a pipeline system that safely carried natural gas into homes. He invented a type of gas meter. Westinghouse's company also introduced a way of supplying electric power called *alternating current.* The Austrian-Hungarian inventor Nikola Tesla, who worked for Westinghouse, came up with the idea.

Westinghouse was born on Oct. 6, 1846, in Central Bridge, New York. As a boy, he worked in his father's machine shop. At 15, he made a spinning *rotary engine.* Westinghouse served in the Union Army and Navy during the American Civil War (1861–1865).

Westinghouse got *patents* (legal protections) for hundreds of inventions. He organized more than 50 companies. He was president of 30 corporations, including the Westinghouse Electric Company. He died on March 12, 1914.

Other articles to read include: **Alternating current; Electric power; Rotary engine; Tesla, Nikola; Train.**

Wheel and axle

The wheel and axle is an important tool. It is made up of a wheel attached to a long rod called an *axle.* When the wheel spins, so does the axle. The wheel and axle is one of six *simple machines* studied in physics.

A machine called a *windlass* uses a wheel and axle. A windlass has one end of a rope attached to an axle. The other end of the rope is attached to the object that needs to be lifted. When someone turns the wheel, the rope winds around the axle and pulls up the object.

A wheel and axle makes lifting easier because the wheel is wider than the axle. The wheel has to turn farther to lift the object connected to the axle. But the wheel is easier to turn.

Other articles to read include: **Automobile; Bicycle; Machine; Motorcycle; Tire; Truck; Winch; Windlass.**

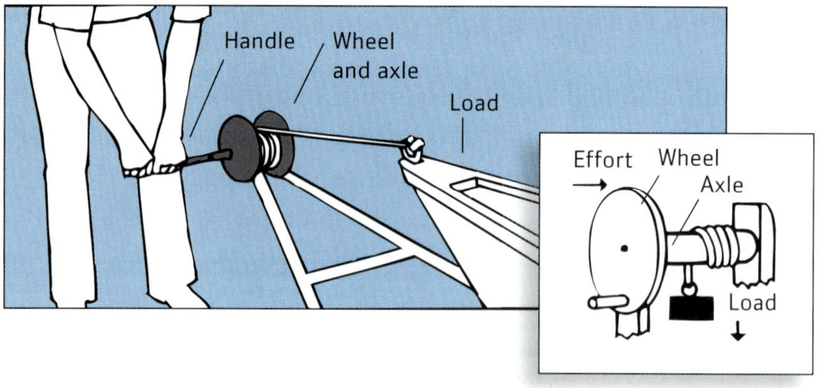

A wheel and axle can make it easier to pull on a load. Turning the wheel requires less applied force or *effort* than does turning the axle. But the wheel must rotate a greater distance.

Whistle

A whistle is a device that makes a sound from moving air or steam. The most common kind of whistle is a tube. It has a hole in its side. The hole has a lip or a sharp edge. Air is blown in one end of the tube. When it hits the lip, the air starts to swirl. The swirling creates a vibration in the air. We hear the vibration as sound.

Steam whistles were once used on locomotives. But they are seldom used today. Police officers and sports officials use small air whistles.

Other articles to read include: **Locomotive.**

A whistle forces air over a lip or sharp edge. Air vibrates as it swirls over the lip, making a whistling sound.

Whitney, Eli

Eli Whitney's cotton gin could clean as much cotton in one day as could 50 people working by hand.

Eli *(EE ly)* Whitney (1765–1825) was an American inventor. He is best known for his *cotton gin*. The cotton gin is a machine that separates cotton seeds from the plant's fluffy fibers. Whitney's cotton gin could clean as much cotton as 50 people working by hand. The machine quickly helped the United States become the world's leading cotton grower. Whitney also became a maker of guns and other weapons.

Whitney was born in Westborough, Massachusetts. Early in life, he showed a talent for making things. When he was 12 years old, he made a violin. In 1792, Whitney went to Savannah, Georgia, to teach and study law. His friend Catherine Littlefield Greene suggested that he build a machine to clean cotton. By April 1793, he had built the cotton gin. It was not the first cotton gin ever invented. But it worked much better than earlier machines.

Other articles to read include: **Agriculture; Cotton gin; Invention.**

Wiki

A wiki is a website that people can easily edit. They can also add material to the website. People far apart can work together on a wiki. Wikis are different from other websites. A wiki's content is usually not "finished." It changes as people edit it. The word *wiki* comes from the Hawaiian phrase *wiki wiki*. It means *fast*.

Some wikis let anyone change their content. Others require that people register to edit. Still other wikis are private. Users must be invited to work on such wikis.

The first wiki was created in 1995. Wikipedia, an online encyclopedia, is one of the most popular wikis. It started in 2001.

Other articles to read include: **Internet; Website.**

The winch on this boat is used for hauling in large, heavy nets filled with fish.

Winch

A winch is a crank. It is used to turn something in a machine. This type of motion is called *rotary (ROH tuhr ee) motion.*

Winch can also mean a crank attached to a drum. Rope is wound around the drum. The rope is attached to a heavy object. By turning the crank, a person can *winch* (pull) the object to a certain position or height.

The simplest winches are turned by hand. Other winches may have an electric motor. *Hydraulic (hy DRAW lihk) winches* are turned by the pressure in a liquid.

Other articles to read include: **Machine; Wheel and axle; Windlass.**

Wind turbines convert the energy of wind into electric power. In this photograph, modern wind turbines tower over a more traditional windmill.

Wind power

Wind power is the use of moving air to do useful work. Wind contains much energy. People have long used this energy to do work. Around 2800 B.C., the Egyptians made sailing ships powered by wind. People in Persia (now Iran) probably made the first windmill during the A.D. 600's. In a windmill, the wind turns a shaft. The turning motion can grind grain. Similar devices can pump water. In modern wind power devices, the spinning shaft makes electric power. Wind power was first used to make electric power in Denmark in the 1890's.

Devices called *wind turbines* convert wind energy into electric power. The turbine connects to long blades. Wind pushes on the blades, spinning the turbine. The turbine's spinning motion powers a generator. The generator converts the spinning motion into electric power.

Wind power works best in areas with strong, steady winds. But even in such places, winds vary from day to day. On some days, there may be little or no wind. For this reason, wind energy requires a backup power system. The backup system can provide power on days when the wind is not strong.

Continued on the next page

Wind energy is *renewable.* Renewable energy cannot be used up, as can fuels such as coal, oil, and natural gas. Also, wind energy is clean. It does not *pollute* (dirty) the environment. However, some people oppose wind power devices. They say the turbines are too ugly or noisy. Others complain that the spinning blades kill birds and bats.

Other articles to read include: **Electric generator; Electric power; Power plant; Turbine; Windmill.**

Windlass

The windlass *(WIHND luhs)* is a simple machine used to lift heavy things and pull loads. A windlass may also be called a *winch.* It is a type of *wheel and axle.*

A windlass has a crank. The crank is attached to a roller. A rope or chain is wrapped around the roller. Turning the crank winds the rope or chain. The winding pulls on a load attached to the rope or chain.

Early windlasses were used to raise water from wells. People lowered a bucket into the well on a rope. The bucket filled with water. Turning the crank pulled in the rope, bringing up the bucket of water.

Modern windlasses are turned by machines. They are used on boats to pull up anchors. They are also used on cranes and elevators.

Other articles to read include: **Machine; Well; Wheel and axle; Winch.**

The windlass is a kind of wheel and axle. It can be used to raise water from a well. Turning the crank handle spins the axle. The spinning winds the rope, pulling up the bucket.

Moving air spins the blades of a windmill. The spinning motion can be used to grind grain or pump water.

Windmill

A windmill is a machine that gets power from the movement of air. Wind contains energy. This energy can be used to pump water, grind grain, or make electric power.

Most windmills have two or more blades or sails. The blades are attached to a bar called a *shaft.* The shaft is mounted on a tower, mast, or other tall structure. When the wind blows the blades, the shaft turns. The shaft's movement can be used to do useful work. The first windmills were built in Persia (now Iran) in the 600's. They ground grain. Other windmills pumped water.

Modern windmills make electric power. They are called *wind turbines.* Wind turbines are becoming an important source of electric power.

Other articles to read include: **Electric power; Power plant; Turbine; Wind power.**

Wire

A wire is a long, thin piece of metal. Some wires are thick and stiff. Others are thin and can bend easily. Wires can be different colors, sizes, and shapes.

Wires are often used to carry *electric current.* Electric current is a flow of electricity. Electrical wires are usually made of copper or aluminum. These metals are good *conductors* of electricity. A conductor carries electric current well. An electrical wire may be a single strand of metal. Or it can be several strands twisted together.

Electrical wires are often covered with an *insulator (IHN suh LAY tuhr).* An insulator is a material that blocks the flow of current. The insulator keeps the wire from damaging anything or shocking people. Wires are often insulated with plastic or rubber. A wire without insulation is called a *bare* wire.

Not all wires are used to carry electric current. Some wires are twisted together into thick, strong cables. Cables help support bridges and other structures. *Optical fibers* are like wires, but they

Continued on the next page

are made from glass. They carry pulses of light, rather than electricity. Optical fibers are used to carry data over the Internet.

Other articles to read include: **Cable; Electric current; Fiber optics; Insulator, Electric; Metal.**

How metal wire is made

1. A chunk of metal called an *ingot* is heated and squeezed into thinner shapes by rollers.

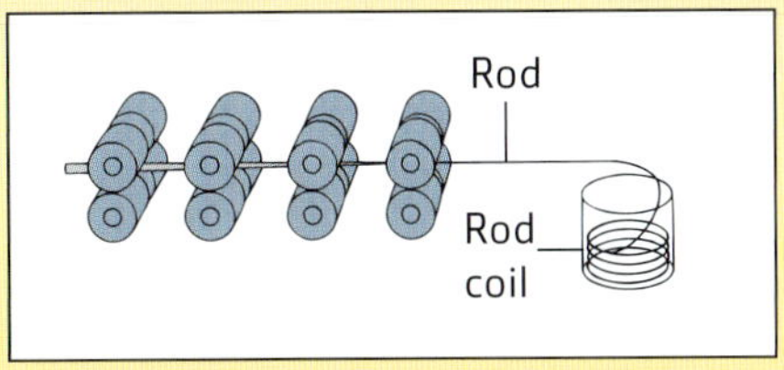

2. More rollers squeeze the metal into a rod. The rod is coiled for easy transport.

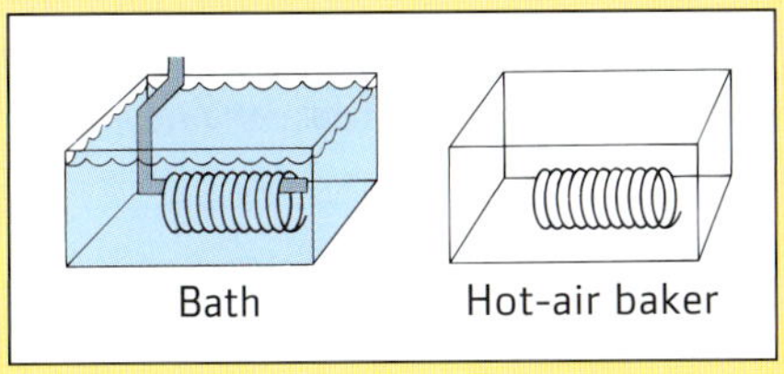

3. The rod coil is cleaned and baked. It is coated in a slippery substance called a *lubricant.*

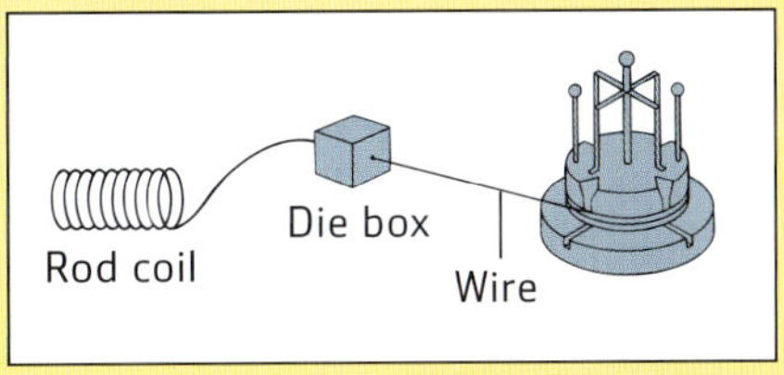

4. The slippery rod is drawn through a small hole in a *die box,* squeezing it even thinner. It becomes a wire.

Wireless communication

Wireless communication is the sending of information using *electromagnetic waves.* An electromagnetic wave is a pattern of energy. It is somewhat like an ocean wave. But electromagnetic waves can travel through air or space. Most wireless communication uses radio waves, which are invisible.

An electromagnetic wave's pattern can act as a code. This code can stand for text, sound, or videos. It can also stand for websites and computer programs. Many devices can pick up and decode the waves. They include radios, mobile phones, and computers.

There are different ways to encode electromagnetic waves. *Amplitude modulation* (AM) changes the height of the waves. The changing height acts as a code. *Frequency modulation* (FM) changes the *frequency* (rate of vibration) of the waves.

Other articles to read include: **Communication; Electronics; Marconi, Guglielmo; Radio; Television.**

Granville T. Woods

Woods, Granville T.

Granville T. Woods (1856–1910) was an African American inventor. His most famous invention involved railroad signals. He invented a railway *telegraph system* in 1887. The telegraph was an early way to send messages through wires. Woods's telegraph helped train crews communicate to avoid crashes.

Woods was born in Columbus, Ohio. When he was young, he learned how to repair railroad equipment. Later, he established his own company in Cincinnati, Ohio. The company made and sold electrical items.

Woods was awarded more than 50 *patents* during his life. A patent is a government document showing ownership of an invention. Woods received his first patent in 1884. It was for an improved steam boiler furnace. Such furnaces powered steamships. He also invented an air brake for trains.

Other articles to read include: **Invention; Telegraph; Steam engine; Train.**

Steve Wozniak

Wozniak, Steve

Steve Wozniak (1950–), an American engineer, is one of the founders of Apple Inc., originally Apple Computer, Inc. Apple makes computer programs and computers, phones, and other electronic devices.

Stephen Gary Wozniak was born on Aug. 11, 1950, in San Jose, California. In 1971, he began working at Hewlett-Packard Company, an electronics maker. Around this time, Wozniak met Steve Jobs. Jobs was another young computer hobbyist. In 1975, Wozniak and Jobs built a simple, inexpensive computer. Jobs encouraged Wozniak to go into business with him. In 1976, the two founded Apple Computer. They began selling computers based on their early design, called the Apple I.

In 1981, Wozniak left Apple. Wozniak had become rich from Apple. He later sponsored music events and taught computer science.

Other articles to read include: **Apple Inc.; Computer; Jobs, Steve.**

Wright, Will

Will Wright (1960–) is an American maker of computer games. He makes games that *simulate* (act like) some part of the real world. One of his most famous games is *SimCity,* made in 1989. In *SimCity,* players make an imaginary city that works like a real city. For example, traffic jams develop if the player does not build enough roads. If the player builds too many roads, there may not be enough money to build other important things, such as hospitals. *SimCity* is one of the most popular computer games of all time.

William Ralph Wright was born in Atlanta on Jan. 20, 1960. As a child, he enjoyed learning and building models. He made his first computer game, *Raid on Bungeling Bay,* in 1984. Wright has made a number of popular simulation games. In *The Sims* (2000), players control the daily life of simulated people. Wright designed a game called *Spore* (2008). It simulates the development of life and civilizations.

Other articles to read include: **Computer simulation; Electronic game.**

Will Wright

Wright brothers

The Wright brothers invented the airplane. Their names were Wilbur (1867–1912) and Orville (1871–1948). Other people had flown through the air on balloons and gliders. But the Wright brothers were the first to fly in an engine-powered airplane. All modern airplanes are based on their work.

The Wright brothers made four flights in their airplane on Dec. 17, 1903. It marked the first time humans flew in an engine-powered aircraft.

As children, the Wrights were fascinated by the study of motion. Their mother encouraged them to experiment and learn.

In 1899, the Wrights began studying the science of flight. They began experimenting with gliders. They thought the biggest problem with flying machines was that they were hard to control. They tested the gliders for several years near Kitty Hawk, North Carolina. Eventually, they figured out how to control a machine in flight.

Continued on the next page

Wright brothers

Continued from the previous page

In 1903, the Wrights built a flying machine with an engine—an airplane. They named it *Flyer.* On Dec. 17, 1903, the brothers made four flights on *Flyer.* The longest, by Wilbur, covered 852 feet (260 meters). It lasted 59 seconds.

For years afterward, most people knew nothing of the Wright brothers' achievement. A few newspapers reported on the Wrights. But the stories were often inaccurate. Many people at the time doubted that flying machines could even exist. In any case, the Wrights liked working in private. They spent several years perfecting their airplane design.

In 1908, the Wrights showed off their inventions in the United States and in France. They made long flights that amazed large audiences. But one flight, on September 17, ended in disaster. An accident caused Orville to crash his plane. Orville was seriously injured, and his passenger died. Orville later recovered and continued flying.

In 1909, the Wrights established a company to build airplanes. Wilbur died of typhoid fever in 1912. Orville sold the company in 1915. But he kept doing research on airplanes for the rest of his life. Orville died on Jan. 30, 1948.

Other articles to read include: **Airplane; Glider; Invention**

Yang Liwei

Yang Liwei (1965–) was the first astronaut launched into space by China. Yang spent 21 hours in space in October 2003. He *orbited* (circled) Earth 14 times, traveling more than 373,000 miles (600,000 kilometers). Yang landed safely in Mongolia after the flight. Before flying into space, Yang was a pilot in the Chinese air force.

People in China call Yang a *taikonaut (TY koh nawt).* That is Chinese for astronaut. Russia and the United States are the only other countries to have launched people into space.

Other articles to read include: **Astronaut; Space exploration.**

Zipper

A zipper is a sliding fastener. Zippers hold parts of clothing together. Zippers are used in many kinds of clothing, especially pants, coats, and boots.

Most zippers have two rows of metal or plastic teeth. The teeth lock together. Each tooth has a raised dome on top and a hollow part on the bottom. As the *slide* is pulled up, it draws the teeth together, one after another. The domes fit into the hollows. The teeth stay locked together this way until the slide is pulled down.

The first zipper with locking teeth was invented in 1917. In the 1930's, zippers became common in everyday clothing.

Other articles to read include: **Textile.**

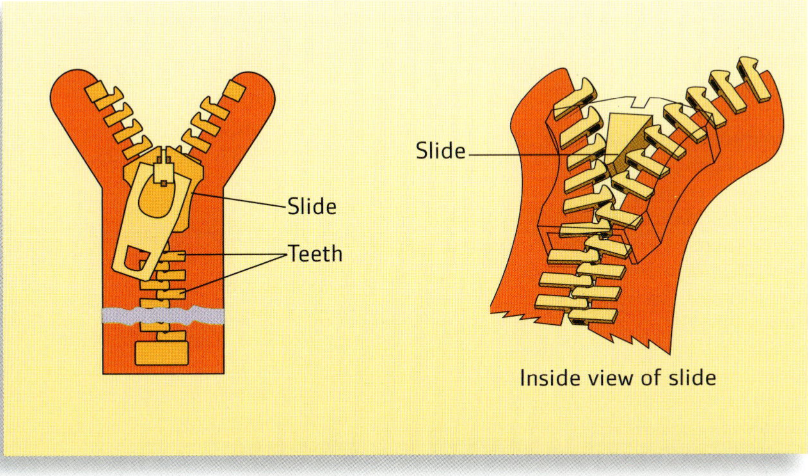

Most zippers have two rows of teeth that lock together (left). The teeth are joined or separated by a *slide.* When the slide moves up, its curved sides pull the teeth together. Moving the slide down acts as a wedge, pushing the teeth apart. Zippers are widely used as fasteners in clothing (below left).

The index is an alphabetical list of important topics covered in this book. It will help you find information given in both words and pictures. The page number or numbers after a heading tell you where to look for information about a topic. For example, there are references to **Atomic bomb** on pages 46 and 211.

When there is an article on a topic in *The Discovery Science Encyclopedia,* the page number or numbers appear in **boldface.** For example, the boldface page for the article on **Blimp** appears along with references to that topic in other encyclopedia articles. When there are many references to a topic, they are sometimes organized under subtopics, as they are under **Computer.**

Sometimes, an index heading refers you to information in other headings in the index. For example, **Bomb** has a "See also" reference to additional information on this topic under **Nuclear weapon.** The "See" reference for **CD** tells you that all the information on this topic will be found under **Compact disc.**

When an entry can mean more than one thing, there are words in parentheses to help you distinguish between these different meanings—for example, **Lock** (canal structure) and **Lock** (safety device).

A page number in *italics* refers to an illustration only. For example, a picture for **Magnetite** appears on 182, but there is no other reference to this topic in the text on this page or the facing page.

A

B

T

The publisher gratefully acknowledges the following sources for photographs. All maps and illustrations unless otherwise noted are the exclusive property of World Book, Inc.

6-7 WORLD BOOK; © Shutterstock
8-9 © Shutterstock
10-11 © Shutterstock; U.S. Air Force; Airbus
14-15 © Shutterstock
16-17 © Shutterstock; © Aaron Vandersommers, Good Year; NASA
18-19 © Shutterstock
20-21 © Shutterstock; Granger Collection; © Peter Chartrand, Liaison
22-23 Johnson Space Center; © Shutterstock; AP Photo
24-27 NASA
28-29 © Alamy
30-31 © Getty; Ohaus Corporation; © Shutterstock
32-33 NASA; © Shutterstock
34-35 © Shutterstock
38-39 © Alamy; © Geraint Lewis, Alamy; © CERN
40-41 © Thinkstock
44-45 © Terry Whittaker, Photo Researchers; U.S. Navy; NASA
46-47 NASA; © Shutterstock
48-49 © Nobel Foundation; © Corbis
50-51 © Roger Wood, Corbis
52-55 © Shutterstock
56-57 © Shutterstock; © Michael Holford
58-59 © Michael Holford
60-61 © Shutterstock; Library of Congress; NASA
62-63 © Image Works; © iStockphoto
64-65 © David Frazier; NASA
66-67 NASA; © Alamy
68-69 © Leonard de Selva, Corbis; © E.R. Degginger; NASA
70-71 © Deutsches Museum; © Alamy; © Science Source; © Getty
72-73 © Corbis; WORLD BOOK; © David Frazier; © Thinkstock; © Shutterstock
74-75 © Shutterstock; © iStockphoto
76-77 © Shutterstock; AP Photo
78-79 © Andrew Syred, Photo Researchers; © Nelson Morris, Photo Researchers; © Shutterstock
80-81 © Alamy; © Shutterstock
82-83 © Michael Philip Manheim, Imagestate; WORLD BOOK; © Shutterstock; © Alamy
84-85 © Alamy
86-87 © Shutterstock; © Alamy
90-91 © Norman Tomalin, Bruce Coleman; © Shutterstock; © Alamy; © Image Works
92-93 © George Eastman House; National Forest Service
94-95 National Forest Service; © Tesla
98-99 © Shutterstock
102-103 © John McLean, Photo Researchers
106-107 © Alamy; Oak Ridge National Laboratory; © Photo Researchers; © Humberto Fernandez-Moran, University of Chicago; © Christina Kennedy, Alamy
108-109 © Alex Segre, Alamy; © Thinkstock; © Alamy
110-111 © Shutterstock
112-113 ESA; © Photo Researchers
114-115 © Shutterstock; © Corning Glass Works; © Alamy
116-117 © Shutterstock; © Thinkstock
118-119 WORLD BOOK; © Shutterstock
120-121 © Getty; © SuperStock
122-123 © Shutterstock; Siemens Westinghouse Power; © Dennis Stock, Magnum
124-125 © John Vanderlyn, Ford Foundation
126-127 © Corbis; © Shutterstock; © Alamy
128-129 © Shutterstock; © Ethan Miller, Corbis
130-131 © Martin Bond, Photo Researchers; © James Amos, Science Source; © Thinkstock; © Shutterstock
132-133 NASA; © Shutterstock; © Art Resource; WORLD BOOK
134-135 © Shutterstock; © Corbis; Granger Collection
136-137 U.S. Defense Imagery; © Shutterstock; Granger Collection
138-139 U.S. Defense Imagery; © Shutterstock
140-141 © Shutterstock; © Bridgeman
142-143 © Shutterstock; © Corbis
144-145 © Alamy © Shutterstock
146-147 James Davis, U.S. Navy; © Corbis; NASA
148-149 Toyota; © Shutterstock; © Miriam Agron, Animals Animals
150-151 © Culver Pictures; © Shutterstock; © Steve Hale
152-153 NASA
154-155 © Getty
156-157 © Art Resource; © Mercedes Benz; © SuperStock
158-159 NASA; © Corbis; © Shutterstock
160-161 © Shutterstock; © Alamy; Keck Observatory
162-163 NASA; © Shutterstock; © Lester Lefkowitz
166-167 © Alamy; © Shutterstock; AP Photo
168-169 © Photodisc; © Alamy; © Alamy; © Shutterstock; © Royal Library; © Her Majesty Queen Elizabeth II
170-171 © Shutterstock
171-173 © Shutterstock; © Thinkstock; © Smithsonian Institution
174-175 © Corbis; © Jeff Daly, Alamy; © Shutterstock
176-177 © Alamy; NASA
178-179 © Ferrari
180-181 © Shutterstock
182-183 © Artstreet; AP Photo
184-185 © Brent Jones; © Alamy
186-187 WORLD BOOK; NASA
188-189 NASA; © Shutterstock; © Corbis; © Francois Sauze, Photo Researchers; © Shutterstock
190-191 © Bill Pugliano, Getty; © Corbis; © Roger Ball, Corbis
192-193 NASA; © Shutterstock
194-195 © Charles O'Rear, Corbis; © Shutterstock
196-199 © Shutterstock
200-201 NASA; © Shutterstock; © Ari Ali, Getty
202-203 Western Reserve Historical Society; © Alamy
204-205 © Shutterstock
206-207 NASA; © Shutterstock
208-209 © Alamy; WORLD BOOK; © Greg Wright, Alamy
210-211 © Patrick Aventurier, Gamma; © Scott Camazine, Photo Researchers
212-213 © Michael Abby, Photo Researchers; © Rick Peterson; NASA
214-215 NASA; © Stock Montage; © Shutterstock
216-217 © Shutterstock
218-219 WORLD BOOK
220-221 © SuperStock; © Shutterstock; © Jim West, Alamy; © Mark Burnett, Photo Researchers
222-223 © Shutterstock; © Malcom Fielding, Photo Researchers; © Art Archive
224-229 © Shutterstock
230-231 © Shutterstock; © Carlos Sanuvo, Bruce Coleman
232-233 © Quebecor World
234-235 © Getty
236-237 WORLD BOOK; © Index Stock
238-239 © Mark Stack, Tom Stack; © Shutterstock
240-241 © Bruce Roberts, Photo Researchers; © David Parker, SPL; © David Woodfall, Peter Arnold; © Hartmut Schwarzbach, Peter Arnold; © Getty
242-243 © Shutterstock; U.S. Navy
244-245 NASA; © Scott Tysick, Masterfile
246-247 NASA; © Shutterstock; ESA; © Raytheon
248-249 © Andrew Haley, Litton
250-251 © Corbis; NASA
252-253 © Shutterstock
256-257 © David Frazier; © Roger Ressmeyer, Corbis; © Shutterstock; © Shutterstock
258-259 © Alcatel-Lucent; NASA
260-261 © Shutterstock
262-263 © Getty
264-265 © Alamy; © Shutterstock
270-273 NASA
274-275 © Getty; NASA; NASA
276-277 © Sovfoto; © E.R. Degginger
278-279 © Shutterstock; WORLD BOOK; © Kip Evans, Alamy
280-281 © Shutterstock; © David Parker, Photo Researchers
282-283 © Getty; © James Amos, Corbis; © Alamy; © Dreamstime
284-285 © Shutterstock; © Art Resource
286-287 © Shutterstock; © Dreamstime; © Getty; © SuperStock
288-289 © AT&T; © Shutterstock
290-291 © Dreamstime; © Shutterstock
292-293 NASA; © Alamy
294-295 © iTech Group; © Alamy; © Shutterstock
296-297 © Guy Croft, Alamy; AP Photo; © Getty; © Corbis
298-299 © SuperStock; WORLD BOOK; © Getty; © Randy Duchaine, Alamy; © Shutterstock
300-301 © Getty; © Goodyear
302-303 © Getty; © Elvele, Alamy; © Alamy; © John Reader, Photo Researchers; © Mary Evans
304-305 © Alamy; © Shutterstock; AP Photo
306-307 © Edward Parker, Alamy; © Alamy
308-309 © Alamy
310-311 © Shutterstock
312-313 © Alamy; © Shutterstock
314-315 © Shutterstock; G. Hudepohl, ESO; G. Lombardi, ESO; © Shutterstock
316-317 © Alamy; © Julian Stratenschulte, Landov
318-319 Granger Collection; NASA
320-321 NASA; © Shutterstock
322-323 AP Photo; © Liu Jin, Getty; © Earl Roberge, Photo Researchers
324-325 © Andrew Syred, Photo Researchers; © Winston Fraser, Alamy; © Shutterstock
326-327 Granger Collection; © Martyn Chillmaid, Photo Researchers; U.S. Navy; © Alamy
328-329 NOAA; © Walter Bohan; © Wolfgang Kaehler, Corbis
330-331 © Shutterstock © Thinkstock; WORLD BOOK
334-335 Granger Collection
336-337 © Mike Hill, Alamy; © David Frazier
338-339 © Shutterstock
340-341 © Getty; © Alamy; NASA
342-343 © Getty; © Thinkstock